DISCARDED
Fordham University Libraries

THE ELITE OF THE ELITE

For my mother and in memory of my father.

The Elite of the Elite
Permanent Secretaries in the British Higher Civil Service

PETER BARBERIS
Manchester Metropolitan University

Dartmouth
Aldershot • Brookfield USA • Singapore • Sydney

© Peter Barberis 1996

All rights reserved. No part of this publication may be reproduced, stored in a retrieval system, or transmitted in any form or by any means, electronic, mechanical, photocopying, recording or otherwise without the prior permission of Dartmouth Publishing Company Limited.

Published by
Dartmouth Publishing Company Limited
Gower House
Croft Road
Aldershot
Hants GU11 3HR
England

Dartmouth Publishing Company
Old Post Road
Brookfield
Vermont 05036
USA

British Library Cataloguing in Publication Data
Barberis, Peter
 Elite of the Elite: Permanent Secretaries
 in the British Higher Civil Service
 I. Title
 354.41006

Library of Congress Cataloging-in-Publication Data
Barberis, Peter, 1948–
  The elite of the elite : permanent secretaries in the British higher civil service / Peter Barberis.
    p.   cm.
  Includes bibliographical references and index.
  ISBN 1-85521-479-2
  1. Civil service–Great Britain. 2. Great Britain–Officials and employees. 3. Executive departments–Great Britain. 4. Administrative agencies–Great Britain. I. Title.
JN425.B37   1995
354.410023–dc20
                                                                95-34896
                                                                CIP

ISBN 1 85521 479 2

Printed and bound in Great Britain by
Ipswich Book Co. Ltd., Ipswich, Suffolk

Contents

List of figures vii
List of tables viii
Preface and acknowledgements x
List of abbreviations xiii
Introduction xv

PART I: THE OFFICE OF PERMANENT SECRETARY

1   Origins and development of the office of permanent secretary 3
2   Advising ministers 22
3   Running a department 44
4   Accounting to Parliament 62
5   A day in the life: permanent secretaries at work 79

PART II: PERMANENT SECRETARIES PAST AND PRESENT – A PROFILE

6   A changing social and educational elite 95
7   Reaching the summit – many are called, few are chosen 118

PART III: PERMANENT SECRETARIES IN WHITEHALL – CAREER PATTERNS

8 An insular order? Permanent secretaries and the outside world	147
9 The dance of the mandarins: interdepartmental mobility within Whitehall	166
10 Strangers in paradise? Permanent secretaries, ministers and their departments	181

PART IV: PERMANENT SECRETARIES AND THE STATE

11 Permanent secretaries and the performance of government	201
12 Permanent secretaries and the constitution	220
Appendix: List of office-holders, 1830-1994	233
Bibliography	257
Index	273

List of figures

6.1	Percentage of permanent secretaries who attended a university	97
6.2	University subjects studied by permanent secretaries and by their peers	103
7.1	Proportion of permanent secretaries who have served in a central department	135
8.1	Careerist permanent secretaries with at least one year's absence from Whitehall after entry to the civil service	162
8.2	Whitehall's openness, as measured by the proportion of permanent secretaries with open or closed careers	164
9.1	Interdepartmental transfers: mobility index, 1872-1984	174
10.1	Departmental service of permanent secretaries and ministers, 1830-1994 (av. no. of months, calculated at six monthly intervals)	193

List of tables

4.1	Appearances before the Committee of Public Accounts	73
6.1	Percentage of permanent secretaries, 1870-1918, who had attended a university, by method of entry to the civil service	98
6.2	Universities attended by permanent secretaries	99
6.3	Universities attended by permanent secretaries and by their peers	102
6.4	Schools attended by permanent secretaries	105
6.5	School education of permanent secretaries and of their peers	107
6.6	Aristocratic connections of permanent secretaries, 1830-1994	110
6.7	Relative social standing of ministers and their permanent secretaries during select periods of office between 1868-1915	112
6.8	Fathers' occupations of post-1945 permanent secretaries	115
7.1	Proportion of civil servants, by final grade reached, who served in a private office	132
7.2	Proportion of civil servants, by final grade reached, who served in central departments	137
8.1	Proportion of careerists, semi-careerists and outsiders appointed as permanent secretaries between 1830-1994	153
8.2	Professional backgrounds of non-careerist permanent secretaries	158

9.1	Number of departments served by careerist permanent secretaries, 1830-1994	172
9.2	Incidence of transfers, by grade, among careerist permanent secretaries appointed between 1919-94	177
9.3	Number of cognate areas served by careerist permanent secretaries appointed between 1919-94	179
10.1	Age upon appointment as permanent secretary	182
10.2	Tenure of permanent secretaryships	185
10.3	Previous service and tenure of permanent secretaryships in certain departments, 1945-94	189
10.4	Turnover of ministers and permanent secretaries in certain departments, 1905-94	196

Preface and acknowledgements

It is some seventeen years since I began to study permanent secretaries. The topic was suggested to me by Professor Maurice Wright of the Department of Government, Victoria University of Manchester. I thank him for that and for his supervision of the ensuing Ph.D. thesis. Rather less than half the present volume emanates from certain sections of the doctoral thesis – mainly the middle chapters of the book. Even these have been recast and completely rewritten. The rest is fresh material, drawing partly upon interviews with permanent secretaries, past and present.

Without co-operation from Whitehall this book would not be what it has turned out to be. Here it would be remiss of me not to mention Sir Robin Butler. In a public lecture he had suggested that academics were partly to blame if, to them, Whitehall seemed unduly inaccessible and fortress-like. It was up to academics, he said, to knock on the door. So I did and I discovered that there had been sincerity in his words. He did not and could not force his colleagues to speak to me. But he and Richard Mottram, then at the OPSS and with a responsibility for promoting more open government, certainly 'oiled the wheels'. A number of current post-holders afforded, upon request, in-depth interviews of between one and one and a half hours' duration. I cannot imagine that this privilege would have been extended to the likes of me in years gone by. Naturally, some preferred not to be mentioned by name. Others had no particular wish for anonymity but acknowledged that to name some but not others would be both anomalous and, by process of elimination, suggestive of those who wished their identities to be protected. So, all interview material is unattributed. This, too, goes for those who had already retired and who were also good enough to give their time.

In addition, over a hundred former permanent secretaries provided biographical and other career details. The process of collecting this information, by correspondence, is one in which I have been engaged at various times over the years. Sadly but inevitably quite a number of these respondents have since departed this life – perhaps to take up permanent permanent secretaryships! Some of them volunteered much more information than I was seeking or expecting – information about themselves, those with whom they worked and about the issues that consumed them in the course of their careers. In a few cases, such correspondence led to personal meetings or telephone conversations. I can only thank them for their time, trouble, and, in one case, hospitality.

Conversely, I experienced very few non-responses and encountered only the occasional carping reply to my enquiries. One of these (which nevertheless answered all my queries) took the form of a warning that the book I was writing would not sell unless it portrayed permanent secretaries as human beings. The same respondent expressed the hope that his name would find no place in the text. On both counts he should find satisfaction with this volume. This is not because I have consciously sought to comply with his or anyone else's wishes. His name finds no place in the text because I had nothing to say about him. No doubt there is much that could but probably never will be said either about that particular individual or about a fair proportion of a breed once described by Churchill as 'slaves of the lamp concealed from the public among the deeper recesses of Whitehall'. And if the reader judges that permanent secretaries are portrayed in this book as human beings it is because that is how most of those who are mentioned by name (and the nameless interviewees) seem to be or to have been – at least to this author. Such judgement may incur the wrath of those uncompromising critics who would insist that a book on permanent secretaries does not deserve to sell if it does portray them as human beings! Still, I have tried to present them fairly and without undue predisposition. Where condemned by the weight of evidence, permanent secretaries and the system they oversee cannot and should not expect to be exonerated. But this should not be to deny their strengths, virtues and (usually) unsung achievements; or to overlook the significance of the wider political context in which they operate. The final two chapters of the book are, in effect, an attempt at some sort of general audit.

I am grateful to the Manchester Metropolitan University for granting sabbatical leave to enable me to complete this volume. This was done through the disposition of research assessment funds. I should like in particular to thank my colleagues Timothy May and David Banks who, between them, read and commented upon drafts of nearly all the chapters. I also thank Tony Butcher of Goldsmiths College, University of London and Helen Ryder of the HM Treasury/Cabinet Office Library for providing me with pieces of factual information; while Dr. Angela Raspin facilitated my access to the (British) National Oral Archive. I pay tribute to the Manchester Central Public Reference Library. The building itself remains an inspiration; the material it contains is an invaluable source. Over many years the staff there have dealt patiently with my countless enquiries and requests.

Needless to say none of the people mentioned in this preface bear responsibility for any points of fact, presentation, interpretation or style upon which this volume may be found wanting. I alone bear full responsibility.

Lastly, but certainly not least, I express my very great thanks to Sara Phillips. She transposed my hand-written script, tables and diagrams into camera-ready copy. To me this qualifies as the eighth wonder!

Peter Barberis
February 1995

List of abbreviations

CAF   Central African Federation
CID   Committee of Imperial Defence
COI   Central Office of Information
CPRS   Central Policy Review Staff
CRO   Commonwealth Relations Office
CSC   Civil Service Commission
CSD   Civil Service Department
CSO   Central Statistical Office
DEA   Department of Economic Affairs
DES   Department of Education and Science
DFE   Department for Education
DHSS   Department of Health and Social Security
DoE   Department of the Environment
DSIR   Department of Scientific and Industrial Research
DSS   Department of Social Security
DTI   Department of Trade and Industry
ECGD   Export Credits Guarantee Department
EEC   European Economic Community
EU   European Union
FCO   Foreign and Commonwealth Office
FDA   First Division Association (Association of First Division Civil Servants)

FMI	Financial Management Initiative
FMU	Financial Management Unit
FO	Foreign Office
HMC	Headmasters' Conference
IMF	International Monetary Fund
MAFF	Ministry of Agriculture, Fisheries and Food
MFP	Ministry of Fuel and Power
MHLG	Ministry of Housing and Local Government
MINIS	Management Information Systems for Ministers
Mintech	Ministry of Technology
MoD	Ministry of Defence
MPBW	Ministry of Public Buildings and Works
MPNI	Ministry of Pensions and National Insurance
MPO	Management and Personnel Office (Cabinet Office)
NATO	North Atlantic Treaty Organization
NBPI	National Board for Prices and Incomes
NEDC	National Economic Development Council
NOA Tr.	(British) National Oral Archive Transcript
ODA	Overseas Development Administration (FCO)
OECD	Organization for Economic Co-Operation and Development
OMCS	Office of the Minister for the Civil Service
OPSS	Office of Public Service and Science
PAC	Public Accounts Committee (Committee of Public Accounts)
P.P.	Parliamentary Papers
PPS	Principal Private Secretary
PSA	Property Services Agency (DoE)
PUS	Permanent Under Secretary
RIPA	Royal Institute of Public Administration
SASC	Senior Appointments Selection Committee
SSRB	Senior Salaries Review Body
TCSC	Treasury and Civil Service Committee
TUC	Trades Union Congress
UN	United Nations

Introduction

Permanent secretaries are the elite of an elite: the most senior of Britain's senior civil servants. They hold the topmost official (i.e. non-political) positions within each of the great departments of state. They are responsible to their ministers for the overall running of those departments; they are among the minister's closest advisers; and they are accountable to Parliament, above all for the regularity of approved expenditure.

The office of permanent secretary has no real counterpart in European and American systems of government (Christoph 1975, p. 43). Its origins are peculiarly British, though widely exported to the Commonwealth. It has inspired many and different images, some born of awe and reverence, others the product of frustration. Bagehot (1928, p. 128) saw the permanent secretary as one 'familiar with disagreeable facts, and though in manner most respectful, yet most imperturbable in opinion'. Having earlier in his career declined the permanent under-secretaryship of the Colonial Office, Sir Henry Taylor (1885, pp. 158-9) nevertheless acknowledged the importance of the position: 'A bad appointment to this office is the deadliest blow that can be dealt... and a good one is the greatest blessing'. More recently Peter Hennessy (BBC Radio 4, 13 January 1994) has described permanent secretaries, collectively, as a 'college of cardinals'. This image conveys a mixture of acknowledgement, enchantment and gentle irreverence – a qualified compliment. With characteristic élan, former Labour minister Tony Benn told a House of Commons select committee that Britain 'is governed by the

Prime Minister and the permanent secretaries...' (TCSC 1986b, q. 491). This was intended as no compliment at all, either to the office of prime minister or to that of permanent secretary.

Yet few beyond the outer circle of government and a gaggle of Whitehall-watchers would know what a permanent secretary is were it not for Sir Humphrey Appleby, the fictional character immortalized in the television programmes *Yes, Minister* and *Yes, Prime Minister*. To the wider public Sir Humphrey *is* the higher civil service, and vice versa. Even to the reasonably well informed, the role and precise functions of the permanent secretary lie subsumed in the opaque imagery of the 'mandarinate', the 'official bureaucracy' or, as is sometimes said, the 'ruling servants'. Few will know about the development of the office of permanent secretary. Scarcely more will know the names of any but a handful of post-holders, past or present. Surprisingly, there has never before been a book specifically devoted to permanent secretaries.

Does Sir Humphrey exist? If not, did he ever exist? Some, including one former permanent secretary (Kemp 1993, p. 29), would reply in the affirmative to both questions. Yet my own meetings with permanent secretaries of the 1990s yielded little evidence of his like within Whitehall today. I have been authoritatively informed that individuals of Sir Humphrey's ilk did hold dominion a generation or so ago. To this extent the television portrayal captures an essential glimpse of a persona that lives vividly in the memory: upper middle class, public school and 'Oxbridge' educated; cultured, clubbable, articulate and full of subtlety; a font of knowledge and wisdom; incorruptible yet capable of deception, manipulation and disingenuity when the mores of Whitehall are challenged by wayward ministerial initiative. And all within the cloak of anonymity, the skein of constitutional propriety.

This, though, even for an age gone by, tells something less than half the story. It projects one particular dimension of one, albeit vital, aspect of a permanent secretary's role – advising ministers. It highlights the *persona dramatis* in which an assured, supercilious adviser effortlessly negotiates his way through the contretemps of an ambitious but often faltering minister. It is good drama and better television but not the rounded picture. It tells little of the broader Whitehall routine of committees, informal networks or day-to-day responsibility for running a large organization. It fails to convey the long hours, the sheer hard work almost invariably involved in becoming and being a permanent secretary. As H.E. Dale once said (1941, p. 66), the work of a civil servant is not the stuff of art!

The four broad aims of this book are reflected in the four sections, or parts, into which the chapters are organized. Part I deals with the office of permanent secretary. It shows what permanent secretaries do and what, in general terms, they have been doing over the last century and a half. It shows the recent change of emphasis in the permanent secretary's role. It examines recent, more radical, proposals for the recasting and even the abolition of the office of permanent secretary. Part II presents a statistical portrait of all post-holders, past and present. It betrays something of their characteristics, collectively. It explains why those civil servants, rather than others, became permanent secretaries. Part III analyzes certain aspects of the development of the higher civil service itself. The vehicle for this is an examination of permanent secretaries' careers. Specific issues include: Whitehall's alleged insularity; interdepartmental transfers; and the extent to which permanent secretaries have had experience of the departments they head. Finally, Part IV looks at permanent secretaries in the wider context of the state. It examines in a general way their contribution to the performance of government. The final chapter considers the position of permanent secretaries within the British constitution, focusing upon the various tensions and ethical dilemmas.

A good deal of the discussion in parts II and III necessarily rests upon statistical data. This requires the demarcation of two analytical boundaries – first, to determine what is to count and what is not to count as a permanent secretary; second, to specify shorter periods within the 150 year span covered by the data.

There is no 'official' definition of a permanent secretary. There are no neat criteria; so there can be no tidiness. Broadly, this study covers civil servants who are or have been i) heads of departments or boards working under the immediate direction of a political chief, not necessarily of cabinet rank; and ii) remunerated commensurately. This leaves a number of loose ends. It means the exclusion of those whose functions are advisory but who have no overall responsibility for a department, such as the Chief Economic Adviser. Neither the Treasury Solicitor and Procurator-General nor the Permanent Secretary to the Lord Chancellor and Clerk of the Crown in Chancery are included, mainly on the ground that they are specialist posts. Included, however, are those who were remunerated at lower levels in posts which were subsequently rewarded on permanent secretary pay scales (e.g. in the Office of Works, Ministry of Transport, Dominions Office). In the rarer cases of downgrading (Privy Council Office, Central Office of Information) only those remunerated at full permanent secretary level are included. Remuneration is in any case a less useful guide for the nineteenth century when there was no universal grading system. The analysis embraces second permanent secretaries, whose inclusion is warranted by their position within the Whitehall hierarchy (see Chapter 1). In this and in other respects the definitions employed here differ somewhat from those upon which earlier studies have been based (Harris and Garcia 1966; Theakston and Fry 1989).

The second analytical boundary concerns the identification of significant periods within the overall time-span – that is, from the 1830s, the 'birth of the modern' (Johnson 1991). Patterns of change are examined through the backgrounds and careers of those who became permanent secretaries in each of seven periods: 1830-69; 1870-99; 1900-18; 1919-45; 1946-64; 1965-April 1979; and May 1979-August 1994. The first period covers what Dicey (1914, pp. 64-5) famously described – in a fashion much disputed - as the age of Benthamism or individualism. It represents the civil service still largely unreformed. The period 1870-99, the beginnings of Dicey's age of collectivism, saw the introduction of open competition: the semi-reformed and quasi-modern civil service. The years 1900-18 marked the more rapid expansion of government with the Liberals' welfare reforms and the First World War; while 1919-45 saw the rise of the 'positive state' and a fully unified civil service (Fry 1969, pp. 11-66). The first three post-war decades brought forth the era, so called, of consensus politics: the zenith of the welfare state and the managed economy (Kavanagh and Morris 1989). This era may be divided into two phases – 1946-64 and 1965-79. These represent, respectively, the consolidation and the calcification of consensus politics. They can also been seen as years during which the higher civil service itself was, first, broadly revered but then becoming the focus of increasingly strenuous challenge. Since 1979 Whitehall officialdom and the administrative tradition of which it is the embodiment has been largely on the defensive. Under successive Conservative governments the 'ship of state', of which permanent secretaries are the principal deck officers, has been steered hard astern, encountering choppy waters in the process.

These chronological boundaries, then, correspond roughly to recognizable phases in the role of the state and of the civil service. Other periods could be chosen with almost equal justification. Indeed, where appropriate the ones adopted are either set aside or collapsed to assist analysis.

Two points of nomenclature require clarification. First, the term permanent secretary is generally used throughout. There used to be a technical distinction between a permanent secretary and a permanent under-secretary. The latter would normally apply where the political chief was a secretary of state. In recent years, though, this distinction has become blurred. There seems to have developed the convention that those who work to a secretary of state may choose to adopt the title either of permanent under-secretary or permanent secretary. The same post may therefore acquire a different nomenclature without there being any formal change of status. This can be confusing to observers but has little serious consequence. In this book the title permanent under-secretary (PUS) is used only to describe a particular post or post-holder so styled. A similar procedure is adopted for posts carrying other titles, such as chairman, director-general or second permanent (under) secretary. The second point of nomenclature concerns titles and decorations. Most modern permanent secretaries have, by virtue of their office, received knighthoods. Some have been raised to the peerage, usually upon retirement. A few (mainly) nineteenth century figures inherited peerages. For ease of presentation, titles and decorations are omitted from the body of the text, except where necessary for purposes of identification or particular emphasis. I trust this gives no offence. Knighthoods and peerages are inserted in the Appendix, an alphabetical listing of all postholders between 1830-1994.

PART I

THE OFFICE OF PERMANENT SECRETARY

1 Origins and development of the office of permanent secretary

Introduction

This chapter shows how the office of permanent secretary emerged in a recognizably modern form during the late-eighteenth and early nineteenth centuries. It sketches the subsequent development of the office under the twin impulses of government growth and popular democracy. There then follows, each in turn, an account of two special permanent secretaryships: the headship of the civil service; and the cabinet secretaryship. This reaches down to the present day and includes brief portraits of some of the more notable incumbents – those who have helped to shape both the offices they have held and the wider civil service itself. The chapter concludes with a description of the formal hierarchy of permanent secretaries.

Origins of the office – the late-eighteenth and early nineteenth centuries

By the 1830s, the office of permanent secretary had, in most departments, emerged in recognizable form. Its genesis during the previous forty or fifty years had been patchy and uncertain, the product as much of surrounding events as of conscious endeavour. As Parris (1969, p. 22) says, it is misleading to talk in any but the loosest sense of a civil service during this period, in that 'it was not permanent, it was not civil, and it was not a service'. Many of the top officials were not permanent: they held their positions at the behest of the party in office, only to yield upon a change of government. This was partly because the boundary between politics and administration was not yet clearly established. There was no clear distinction of personnel between civil and political office-holders. Nor was there any conception of a 'service', implying routine pay scales and other conditions of employment. Indeed the notion of an employment contract for servants of the state was still in its infancy (Chester 1981, pp. 123-68). There were government departments, but no notion of a unified service. This, the most ambitious of the mid-nineteenth century reform proposals, did not come to fruition until the early decades of the twentieth century.

The deep-grained departmentalism prevented any orderly pattern in the emergence of the office of permanent secretary. A Commissioners' report with reference to the Home Office and the Foreign Office concluded that 'for the necessary official business of each department, one under-secretary is sufficient', and that:

> for the obvious reason of preventing the confusion and serious consequences that may arise in business of such high importance from frequent changes, such office ought to be made stationary.
> (Commissioners for Fees etc. 1786, p. 10)

The secretaries of state were not prepared formally to accept that an under-secretary should be permanent, though the Home Office in practice soon adopted this arrangement (Sainty 1975, p. 5). The position at the Foreign Office was less clear-cut. According to Tilley and Gaselee (1933, p. 26), William Fraser may be described as permanent under-secretary for the period 1782-9. This is at odds with the official Foreign Office list which, first published in 1852 and which until 1901 listed all previous post-holders, identified George Aust as the first incumbent. Aust was appointed in 1790. But this was disputed by at least one contemporary, Sir James Bland-Burges, the political, or parliamentary, under-secretary. Burges adamantly denied the existence of any equivalent permanent post (Hutton 1885, p. 287). This is consistent with the assertion that George Hammond's second appointment in 1807 established 'a continuous sequence of permanent under-secretaries for Foreign Affairs' (Parris 1969, p. 43). Others, though, opt for a later period. Middleton (1974) sees John Backhouse as a pivotal figure in the emergence of this particular permanent under-secretaryship. Backhouse held the position between 1828-42. This gels with the observation that, while it had gradually hardened into custom, the distinction between the permanent and parliamentary under-secretaries at the Foreign Office became formally enshrined only from 1831 (Collinge 1979, pp. 10-11).

The aim here is not to resolve these disputes, but to illustrate the sometimes shadowy and indeterminate emergence of the office of permanent secretary. Of course, the Foreign Office is an extreme example of these uncertainties. The experiences of other departments nevertheless demonstrate the unevenness with which it took root across Whitehall. At the Admiralty, John Barrow was appointed Second (i.e. permanent) Secretary in 1804 following the fall of Addington's administration. He displaced Benjamin Tucker 'whose services Lord Melville... deemed it right to dispose of on account of his well known partisanship' (Barrow 1847, p. 254). Barrow, like George Hammond at the Foreign Office, was in turn replaced in 1806 upon the creation of the 'ministry of all talents'. But he was reinstated with the return of the Tories under Lord Portland the following year. He remained in post until his retirement in 1845. Barrow's presence, sensitivity and lack of political ambition secured his permanence, establishing the office as a distinct entity (Lloyd 1970, p. 82).

At the War Office, the American War prompted the appointment in 1775 of a Second Secretary, Matthew Lewis. Lewis worked closely with the Secretary at War. He retained this position until his retirement in 1803, during which time 'the development of the post into that of permanent administrative head seems clear' (Gee 1954, p. 125). At the Board of Trade, Thomas Lack was appointed in 1810 to the dual positions of Clerk and Assistant Secretary. From 1822 the latter was recognized as a distinct entity, enjoying a further enhancement in status in 1825 (Sainty 1974, p. 42). Here, as in the War Office, the energies of the incumbent were in large part responsible for the development of the office of permanent secretary. Where the incumbent played a less visible role, recognition of the office was either delayed or else it remained associated with more routine functions. Such was the case at the Board of Control (India Board), although from 1813 the Assistant (Permanent) Secretary was authorized to sign 'orders and explanations' (Foster 1917, p. 69).

A Minute of 1805 created the post of Assistant Secretary to the Treasury. This arose from the need both to relieve the parliamentary secretaries from a growing burden of work and to supervize the chief clerks. The appointee, George Harrison, is often regarded as the first permanent secretary of the Treasury (Torrance 1968; Sainty 1972, p. 59). Against this Roseveare (1973, pp. 87-8) argues that not until 1859 was the position elevated from that of running one of the divisions to that of having undivided responsibility for the supervision of the department and of chief adviser to the Chancellor of the Exchequer.

If the duties of permanent secretaries varied as between departments, it was almost everywhere established by the 1830s that the incumbent should remain in post when there was a change of government. Thus some members of the incoming Whig government in 1835 tried, but failed, to displace on political grounds Barrow at the Admiralty and Robert Hay at the Colonial Office (Kriegel 1977, p. 292). Barrow, as we have seen, stayed, while Hay's departure the following year was on grounds of ill-health. There was by now a clear categorization of personnel: politicians and administrators were easily distinguished from one another. As will be seen in a later chapter, individuals continued to cross the boundary between politics and administration. They would continue to do so down to the end of the nineteenth century and indeed after. But there was now a perceptible boundary to be crossed. On the other hand, the precise functions of the permanent secretary were still by no means clearly established or universally understood. In particular, the changing relationship between the permanent and the parliamentary secretaries was a central feature in the development of the former.

Development of the office of permanent secretary from the mid-nineteenth century

As with its emergence, there was no uniform pattern in the subsequent development of the office of permanent secretary. Nor did it proceed everywhere smoothly or trouble-free. In 1877 the permanent secretaryship at the Admiralty was abolished and the duties transferred to a Naval Secretary, Admiral Hall. There had for some time been disquiet about the lack of sufficient service input to the running of the department. But with increasing need for co-ordination the permanent secretaryship was resurrected five years later. Only by chance did the position fall, temporarily for a two year period, to a naval officer, Captain (later rear-Admiral) George Tryon. The original appointee, Robert Hamilton, a career civil servant, had been in post only days when he was sent to Ireland to replace the (Permanent) Under Secretary, Thomas Burke. Burke, together with his political chief Lord Frederick Cavendish, had been a victim of the Fenian atrocities in Phoenix Park in May 1882. He thus became the first and only permanent secretary to have been assassinated. That he, rather than Cavendish, was the principal target is some testimony to his own conspicuousness. It is yet greater testimony to the visibility of this particular permanent secretaryship, in which a succession of occupants adopted high and often controversial profiles over the next four decades until the partition of Ireland in the early 1920s (O'Halpin 1987).

These examples are, of course, atypical and exceptional. In the Whitehall mainstream the office of permanent secretary was by now deeply embedded. The growth and increasing complexity of government secured its consolidation; the notion of 'constitutional bureaucracy', a by-product of popular democracy, shaped the context in which incumbents operated.

The growth of government brought increasing complexity and division of functions (Fry 1979; Greenleaf 1983; 1987). It was partly responsible for the demarcation of responsibilities between the permanent and the parliamentary secretaries; and for the advance of the former at the expense of the latter. Even by the 1870s, though, the demarcation of roles remained slightly unclear – for example at the Colonial Office (Blakeley 1972, p. 159) and at the Home Office (Pellew 1982, pp. 26-7). But by this time the permanent secretary had, in most departments, outstripped in importance his parliamentary counterpart (Theakston 1987, pp. 19-29).

The mid-nineteenth century was, above all, the age of the cavalier, enthusiast permanent secretary. Men such as Charles Trevelyan (Treasury), James Kay-Shuttleworth (Education Department), James Stephen (Colonial Office), Rowland Hill (Post Office) and Edwin Chadwick (Poor Law Board; General Board of Health) had high profiles. Each in their own way made contributions to public affairs with equal and greater resonance than did the politicians they nominally served.

Trevelyan had served in India with public distinction throughout the 1830s. His appointment in 1840 marked the beginning of an equally distinguished nineteen year spell as head of the Treasury. He used this position to administer relief works in Ireland during the famine of the mid and late-1840s. He is immortalized in the investigations and famous report on the civil service of the mid-1850s, co-authored with future Chancellor of the Exchequer Sir Stafford Northcote. As an attack on the *status quo* the report inevitably brought him into open controversy. Besides, he possessed an 'almost always irresistible temptation to make his own views public' (Wright 1969, p. xxi). Notoriety followed him when he left the Treasury in 1859 to become Governor of Madras.

James Stephen headed the Colonial Office between 1836-48. His profound influence on policy, sometimes thinly veiled, brought him the nickname 'Mr Over Secretary Stephen'. He was nevertheless sensitive to the proprieties of his position. In 1845, when about to come under attack in Parliament, he wrote: 'Silence is my only defence because any other vindication would have involved a breach of confidence' (Hughes 1958, p. 30). He accepted the judgement of Lord Stanley on a previous and similar occasion that 'your official situation imposes upon you the obligation of silence' (Ibid, pp. 32-3).

Hill and Chadwick showed less restraint. Hill had been involved in a bitter feud to secure the introduction of his penny post scheme (Hill 1940). He 'could not accept that his role as a civil servant was to implement the decisions of his political master' (Daunton 1985, p. 32). This did not prevent his appointment in 1854 as sole Permanent Secretary at the Post Office, having for eight years previously been Secretary to the Postmaster General and *de facto* Joint Secretary with his *bête noire*, Col. Walter Maberly. But he continued to spare his adversaries little. In return he received while permanent secretary three apparently serious assassination threats (Hey 1989, p. 83). Edwin Chadwick's Benthamite zeal, his proclivity for centralized supervision, brought him and the New Poor Laws into similar head-on conflict with powerful, predominantly Tory, interests. Hostile and even otherwise sympathetic politicians were unwilling to allow much latitude to the position of Secretary to the (Central) Poor Law Board which he held between 1834-47 (Finer 1952, pp. 96-153). By sheer energy, tenacity and force of personality he grabbed more leeway than his superiors were wont to concede. Yet he was obliged to continue his struggle under the fetters of three supervizing commissioners, to whose ranks Chadwick aspired but was consistently denied by successive governments. At the General Board of Health, to which he was Secretary between 1848-54, he was subject to similar attentions. His apparent excesses were a major factor in his removal and, ultimately, in the Board's demise (Lewis 1952, pp. 358-75).

Having been associated with Chadwick as an assistant Poor Law commissioner, James Kay-Shuttleworth began in 1839 a ten year stint as (Permanent) Secretary to the Education Department – or, to be correct, the Education Committee of the Privy Council. Here he pressed his case for reform almost (but not quite) regardless of the sensibilities of his political masters. He was a 'street-fighter', never searching for bureaucratic obscurity. His ultimate loyalty was 'to his cause, not to the government he served' (Selleck 1994, p. 158). Inevitably he was embroiled in wider controversy. He became the subject of open public attacks. Yet while retaining manifest Benthamite liberal sympathies, he survived and adapted to Peel's incoming Tory government in 1841. Perhaps the latter moved more to accommodate Kay-Shuttleworth on education reform than he to the new government. Increasingly, it was as an unobtrusive, manipulative power behind the scenes that he generated hostility among offended interests (Selleck 1994, p. 234).

The policies and personalities of all these men were the source of aggravation as much as were the constitutional proprieties of their positions. And for every Hill, or Chadwick, there were three or four permanent secretaries who remained unknown to the wider public. But those who were so inclined could and did play active, overt, roles in policy-making. They knew what policies they wanted and worked unstintingly to such ends. Provided they did not overstep the mark, they could act as protagonists in a relatively open tug-of-war, each participant fighting his corner. That this should have survived the separation of administration from politics is one of the quirks of the nineteenth century. It is a further illustration of the untidy pattern of events. It is a reminder, too, that the nineteenth century reformers of the civil service were moved primarily by questions about efficiency, economy and the curbing of patronage. They accepted prevailing constitutional orthodoxies which had little place for the neat separation of personnel which emerged separately as the product of the disciplined mass parties of the late-nineteenth century (Greenaway 1985). Only as events unfolded, then, did the administrative reforms come to be associated with a politically non-partisan, anonymous service.

As government grew, so it became ever more necessary to secure consistently high calibre people to fill top and other senior posts. The prevailing system of patronage was ill-suited to meet such need from within the service. Trevelyan and Northcote in their famous report acknowledged that there would be a time lag between reform of the recruitment process and the supply in sufficient numbers of good quality senior career civil servants (Northcote-Trevelyan 1854, p. 7 and p. 15). In the meantime, it would be necessary to appoint from outside. Often, these were people already eminent in other walks of life, men of independence who would not take easily to obedient anonymity. In the absence of formal constitutional constraints they could remain proud. But increasingly – certainly well before the close of the century – this was to become more difficult. What made it more difficult was the rise of popular democracy – in particular the consolidation of organized parties linked, however loosely, to a mass electorate by the nexus of 'policies for votes' and 'votes for policies'.

Popular democracy was thus the mainspring for the modern constitutional bureaucracy. It meant that policies and the responsibility for policies should lie with those who had been directly elected. It would be undemocratic for those who had not been elected (i.e. civil servants) to remain at the forefront. Thus public responsibility for the policies and work of a department came to rest with ministers, while civil servants sank below the parapet. Such at least was the formal position as it had come to be established by the early 1870s (Parris 1969, pp. 80-105). The transitional period was one of adjustment for many permanent secretaries. Louis Mallet, PUS at the India Office 1874-83, expressed his frustration at the need to torture policy objectives to the demands of political expediency, while unable to make public protest (Mallet 1905, p. 148).

As noted earlier, by no means all or even the majority of permanent secretaries had ever been bull-headed zealots. By now few indeed sought public attention. Rarely did permanent secretaries emerge from the shadows. Rather, they performed their tasks quietly and with apparent subordination to their ministers. But if this now became the norm, it did not mean that they shrank from their policy-making role. Far from it. They simply performed under the cloak of anonymity. Indeed the advent of modern ministerial responsibility may have enhanced the influence of permanent officials. This may help to explain how quickly permanent secretaries adapted, even those who were drawn in from the public world in other walks of life. And, as will be seen in Chapter 8, a good number of permanent secretaries continued down to the First World War to be recruited from outside Whitehall.

Occasionally, difficulties continued to arise. This was so especially in sensitive and controversial areas of policy. Thus first George Kekewich in 1902 and then, eight years later Robert Morant, found themselves removed from the Education Department. The former was simply unable to reconcile himself to policies with which he had little sympathy and was disinclined to compromise (Kekewich 1920, pp. 227-37). Morant, an abject elitist but one of the foremost public servants of his or any generation, chimed out more than an echo of Chadwick half a century earlier. Like Chadwick, he failed to curb his interventionist disposition, offending powerful local interests (Holmes 1951; Judge 1984). He met his downfall by giving wide (internal) circulation to a memorandum by one of his inspectors, Edmond Holmes, father of Maurice, a future permanent secretary of the Department. The Holmes circular was considered controversial. Its inevitable leaking pitched the minister, Walter Runciman, into a political storm. Morant's circulation of the document was unauthorized and he had failed to keep his minister fully informed (Cross 1977, pp. 17-29). Already deeply unpopular, Morant had to go. He was nevertheless soon to head Lloyd George's new National Insurance Commission.

A few years before all this Francis Mowatt, Joint Permanent Secretary at the Treasury, had clearly been in breach of what had by now become the acknowledged mode of conduct for senior officials. In 1903 Joseph Chamberlain launched his Tariff Reform League. His protectionist proposals struck at the foundation of the free trade philosophy with which the Treasury was associated. In resisting Chamberlain Mowatt was not content, as were his senior colleagues, merely to stiffen Chancellor Charles Ritchie through the medium of private counsel. He made little effort to contain his utterances within the portals of the Treasury. He remonstrated face-to-face with Chamberlain on the streets. He 'schooled' the young Conservative MP Winston Churchill in the name of the anti-protectionist cause. This was neither the first nor the last occasion upon which he beefed-up Churchill with information detrimental to the government (Gilbert 1991, p. 154). It was not decisive in Churchill's crossing the floor of the House the following year but it turned up the heat for Prime Minister Arthur Balfour. It made more precarious the already fine balancing act in which the premier was engaged as he tried to reconcile the warring factions within his party. Balfour regarded Mowatt's behaviour as 'that of a partisan and consequently subversive of all the loyalty which has characterized the Civil Servants of the Crown, no matter how much the measure is contrary to their individual opinions' (Bahlman 1993, pp. 436-7). Balfour must have regretted having allowed Mowatt to continue beyond the normal retirement age. But it was decided that the errant permanent secretary's removal now would bring only further embarrassment to the government. In the event Mowatt went of his own accord later the same year and continued to campaign publicly, without inhibition.

In even more momentous circumstances, the anti-appeasement crusade of Robert Vansittart led to his eclipse in the Foreign Office during the late-1930s with the government's increasingly frantic efforts to avert war (Vansittart 1958, pp. 496-7; Colvin 1965, pp. 141-9 and 170-5; Rose 1978, pp. 188-218). Upon his removal in 1938 as PUS he was made Chief Diplomatic Adviser. In this nebulous role relations were strained with his successor, Alexander Cadogan. Cadogan accused Vansittart of trying to be a super PUS (Dilkes 1971, p. 67).

Even allowing for the gravity of events in which he was involved, the swashbuckling Vansittart was untypical of civil servants in his own day. In his unrelenting tenacity, his robust independence and his unwillingness to fall in with the policies of his ministers, Vansittart, too, was a throwback to the crusaders of the mid-nineteenth century. Whatever the moral verdict about appeasement his position, constitutionally, became untenable, especially after Neville Chamberlain assumed the premiership in 1937.

Vansittart's stock was already low following the Hoare-Laval pact in 1935, widely seen as yielding to Italian territorial demands in Ethiopia. In framing the pact, Foreign Secretary Hoare had undoubtedly been prompted by Vansittart. The ensuing outcry brought Hoare's resignation, but not that of Vansittart, despite widespread public calls. Ironically, he was saved by the fact that his immediate removal would have been a public signal that policy was being driven by officials. Yet Vansittart's sponsorship of the Hoare-Laval pact was the product of his broader aim to disengage Italy from Germany and so to confront the Germans with a united Europe (Rose 1978, p. 176). This the government was unwilling to make known, for fear of offending Hitler. At the root of his eventual removal as PUS lay a forthright opposition to German expansion – an opposition held to be a hindrance to the policy of appeasement. Moreover Anthony Eden, who succeeded Hoare, felt Vansittart's presence to be a threat to his authority. For it is the job of a permanent secretary to support the minister. Vansittart tried, consistently if never to full effect, to undercut his political masters whenever he felt justified. This he did, not least by the surreptitious leaking of sensitive information, usually via an intermediary, to government critics such as Winston Churchill and Hugh Dalton. Vansittart's imperiousness, his upper class disdain for certain of the political leaders, military chiefs and others made his antics the more difficult to bear and no less easy to contain. Eden described him as 'a sincere, almost fanatical crusader, and much more a Secretary of State in mentality than a permanent official' (Avon 1962, p. 242).

Other permanent secretaries since Vansittart have been eased out, sometimes to head another department. Very occasionally, departures have been involuntary and comparatively brutal, if not necessarily taking the proportions of a public execution. At other times permanent secretaries have left quietly and of their own accord. The vast majority, though, have remained within the fold, uneasy maybe with the direction of policy, probably having mobilized all the forces at their disposal to secure their preferred options. But always within the confines of Whitehall. They remain at the helm, finally subjugating their differences to the task of serving the minister and the government of the day. As will be seen in the final section of this book, critics have alleged that in recent years top mandarins have been too ready to comply with ministers' wishes. Certainly not since Vansittart has a permanent secretary so sustained, as he did for several years before his removal, such a public posture of incongruence with constitutional propriety.

Less senior officials continue from time-to-time to leave Whitehall on well publicized matters of principle or in a blaze of controversy. The case of Clive Ponting is the most spectacular in recent times. Ponting, an assistant secretary in the Ministry of Defence, left the civil service in 1984. He had disclosed to a backbench Labour MP, Tam Dalyell, certain confidential documents associated with the sinking in 1982 of the Argentine warship, *General Belgrano*, during the Falklands campaign. In January 1985 he was acquitted of charges brought against him under the Official Secrets Act (Norton-Taylor 1985; Ponting 1985). Exceptional as is such behaviour in an assistant secretary, it would be almost inconceivable of a permanent secretary. For one thing, it is unlikely that an official so inclined would ever reach permanent secretary level. Such individuals would probably fail to achieve promotion or, like Ponting, leave Whitehall. For another thing, permanent secretaries are the gatekeepers. It is they to whom other senior officials will normally turn when there is a crisis of conscience. Sometimes – certainly if it is a permanent secretary who is experiencing such a crisis – the head of the home civil service will become involved. It is necessary, therefore, to say something about the emergence and development of this special permanent secretaryship.

The headship of the civil service

Warren Fisher became in 1919 Permanent Secretary to the Treasury and Permanent Head of the Civil Service. He was the first specifically designated head of the civil service, though the Treasury post had, since the mid-nineteenth century, acquired a *de facto* status superior to that of other departmental headships (Wright 1969, pp. 367-8). Fisher's brief included the Foreign Office, though not the diplomatic service which at that time was a separate entity. Fisher did not, as is sometimes assumed, play any part in the process by which the official title was conferred (Hamilton 1951). The cards had been shuffled and dealt, so to speak, before he took up post. The Cabinet Finance Committee which had endorsed his appointment also ratified the new structure in which he was to operate. The initiative was probably taken by John Bradbury, one of the joint permanent secretaries to the Treasury (O'Halpin 1989, pp. 30-9).

If Fisher did not shape the cards he was dealt, he certainly played his hand for all it was worth. Remaining scrupulously within bounds of constitutional propriety, restrained by Whitehall's internal realpolitik, he forged a role for twenty years as head of the civil service which left a powerful legacy. He did not always get his way. As his biographer puts it, he was not the pope of Whitehall (O'Halpin 1989, p. 292). But he inspired a generation and more of top mandarins – as much by his behaviour and lofty ideals as by the concrete changes he wrought. In later chapters the extent and limitations of some of his achievements will be examined more closely – for example in connection with top appointments, in facilitating interdepartmental transfers and in developing the role of the permanent secretary as accounting officer.

Fisher's two immediate successors were Horace Wilson (1939-42) and Richard Hopkins (1942-45). In their different ways both have their places in the annals of Whitehall. Wilson is best remembered as Neville Chamberlain's appeasement-struck confidant during the late-1930s. This, though, is to overlook his earlier career, including that in the Ministry of Labour where he had been Permanent Secretary between 1921-30 (Lowe and Roberts 1987). Hopkins was an expert in public finance. Legend has it that he was the only person who could hold his own in debate with Maynard Keynes on a subject of the latter's choosing (Harrod 1951, p. 422). But neither Hopkins nor Wilson distinguished themselves as heads of the civil service. Wilson's association with appeasement had weakened his own authority and that of the position he held. The latter, linked to the Treasury role, further suffered as the Treasury itself became partly eclipsed during the early years of the Second World War by the Economic Section of the Cabinet Office. For a time the Economic Section maintained a spirit of independence, though it had ceased to be a serious rival long before its eventual transfer to the Treasury in 1953 (Cairncross and Watts 1989).

There was also a reaction to the alleged excesses of Warren Fisher. Fisher, too, had been implicated with appeasement, although subsequent scholarship has shown this to be untrue. From the mid-1930s, he did as much as anyone to crank up the Whitehall machine for the war he believed to be inevitable (Watt 1965; Peden 1979). More justifiably he was judged to have interfered perhaps detrimentally, and certainly without authority, in foreign policy and in the making of certain diplomatic appointments for which the Foreign Secretary claimed sovereignty (Selby 1953, p. 6; Avon 1962, pp. 319-20). Consequently, under reforms instituted in 1943 by Foreign Secretary Anthony Eden, the Foreign Office was formally separated from the home civil service (Foreign Office 1943, paras. 5-8, pp. 3-4).

But the animus went deeper than this. In 1926, Sir Henry Craik had declared the position of head of the civil service to be 'a ludicrously absurd... new fangled piece of mountebankism' (HC Debs. 1926, 5th Series, vol. 194, col. 296). Craik, himself a former senior official, held that overall responsibility for the civil service should rest with the democratically elected government. In response, the title of the post was changed from *Permanent* Head to *Official* Head of the Civil Service. Nevertheless, similar misgivings were evident in a subsequent parliamentary debate in November 1942 (HL Debs. 1942-43, 5th Series, vol. 125, cols. 223-325).

For all these reasons, Edward Bridges, upon assuming the dual role in 1945, deliberately soft-pedalled the use of the term 'Head of the Home Civil Service', as was now the designation (Bridges 1964, p. 176). But he did not soft-pedal his exercise of the role. He carried the torch lit by Fisher. Less innovative, less warrior-like than Fisher, Bridges was more subtle, more insightful and, in his own way, equally creative. He was driven by an equally strong sense of public duty – an adherence to the most demanding standards of probity, public-spiritedness and constitutional propriety. These were among the central values he sought more deeply to implant into the Whitehall culture (Chapman 1988).

When Bridges retired in 1956, the Treasury was reorganized. He was replaced by three joint permanent secretaries, reduced to two upon subsequent reorganization in 1962. One of his immediate successors was Norman Brook. Brook assumed the title Head of the Home Civil Service between 1956-62. He, too, was one of Whitehall's legendary heavyweights. A confidant of Churchill and, later, Harold Macmillan, he was more the formidable operator than the bequeather of any great tradition of public administration. Yet even his considerable powers must have been taxed by the triple role that he was given. For not only was he Head of the Home Civil Service and Joint Permanent Secretary to the Treasury, but he was also Cabinet Secretary. The latter position he had held since 1947, having for two years before that been an additional Cabinet Secretary alongside Bridges while Bridges was also wrestling with the demands of the Treasury job. In truth little was required of Brook in economic and financial matters, his brief at the Treasury being on the Pay and Management side. The same is true of Laurence Helsby who in 1963 followed Brook at the Treasury and as Head of the Home Civil Service. But there was now a separate Cabinet Secretary, Burke Trend.

By this time the tide was beginning to turn against the Treasury. The Department of Economic Affairs (DEA) was set up in 1964 as both complement and counterweight, though more the latter than the former. The Fulton Committee reflected a growing belief that the Treasury should also be relieved of its overall responsibility for management and personnel matters (Fulton 1968, paras. 244-53, pp. 79-82). The Civil Service Department (CSD) came into existence in 1968. The Permanent Secretary of the CSD was also Head of the Home Civil Service. The first post-holder was William Armstrong, previously Joint Permanent Secretary to the Treasury.

A man with a mission, William Armstrong sought to establish the CSD as one of the central lynchpins in the Whitehall machine. For a time he succeeded. Only when he began to get embroiled in wider policy issues during the second half of Edward Heath's premiership did his star begin to wane. This was most apparent during the miners' strike of 1973-4. Mockingly hailed as deputy prime minister, he was drawn increasingly close to Heath. He became publicly associated with policies that were seen as failures. This was too much for Armstrong and too much for his position as a civil servant. In truth he did little more than to present unambiguous advice to a premier and senior cabinet ministers who had lost their way and were glad to have guidance. In this Heath the bureaucratic politician had given ample rein and indeed active encouragement to Armstrong the highly political civil servant (Campbell 1993, p. 491). Discredited and recovering from a breakdown, Armstrong formally left the civil service several months after the fall of the Heath government in March 1974.

With echoes of Horace Wilson, Armstrong's demise weakened the headship of the civil service. Moreover, the writing was on the wall for the CSD. Armstrong's two successors, Douglas Allen and Ian Bancroft, had an uphill battle. Like Armstrong they encountered sometimes stout resistance from some of their fellow permanent secretaries and from others in their attempts to refashion Whitehall along certain of the lines suggested by Fulton. Unlike Armstrong they were also fighting for the existence of their department.

The CSD was wound up in November 1981 following an animated exchange between Bancroft and Prime Minister Margaret Thatcher. Bancroft's ensuing redundancy – and that of the Second Permanent Secretary, John Herbecq – gave a further ad hominem veneer to a decision which had been the climax of longer standing and deeper rumblings (Greenaway et al 1992, pp. 139-63). Less than twelve months earlier, the Treasury and Civil Service Committee had devoted an entire report to the future of the CSD. It received divided counsel from witnesses but concluded that the Department should be revitalized, not abolished (TCSC 1980, para. 39). The English Committee had already noted that the CSD had lost its initial drive (Expenditure Committee 1977a, para. 73, p. xxxix). It proposed the transfer of some of its functions back to the Treasury, even hinting at its abolition (Ibid, para. 72). In the event, some of the CSD's functions did go to the Treasury, others to a newly established Management and Personnel Office (MPO) in the Cabinet Office. Consequently and for the first time there were now two joint heads of the home civil service – Douglas Wass, who was also Permanent Secretary to the Treasury, and Robert Armstrong (no relation to William) who, since 1979, had been the Cabinet Secretary. When Wass retired in 1983 Robert Armstrong became sole Head of the Home Civil Service. He continued to combine this role with that of Cabinet Secretary. So too has Robin Butler, who succeeded Armstrong in 1988.

In circumstances largely not of their own making, first Robert Armstrong, then Robin Butler found themselves at the centre of public controversy.

Armstrong was sent during 1986-87 to defend in an Australian court the British government's decision to try to prevent publication of the book *Spycatcher*. These were the memoirs of a former secret service officer, Peter Wright. It was unusual for a civil servant, however senior, to be the front man. Armstrong did not expect to be given the task (Hennessy 1988, p. 31). In fact there was a precedent of sorts – that of Horace Wilson sent by Neville Chamberlain to negotiate face-to-face with Hitler in 1938 as a prelude to the Munich agreement. There was, moreover, to be a sequel, again of sorts.

In 1993-94 a number of senior officials (and senior ministers including prime ministers, past and present) gave testimony to a committee of enquiry chaired by Lord Justice Scott. The committee had been established by the government to examine aspects of the process by which, allegedly, ministers had circumvented their self-imposed embargo upon arms' sales to a hostile power (Iraq), misleading Parliament and the public in the process. Among other things, public attention focused upon the advice given by officials to ministers. What advice had been given, by whom to whom; and with what knowledge had ministers proceeded? As Head of the Home Civil Service and Secretary of the Cabinet, Robin Butler, inevitably, was invited to give evidence. He betrayed all the signs of one deeply disturbed by certain of the allegations and by the attendant publicity. He sought to vindicate Whitehall's procedures and the behaviour of the officials involved. Specifically, he took issue with the mass media. He objected to its sensationalist and distorted presentation of the evidence given to the Committee. This was true, but his saying so brought only further lampooning amidst press counterclaims of undue defensiveness and complacency. It cannot have been a comfortable episode for a civil servant weaned on the canons of anonymity or, at worst, discourse with a critical but friendly, well informed and strictly limited public. Perhaps the likes of Hill or Chadwick might have fared better. They would at least have been accustomed to the sensation of public bombardment. But not the modern mandarin. Perhaps none this century have been so brutally, so involuntarily, exposed to a hostile mass audience as were Robert Armstrong and Robin Butler.

In another sense this higher public profile has been at once both self-induced and the product of secular institutional developments. From William Armstrong onwards, successive heads of the civil service have made themselves more readily available to the media – more so than either their predecessors or their permanent secretary colleagues in the departments. William Armstrong, in particular, cultivated a more conspicuous presence. So, too, has Robin Butler. Many would see this as inevitable, even desirable, in the context of more open government. The head of the home civil service is, after all, a figurehead – an authority figure with a leadership role. As the official (i.e. non-political) spokesperson for almost the entire civil service the incumbent will find the public domain to be the natural forum in which to expound upon the changing climate, shape and workings of the Whitehall machine.

This greater transparency has brought into question a wide range of issues concerning the role of the higher civil service. Some of these questions will be examined in the final chapter. It has also drawn attention to the wisdom of linking the headship of the civil service with the cabinet secretaryship, or indeed with any other permanent secretaryship. Personalities aside and apart from random sparks such as the *Spycatcher* trial or the Scott Inquiry, there are deeper issues. The arguments and counter-arguments have been expatiated (TCSC 1986a, paras. 5-44; TCSC 1986c, paras. 31-6; TCSC 1988a, paras. 54-60). Is the headship of the civil service compatible, in principle, with concurrent tenure of another permanent secretaryship? Even if compatible, is not the range of responsibilities too wide, the sheer workload too great? As against these considerations, one may question whether, in the absence of a high-powered personnel department, an unattached head of the civil service could be effective. And if the role is to be attached to some other, then does not the cabinet secretaryship provide the most appropriate coupling? Such seems to be the latest thinking of the TCSC (1994a, para. 243).

The cabinet secretaryship

The cabinet secretary occupies a central position commanding a panoramic view of the Whitehall landscape. The Cabinet Office, which the cabinet secretary heads, is the gearbox of central government. It is staffed mainly by high-fliers on loan or secondment from other departments. Just how high they fly and how important the Cabinet Office is to their progress through the hierarchy will be seen in a later chapter.

Neither the secretaryship nor the Cabinet Office always enjoyed such status. The position and the institution were built upon the example of the Committee of Imperial Defence (CID). The CID was established in 1902 in the light of perceived shortcomings in the military co-ordination of the Boer War (Wilson 1975, pp. 27-35). It was equipped, from 1904, with a secretary and support staff to achieve better liaison between the services and to provide a firmer administrative framework for defence strategy. In similar circumstances the Cabinet Secretariat was formed in December 1916 in the early days of David Lloyd George's premiership. The First World War involved massive civil as well as military deployment, whereas the Boer campaign had been essentially a military matter. So, the Cabinet Office and the cabinet secretary would have an across the board involvement. The first incumbent, Colonel Maurice Hankey, had, unlike Fisher as Head of the Civil Service, a direct role in the creation of the position he was to occupy (Naylor 1984, pp. 8-9). He continued as Secretary of the CID, to which he had been appointed in 1912. In 1923 he became also Clerk of the Privy Council when Almeric Fitzroy was obliged to resign following allegations that he had been harassing women in Hyde Park. Hankey was to carry these three roles until his retirement in 1938, when they were separated.

Hankey's long tenure of the cabinet secretaryship was a factor in the development of the office. So, too, were his personal qualities. Tactful, shrewd, reticent in public, his craft was quiet persuasion. He nevertheless wielded considerable influence behind the scenes – as much and more than 'all but the most determined Cabinet ministers' (Watt 1965, p. 6). Yet this was a personal achievement, not a mark of Cabinet Office supremacy. For its early years were blighted by controversy and uncertainty. Initially it ran alongside Lloyd George's political secretariat, or Garden Suburb, with which it was often confused (Turner 1980). During the war the latter was the hub of ideas and policies. The cabinet secretary and the Cabinet Office were concerned with the more bureaucratic task of co-ordinating and supervizing the implementation of cabinet decisions. Upon the fall of the Lloyd George Coalition in 1922 the Garden Suburb disappeared. There had already been strenuous public calls, orchestrated among others by former cabinet minister and press baron Lord Beaverbrook, for the demise also of the Cabinet Office. Warren Fisher, sensing the opportunity, proposed its absorption within the Treasury. It nevertheless survived a Commons' vote shortly before Lloyd George's fall. And during his brief premiership, Andrew Bonar Law, ironically a close associate of Beaverbrook, ensured the permanence of the office and the institution. Ignoring the red-bloods of his party, he found the new arrangements too useful to abolish. The cabinet secretary and the Cabinet Office were now secure, the latter operating for a time with lower staffing levels.

In defending his creation, Lloyd George had claimed that the Cabinet Office's role was procedural – a 'recording machine' in the service of ministers and not an influence upon policy (HC Debs 1922, 5th Series, vol. 155, cols. 263-76). The Haldane Committee on the Machinery of Government, too, had recommended that the cabinet secretaryship be made permanent, though in an administrative rather than a policy role (Ministry of Reconstruction 1918, paras. 10-11). But procedural horizons were to prove almost infinitely flexible. It is difficult to know precisely when the functions of the Cabinet Office, as distinct from the cabinet secretary, became more policy than procedure orientated. If Hankey had long established himself at the centre of affairs, then the Cabinet Office may only have become fully developed as a high-powered policy machine under his two successors, Bridges and Brook.

The cabinet secretary retains the original 'procedural' functions: agenda preparation for cabinet and cabinet committee meetings; taking and drafting of minutes; circulation of papers; communication to departments. Misleadingly, the incumbent is sometimes referred to as the prime minister's permanent secretary. But the cabinet secretary serves the cabinet as a corporate body. In modern times the legendary door between the cabinet secretary's room and the prime minister's office has remained locked, save on rare occasions. This symbolizes a rather greater distance than normally there would be between a departmental minister and permanent secretary. Nevertheless there inevitably develops a more or less close personal relationship between cabinet secretary and prime minister. Some relationships have been closer than others. Notably close were those between Hankey and Lloyd George, between Brook and Churchill and, to a lesser extent, between Burke Trend and Harold Wilson in the 1960s (Pimlott 1992, p. 347; Ziegler 1993, pp. 184-5). There also developed a very close liaison between Thomas Jones and Stanley Baldwin. Jones was Deputy Cabinet Secretary but the division of work between himself and Hankey allowed Jones to operate in certain respects as a parallel cabinet secretary. Jones's association with Baldwin carried beyond his formal retirement from the civil service in 1930 (Middlemas and Barnes 1969, p. 169; Ellis 1992, p. 315).

It should not be supposed that either the cabinet secretary, or any other individual civil servant, has ever singlehandedly engaged or monopolized access to the levers of power. From the 1960s, especially, political leaders have cultivated and drawn upon alternative sources of advice and support (see the next two chapters). In this and in other ways Whitehall has become more fragmented. But the Cabinet Office and the Treasury remain the two central pillars of Whitehall. From time-to-time their respective positions of supremacy have been challenged. The examples of the Economic Section, the Garden Suburb, the DEA and the CSD have already been mentioned. To these one could add the short-lived Office of the Minister for Economic Affairs in 1947 and the Central Policy Review Staff (CPRS), set up in 1970 but disbanded in 1983 (Blackstone and Plowden 1988). Only the Policy Unit, set up in 1974 by Harold Wilson, has survived. It is not, in any case, entirely part of the official civil service. It is in some ways an alternative to the permanent bureaucracy.

Since Fisher's attempted coup in the early 1920s, the Treasury and the Cabinet Office have usually maintained the mutual posture of peaceful coexistence. Perhaps each is respectfully aware of the other's might. More than this, their spheres of influence, while intersecting at many points, revolve around different axes, working through different trajectories.

The hierarchy of permanent secretaries

The post of Cabinet Secretary and Head of the Home Civil Service currently comprises one of the three top permanent secretaryships in Whitehall. The other two are the Permanent Secretary of the Treasury, now confined to matters of economic and financial management, and the PUS of the Foreign and Commonwealth Office (FCO). The latter has also, since the 1960s, been Head of the Diplomatic Service. The post of Cabinet Secretary and Head of the Home Civil Service carries by a small margin the highest ceiling, but all three enjoy a salary differential over other permanent secretaries.

Aside from these three, heads of all other major departments are, at the time of writing, paid on a common scale. This has been known as grade 1 since the introduction in the 1970s of the open structure. Not all grade 1s are permanent heads of department: the grade is also used for certain senior advisory and other miscellaneous posts. However, under arrangements announced but yet to come into effect, this commonality looks set to disappear. Acting upon the recommendations of the Senior Salaries Review Body (SSRB), the government agreed early in 1995 to pay increases which included a lifting by some 27 per cent of the upper ceiling (i.e. that currently enjoyed only by the Head of the Home Civil Service). Announced simultaneously with low single figure pay increases for other public sector employees, the deal naturally fuelled controversy about disparities and about equity of treatment. But the SSRB and the government acknowledged what had also long been the case – that top mandarins' salaries were considerably lower than those of their counterparts in the private and in the recently privatized sectors. It would be necessary to pay more if Whitehall was to attract greater numbers of outsiders, something for which critics have pressed over many years (see Chapter 8). It would also be necessary to pay more in order to retain existing mandarins and to remove certain anomalies. At least one executive agency chief executive, recruited from outside the civil service, had been receiving a salary higher than that of the permanent secretary under whose wing he operated. Yet of equal significance is the nature of the new procedures for determining permanent secretaries' salaries. A committee will recommend an individual scale for each permanent secretaryship. The committee will be chaired by an outsider, Sir Michael Perry, Chairman of Unilever. Other committee members will include the Head of the Home Civil service, the Permanent Secretary to the Treasury, and two other business leaders. The scale for each permanent secretaryship will be drawn from a broad range (£90,000-£150,000 pa. from 1 April 1995). No longer will all mainstream departmental permanent secretaries be remunerated at the same level. It remains to be seen what implications this will have for the hierarchy of permanent secretaries and for the pattern of top level interdepartmental transfers (see Chapter 9).

A further feature of the Whitehall hierarchy has emerged with the creation in certain departments of second permanent secretaryships. Second permanent secretaryships are largely a modern phenomenon. George Barnes was a second secretary at the Board of Trade during the First World War. And Cyril Musgrave was Second Permanent Secretary at the Ministry of Supply for twelve months before his elevation to the permanent secretaryship in June 1956. But not until the 1960s did such positions find an established place in the hierarchy of some of the larger departments. By the mid-1970s there were sixteen such posts; today there are only half that number. These posts should not be confused with joint permanent secretaryships. The Treasury, as noted earlier, had joint permanent secretaries between 1956-68. Joint permanent secretaries existed there also between 1902-08 and between 1913-19. The practice, never widespread, was nevertheless more deeply rooted within certain other departments during the nineteenth century. The most notable examples were the Post Office (between 1836-54), the Privy Council (1821-59) and the Board of Trade (1829-67). Aside from the Treasury, such arrangements during the present century have usually been short-lived, expediential and occasioned by irregularities.

The essence of a joint secretaryship is that the post-holders enjoy equal status and (usually) equal pay. Second permanent secretaries receive a salary slightly lower than that of a permanent secretary. Currently it is approximately 90 per cent of the latter, though the proportion has varied. Variations are likely to be greater in future as a consequence of the new salary arrangements described above. The second permanent secretary is hierarchically subordinate to the departmental permanent secretary. In practice, there is often a lateral division of responsibilities. The second permanent secretary is usually also an accounting officer, responsible for a large area of the department's work. The position is therefore more than simply a deputy to the permanent secretary. The second permanent secretary is, in effect, another type of permanent secretary. If not exactly indistinguishable from that of permanent secretary, the office of second permanent secretary has a very similar brief, including that of advising ministers, the subject of the next chapter.

2 Advising ministers

Introduction

Traditionally, the task of advising ministers has been the most central of the permanent secretary's functions. It has also been the most controversial. This is an inevitable consequence of the sharp disjunction between the political and the official levels of government (Roll 1985, p. 186). Nowhere is this disjunction sharper than it is in Britain. Yet while there is a neat separation of personnel and of public projection the role of top British civil servants also entails a vital fusion of politics with administration (Thomas 1978, pp. 33-71). Permanent secretaries operate within the crucible of ministerial sensibilities. Whatever bears upon the minister must bear also upon the permanent secretary.

The role of all top officials is therefore shaped – warped according to some – by the notion of ministerial responsibility (Pyper 1991; Ponting 1989, p. 16). This role is the product of three interacting features which give special character to relationships between ministers and civil servants: the formal accountability of ministers to Parliament; the anonymity of officials – or at least their reticence in public on matters of high policy; and the permanence of the bureaucracy. These three factors came together historically for some of the reasons mentioned in the last chapter. They are often seen as mutually reinforcing, each being inherent to the other like the 'distinct but not separate' dimensions of the Holy Trinity.

None of this is to deny the existence of the critics – those who do not accept, for example, that the accountability of ministers establishes either the imperative of official anonymity or the necessity for bureaucratic permanence. Nor is it to obscure the fact that, descriptively, few would claim the prevalence today in anything like their pure forms the traditional notions of ministerial responsibility and the public non-persona of senior officials. The validity of some of these critiques and of accompanying proposals for reform will be examined in the final chapter. For the moment the focus is upon the advisory role of permanent secretaries to ministers. In order adequately to explain this it is necessary first to flesh out some of the implications of the constitutional position in which all senior civil servants are placed. There then follows a brief discussion about how ministers relate to the official Whitehall machine. This provides a platform for an examination of the advisory role – how, in what ways and on what sort of things permanent secretaries have advised their ministers. All this is to be seen in the context of more or less perpetual change. The chapter therefore concludes with an analysis of the changing advisory role played by permanent secretaries. The vexed questions of their influence upon ministers and their contribution to the performance of government are taken up in the penultimate chapter.

The constitutional yoke

It is well known that Britain does not have a unified, written constitution. There is no formal document or collection of documents which either purports to be a constitution or which could readily be invested with the status of a constitution. There are isolated statutes and miscellaneous other documents to which reference may be made from time-to-time in moments of difficulty or controversy. But much rests upon common understanding, convention, custom and practice. This gives a flexibility which for some is a source of abiding strength but which for others is a fundamental weakness. More particularly, this flexibility and the absence of a detailed written constitution can sometimes make it difficult to specify what exactly is the formal position of civil servants – at least in terms that would receive universal acclaim. Countless texts, monographs and speeches have nevertheless been devoted to the subject. We can talk in a loose sense about a 'constitution' which rests heavily upon convention and understanding even if it is not a written constitution the like of which exists in most other countries. It is therefore possible to set out the main elements. This may best be done by addressing three questions: what is the prima facie constitutional position of the senior civil servant as generally understood, particularly that of the permanent secretary; what are the characteristics of a good adviser; and what tensions are likely to be encountered in performing an effective advisory role?

As noted in the last chapter, it was established by the middle of the nineteenth century that the position of permanent secretary was subordinate to that of the democratically elected politician. Fundamental to this is the ultimate prerogative of the minister to decide – to override, reject or to draw selectively upon the advice of senior officials. There is however a distinction between, on the one hand, rejecting advice after due reflection and, on the other hand, declining to give due consideration to advice properly tendered. It was alleged in 1993 that Home Secretary Michael Howard had made policy decisions without having given proper consideration to the advice available from the appropriate officials in his department (*The Guardian*, 11 November 1993). Clive Whitmore, the PUS, denied a specific allegation that he had received a letter of complaint from those officials who apparently felt aggrieved (*The Guardian*, 12 November 1993). He also claimed that, while not always accepting the advice offered, ministers at the Home Office had at least given ear to alternative soundings. This has not allayed critics who continue to insist that there has been a growing tendency among ministers to ignore uncongenial advice and factual data – if not in the Home Office, then elsewhere in Whitehall (Plowden 1994, p. 104). But even if such allegations were to be borne out it is a moot point as to whether there would have occurred any strict constitutional impropriety. Nor, if true, would it be without precedent. Austen Chamberlain, during his first spell as Chancellor of the Exchequer (1903-05), seems not to have taken the top Treasury mandarins fully into his confidence. They were left guessing as to his intentions (Bahlman 1993, p. 453). With perhaps as much bravura as accuracy Margaret Thatcher once dismissed allegations that a leak had emanated from her officials in Downing Street. This she did with the comment: 'they never know anything, so how could they leak?' (Prior 1986, p. 134).

It may be unwise, even detrimental to good government, for ministers not to give careful consideration to official advice before making a decision. It is certainly contrary to the conventional practice to which most ministers adhere most of the time. It also rests uneasily with the guidelines issued to ministers, *Questions of Procedure for Ministers*. This states that: 'Ministers have a duty to give fair consideration and due weight to informed and impartial advice from civil servants, as well as to other considerations and advice, in making decisions' (Cabinet Office 1992, para. 55). But 'fair consideration and due weight' may be capable of interpretation. Moreover the constitutional status of the document is unclear. There is no formal sanction and much lies at the minister's discretion. It is therefore by no means clear that a constitutional impropriety would arise unless ministers publicly named and blamed officials for ensuing policy failures or, for that matter, implicated them personally in the event of success. Here there is a fine line between public plaudits (or brickbats) for the official machine and the disclosure of contributions made by individual civil servants to specific policies. It has until recently been the accepted wisdom that the advice tendered to ministers by civil servants at all levels should remain confidential. The more vigorous proponents of open government would dispute the necessity for this but it remains the working assumption. It has had little to do with the Official Secrets Act. It is much more about the extent to which confidentiality has been and continues to be a practical necessity for free exchange, hence mutual trust, between minister and mandarin and to allow the latter to inspire equal trust in a new minister and a new government.

Behind these closed doors it is legitimate for the permanent secretary to give strong, uninhibited, advice to the minister. In all save the rarest of circumstances the minister will at least listen. The minister may not be moved and the permanent secretary may try again, perhaps taking a different tack. This, too, is legitimate provided the permanent secretary keeps within the bounds of Whitehall. Clearly the activities of Mowatt and Vansittart, noted in the last chapter, are beyond the pale. Both permanent secretary and minister know that in the end the minister, if resolute, must prevail. In retirement and with rueful acknowledgement Vansittart reflected: 'I conceded no superiority to politicians except that in a clash they must win' (1958, p. 399). It is the bureaucratic equivalent of the shopkeeper's lament that the customer is always right. It calls for some fine judgements. As a permanent secretary of the 1990s put it: 'at some point – and it's one of the most difficult things to know when – you have to salute the flag and get on with it'.

The ability to swing behind a policy against which permanent secretaries have previously been counselling their ministers is something not easily understood by those who are unversed in the ways of Whitehall. Nor is it always fully accepted by those who do know the system. It is one of the most distinct qualities of the top British mandarin. Charles Hill, Conservative Minister for Housing and Local Government in the early 1960s, recalled that on one fairly important policy issue he had decided against the advice received from his department and from its permanent secretary, Evelyn Sharp. Sharp had presented strong arguments, strongly held. Hill therefore felt it more appropriate to ask his private secretary to draft the paper he intended to put to the cabinet. This upset Sharp even more. She confounded him by producing, within twenty-four hours, a paper in support of the minister's proposals that was 'terse, clear, strongly argued and very convincing'. As Hill noted: 'She had had her say, the internal argument was over... from now on her job was to help me persuade my colleagues of its wisdom' (Hill 1964, p. 232). More recently Douglas Wass, Permanent Secretary to the Treasury, held views about the handling of the economy which differed from those of the Thatcher government in the early 1980s. This has been acknowledged by the then Chancellor of the Exchequer, Geoffrey Howe. Yet it did not affect Wass's willingness 'to commit himself wholeheartedly to the task in hand' (Howe 1994, p. 284).

An area of grey emerges though if, before a decision has been taken, the permanent secretary begins to mobilize other permanent secretaries and, through them, other ministers. Here there lurks an uncertainty as to where exactly the permanent secretary's loyalties rest. Are they exclusively to the departmental minister? Are they to the government as a whole, the prime minister or to the head of the civil service? Or are they to some more rarefied notion of state, constitution or ethical touchstone? These and related matters will be discussed at greater length in the final chapter. But for immediate and practical purposes there is no definitive answer to these questions. In the wake of the Ponting Affair (see Chapter 1) the then head of the home civil service issued in February 1985 a memorandum seeking to clarify the duties and responsibilities of civil servants in relation to ministers. The Armstrong Memorandum, as it has come to be known, was issued following consultation and with the agreement of the departmental permanent secretaries of the day. It has since been incorporated into the Civil Service Management Code, issued in 1993. It states that:

> The Civil Service as such has no constitutional personality or responsibility separate from the duly elected government of the day.... The Civil Service serves the Government of the day as a whole, that is to say Her Majesty's ministers collectively, and the Prime Minister is the Minister for the Civil Service. The duty of the individual civil servant is first and foremost to the Minister of the Crown who is in charge of the Department in which he or she is serving.
> (HM Treasury 1993, Section 4.1, Annex A, paras. 3-4).

It is, in effect, a restatement of the traditional position as commonly understood. The very necessity for its formal expression may well be indicative of a lack of consensus. As such it has been widely condemned as inadequate, lacking in imagination and failing to grapple with the tensions and dilemmas that are seen as confronting the modern civil servant. For example, it appears to acknowledge no potential conflict between loyalty to the minister and loyalty to the government as a whole. Still, in the absence of anything else the Armstrong Memorandum has been the only authoritative document on the subject. This may change with the introduction of a new code following pressure from the FDA and the TCSC (see Chapter 12) – but only slightly. The proposed code restates the duty of all civil servants to serve the government of the day while recognizing the need to discharge public functions 'reasonably and according to the law', including international law, the administration of justice and the ethical standards of certain professions (Cabinet Office 1995, p. 49). It does not specify whether and in what circumstances these are or could become higher calls of duty than to the departmental minister in the event of a conflict of loyalty. Perhaps it would be difficult and indeed inappropriate for a code to make such specification.

The working assumption, then, is that the primary and immediate loyalty of the permanent secretary is to the minister. This is what permanent secretaries believe: it is the benchmark from which deviation requires special justification – and then only within the confines of Whitehall. And when, having heard the arguments, the minister decides upon a course of action then the permanent secretary and other senior mandarins must accept the decision even if it is not their preferred option. Ideally, they should perhaps learn to internalize it, though this may be asking too much. Not all have the supreme gifts of an Evelyn Sharp. It may mean making the best of government election pledges – pledges which may be ill-fitted for ready implementation and with which even the minister may not be wholly enamoured. Ian Bancroft, former Head of the Home Civil Service, has described some such pledges as 'garbage'. He says that it then becomes a question of 'handling matters so that somehow or other the garbage is made into something edible' (Hennessy 1989, pp. 509-10). A special responsibility falls upon the permanent secretary. The minister will usually look above all to this official to ensure that the department swings behind the policy, or decision, that has been made. This brings into play a complex of internal management issues that are the subject of the next chapter.

What gives extra piquancy to the constitutional position of all civil servants is their permanence. Permanent secretaries may be called upon one day to put their weight behind policies which are different from, at odds with or even the antithesis of those for which they have been striving the previous day. Of course, there is more than an element of caricature about this if taken literally. Yet shifts of direction can be severe – not only upon a change of government but upon the more common occurrence of a ministerial reshuffle. Bureaucratic sensibilities blow little wind in the sway of forces that shape such reshuffles. Far from strengthening the civil service, ministerial reshuffles are often unwelcome (Alderman and Cross 1979). The logistics attending their execution – the speed and secrecy, notwithstanding perhaps many months of speculation – exacerbate the disruption. The departmental permanent secretary may hear an authoritative whisper, or get a private reassurance from the minister who is confident of staying. Usually there is little warning as to the identity of the new minister. The permanent secretary will be involved where reshuffles are accompanied by departmental reorganization – though not always (Alderman and Carter 1992, p. 522). For all concerned, reshuffles can occasionally bring trauma and always a heavier workload as top officials brief the new minister and adapt to a new style. Those who represent British interests abroad are equally sensitive to the disjunctions that sometimes ensue. The case has been made (in jest) for a psychological disturbance allowance (Henderson 1994, p. 60).

What, then, are the characteristics of one who is able successfully to take all this on board? It is necessary, in the time-honoured phrase, to 'know the minister's mind'. Richard Crossman had a tempestuous, love-hate relationship with Evelyn Sharp, his permanent secretary at the Ministry of Housing and Local Government (MHLG) in the 1960s. After a few months though Crossman, like Charles Hill before him, was acknowledging the value of Sharp's 'skill and speed of drafting and her power to take an idea of mine and think it through and write it out' (Crossman 1975, p. 185). This, as Evelyn Sharp's career would testify, is not a licence simply to serve up advice reckoned to be congenial to the minister; or, more perversely, to do the opposite. Rather, it is the duty of the permanent secretary to ensure, so far as possible, that the minister is aware of all the salient facts and considerations, palatable or otherwise. This may include frank and fearless, but usually friendly, exchanges. A good permanent secretary need not abandon that which he or she considers right until overruled by the minister. When a minister overrules, it is usually (not always) on account of some political calculation or other value judgement. William Harcourt, the late-nineteenth century Liberal leader, thought that it was the function of ministers simply to tell civil servants what the public would not stand (Greenleaf 1987, p. 184). This is a facile interpretation. Then, as now, senior mandarins would also have remained sensitive to the political climate. Ministers expect to be warned of the political as well as the administrative and technical aspects of any course of action under consideration. They will be justified in complaining (privately, not publicly) if officials have failed to apprise them of obvious pitfalls. The permanent secretary will take the rap. It is the job of officials to spot problems before they become acute – to help keep the minister one jump ahead and, more generally, to make for 'better' or better-informed decisions. It is the job of the permanent secretary sometimes to do this, always to see that it is done. This implies a wider vision and long sightedness.

This longer term vision begets a number of finely tuned tensions inherent to the advisory role. Knowing the mind of the minister may often mean knowing the mind of one necessarily absorbed with the short term. To this extent and in the cause of faithful service to the minister the short term can become omnipresent to the detriment of good governance. One former permanent secretary considered it to be his duty to push ministers from a short term to a medium term view and to look at strategy (Cubbon 1993, p. 11).

Therein lies a further tension. In interposing an alternative perspective – one that is complementary let alone one that rests uneasily alongside ministerial inclinations – the permanent secretary may appear obstructive. Much will depend upon the circumstances and upon the way in which things are handled, by both parties. A well intentioned warning may be a clever piece of manoeuvring in the eyes of the beholder. If, alternatively, the permanent secretary permits undue 'trimming', as distinct from inadvertence, then there may be a loss not only to the performance of government but also to the principle of bureaucratic impartiality. Yet what would be the good, it may be asked, in suggesting courses that were the negation of government objectives? In helping ministers to move in the direction of their (and presumably the electorate's) choice it is therefore necessary, as one former permanent secretary put it, to 'take on in some degree the coloration of the party in power' (Part 1990, pp. 106-7). It is another tricky balancing act. Just how tricky is evident in the fact that the bureaucracy was often condemned during the 1960s and '70s for blocking or parrying the efforts of ministers, while in the 1980s and '90s it has been almost equally berated for its obsequience.

Ministers know that they are birds of passage. Permanent secretaries know it too. As already mentioned, a change of government or a ministerial reshuffle may bring a new political chief to the helm at a moment's notice. The permanent secretary must to the last remain loyal to the one currently in situ while knowing that a new face could herald a change of emphasis or direction. The tension here is heightened to the extent to which top officials should and do (temporarily) take on some of the government's coloration. But lines of policy, courses of action, can no more be halted and set off again without some loss of momentum than can a car at full speed be brought to an instant halt and then started up again in top gear. There may then be the tendency never to move out of low gear – to hold back in anticipation of the possible. Evelyn Sharp, then a deputy secretary, acknowledged that this was so in the MHLG during the latter stages of the Attlee government. The minister, Hugh Dalton, was equally aware both of the government's precariousness and of his officials' predicament (Pimlott 1985, p. 595).

All this can induce a certain world-weariness, even cynicism, among long-toothed permanent secretaries. In a sense it is inevitable, but no less frustrating for ministers if it becomes too obvious. Barbara Castle (1993, p. 368) reflected upon Thomas Padmore at the Ministry of Transport during the 1960s: 'I longed for a permanent secretary who would guide my new initiatives because he believed in them, instead of just accepting them'.

With all these ambiguities and tensions it is not surprising that the advisory role of permanent secretaries has often been the focus of so much controversy, so many differing prescriptions and almost as many misapprehensions. Before looking at the way permanent secretaries advise ministers it will be useful briefly to consider the Whitehall machine from the perspective of ministers.

Ministers and the Whitehall machine

While in constitutional terms the minister is the prime mover, or at least the fulcrum, of departmental activity there is an implicit contract. The department, through the permanent secretary, will allow itself to be directed by the minister so long as the minister understands that, in so doing, its compliance should be acknowledged. Departments do not like being taken too much for granted. If they are, life can be made difficult for the minister. The minister may still prevail, but at the expense of much trouble, energy and perhaps depletion of political capital. It is far better to carry the department.

It has been acknowledged that: 'the Civil Service is not the property of any single Administration...' (Cabinet Office 1994, p. 4, para. 1.8). This is to say that, questions of day-to-day loyalty notwithstanding, neither permanent secretaries nor their departments are exactly pieces of putty in the hands of ministers. It is also to say that there is an underlying dependency: ministers rely on their top officials. This has been given vivid expression by Michael Heseltine (1990, p. 11):

> I freely admit to the moments where the pure gold of the perceptive permanent secretary shone through... You are tired. It is late... you ramble, hesitate and suddenly the voice at your elbow takes over: "I think that's most helpful Secretary of State. We'll proceed as you have outlined which, if I follow your argument correctly, I would summarise as follows..." And the permanent secretary pours out a string of elegant phrases and concise instructions as tears of gratitude well up within you.

Heseltine is not a weak minister. Nor was Hugh Dalton. Yet he, too, upon being shown the way out of a tight corner, would 'sigh with relief and put his initials at the bottom' (Pimlott 1985, p. 426). Richard Crossman saw things rather differently. He described a sensation akin to 'floating on the most comfortable support'. He was conscious of a great departmental machine devoted to his sustenance. He added that, were he to challenge and try to redirect policy 'there would be no formal tension at first, only quiet resistance – but a great deal of it' (Crossman 1975, p. 31). An echo of this can be found among those who have held office more recently, albeit from a smaller minority of ministers (see Clark 1993, p. 240).

Many politicians have taken to heart Arthur Henderson's widely quoted line that the first forty-eight hours determine whether the minister will run the department or whether the department runs the minister. With this in mind some have employed theatrical gestures, no doubt to the amusement of the knowing permanent secretary. A few have tried to sustain a war of attrition built upon constant suspicion and with the occasional, or more than occasional, showdown.

From the ministerial perspective, part of the problem lies in the 'loneliness of the short-distance runner' (Castle 1973). Even with the advent of political and other temporary advisers, ministers can sometimes feel lonely, detached and vulnerable. Ministerial life is often relatively short – an average since the First World War of approximately two and a half years in any one position (Alt 1975; Rose 1991). Ministers need to make their mark quickly. Understandably they often want to go faster and further than civil servants think either prudent or possible, especially with a major initiative which impinges upon other policy areas. This will usually involve the permanent secretary in the task of seed-sowing outside the department. To the minister, this may seem like the classic Whitehall conspiracy – especially if, as a result, the permanent secretary begins to express increasing doubts about the way forward. On occasion there may indeed be a conspiracy of sorts – usually where a minister lacks support among cabinet colleagues. Permanent secretaries are highly sensitive to the political fortunes of their ministers. This can work both ways. Some ministers, after what they consider to have been lukewarm support from officials, may notice a more fulsome response as they ascend the 'greasy pole'. Conversely, the first tremblings of a ministerial career passing its meridian will often percolate through the permanent secretary – in the manner of nuance and subtlety rather than facile transmission. The Whitehall grapevine is never more efficient than when disseminating the political barometer.

One of the most difficult things for a minister is to engage with the Whitehall machine without becoming ensnared in its disarming embrace – to forge its many positive but potentially wayward talents to the ministerial perspective. The permanent secretary is there to help the minister to do this. It will help if the minister has clear ideas and if these ideas are the product of careful thought. The permanent secretary will increase in confidence and therefore in the ability to assist if the minister can also win political battles and is skilful in presenting policies to the public. Better still if the government remains strong for a sustained period and without being blown off course by unforeseen crises or undue drift. In many ways, these conditions were fulfilled during the 1980s. It was widely believed that the bureaucracy had become a much less potent force: that its grip upon ministers, thought by some previously to have been unacceptably tight, had been broken (Middlemas 1991, p. 422). This was the more plausible with a prime minister, Margaret Thatcher, who made little secret of her disdain for officialdom. Yet the adversarial paradigm upon which such views are predicated is generally much further from reality than the alternative model of mutual co-operation between ministers and officials. Certainly relationships passed through some 'choppy waters' during the 1980s. This has been acknowledged both by the present head of the civil service and by a permanent secretary whose career embraced the first two years of the Thatcher era (Butler 1990, p. 3; Nairne 1994, p. 5). But most of the departmental ministers of the Thatcher years seemed to have enjoyed productive relationships with their permanent secretaries. Many, like Heseltine, have acknowledged their debt to those whose efforts helped to secure the policies they wanted, even though some of the mandarins may have had misgivings about the objectives to which they were lending assistance (Barberis 1994).

From a comparative perspective it has been observed that Britain remains a political system with ' a relatively low level of administrative power and control' (Peters 1989, p. 59). The bureaucratic machine is nevertheless a very powerful instrument. Whether for good or ill depends in fair measure, even from the ministerial perspective, upon ministers themselves. For the unwary, the inept, the heavy-handed or simply the unlucky the pressure of the bureaucracy can seem like a 'relentless... tide that is always coming in' (Haines 1977, p. 25). Those who have tried to fight it have rarely triumphed. Their achievements have usually been modest – less than their talents would have promised. Such was the fate of Labour ministers Richard Crossman and George Brown. They were defeated not by the bureaucracy but by themselves. Margaret Thatcher is an exception to the rule. She waged war upon the bureaucracy and won – mostly and for most of the time. She nevertheless had more natural allies at various levels and worked more closely than is often supposed with top mandarins, including those who were by no means wholly of her own disposition. More commonly ministers have been successful where they have befriended the bureaucracy while establishing an unchallenged authority. One of the classic examples was Labour's early post-war Foreign Secretary, Ernest Bevin. In a tribute which explains much about his ability to use the Whitehall machine Bevin's biographer says: 'He... always had enough ideas of his own not to mind picking up others from a staff which he expected to argue the case for alternative courses of action ' (Bullock 1983, pp 101-2). If Bevin was a civil servant's minister he was also the politician's politician. His achievements rank among the most considerable of any of the twentieth century foreign secretaries.

It would be easy to conclude from all this that when things go wrong between a permanent secretary and a minister the latter is always at fault. Breakdowns are not frequent but they do occur. Things can go wrong for a variety of reasons. It is as difficult to categorize and analyze these reasons as it is to ascertain culpability. The chemistry of personalities is usually an ingredient. The bottom line is that a minister must have confidence in the permanent secretary. Barbara Castle, as previously noted, had no confidence in Thomas Padmore. She tried to get him removed. But Padmore did not retire until after Castle herself had taken another cabinet post. Margaret Thatcher tried in the early 1970s to remove her permanent secretary, William Pile, from the DES (Young 1990, p.72). Pile held on, retaining the support of Prime Minister Heath, no doubt on the advice of William Armstrong. Amid more intense publicity, Peter Kemp was forced to take early retirement in 1992. Rumour had it that he did not carry the confidence of the new minister, William Waldegrave. The official version was that

Kemp's job had changed (which was palpably true) from the specific role of Next Steps Project Manager, to which he had been appointed, to something more like a standard departmental permanent secretaryship. For the latter he was thought to be unsuitable. No other post of comparable standing could be found for him in Whitehall.

Rifts between a minister and a permanent secretary can sometimes be absorbed and localized. The minister may by-pass the permanent secretary, or at any rate look to other officials and to other sources for first-line support. A mutually acceptable *modus vivendi* may still be possible. Serious rifts, though, may send more profound shock waves through the system. The head of the civil service then has to decide whether to move the permanent secretary or whether to sit it out, perhaps in anticipation of an imminent cabinet reshuffle or the retirement or voluntary resignation of the permanent secretary. Much depends upon the nature, the intensity and the wider consequences of the rift. A permanent secretary known to have quarrelled with one minister may be difficult to sell to another. A move that is acceptable on all other considerations may bring a permanent secretary to a department in which he or she has no experience and little affinity. This is not ideal but it is a price Whitehall has sometimes been willing to pay. It pays the price because it is at the very least highly desirable that there should exist between minister and permanent secretary a good working relationship – the bedrock of the advisory role.

Giving advice

It has been said that it is difficult to convey to someone who has not experienced it just how close a permanent secretary and a minister can become (Wass 1984, p. 58). This echoes William Beveridge's famous remark likening the relationship to that between husband and wife in that they should be divided by no secrets. The permanent secretary can be and often is 'a sort of political neuter and father-confessor figure' (Theakston 1987, p. 105). This role is facilitated by the fact that the permanent secretary is not a Parliamentary or party politician. Ministers have often seen more frequently and talked more freely to their permanent secretaries than to their political colleagues (Headey 1974, p. 153). Former permanent secretary Idwal Pugh believes that the ideal relationship exists 'when you meet late in the evening over a whisky or a cup of tea and talk about this and that' (Crosland 1983, p. 266).

Some develop enduring personal friendships, while other relationships never exceed strict professional necessity. It is, of course, an interactive process shaped as much by the imperatives of office as by individual human proclivities – and then more by those of the minister. A permanent secretary of the 1990s explained: 'unless the minister wants to develop a close relationship – and some I've been closer to than others – it's a business relationship rather than a close one'.

Three more general points may be made about types of relationship. First, at any given point over the last hundred or so years, there have coexisted various patterns in the daily relationships between permanent secretaries and ministers. Some have been close, overlaid and even preceded by existing friendships. Others have always been more businesslike. Second, there is no reason to suppose that either arrangement is any more or less satisfactory for the conduct of government so long as it suits the parties concerned, especially the minister. Third, while difficult to measure, there has probably been a growing tendency toward the businesslike pattern over the last two or three decades. There are various possible reasons for this tendency, such as it may be. A more businesslike approach may be a consequence of the rise of the career politician (Riddell 1993). This perhaps ties in with a certain social decomposition both in the political and in the administrative elite (see below, Chapter 6). It may reflect a greater readiness among some ministers to look for support beyond the civil service. It may also reflect a greater complexity (discussed below) in the pattern of relationships at senior level within Whitehall. Permanent secretaries now share their ministers, as it were, with other senior officials. And, as ever, the private secretary is usually closer to the minister than is the permanent secretary.

Private secretaries have been described by one of their number as the 'impresarios of Whitehall' (Henderson 1984, p. 1). They are constantly on hand, go everywhere – indeed live virtually at the minister's hip. They will often be the first to detect the initial rumblings of a political earthquake which may come to engulf the minister, especially if the epicentre happens to be some private or personal scandal. Richard 'Sam' Way was PUS at the War Office in 1963 when there emerged the scandal that was to cost minister John Profumo his job and the government a serious embarrassment. Profumo had had an affair with one Christine Keeler who was also conducting an affair with a Soviet diplomat. For some the situation was pregnant, if nothing else, with security implications. What sunk Profumo was his having to be forced to concede a sexual relationship when initially he had steadfastly maintained – both publicly in the Commons and privately to premier Harold Macmillan – that there had been no such affair. Way had no reason to doubt his minister's initial denials until he saw the press reports. On reflection, he realized that the private office must at an earlier stage have known a good deal about what was happening (National Oral Archive Transcript (NOA Tr.), pp. 37-8). Interestingly, Way implied no impropriety on the part of the private office in his not having been informed at the outset. Neither at the time nor later did he attempt to discover how much these uniquely placed but nevertheless more junior officials had known and about which he had initially been left uninformed.

Such occurrences are not common but they do happen from time-to-time. It should not be supposed that the minister's private office is some sort of fortress, still less an army of ministerial allies pitched into battle with the permanent secretary. The permanent secretary will have a say in the staffing of the private office. Such appointments continue to be significant in the promotion chain which may lead to a permanent secretaryship (see Chapter 7). Moreover, as a former permanent secretary has said, a good private secretary can do more than perhaps anyone else in Whitehall to get a minister and a permanent secretary on 'valid' terms with each other (Redcliffe-Maud 1981, p. 52). Above all, the private secretary is not a surrogate permanent secretary. There will certainly be a heavier reliance upon the private secretary for many of the day-to-day matters that command the minister's attention. But there are some things which the permanent secretary can do and which the private secretary cannot do, especially when it comes to pulling the big levers that will mobilize the Whitehall machine. Only the prime minister's private office carries a punch anything like that of a permanent secretary.

There is a further and telling aspect to this dissection of relationships. One of the permanent secretaries of the 1990s put it like this:

> What you have to avoid as the permanent secretary is becoming a glorified principal private secretary to the secretary of state. That's something which could happen all too easily... where there's a great deal of policy development going on into which the permanent secretary is drawn, and also where we get quite a lot of crises of a policy kind. You have to respond to some new kind of situation out there in the world outside – or a crisis of an operational kind, which again draws you in... And you spend quite a lot of time just sitting with the secretary of state.

Another permanent secretary expressed it rather differently:

> ...the arrangement I have with my minister is that he knows I have a big department to run and that I'm more valuable to him sitting here making sure it all works in two or three weeks' time than sitting in his room all day.

This same permanent secretary acknowledged that, if called by the minister, he would not say 'no I'm not coming'. To this extent the style and disposition of the minister are important factors. Some permanent secretaries are never out of their minister's office because the minister wants them there. Others see their ministers only occasionally, perhaps once or twice per week. None could abstain from contact for eighteen months as did Warren

Fisher with Chancellor of the Exchequer Winston Churchill in the 1920s (Chapman 1988, p. 30). This was quite untypical of an era when permanent secretaries probably saw as much if not more of their ministers than do their present day descendants – bearing in mind the points made earlier about varying personalities and circumstances. In any case at the Treasury Fisher was supported by three controllers (permanent secretary level) who did have regular contact with the Chancellor. As Head of the Civil Service, Fisher tended to work directly to the Prime Minister. Besides, Fisher and Churchill did not get on, having clashed before. Fisher derided Churchill as 'a lunatic' (O'Halpin 1989, p. 127).

Normally, most permanent secretaries will see their ministers daily, sometimes more than once a day, seldom less than twice a week when Parliament is in session. They come into contact with junior ministers, too. Such contacts are less frequent – perhaps once a week – and only when there is a particular reason. These are the generalities within and around which there are many individual variations.

It is rare nowadays for a permanent secretary to accompany the minister outside Whitehall. Here there seems to have been a distinct shift over the last couple of decades. It can be seen most clearly at the FCO. During the Wilson and Heath governments it was the custom for the PUS to travel abroad with the Foreign Secretary (Greenhill 1993, p. 155). Now the PUS is much more likely to remain in Whitehall to 'mind the shop' (Dickie 1992, pp. 50-1). This itself says quite a lot about the changing roles of permanent secretaries and in particular about their changing advisory roles.

Changing advisory roles

On what sort of matters do permanent secretaries advise ministers? How has this changed over time? And why?

It would be easy but rather misleading to equate 'advice' with 'policy'. According to one former permanent secretary policy advice is rather a misnomer because ministers think in terms of 'ideas and prejudices and headlines rather than policies' (Cubbon 1993, p. 9). And if ministers think in such terms so too, in some measure, must permanent secretaries. In a sense this may be as unfair to ministers as it is to permanent secretaries. Both are prisoners of their environment. Ministers must be ready to respond to media comment, be it about a general policy decision, an apparent failure of policy or a criticism about the operation of some more specific aspect of the department's work. The permanent secretary must be ready, at short notice, to help the minister deal with such excursions. One of the current permanent secretaries said: 'Permanent officials are partly there actually to prop up ministers and keep them cheerful – and the permanent secretary has an important role in that respect for the minister'. The same individual acknowledged that it was only upon his becoming a permanent secretary that he was again reminded (from his days as a private secretary) 'just how stinkingly difficult it is to be a minister'. The more extensive, better informed and heightened media probings of the last couple of decades have undoubtedly added to the burdens of ministerial life. They may also have amplified the permanent secretary's propping up role.

Ideas and prejudices, as Cubbon calls them, are, of course, meat and drink to politicians. They are necessarily also part of the permanent secretary's diet, though in a different sense. Even so, beyond a certain point they may leave the modern mandarin feeling somewhat uncomfortable. Politicians have complained, for example, at the inability of senior officials to write good speeches – to project policies in political terms (Castle 1980, p. 174; 1984, p. 432). This is not always true. Macmillan's iconoclastic 'Winds of Change' speech to the South African Parliament in February 1960 contained a large input from a former permanent secretary, John Maud, and was polished up by Cabinet Secretary Norman Brook (Horne 1989, pp. 194-5). Lloyd George's budget speech of 1912 was based upon a memorandum from his permanent secretary, John Bradbury, which stated the case for Liberal finance 'with a degree of partisan commitment that no politician could have exceeded' (Grigg 1985, p. 34).

Permanent secretaries continue occasionally to have a hand in the preparation of speeches and other departmentally related public statements made by their ministers. But theirs will rarely be the major contribution. More commonly they will cast a watchful eye, perhaps redrafting as necessary if (but only if) there is an important and sensitive issue at stake. And for the pot-boiling political speeches, the Whitehall bureaucracy will check only for factual accuracy. The main inputs come from elsewhere. Top mandarins no longer, if ever they did, have anything like a monopoly. So, too, in broad policy – and for two main reasons. First, the increasing tendency of ministers to supplement official advice with policy inputs from other sources. Second, fragmentation within the Whitehall bureaucracy itself.

The first of these two factors requires only brief comment in the present context. There has undoubtedly developed during the 1980s and 1990s a greater tendency among ministers to draw upon sources of advice adjacent to and outside the regular civil service. The permanent bureaucracy has, in turn, learnt to share its advisory role with other, alternative, input sources. Specifically, those adjacent to and working alongside the regular bureaucracy include temporary political, specialist and other personal advisers to ministers. Those outside Whitehall comprise part of what are commonly called 'policy communities', operating through the medium of 'policy networks' (Wright 1988; Marsh and Rhodes 1992). Increasingly prominent have been a certain variety of think tanks, or independent research institutes.

Temporary advisers have a far longer history than is often supposed. They became semi-institutionalized under Harold Wilson's first premiership. They were at first regarded with suspicion by civil servants, not least by permanent secretaries. They were accorded tentative but then more fulsome accommodation (Donoughue 1987, pp. 22-4). They came of age during the 1980s and now seem to work harmoniously alongside the 'regulars'. Individual ministers are permitted up to two political advisers, though there may be other specialists in addition. The Prime Minister's Policy Unit (see above Chapter 1) has been the location for some of the most influential of the political advisers. It is difficult to know precisely how influential they are or have been in providing policy advice for ministers. Certainly during the 1980s individuals operating within the Policy Unit such as John Hoskyns, Norman Strauss, Ferdinand Mount and others, such as Alan Walters, exercised considerable leverage, if only for limited periods (Jones 1987). Others again, such as Alfred Sherman, Lord Harris, Arthur Seldon and Madsen Pirie had direct or indirect influence at the highest levels while maintaining their association with independent think tanks. Sherman was a co-founder of the Centre for Policy Studies, Seldon and Harris founder members of the Institute of Economic Affairs. The community of think tanks, again, is no recent phenomenon. But these bodies have had a higher profile during the 1980s and '90s than hitherto. Certain of those among the right wing variety carried a profound resonance during the 1980s (Cockett 1994). Generally, though, their pitch is the broader intellectual climate – the underlying assumptions and epistemic communities within which and through which policy ideas emerge (Stone 1993).

Perhaps more pertinent to the advisory role of the permanent secretary is the second broad factor mentioned above – fragmentation within the bureaucracy itself. Here the changes have been more subtle, less perceptible and, where noticed, sometimes misunderstood in their evolutionary context.

The modern permanent secretary is rarely, even within the confines of the official machine, a conspicuous policy initiator – certainly not in the manner of Hill, Chadwick or Kay-Shuttleworth in the heady days of the nineteenth century. Such figures really could, and did, change things, almost singlehandedly. The permanent secretary of today is one, albeit critical, strand in a multicentric complex. In conjunction with the greater availability of advice to ministers from sources adjacent to and outside the regular civil service this constitutes a notable dimension of fragmentation. It has also been seen as the harbinger of a less significant existence for and even the eventual abolition of the office of permanent secretary (see Chapter 5).

Perhaps the most telling comparisons are those with permanent secretaries of the middle decades of the present century. At the Home Office Charles Cunningham, PUS between 1957-66, was the sole channel through which the secretary of state received advice. A frustrated Home Secretary

Roy Jenkins has described how he would receive from Cunningham one clear recommendation expressed in a few hundred words of lucid prose. There were no supporting documents, no allusion to possible alternative courses of action. Instead: 'all wrinkles had been smoothed away by the firm and skilled hands of the permanent under-secretary' (Jenkins 1991, p. 182). Cunningham's penchant for drafting personally all answers to Parliamentary questions is legendary.

Cunningham was by no means the only permanent secretary of his era to monopolize or dominate the advisory role. Eric Bowyer, head of the Ministry of Pensions and National Insurance (MPNI) between 1955-64, used to have premeetings in which he decided the departmental line to be put to the minister. It was woe betide anyone who didn't toe the line: they were simply excluded from further meetings (private information). Edward Playfair was himself a permanent secretary of the same era. He claims that one of his peers simply refused to tell his political chief that all the under secretaries and assistant secretaries were of the opinion that 'the decision to which the minister was committing himself was utterly unworkable and politically harmful' (Playfair 1965, p. 264). As the newly appointed Minister of Housing, Harold Macmillan was told bluntly by departmental head Thomas Sheepshanks that it was unconstitutional for a minister to consult anyone other than the permanent secretary (Macmillan 1969, p. 401).

There was indeed some substance to Sheepshanks's position. A cabinet paper issued in 1949 had stated that: 'The minister is entitled to look to a single person who can advise him on policy... and that duty must be discharged by the permanent secretary' (Theakston 1987, pp. 74-5). Some permanent secretaries were, as we have just seen, jealous guardians of this prerogative. Others no less jealous were unable to hold the line. Sheepshanks was effectively by-passed by Macmillan who began to work through other officials, notably Evelyn Sharp. Ironically, Sharp was equally jealous and on the whole more successful in resisting similar tendencies when she served Richard Crossman a decade later (Crossman 1975, p. 627). At the Ministry of Transport Barbara Castle, unable to remove Thomas Padmore, turned to others in the department and even to the permanent secretary of another department (Castle 1984, p. 94). During the earlier post-war years Donald Fergusson, Permanent Secretary at the Ministry of Fuel and Power 1945-52, maintained a Cunningham-like monopoly over advice to ministers. This he had to change when Hugh Gaitskell became minister. But Fergusson felt uncomfortable with the arrangement and reverted to a tighter control under Gaitskell's successor, Philip Noel-Baker (Williams 1979, p. 147).

Not all permanent secretaries of the period were immutable, or ungracious when forced to yield. Edward Boyle was a minister in successive Conservative governments of the 1950s and 1960s. He says that no one would have thought it odd for him occasionally to have preferred the advice of a junior official to that of the top administrators – at least on what he called 'category 3' decisions, such as those arising from MPs' letters or Parliamentary debates (Boyle 1980, p. 10). As Chancellor of the Exchequer between 1951-55 R.A. Butler had the habit of calling up mid-rank officials. He did so without causing any apparent consternation further up the hierarchy (Seldon 1981, p. 165). As Minister of Health in the 1940s, Aneurin Bevan used to wander, unannounced, into officials' rooms. This worked satisfactorily because the permanent secretary, William Douglas, could accommodate such irregularities (Foot 1973, pp. 40-3). One former permanent secretary from the 1970s recounted how, working at deputy secretary level in a large department during the 1960s, he was enjoined to report directly to the secretary of state. The PUS was at first unaware of this. He was not enamoured when after a time he found out. But the secretary of state was strong and the PUS had the good sense and the good grace neither to disturb the arrangement nor to berate the then deputy secretary (private information).

These examples are sufficient to show two things. First that the middle decades of the twentieth century saw many permanent secretaries more or less monopolizing channels of advice to their ministers. This period may have been the heyday of rigid hierarchy. Second, there were nevertheless exceptions, usually where ministers forced the issue or where permanent secretaries themselves permitted a more relaxed regime.

What, then, can be said about the earlier decades of the present century and about the late-nineteenth century? Similar examples can be found of permanent secretaries willingly acceding to arrangements which allowed ministers a more varied flow of advice from within the department. As Secretary of State for War in Gladstone's final administration of 1892-94, Henry Campbell-Bannerman had as his PUS Ralph Thompson. He got on well with Thompson, but worked more closely with Arthur Haliburton and Ralph Knox, assistant secretary and accountant-general respectively, both future permanent secretaries (Wilson 1973, p. 171). In Ramsay MacDonald's second Labour government, 1929-31, Minister of Transport Herbert Morrison generally worked through his permanent secretary, the formidable Cyril Hurcomb. But he also got much advice from further down the line. This was successful because Morrison never played civil servants off against one another and because Hurcomb gave his blessing (Jones and Donoughue 1973, p. 132).

There is a further and more general point to be made here. It has been suggested that, even up until 1939, there was less of a gulf between technical experts and what, with increasing disparagement, were called generalists (Johnson 1981, p.132). Certainly in the mid-nineteenth century specialist advisers and inspectors had enjoyed a freedom of expression that they were never to recapture. They could be stifled only by the strongest permanent secretaries. And some of the permanent secretaries were themselves specialist professionals (see Chapter 8). Even in the late-nineteenth century the technical expert was often able to: 'initiate and, by judiciously cultivating the legal adviser and permanent secretary, submit measures which greatly extended government activity...' (Macleod 1988, pp. 12-3). Some of the weightiest characters in Whitehall during the nineteenth and early twentieth centuries enjoyed status, influence and even fame without being permanent secretaries. Occasionally, though not often, they were paid higher salaries than the permanent secretaries under whose wing they nominally operated. Among the many such figures of note were John Simon (health reform), Michael Sadler (education) and Josiah Stamp (public finance). These are not of course pure examples. Stamp, for instance, left the civil service as an assistant secretary in 1919 when rising fifty and made his most notable contributions to public life as an industrialist. It is tempting to muse whether the permanent secretaryships held by the Hills, the Chadwicks and the Kay-Shuttleworths of the mid-nineteenth century were strictly necessary to their achievements. Yet things were already becoming more regularized well before the century's end. Simon resigned in 1876 his post as Medical Officer to the Local Government Board, unable to work within the increasingly tight rein imposed by the 'lay' bureaucracy (Lambert 1963, pp. 570-5). The permanent secretary, John Lambert, engineered Simon's downfall. Simon was no Chadwick: his departure was met not with applause or relief but with public anguish at the nation's loss.

It is possible to identify four broad phases in the evolution of the permanent secretary's advisory role. First, the mid-nineteenth century, which can only be described as variable, shaped more by personality and chance circumstances than by anything else. Second, in the late-nineteenth and early twentieth centuries there was a more ordered pattern in the tendering of advice, increasingly but by no means solely through the permanent secretary at the head of a sometimes surprisingly flexible senior hierarchy. The third period, from around the 1920s to the 1960s, was the closest approximation to hierarchical rigidity and high-handed monopoly. The monopoly which many permanent secretaries exercised in the flow of advice to ministers could be and sometimes was relaxed – occasionally upon the initiative of a confident permanent secretary but more typically by the assertiveness of a strong or a dissatisfied minister. And fourth, since the 1960s, this monopoly, such as it was, has been challenged and finally broken, probably for ever. The Major government has signalled its wish for structures designed, among other things, to give greater access to ministers and heads of department for officials down to assistant secretary (grade 5) level (Cabinet Office 1994, p. 38, para. 4.22). This confirms not so much a reversion to any of the earlier patterns as the development of a new and different advisory role for the permanent secretary – at least in the specific aspect of policy advice.

If permanent secretaries are rarely the initiators, still less the proselytizers (vis-à-vis ministers) of detailed policy proposals what, then, is their role? In a sense, they have become policy managers rather than policy makers or originators. It is rare nowadays for a permanent secretary to initiate a major policy – an idea clearly acknowledged as his or hers – and push it through, even under the cloak of ministerial authority. They pitch in, they make their distinctive contributions – but as one of a greater number of participants. Their more typical, vital but less distinct contribution is to harmonize the contributions of others. As one of the current permanent secretaries explained:

> It's a very different job now from sitting there reading through a file, having a better idea than the one in the file and going to the secretary of state to persuade him... It may still happen, but the important job is strategic management – keeping the department's and the government's policies in line and moving forward in a sensible, coherent way.

Another contemporary permanent secretary describes the role as that of broker – 'trying... to come up with a solution which answers all the various problems that are on the table and not just one, or some'. Another said: 'In a sense I'm not allowed to care what the solution is! Of course, I do and I will say if I think this is better than that – but what we really want is... a resolution'. Yet another, in a smaller department, gives a slightly different spin:

> All the policy advice doesn't come through me. What I try and do is ensure that I see it all, and I try and ensure that it is properly orchestrated. And, of course, if it's not correct in my view, then I leap in and say "I don't agree with this".

In the larger departments the permanent secretary does not always even see all the advice that goes from other officials to the minister. But, through the medium of other very senior colleagues and by means of more systematic management controls, the permanent secretary should be confident that a broad coherence is maintained. This does not mean the suppression of alternative perspectives – rather to ensure that, however many shafts of light there may be, they are projected onto the one canvas. Perhaps the orchestration, or conductor, analogy is the most apt. The permanent secretary will set out the composer's score for those who are going to do the playing. Like the orchestrator, the permanent secretary will have added some embellishments, sometimes to a greater and at other times to a lesser extent. Like the musical conductor the permanent secretary will bring in the different sections of the orchestra where appropriate to get a result that broadly follows the composer's markings while allowing a certain latitude for artistic interpretation. Occasionally, unlike the conductor, the permanent secretary will descend from the podium and join the orchestra, making a distinctly audible contribution. The conductor/soloist is less frequently heard now than in the past. The precise frequency will vary – within limits – according to the inclination of the permanent secretary, the style of the minister and the nature of the policy in question.

It is, of course, to the permanent secretary that the minister will turn for remedial action if there is a feeling that the advice being tendered by other officials in the department is slanted, or is in any way unsatisfactory. It is also, as ever, the permanent secretary upon whom the minister will rely for support when difficulties arise. This propping up, or fire-fighting role has probably changed little down the years. On the other hand, some ministers (by no means all) have begun to take a greater interest in the management of their departments. This is also an aspect of the permanent secretary's job which has been in greater evidence in recent years. In a sense it is another aspect of, rather than a completely different area of activity from, the orchestration or management of policy advice. The next chapter therefore concentrates on the permanent secretary's task of running a department.

3 Running a department

Introduction

If there has been a change in the advisory role of permanent secretaries there has been a change no less significant in the way they run their departments. Some would argue that only in recent years have permanent secretaries begun to give due attention to this aspect of their work. The Fulton Committee (1968, p. 12, para. 18) complained that senior officials 'tend to think of themselves as advisers on policy to people above them, rather than as managers of the administrative machine below them'. This was a reformulation of similar sentiments uttered by the Plowden Committee (HM Treasury 1961, p. 16, para. 47). On the face of it, neither committee seems to have cut much ice. Shortly after his retirement Peter Carey (1984, p. 82) wrote that the first genuinely managerial job he had had was upon becoming a permanent secretary. His career in Whitehall had given him no preparation for this role. Carey, who headed the DTI (later the Department of Industry) from the mid-1970s, considered this to have been a cardinal weakness in the system. His analysis seemed to have been vindicated when the Ibbs Report pronounced that while most senior civil servants were responsible both for policy and management the former continued to receive higher priority. This, it claimed, was: 'not only because it demands immediate attention but because that is the area in which they are on familiar ground and where their skills lie, and where ministerial attention is focused' (Efficiency Unit 1988, p. 3).

The implications of these observations seem clear enough. Permanent secretaries of yesteryear were more or less oblivious to management. Those of today, while more sensitive to such responsibilities, have failed fully to meet the challenge, partly because of the imperatives of the system, notably the demands of ministers. Yet, in another sense, some of these very impediments have, in recent times, also impelled permanent secretaries towards a more distinctly managerial role. The policy orchestration, or brokerage, role described in the last chapter implies the management of a team of policy-mongers. The attempt to separate policy from operations has involved the permanent secretary in a bigger management as well as in a different policy role - precisely because it is not possible to divorce operations from the kind of policy, or at any rate political, work which typically draws in the permanent secretary. Within the context of ministerial responsibility, operational issues are potential policy issues. The very focus upon ministers has thus pulled permanent secretaries closer to the hub of operations. Some ministers have also begun consciously to interest themselves in the strategic delivery of services as well as, and as distinct from, the knee-jerk response to transitory crises.

For these reasons alone permanent secretaries have been obliged to give a higher profile to their managerial roles. A growing number have themselves made the running. Much depends upon what is meant by 'management' and what exactly are held to be the salient elements in the managerial role of the modern permanent secretary. Is there a distinction between running a department and managing a department? Is it true to say that permanent secretaries in the past had no conception of management, in any sense? In what sense, then, do contemporary permanent secretaries really manage their departments?

In dealing with these and other questions this chapter will examine the changing management role of the permanent secretary through three points of reference. First, by establishing what kind of departmental role permanent secretaries played in the hallowed Whitehall tradition. This will show how that role developed down to the 1970s. Second, by sketching some of the broad impulses and specific initiatives during the 1980s and 1990s which have begun significantly to change the Whitehall landscape - the new managerialism. Third, by showing how these impulses have affected the management function of permanent secretaries.

The Whitehall tradition

By the mid-nineteenth century most permanent secretaries had established themselves at the head of an official hierarchy, responsible to the minister for the day-to-day running of their departments. This had not in all cases been achieved without blood-letting. Henry Unwin Addington, PUS at the Foreign Office, fought and won an internal battle in 1848 vis-à-vis his Chief Clerk, George Lenox-Conyngham (Cromwell 1960; Middleton 1977, pp. 134-5). At stake was the right of a subordinate official to demand the imprimatur of the secretary of state before complying with an instruction issued by the PUS. More typically, relations were harmonious, the authority of the permanent secretary undisputed within the formal hierarchy. This did not always mean a vertical division of labour. On becoming PUS at the Colonial Office in 1860, Frederic Rogers found the work divided between himself and his immediate subordinates on a functional (i.e. geographical) basis. This he later changed: 'I shall have the top and the others all the bottom... instead of dividing the world between us' (Marindin 1896, p. 276). At the Home Office, even to the 1890s, the PUS and the assistant under-secretary 'simply shared out in a rather haphazard way the work which came up from heads of department' (Pellew 1982, p. 60).

If the precise distribution of work was sometimes haphazard the administrative process itself was in most departments already quite heavily bureaucratized. The efforts of individual permanent secretaries were instrumental in this process. At the Colonial Office back in the 1840s, the flamboyant James Stephen had devised procedures which enabled subsequent generations to trace 'sources and motives for actions and policies' (Knaplund 1953, p. 17). If careful record-keeping is one aspect of bureaucracy, then a degree of depersonalization and routinization are further hallmarks. Kay-Shuttleworth believed that the internal administration of the Education Department should '...be rendered in all respects independent of my person which the accident of ill-health might any day withdraw' (Selleck 1994, p. 246). John Lambert worked in various ways to routinize the work of the newly formed Local Government Board during the 1870s (Bellamy 1988, pp. 123-31). He imposed common recruitment, standardized files and explicit lines of authority to ensure that the department spoke with one voice. This, as noted in the last chapter, meant the gradual subordination of technical experts.

As a consequence of all this there was a growing tendency for matters to be passed up through the hierarchy - a characteristic in particular of public bureaucracy. This was so especially where the work was of a legal or quasi-legal nature. The imprint of ministerial responsibility left its mark, too. Permanent secretaries of the late-nineteenth and early twentieth centuries were often caught between two conflicting tides: the one demanding their close attention and supervision; the other - the sheer volume of work going on in their departments - beckoning a greater delegation. Arthur Godley, PUS at the India Office between 1883-1909, spent a third of his time during the early years seeing mostly his secretaries of department (equivalent to today's under secretaries, or grade 3s). This was partly because he was not at first entirely confident of their abilities. Nevertheless, throughout his permanent secretaryship he personally directed the preparation of almost all important dispatches (Kaminsky 1986, p. 17). This was an ever increasing burden, the volume of correspondence increasing by over 50 per cent during his first decade as PUS. The expansion of work in the Home Office during the early years of the twentieth century did bring greater delegation. No longer could the PUS sign, or even supervise, all correspondence of importance. Yet the department remained small enough down to 1914 for 'one man to control his staff in a very personal way' (Scott 1959, p. 28). In the Admiralty, Oswyn Murray, Permanent Secretary 1917-36, maintained Pepys's touchstone that 'not even a cat should swing in the Navy Office but he should know of it' (Murray 1940, p. 118). He died in post, exhausted, having worked nearly three years beyond the normal retirement age.

As noted in the previous chapter, the middle decades of the present century marked the closest approximation to the permanent secretary as the monopolizer of channels of advice to ministers. Similarly these were the years in which the Whitehall tradition of internal departmental administration came nearest to a top-heavy bureaucratization revolving around the permanent secretary. For incumbents who were so inclined it remained possible to maintain close personal supervision. At the Colonial Office, George Gater, imported from local government in 1939 by Neville Chamberlain, was, according to one of his successors, 'an absolute monopolist: he insisted on bottlenecking everything' (Poynton, NOA Tr., p. 32). This was not always conducive to the efficient conduct of business. At the same time, an onerous burden upon ministers was sometimes the consequence of a permanent secretary's inability or disinclination to keep on top and weld together the contributions of multifarious sectional interests within a department. Such, on one account, was what went wrong in the Foreign Office during the 1930s (Cross 1977, p. 188). Perhaps this was Vansittart's greatest failing. Whatever the case other permanent secretaries may have seen in it a salutary lesson: beware of letting go.

For the most part permanent secretaries down to the 1960s tried to maintain a fairly tight grip. How did they do this? And how does this square with the notion that they kept their distance from any activity that could be called management?

In the first place, maintaining a tight grip often involved a Herculean effort. As will be seen in Chapter 5, all permanent secretaries worked long hours - some to excess. Second, it was still just possible by sheer force of character to galvanize a department in a fairly personal way. This would usually mean leading from the front so that, even without intervention in every detail, the department knew the permanent secretary's mind as clearly as the permanent secretary knew the minister's. With Evelyn Sharp at the MHLG 'everything bore the stamp of her spirit and drive and she somehow kept her finger-tips on all that was going on of any importance' (Hill 1964, pp. 230-1). Third, even among monopolizers there was a subtle shift from direct supervision to the arm's length co-ordination of the efforts of others. Charles Cunningham, one of Evelyn Sharp's contemporaries and PUS at the Home Office during the 1950s and '60s, later reflected: 'one of the things I tried to do was to bring (different) parts of the office more closely in touch with one another than they had been hitherto' (NOA Tr., p. 21). Fourth, many permanent secretaries of this period instituted regular meetings of senior staff. Harold Caccia did so in the Foreign Office where he was PUS between 1962-65 (Greenhill 1993, p. 110). In the Ministry of Supply, Archibald Rowlands established Friday afternoon meetings of all deputy secretaries and under secretaries 'to talk over all the aspects of the Ministry's work' (Musgrave, NOA Tr., p. 13). Rowlands was permanent secretary between 1946-52 of what was then one of Whitehall's largest departments. It was said of him that he seemed less the Ministry's permanent secretary, more its managing director (*The Times*, 24 August 1953). Meanwhile at the Home Office it fell to Arthur Peterson, PUS between 1972-77, to introduce regular set piece meetings and other 'managerial devices' (Peterson, NOA Tr., pp. 34-5). It was now possible for the PUS to keep on top of the department without the need for constant, active supervision.

A fifth and further way in which permanent secretaries were and are able to reconcile their departmental responsibilities with an ever growing volume and complexity of work was by being selective in their efforts. Permanent secretaries have been inclined, sometimes out of personal interest, to direct their attention to certain areas of work. At the Ministry of Supply in the mid-1950s James Helmore freed himself as much as possible from other things to concentrate on aircraft policy (Musgrave, NOA Tr., p. 14). This is perhaps an extreme example of what happened or of what was possible. Often, sheer necessity would claim the permanent secretary's attention, especially in areas of work likely to come within the orbit of the minister. Conversely, less politically sensitive or more specialized areas could escape the permanent secretary's gaze. There was nothing novel about this. Permanent secretaries always had and continue to have a large degree of discretion in shaping the roles they play.

This element of discretion gives a clue to the second question posed above - how to reconcile the hierarchical control with the alleged neglect of management. Some permanent secretaries were very sensitive to the goings on in their departments. Others were much less sensitive. Those that were sensitive did not so much manage as preside over their departments. They would know most if not all the staff in the administrative grades and some in the executive, specialist and even clerical grades. They would usually, as we have seen, hold regular meetings. They would, in short, have known much of what was going on in all but the largest departments down to the 1960s, if such was their inclination. To suppose otherwise would be a mistake and a distortion of the base from which to compare subsequent developments. What would pass as rudimentary management probably existed without being known as such - in part a reflection of changing fashions in terminology. What did not exist were the more elaborate, more systematic control mechanisms of a later age. And where the permanent secretary took little interest in the operational routine of a department, then no one else at senior level was obliged to play a complementary role. In this case nobody in any sense of the word managed the department. It would simply run by its own momentum. People had their tasks, they knew their jobs and they got on with it. Only when something went wrong, or where a political or policy initiative reverberated through a ministry, would the day-to-day activities of certain sections come to the notice of the permanent secretary. Throughout Whitehall there was little, if any, proactive management. There were no performance targets or output indicators. There were budgets but no semblance of management accounting. The words of Frederick Hoyer Millar, PUS at the Foreign Office during the 1960s, reflect the prevailing climate:

> Well, I suppose one was there to keep the machine going, really, and advise the Secretary of State and carry out his instructions. I can't think what else. Oh, and also to ensure that your department was in touch with the rest of Whitehall.
> (Inchyra, NOA Tr., p. 13).

By the late-1960s things were beginning to change. On one interpretation, a new generation of mandarins who had served in the forces during the Second World War started to claim senior positions in Whitehall. They were more management conscious (Part 1990, pp. 39-40). Some, such as Richard 'Otto' Clarke at Mintech in the late-1960s gave public expression to this new awareness (Clarke 1971). The head of the civil service did likewise. William Armstrong was later vilified as having conspired to defeat some of the central reforms recommended by the Fulton Committee (Kellner and Crowther-Hunt 1980, pp. 59-77). But he understood and tried to nurture within Whitehall the then tender plant of management. He foresaw by a decade or more the emphasis upon financial accounting and value for money (Armstrong 1970, pp. 16-7). These were to be among the leitmotifs of the 1980s and the 1990s - manifestations of the new managerialism which was to shake the Whitehall tradition to its roots.

The new managerialism

For all William Armstrong's foresight it would be at best a half truth to claim that he perceived or would have welcomed without reservation the full wind of change that has blown through Whitehall during the 1980s and '90s. Any such claim for most of Armstrong's permanent secretary colleagues would fall well short of half the truth. This was evident in the predominantly negative response of the senior echelons to the Fulton Report of 1968. The Fulton Committee misjudged many things in its analysis of Whitehall's undoubted shortcomings. For example, as we have just seen, some permanent secretaries did spend at least some of their time looking downwards into their departments - more than Fulton led the public to believe. Fulton's intemperate tone provoked in certain of the top mandarins a reactionary posture which belied the broad disposition across Whitehall as much as the hard veneer of the report belied its basic contents. In any case, Fulton said nothing original about the civil service. It proposed hardly anything that had not already been suggested. A careful rereading of the report scarcely supports any specific claim that the reforms of the 1980s and the 1990s were 'all in Fulton'. What Fulton did contain was an analysis which, if distorted in much of its detail, nevertheless captured an element of the Whitehall mystique. If a few permanent secretaries of the day were already doing more to run their departments they were probably the only senior mandarins who were. Progress through the Whitehall hierarchy provided little deliberate preparation for this aspect of the work. Again, if some of Fulton's more celebrated proposals now seem inappropriate or half-baked, the report projected a broad vision which embraced the spirit if not the letter of later reforms. Like Holy Grail it contained more artistic than literal truths. As such, and above all, it provided not a blueprint but a focus and an inspiration for future reformers.

There is a voluminous and still growing literature on the Whitehall management reforms of the 1980s and 1990s (Metcalfe and Richards 1990; Massey 1993; Pollitt 1993; Greer 1994; Zifcak 1994; O'Toole and Jordan 1995). Here it is necessary only to sketch the main elements so that in the next and final section of this chapter it will be possible to examine the implications for the changing managerial role of the permanent secretary.

As the 1980s dawned the initial post-Fulton momentum seemed to have disappeared. There was debate about who to blame. Few doubted Kellner and Crowther-Hunt's description (1980, pp. 78-99) of the 'lost reforms'. Yet already Margaret Thatcher had re-introduced Derek Rayner to Whitehall, this time as the Prime Minister's Adviser on Efficiency, supported by a newly created Efficiency Unit. Rayner and his team were to conduct a series of scrutinies intended to demonstrate to departments how it was possible to achieve savings by taking a critical, clinical, look at procedures, methods and assumptions. The ultimate hope was to fire departments with the enthusiasm to introduce, unprompted, their own scrutinies rather than have the Efficiency Unit itself toiling 'against the collar'. Under the auspices of Thatcher and concerned as they were with savings the scrutinies inevitably bore the mark of

Conservatism. In fact they were also the product of secular currents within Whitehall, especially in their operation (Bray 1988). Early results were inauspicious (Metcalfe and Richards 1984). The scrutinies brought no attitudinal sea-change, rather a finely calibrated shift of consciousness towards the relationship between costs and benefits, inputs and outputs.

Meanwhile at the Department of the Environment (DoE), Michael Heseltine, during his first spell as Secretary of State, 1979-83, had introduced Management Information Systems for Ministers (MINIS). In essence this was a mechanism by which ministers could monitor systematically what was going on in their departments. Its potential could be cashed in by permanent secretaries as much as by ministers. It entailed procedures for reporting progress on current activities, horizontally and vertically within a department. Such an exercise would require explicit appraisal, updated regularly, based upon the systematic collation of information - itself something of an innovation in Whitehall. Not all ministers shared Heseltine's enthusiasm; nor all permanent secretaries. Some departments adopted paler versions; some remained aloof. But it was a signal for further changes.

More wide-ranging was the Financial Management Initiative (FMI). Introduced in 1982, FMI was essentially an exercise designed to combine resource allocation with cost control. As such it required the setting of objectives, performance targets and output indicators linked to specific budget heads. It came to incorporate and even to eclipse certain of the earlier developments, such as MINIS. Responsibility was to be more transparently located to individuals in charge of particular areas of work. With these mechanisms it was hoped to maintain broad but more effective financial control by way of increasingly meaningful decentralization. Its embrace of all areas of work was a further feature. Against such ambitions, initial achievements were comparatively modest. Five years after its launch the Public Accounts Committee noted that progress had been uneven and in some areas highly qualified (PAC 1987). Yet without doubt it brought a perceptible culture change, especially for permanent secretaries. A Financial Management Unit (FMU) had been set up jointly by the Treasury and the Management and Personnel Office (MPO) of the Cabinet Office. The FMU's job was, among other things, to help permanent secretaries to apply FMI principles within their departments. Whether they liked it or not, permanent secretaries found themselves playing a critical role. In his valedictory in December 1987 the head of the civil service described FMI as the single most important development of the previous eighteen years (Armstrong 1988, p. 12).

Within weeks of Armstrong saying this there was launched an initiative which was to resonate even louder than FMI. In February 1988 the Efficiency Unit published *Improving Management in Government: The Next Steps*. It was written by Kate Jenkins, Karen Caines and Andrew Jackson, three members of the Unit working under the tutelage of Robin Ibbs who had succeeded Rayner as the Prime Minister's Special Adviser on Efficiency. The document became popularly known as the Ibbs Report. The reforms heralded by Ibbs have been widely seen as constituting perhaps the most conspicuous change in the Whitehall landscape for over a hundred years. The title *Next Steps* was significant in that it was regarded as an incremental progression, not a quantum leap. Its publication invoked the ghost of Fulton, hitherto assumed to have been laid to rest. Some of the ideas bore a resemblance to Fulton. Most notably Ibbs, like Fulton, diagnosed a managerial deficiency. Like Fulton, Ibbs sought as one of the remedies a division of labour between policy and operational work. The one would be the business of those in the core departments, including permanent secretaries; the other would be the day-to-day responsibility of newly created executive agencies. Each such agency would be headed by a chief executive and operate at arm's length from its sponsoring department. The department would pull the strings of broad policy, in the formulation of which chief executives would be involved. Agencies would, within budget limits, have much greater freedom, encouraging a sense of distinct identity among personnel. These freedoms would embrace delegation in recruitment and discretion over pay and conditions of service. The notion of a career in a unified civil service was pronounced to be an anachronism, a signal departure from Fulton (Efficiency Unit 1988).

With these proposals Ibbs claimed potential for improvements both in policy and in the operation and delivery of services. What is striking is the speed and extent to which Ibbs's proposals have been turned into reality. Early scepticism about the likelihood of substantial action soon gave way to an acknowledgement, often accompanied by anxiety, that something significant was happening. Within five years some ninety-two executive agencies had been established in which 62 per cent of all civil servants were engaged (Cabinet Office 1993). By this time the misgivings of the critics were being matched and overtaken by greater concerns for the implications of a further initiative - the programme of contracting out. This was initially announced under the guise of yet another initiative, the Citizen's Charter, officially launched in July 1991. The intention was that the quality of public services would be enhanced by empowering the citizen to obtain better 'value for money within a tax bill the nation can afford' (Cabinet Office 1991, p. 4). This was to be achieved by, among other things, the setting and publishing of required performance standards and, where possible, the creation of choice between competing providers of services. The latter was given further force by the government's proposals to increase competition by contracting out. It saw the private sector as providing the model:

> They (the private sector) stick with what they know best. And they buy in specialist contractors to provide new ideas, more

flexibility, and a higher level of expertise than could exist in a purely in-house operation. Public sector bodies are increasingly doing the same.
(HM Treasury 1991, p. 1).

By May 1994, an estimated £1.3bn of activities had been examined, from which the government claimed annual savings of £150m, with more expected (Cabinet Office 1994, p. 15, para. 2.25). A number of organizations such as the Royal Ordnance Factories had already been transferred to the private sector. It is as yet difficult to know whether this represents a plateau or the harbinger of heightened activity. The government seemed equivocal as it sought to keep this and other issues to the fore with the publication in July 1994 of the White Paper, *The Civil Service: Continuity and Change*. Some saw this White Paper as further evidence of the shift towards business management methods, while others detected signs of increasing caution. It signalled a greater emphasis upon individual departments taking responsibility for efficiency plans (Cabinet Office 1994, p. 2, para. 1.4 and p. 23, para. 3.12). It confirmed the government's wish that all executive agencies should be responsible for their own pay and grading (p. 26, para. 3.26). At the same time the government seemed anxious to allay some of the fears expressed by critics about the implications of developments that had been taking place since the Ibbs report. It wanted senior staff to continue to be seen as a cohesive service (p. 36, para. 4.16). It talked about the need to sustain key civil service values and corporate wisdom.

At the same time, certain organizational changes in Whitehall during the late-1980s and early 1990s have had a bearing upon the overall management of the civil service. The MPO of the Cabinet Office was abolished in 1987, its responsibilities divided between the Treasury and the newly established Office of the Minister for the Civil Service (OMCS). The latter, too, operated under the wing of the Cabinet Office. The Treasury retained responsibility for pay and management, an arrangement undisturbed by further reorganization in 1992 in which the OMCS was replaced by the Office of Public Service and Science (OPSS). This now embraces more or less all the Cabinet Office's civil service management work, including the Citizen's Charter Unit, the Efficiency Unit, the Next Steps Programme Team, the Public Appointments Unit, the Top Management Programme, the Management Development Group and the Machinery of Government Division. It has general oversight of the work of the Civil Service College, the Occupational Health Service, and Recruitment and Assessment Services - all now executive agencies. The science and technology responsibilities include the work of the research councils and the implementation of policies outlined in the government White Paper *Realising Our Potential* (OPSS 1993). With this rationalization the permanent secretaryship of the OPSS assumed more the form of a standard departmental head. It precipitated the departure of Peter Kemp (see Chapter 2).

Two broad issues arise from all this. First, there are the procedural implications in Whitehall as central government departments (and executive agencies) are engaged constantly in the application of a whole new range of techniques. These include periodic market testing to establish their continued suitability to provide services and functions for the conduct of government. Second, there is the management of relationships between core departments and executive agencies - or for that matter private contractors - who deliver services on behalf of the 'enabling department'. The creation of executive agencies and the emphasis upon market testing together mean the end of the traditional hierarchical command bureaucracy of which permanent secretaries formed the apex. That Whitehall never bore in anything like pure form all the traits of such bureaucracy is not to deny the significance of what has been happening. There is in process a shift, first to management *by* contract; second, to management *of* contract (Greer 1994, pp. 77-80). Whether or not desirable, the developments of which these shifts are the result have had and will continue to have a profound effect upon the managerial role of the permanent secretary.

New roles for old?

In understanding the full implications of the new managerialism for the role of the permanent secretary it is useful to lay bare the underlying, quasi-philosophical, premises upon which are based many of the initiatives described above. There is at one level an often implicit utilitarianism (O'Toole 1990). This manifests itself in, among other things, a greater concern for measuring costs and benefits and for the specific, tangible, outcomes of performance rather than with the broader but necessarily vaguer notions about 'public interest', 'community' or 'common good'. These broader notions were arguably the stock-in-trade of the senior mandarins of yesteryear. They may still be upheld by current post-holders, though arguably (see Chapter 12) with less resolution and certainly not to the exclusion of more immediate concerns for performance indicators and other management techniques. A further manifestation of the utilitarian disposition is the perception of all participants as self-interested actors. In the language of a certain variety of public choice theory this includes senior civil servants whose empire building and budget inflating tendencies constitute a market distortion. Such, on one account, is the rationale behind *Next Steps* (Greer 1994, p. 15). Taken to its logical conclusion permanent secretaries would be the poachers, not the gamekeepers. They would be treated as mercenaries rather than as the altruistic gladiators. Their role would be the more technical one of regulating the boiler house rather than that of deck officers of the ship of state.

This, of course, is a caricature and is to anticipate much that has not yet happened and may not happen. But it suggests a possible and plausible general direction of change. More immediately, many permanent secretaries have assumed a distinctly managerial orientation. A number of discernible managerial tasks fall to permanent secretaries in consequence of the new managerialism. Specifically, permanent secretaries have been heavily involved in the process by which executive agencies are selected, established and subsequently monitored. Each agency has a framework document, revised usually at three yearly intervals; an annual business plan; and a longer term corporate plan. Permanent secretaries have key roles in formulating these documents - in effect the contracts by which agencies deliver on behalf of departments. This alone will ensure their continuing involvement. It has already pushed many permanent secretaries towards a strategic management role in which they maintain a synoptic overview rather than a detailed engagement in any particular operational area. The Department of Social Security now has a management board. The board comprises senior people in the department, including the executive agencies. Michael Partridge, Permanent Secretary of the DSS, says:

> We have taken a deliberate view that I am just Chairman of the Board, the Board runs the department. And I'm, so to speak, the disinterested Chairman of a holding group of companies. And my job is to ensure that all the Board reaches agreement, and the Department as a whole moves along. But I'm not a traditional permanent secretary laying down the laws as to what is going to happen. They have to reach decisions on how best to run the Department, and I help them as Chairman to reach those decisions. That is very different from the traditional Whitehall role of a Permanent Secretary.
> (BBC Radio 4, 6 January 1994).

On the other hand, one of Partridge's opposite numbers in another department was quite emphatic: 'We are not a board of directors... but we try to run it on a consensus basis'. Another said simply: '... the idea that the thing works as a complete hierarchy is rubbish. I mean, it just doesn't'.

The size of a department is one factor which influences the precise managerial role played by the permanent secretary. Another is the nature of the department's work. Social security in Britain is a quasi-unified system under the wing of one department. The DSS has overall responsibility for a wide range of benefits, now mostly delivered through the medium of executive agencies. *Next Steps* has therefore had a profound effect upon the

Department and upon the role of the permanent secretary. In contrast, the Department of Health has never had the direct operational task of providing medical care. Again, in the MoD there has always been a near parallel senior structure operating under the chiefs of staff. The same was true of the old service departments - the Admiralty, the Air Ministry and the War Office - prior to their coming under the MoD in 1964. So, the precise managerial implications of *Next Steps* for permanent secretaries have varied because they head departments which have been affected to different degrees and because those departments have proceeded from different base-lines. But these are variations of extent, not of fundamental substance. Within all departments there are a number of specific managerial functions which, one way or another, are the responsibility of the permanent secretary. These include: representing the minister; representing the department; personnel management; conflict resolution and co-ordination. These aspects of the permanent secretary's management role warrant further comment.

Ministers look to their permanent secretaries to 'square' the department. It is the permanent secretary's task to see that, once an initiative has been taken, then 'it does not take too long for the change… to be understood in all parts, and at all levels, of the department' (Nairne 1990, pp. 8-9). It is the permanent secretary to whom the minister will turn if he or she feels that the department is not fully behind a policy or if something is being lost in transmission. Similarly the permanent secretary will also be expected to resolve difficulties where the minister feels that the advice coming up from other officials is slanted, or is in some way deficient. It is a role which the advent of ministerial special advisers has in no sense diminished. Rather, it has been given greater emphasis by fact of the greater variety of advisory inputs, as noted in the last chapter. No one is in quite the same position as the permanent secretary to swing a department behind a new policy or other initiative. It will fall to the permanent secretary to achieve this, if necessary, by effecting a redeployment of personnel. All permanent secretaries take very seriously their role as the minister's agent in the department. One permanent secretary explained how, in meetings, he always sits next to the minister on one side of the table with his senior colleagues on the other side. This is not the universal practice and is mainly a matter of personal style. Ministers, too, have individual styles. Tony Benn, for example, would always sit at a conference table with the permanent secretary on the other side - even with only the two people in the room (Part 1990, p. 172).

While representing the minister to the department, the permanent secretary also represents the department to the minister and, on occasion, to a wider public. The permanent secretary is the official figurehead of the department. Other officials will look to the permanent secretary to apprise the minister where they feel that issues have not been given a proper airing or where there is felt to be some sort of corporate injustice. This can place the permanent secretary in a delicate position, especially where officials consider the minister or the government to be culpable. One permanent secretary confessed:

> Hypothetically speaking, the government may have done things in relation to staff which I personally think are disgraceful... but as a permanent secretary I would not be in a position to make that clear. And you can't really make that clear to staff. A nod and a wink to the staff is not a good idea... and what you say to them and what you say to the minister in private can be two very different things.

Occasionally dissension within a department may, if not resolved, spill over into the public arena. This has happened, as noted in the last chapter, where staff have felt that their offerings have been neglected by ministers. Permanent secretaries are now generally obliged to play a more active role as public figureheads, if only because of the more intense probings of journalists. Of course, they are by no means the only civil servants who have contact with the media. Indeed they will usually be less involved personally than many of their senior colleagues. But on major matters they can often speak with an authority, if not necessarily a detailed knowledge, that is unique among senior officials. Normally they are not mentioned by name in any ensuing report, especially if it is a policy matter. There is, however, a growing tendency for permanent secretaries to be quoted from time-to-time in connection with questions of internal management. It reflects the more general climate of openness and greater sensitivity to public relations. As noted in Chapter 1, it is a task that naturally and quite frequently now attaches to the head of the home civil service. Certain of the departmental permanent secretaries, such as Terence Burns at the Treasury, seem also to have cultivated the media, though to a lesser extent.

This figurehead role has also to do with upholding morale, an aspect of personnel management. At one level, personnel management depends less upon the permanent secretary than upon the heads of particular operational units. This has been underlined with the advent of agencies whose chief executives have an explicit responsibility for personnel. But permanent secretaries have a big say in the appointment of those chief executives. And within the departmental core, all permanent secretaries are involved in making appointments down to grade 5 (assistant secretary), some retaining control down to grade 7 (principal) level (Efficiency Unit 1993, p. 32). One permanent secretary considered his involvement in the making of such appointments as being his most significant contribution to the quality of the department. Another said that he did all the succession planning himself.

If they are to be effective in upholding morale, then it is seen as increasingly important for permanent secretaries to keep in touch with the departments they head. This has never been a problem in connection with those officials whose work is policy orientated, or who have a role advising ministers. But this is no longer enough. Permanent secretaries are increasingly sensitive to the need to get out of their offices in Whitehall and 'meet the troops'. This is not without its difficulties. What to the permanent secretary can seem like a mutually informative exchange may take on the appearance of a bromide royal visit to those 'out in the sticks'. One permanent secretary described his approach: 'I saw them all, gave them all a handshake and sat down, asking what they do and how they do it and what's bad, what stresses them, what pleases them... I'm beginning to do that'. This may allow the permanent secretary better to know the department, but it does not necessarily improve morale unless it is possible to redress the grievances inevitably articulated. Moreover it is by no means clear that such contacts, if pursued extensively, will continue to rest easily with the strategic management role. Of course, the permanent secretary who neglects the outposts is open to allegations of remoteness. Either way, the permanent secretary cannot win. Another of the current incumbents puts it like this:

> ...you've got a big time management problem and you must put your effort where it adds most value in relation to the minister. But you are also in charge of all these people and you have to make them feel that you love them. And I find that, personally, an extremely difficult thing to do... So, I pass the message down - "it isn't that I don't care, it is that I actually think you're doing it so well you don't need my help". Back then comes the message - "we don't really believe that" - you know, he doesn't love us enough.

It may or may not be a reflection of neglect by the permanent secretary if a department appears disgruntled. The same is true where a department is internally disunited, where different elements are competing for supremacy. Here there is a nice distinction between creative tension and centrifugal debility; or between a consensus that calcifies and a harmony that lends colour and vitality. It is a tricky line for the permanent secretary to pursue, even among senior colleagues. The senior staff meetings that were still a novelty in the 1960s are now everywhere an institution. All permanent secretaries try in this way to keep at least some sort of continual overview. As one of them says: 'the worst thing is not to be driving the agenda but to be sitting waiting and then other people take the initiative and you get buffeted about all over the place - ministers get unhappy and the department gets unhappy'.

This connects with the phenomenon of the so-called departmental view. It is difficult to say precisely what *is* a departmental view. It is not something tangible, committed to a single document or authoritative statement. Its very existence may be a matter of dispute, though invariably its presence is felt by civil servants and ministers alike. In a famous passage never since surpassed Edward Bridges (1950, pp. 15-6) described the departmental view as:

> ... a store of knowledge and experience in the subjects handled, something which eventually takes shape as a practical philosophy... the result of nothing more startling than the slow accretion and accumulation of experience over the years. ...And so by trial and error something has come about which differs greatly from the original plan; it is something shaped by many hands. It is quite different from anything which any single man or woman could have produced...

Occasionally, as Bridges acknowledged, the departmental view may bear the mark of an outstanding individual, as likely as not a permanent secretary. Invariably and perhaps more now than in Bridges's day it is much more deeply rooted than that. This is how it often seems to ministers who face 'an accumulation of experience and tradition which goes back at least one hundred years' (TCSC 1986a, p. xviii, para. 5.1). It may be felt as a steady pull towards an indeterminate centre of gravity; or it may find more explicit expression in the parameters of tolerance - policies or initiatives the department would prefer not to entertain. As heads of departments and as the agents of ministers this can be difficult for permanent secretaries. Not surprisingly, some of them are wary about the existence or development of a departmental view. One current post-holder was quite emphatic: 'Yes, there very often is a departmental view but if someone uses those words to me I stamp on them because... we are here to do that which ministers want us to do'. Others take a more relaxed view: 'Yes - departmental views do develop. A lot of policy development begins with officials. We perceive the need for new policies in certain areas sometimes before ministers do because we are actually dealing with business day in and day out... a department can pursue a major line of policy over a period of time'. The same permanent secretary was quick to point out that ministers, too, are involved in this process. But it may not always be easy for the permanent secretary to maintain a coherence of perspective among senior colleagues. There is some evidence that officials at grades two and three (deputy and under secretaries) do not always perceive permanent secretaries as sharing their values as to the relative importance of different personal attributes (Efficiency Unit 1993, p. 23). In a different way, one former permanent secretary has said that his own personal performance indicator was the absence of leaks from within the department (Cubbon 1993, p. 12). On this criterion the performance of some of his peers over the last decade or so must be found wanting. At the same time, there are more fault-lines. As one of the present incumbents acknowledged, there is a tension between, on the one hand, developing a culture in which individuals lower down the line assume a specific responsibility and are encouraged to take decisions and, on the other hand, the traditional public service ethos in which no decision may be better than a decision that turns out badly. Moreover, the greater the number of decision making points, the greater are the chances of unevenness and lack of coherence.

Now, perhaps more than ever, there is a premium upon the permanent secretary to maintain a coherence within the department. Now, certainly more than at any other time this century, the capacity of the permanent secretary to achieve this is under threat. The vanguard of this threat is Whitehall's growing fragmentation. Chief among the sources of this fragmentation are the creation of executive agencies and the likely consequences of extensive market testing.

Publicly, Whitehall has absorbed these initiatives with typical sang-froid. Robin Butler has given assurances that the creation of executive agencies 'does not imply... a fragmentation of the Civil Service or the end of the Civil Service as a unified Service and I think it is important that it should not' (TCSC 1989, Q. 320). Not all permanent secretaries are as sanguine. One expressed anxieties as to whether there had been sufficient thought given to the implications of recent changes for orderly government:

> It's rather like having a car and a little mechanical knowledge... you put your head under the bonnet, you see a bolt and you loosen it, or you see a screw and you tighten it up... but unless you understand it you don't know. And I'm afraid we're doing a bit too much of that in government at the moment.

Another expressed a more specific misgiving:

> One of the problems is that the agency chief executives are going to concentrate on delivering what they have been asked to do... but they don't – because they have very little contact with ministers – they don't think about the politics of it.

Of course, some agency chief executives have more contact with ministers than do others. Some permanent secretaries encourage it more than others. Some permanent secretaries have a stronger hand than others in the running of those executive agencies within their purview.

More generally, a recently retired permanent secretary has expressed publicly his doubts as to whether executive agencies, as halfway houses between privatization and a politically accountable department, have a sufficient theoretical grounding to enable them to survive (Chipperfield 1994, p. 12). But the lack of a theoretical base has in itself rarely been an obstacle to the survival of institutions in the British tradition of public administration. There seems little prospect of executive agencies' demise, even upon a change of government.

It should not be supposed that even the more sceptical permanent secretaries find these changes personally threatening. They are perhaps less exposed than are some of their senior and mid-ranking colleagues (Barberis 1995, p. 107). But they have been and will continue further to be affected. Only time will tell whether individual agencies develop a momentum and assume an identity which poses a problem of managerial control. Agency chief executives are, as Robin Butler recognizes (1990, p. 8), a new breed of civil servant. Already those charged with some of the more politically sensitive operations have a higher public profile than the permanent secretaries to whom they report. They are designated accounting officers, previously the sovereign function of the permanent secretary. It is to this role of the permanent secretary, then, that attention is now turned in the next chapter.

4 Accounting to Parliament

Introduction

Chapters 1 and 2 outlined the notion of ministerial responsibility and its general implications for the office of permanent secretary. Central to the traditional notion is that the permanent secretary is responsible to the minister, privately not publicly; and that the minister, not the permanent secretary, should answer to Parliament and the wider public on behalf of the department. To this there is one formal exception, together with other practices by which the constitutional separation of roles has become frayed at the edges. The formal exception is that the permanent secretary is accountable and directly answerable to the House of Commons' Committee of Public Accounts – or the Public Accounts Committee (PAC) as it is more commonly known. Additionally, it is the custom that permanent secretaries should appear before other Parliamentary and miscellaneous official committees of enquiry. Various ad hoc select committees have long been active, though their wider embrace and more systematic remit is a feature mainly of the last two decades.

This chapter is, accordingly, organized into three sections. The first section describes the long, sometimes difficult, route by which permanent secretaries became accounting officers. It shows how, having been established more or less universally in Whitehall by the 1920s, these arrangements prevailed almost unchallenged for half a century. The second analyzes the growing criticisms and increasing tensions, not least those arising from the designation of chief executives as accounting officers for their respective agencies. The third section focuses upon the modern Parliamentary select committees – the extent and the precise ways in which they have affected or are likely to impinge upon the permanent secretary.

Permanent secretaries as accounting officers: the battle for a principle

To whatever extent laissez-faire principles pervaded contemporary thought, mid-Victorian government was conspicuous by a steady growth. And growth was accompanied by continual sensitivity to the inevitably increasing levels of public expenditure. None was more sensitive than William Gladstone. In the second of his four spells as Chancellor of the Exchequer and following an earlier recommendation from the Committee on Public Monies, Gladstone successfully moved the House of Commons for the creation of a permanent committee of public accounts (HC Debs, 3rd series 1861, vol. 162, col. 318). Its job would be to examine the regularity of expenditure against approved estimates. The PAC was soon to be served in its investigatory work by the Exchequer and Audit Department (now the National Audit Office), headed by the Comptroller and Auditor General.

The Exchequer and Audit Act, 1866, gave the Treasury a formal authority of prior scrutiny in the formulation of departmental estimates, at least where increases of expenditure were involved. This was part of the gradual if faltering process by which the Treasury began from the mid-nineteenth century to exercise greater financial control (Wright 1969; 1972). The 1866 Act also required that one person from each department should sign the accounts documents for that department as a whole. It laid upon the Treasury the duty to nominate who would be that person. The Treasury, however, left departments to nominate their accounting officers. Few departments at that time possessed either a culture or an organizational structure conducive to ready compliance. This the PAC found unsatisfactory. The Treasury redoubled its efforts. A Minute of 1872 laid down that the permanent heads of department should be nominated as accounting officers – that is, responsible for the appropriation accounts presented to the Exchequer and Audit Department. But the practice continued to fall some way short of the ideal. Fifteen years later, Reginald Welby, Permanent Secretary to the Treasury, explained to the Royal Commission on Civil Establishments (Ridley Commission) that he had no power to nominate who should be the accounting officer for a department. He could only insist that the permanent secretary assume a responsibility for the accounts, though the Treasury would not, he said, approve the signature of the political chief together with 'merely that of quite a subordinate officer under him'

(Ridley 1888, Q. 10, 807). Only in the Post Office, where there had been 'grave irregularities', had the Treasury really been able to call the shots.

Down to 1914 and even shortly after the Great War there were as many exceptions as adherences to the principle that the departmental accounting officer should be the permanent secretary. Only eight of the twenty-two heads of the main departments were also the accounting officers (PAC 1920, Appendix 34, pp. 402-3). In the departments of the secretaries of state (Colonial Office, Foreign Office and Home Office) an assistant under-secretary or chief clerk performed this function. In the other eleven cases the accounting officer was the accountant-general, usually operating at a level equivalent to a modern under secretary. These eleven included the three service departments (Admiralty, Air Ministry and War Office) which had agreed the principle – and were in process of adopting the practice – of placing the responsibility firmly with the permanent secretary.

There were a number of reasons for this continued failure to square the circle. First and above all, departmentalism remained strong during the late-nineteenth and early twentieth centuries. When under threat it could prove obdurate. The prospect of the Treasury or of any other external agent nominating an accounting officer was seen as a threat. Second, the sense of threat was sharpened by the legacy of Treasury insensitivity, particularly that of Ralph Lingen (Roseveare 1969, pp. 209-10). Lingen was Permanent Secretary to the Treasury between 1869-85. His heavy-handed insensitivity towards other departments cast a shadow over relationships from which his more emollient successor, Reginald Welby, found it difficult to escape. It must have been with an air of wistful resignation that Welby agreed with the Ridley Commission that: 'however good the financial criticism of the Treasury may be, it ought never to supersede an effective criticism within the Department itself' (Ridley 1888, Q. 10, 808). This betrays a third and final factor. The Ridley Commission had already pronounced: 'To say nothing of the fact that the permanent secretary has already quite enough to do, we deprecate the multiplication of finance branches' (1887, para. 100, p. xxii). The realpolitik underpinning this statement was quite simple: the politicians were not yet won over. Nor were all the permanent secretaries.

While the prosecution of the Great War made difficult any further advance towards uniformity, its aftermath brought a stronger injection of centralization and stringency. This assisted but did not in itself make inevitable the designation in every department of the permanent secretary as accounting officer. This achievement was the work largely of Warren Fisher, with the help of some powerful allies.

The critical issues were rehearsed in evidence submitted to the PAC and in corresponding reports issued by the Committee in 1920 and 1921. Acknowledging the continued importance of the departmental finance officer, or accountant-general, Fisher was nevertheless adamant that responsibility should rest squarely with the permanent head. The latter, he argued, should never be able to say 'it was not me' (PAC 1920, Q. 5299).

The PAC remained unconvinced. Its reasoning is worth recalling in the light of the debates that were to resound some seventy years later. The Committee was impressed by two considerations. First, that the added responsibilities would be too great a burden upon permanent secretaries, at least in the civil departments. This, it conceded, was not the case in the service departments. Here the permanent secretaries were absolved from responsibility for large areas of work which came under the jurisdiction of the military chiefs. Second, the arrangement proposed by Fisher would confront the Committee each year with an accounting officer who did not have detailed knowledge of finance. Conversely, the person who possessed such knowledge would appear only as a subordinate to be referred to on points of detail (PAC 1921, paras. 10-11). Fisher seemed to have been defeated. Not until 1925 did the PAC finally and formally relent. By this time Fisher had already won his battle, with the help of his permanent secretary colleagues and with the assistance, passive if not active, of the premier.

In February 1920 the Cabinet had approved recommendations, derived from a report by the Council of Financial Officers (Baldwin Council), which sought to prevent permanent secretaries becoming divorced from finance (O'Halpin 1989, p. 48). The cabinet clearly failed to grasp its significance (Ibid. p. 49). Later that year Fisher moved to exploit the situation as his own thinking began to crystallize. He sought and got from nearly all his fellow permanent secretaries consent for the view that, in principle, they should be the departmental accounting officers. Fisher would nevertheless also have needed at least the passive support of Prime Minister Lloyd George. Lloyd George's inclination towards stronger financial control predated the Great War (Wiemann 1971). He is said to have been the only minister of his day who could overcome the Treasury (Taylor 1964, p. 126). At the same time while he, more than any other Liberal, did much to conciliate the Labour Movement, he was also anxious to neuter Labour as a potential governing party (Morgan 1979, pp. 213-4). We can only speculate as to whether Lloyd George, in giving Fisher his head, saw the opportunity both to rein-in some of his Coalition colleagues and to provide a bureaucratic bulwark against the potential profligacy of any future Labour government. Fisher's strategy was clear enough. He had said quite bluntly: 'Pin it on him (i.e. the permanent secretary)... and you have got him as an ally for economy' (PAC 1920, Q. 2183).

The arrangements so established undoubtedly strengthened the hand of the Treasury. They also gave permanent secretaries a surer footing in resisting any unauthorized or irregular financial manoeuvres promulgated by their ministers. They did not involve any procedural novelty. The developments of the 1860s and the 1870s had given accounting officers the liberty to demur where they felt a transaction was not supported by legislation or other requisite authority. If, upon representation, an initial transaction was reaffirmed by the minister, the accounting officer would be bound to comply. But compliance would be accompanied by a memorandum apprising the Audit Department of the accounting officer's misgivings. The accounting officer would thereby be absolved. Without such a memorandum, the accounting officer could be implicated in the event of expenditure subsequently deemed 'irregular'. Then there would be the technical possibility of a surcharge upon the person of the accounting officer.

Where and for so long as the accounting officer had not been the permanent secretary then the measure of independence thereby accorded to the former constituted a manifest fault-line in the authority of the latter. The near universal absorption of the accounting officer role was therefore a milestone in the tighter grip that permanent secretaries were able to maintain within their departments during the middle decades of the twentieth century. This is not to say that all accounting officers were fully blown permanent secretaries. There were and are smaller departments, sometimes subordinate to larger ministries, headed by civil servants below permanent secretary level. They, too, are in some cases accounting officers (see Table 4.1 below). But all departmental heads who are full permanent secretaries are accounting officers. In fact one major department – the Foreign Office – continued for some time to resist. During the early 1920s, Eyre Crowe had blocked Fisher's efforts to bring the FO in line. Not until Cadogan succeeded Vansittart in 1938 did the PUS become the accounting officer (Cromwell and Steiner 1984, p. 96). Elsewhere in Whitehall, Fisher's success in the early 1920s was consolidated in the years and decades that followed. In particular, whatever the routine tensions between the Treasury and the spending departments, there seems to have been relatively little friction at permanent secretary level.

This is not to suggest that the departmental permanent secretaries of, say, the 1940s, '50s or '60s enjoyed relationships with the Treasury that were entirely trouble free. To an extent they were cast into different not to say adversarial roles. None of the parties were noted for their obsequience. Evelyn Sharp, as a member of the Plowden Committee in the early 1960s, was known to be suspicious of the iniquities of Treasury control (Theakston 1993, p. 144). But more often than not there was a good deal of mutual acknowledgement, no doubt in part a product of the subtle and sensitive approach adopted by Bridges and his successors, if not by Fisher. It probably also reflected the relative social cohesion, the *esprit de corps* and the policy of interdepartmental transfers which was to an extent a legacy from the Fisher era (see chapters 6 and 9). It owed something, too, to the accounting officer function which established or reinforced the Treasury as the centre of gravity in the minds of permanent secretaries. When examining expenditure control the Commons' Estimates Committee (1958, para. 41), while critical on a number of points, seemed satisfied that there existed a joint ownership of financial responsibility. Six permanent secretaries from the spending departments gave evidence: Alan Hitchman (MAFF); John Hawton (Health); Cyril Musgrave (Supply); Richard Powell (Defence); John Lang (Admiralty); and Frederick Hoyer Millar (Foreign Office). None bore witness to any deep-seated antagonism. John Hawton reflected the prevailing mood when he said: 'I do not see the Treasury as some extraneous body with whom we deal and negotiate like two diplomatic bodies' (Estimates Committee 1958, Q. 1257). Fisher would have been well pleased.

The broader significance of all this should not be misunderstood. The arrangements were not specifically designed and were in any case quite inappropriate to foil policy initiatives for which there was the political will. The mid-twentieth century saw some of the sharpest advances in state activity with a consequent escalation of public expenditure. No doubt some permanent secretaries of the time were uneasy. Their roles as accounting officers did not equip them to prevent increased expenditure, rather to ensure its regularity in accordance with Parliament's wishes. Increasingly there developed a focus upon economy – prudent expenditure in the service of agreed policies, later canonized in the slogan 'value for money'. In effect the notion of the permanent secretary as accounting officer reflected the inseparability of finance from policy. This was to enhance the potential for occasional friction between permanent secretaries and their ministers. At the same time, the increasing areas of work in which their departments became involved brought into question the capacity of permanent secretaries to answer to the PAC for matters about which they personally had little detailed knowledge. The 1960s and the 1970s saw the creation of many giant departments, or super ministries. These years also marked the beginning of a more widespread challenge to the arrangements that were completed half a century earlier.

The system and its critics

No permanent secretary takes lightly the responsibility of accounting officer. For some the sense of responsibility is great, even awesome – especially for those who head departments with large and wide-ranging budgets. Appearance in person before the PAC provides the main focus. It has done so for as long as permanent secretaries have assumed the accounting officer's role. An element of pride – and theatre – is often a feature. Cyril Musgrave, who headed the Ministry of Supply in the late-1950s, said: 'It was a point of honour that you put yourself in the position to be able to answer them and that the number of occasions on which you had to ask to refer back to papers or to other officials was kept to the absolute minimum'

(NOA Tr., pp. 22-3). Any such appearance, he said, meant working long hours for weeks beforehand. He thought that the responsibility resting on one individual to be 'unduly severe' (p. 23). He recalled a moment of light embarrassment when he was unable to inform the Committee what price his department paid for sparking plugs! For some permanent secretaries, appearance and the preparation for an appearance before the PAC has always taken precedence over all other matters (Cooper 1987, pp. 16-7). This still seems to be so. A present incumbent said: 'When I go to the PAC we have lots of rehearsals. We spend a lot of time... trying to make sure we have all the information. Colleagues sit around a table and throw all the nasty questions'. Another who, as head of a big spending department, made several appearances in quick succession, described the effort involved as 'pure misery'. Each appearance required from him 'the best part of a fortnight – and I mean a solid fortnight – to get wound up!' Such frequency of appearances is unusual but by no means without precedent. Not all permanent secretaries make quite such time-consuming and apparently all pervasive preparations. A colleague in another department said that he usually put in two full week-ends' work prior to each visit to the PAC.

No permanent secretary can afford to be found wanting before the PAC. This is so especially now with the exposure of PAC proceedings, along with those of other select committees, to the broadcasting media. The permanent secretary must appear assured, self-confident, able to deal effectively with the occasional 'bouncer'. Permanent secretaries must also remember that they are civil servants. They must not try to dispatch too many of the bouncers to the boundary – or, if they do, they should employ only the orthodox strokes. Montague Alfred, brought in at permanent secretary level with no previous experience of Whitehall, ignored these strictures. He did so to his own peril.

Montague Alfred was Chief Executive of the Property Services Agency (PSA) and Second Permanent Secretary in the DoE. Cases of fraud and corruption had been brought to light, mostly having taken place before Alfred's appointment in 1982. A special committee jointly chaired by one of the department's former permanent secretaries, Geoffrey Wardale, had made some extremely critical observations. The Wardale Report was duly presented to the PAC which then took evidence from Alfred, among others. At stake was the efficacy of higher financial control within the PSA. Alfred gave his evidence over two days, part of it in private since police prosecutions were still in process against certain of the private contractors involved (PAC 1984, Qs. 2280-2344). The PAC felt Alfred to be too complacent, even mildly dismissive of the gravity of the charges. In his defence he criticized the Wardale Report, in particular its terms of reference. In so doing he implicated his Secretary of State, Patrick Jenkin. Alfred had to go. Jenkin explained: 'I reluctantly concluded that his answers were inconsistent with the Government's policy on the Wardale Touche Ross report' (H C Debs 1983-84, Sixth Series, vol. 56 – written answer col. 75).

The incongruence between Alfred and his political chief was decisive. Almost equally important was his apparent failure to take sufficiently seriously the concerns of the Commons' most venerated and long-standing select committee. Alfred's performance may be contrasted with that a few years later of Michael Partridge, Permanent Secretary of the DSS. The department was preparing to introduce its Operational Strategy. This involved completion of one of the largest computerization programmes ever undertaken in Europe. The PAC had long been critical of certain aspects of the programme. The Comptroller and Auditor General had alleged apparent slippage in many of the projects – allegations which Partridge was keen to counter. The situation was ripe for confrontation. But Partridge won the day with subtlety. He remained, as one observer noted: 'wonderfully placatory and disarming, as time and again he seemed to agree with the questions – "that is a good point, actually", he would say to an argument which he clearly thought was not at all a good one' (Fallon 1993, p. 146).

Perhaps the sharpest conflicts likely to arise for the permanent secretary in the role of accounting officer are those with an exuberant, expansive minister. As noted above, it remains the prerogative, indeed the duty, of the permanent secretary to lay before Parliament via the Comptroller and Auditor General a note of dissent in cases of irregularity or impropriety. These are distinct from the more routine and non-contested cases in which the permanent secretary draws attention to the fact that there has been a financial loss, or some special payment. This may involve a temporary advance already agreed with the Treasury but still requiring Parliamentary approval by means of a supplementary estimate or excess vote. Irregularities, though, are more fraught. Conflict usually rests in the fact that different perspectives of judgement are in play, flagrant abuse or attempted fraud by ministers being rare. What to the minister seems simply an exercise of discretion over a relatively small matter in a large department with an ample budget may, to the permanent secretary, be a perversion of the purpose for which moneys were initially approved by Parliament. Sometimes disagreements are more about technicalities than about intentions or ultimate objectives. Thus Eric Bowyer in the early 1960s felt that his minister had no authority to make certain payments to disabled war veterans (Boyd-Carpenter 1980, pp. 131-2). Where more fundamental policy issues are concerned, differences of perspective can take a less friendly turn. Peter Carey, Second Permanent Secretary at the Department of Industry, objected in 1975 to the use of Section 7 of the Industry Act, 1972 to establish three workers' co-operatives (Wright 1977, p. 298). His minister, Tony Benn, felt unfairly thwarted (Benn 1979, pp. 158-9). Benn fared little better with Carey's 'senior' partner, Antony Part. Part (1990, p. 175) says that he wrote three memoranda of warning to Benn during their eighteen months working relationship.

More recently and perhaps more spectacularly, Tim Lankester, then Permanent Secretary at the Overseas Development Administration (ODA), issued a disclaimer over the Malaysian Pergau Dam project. Lankester believed that financial support for this project did not represent good use of public money. It also involved an alleged contravention of guidelines which sought to prevent the linking of aid to developing countries with pursuit of the defence or business interests of the donor nation. The case caused a political storm as it received widespread publicity during 1993 and 1994. There were loose parallels with the even more emotive question of arms sales to Iraq, the subject of the contemporaneous Scott Inquiry. Lankester's note of dissent was only one aspect of the Pergau Dam Affair. But it added zest to the ensuing political battle of words, no doubt unintentionally so far as Lankester was concerned. What was notable was Lankester's recoiling not only from his own minister, the Foreign Secretary, but also, implicitly, from the Prime Minister. The PAC (1994b, p. xiii, para. 48) accepted that Lankester had given clear advice that support for the project would not be an effective use of the aid budget – especially at prices well above initial estimates. Perhaps one of the most interesting things was that no attempt was made to persuade Lankester as to the economic viability of the project when once he had indicated his views (Ibid. Qs. 14-5). The Foreign Secretary noted Lankester's formal memorandum of reservation, exercised his own prerogative to overrule it and proceeded. But Lankester had laid down a marker.

These kind of cases are, it must be stressed, exceptional. Most senior ministers, with their extensive experience of Whitehall, understand the predicament of the permanent secretary. For the most part potential difficulties are resolved with a quiet word – at least so far as irregularities are concerned. One of the permanent secretaries of the 1990s with long experience as an accounting officer in more than one department said that he had never had such problems with ministers. But he acknowledged that 'it occasionally happens that, for political reasons… a minister will want to do something which clearly involves expenditure which, in the view of officials, isn't going to produce value for money'. This is a much greyer area. It is something which, previously implicit, has received more overt expression in recent years. It was part of the shift of emphasis with which, following the National Audit Act, 1983, the National Audit Office replaced the Exchequer and Audit Department. This shift of emphasis has technically altered neither the status nor the procedural arrangements by which accounting officers discharge their functions. All accounting officers continue to receive from the Treasury a memorandum detailing their specific responsibilities. This has long been the practice following a case of embezzlement and an ensuing recommendation from the PAC in 1937. The Treasury memorandum, revised in 1990, requires the accounting officer to ensure the provision, at all levels, of such organization and procedures as are necessary: 'to avoid waste and extravagance and to seek economy, efficiency and effectiveness in the use of all resources made available to the department' (PAC 1990, p. iv, para. 6). But, in contrast with matters of irregularity or impropriety, notes of dissent issued by accounting officers about value for money are not required to be laid before the National Audit Office. For some this is an anomaly and there is growing pressure to standardize arrangements for all notes of dissent.

The Treasury memorandum is, as one permanent secretary said, 'a salutary stick to have in your hand from time-to-time... if they (ministers) look as if they might be going to kick over the traces'. Together with the presence of the PAC the Treasury memorandum can also help the permanent secretary in the internal direction and management of the department (Cooper 1987). But this begs a number of questions. Is the permanent secretary suitably equipped by way of routine internal management control if it is thought necessary to bring such external threats to bear? To what extent is it reasonable to expect any one permanent secretary personally to account for the large sums and miscellaneous character of expenditure covered by even the medium sized departments, let alone the largest ones? Does the sheer effort personally expended in the preparation, appearance and aftermath of a PAC meeting constitute the best use of the permanent secretary's time? Could not there be a greater delegation and diffusion of responsibility? Is there not in any case an inherent conflict in the permanent secretary's dual responsibilities for policy and finance?

Some of these questions are, it will be remembered, ones which exercised the PAC in the early 1920s. As noted above, the Committee was not wholly mollified but was in the event outflanked by Warren Fisher. The system in the 1990s is by no means exactly the one bequeathed by Fisher. Even since the days of Cyril Musgrave in the 1950s things have changed. No modern permanent secretary would be even mildly embarrassed by an inability to recite the price of sparking plugs. The permanent secretary of the 1990s is more likely to be accompanied by a subordinate, though still quite senior, official possessing command over such detail. Why then not make the subordinate one of a number of accounting officers?

It has been claimed that the notion of the permanent secretary as accounting officer has lost its original significance and survives only as one of the 'reassuring myths of British government' (Ponting 1989, p. 22). In particular, says Ponting, there is no real comeback on the permanent secretary when things go wrong. With this Montague Alfred would certainly disagree. Much hangs upon the notion of responsibility. Perhaps the real force of the responsibility lies in the requirement to 'find out and answer', rather than in retribution directed to the person of the accounting officer. Is it still appropriate, then, that the accounting officer should be the permanent secretary? Here the creation of executive agencies has brought a potentially important change from the arrangements devised by Warren Fisher. Chief executives are now the accounting officers for their agencies. This was foreshadowed in the Ibbs Report (Efficiency Unit 1988, para. 22). Its realization followed a fierce battle in which the Treasury, under its then Permanent Secretary Peter Middleton, fought a stout rearguard action (TCSC 1988b, Qs. 369-73). Middleton's successor, Terence Burns, seems much less troubled about the possible loss of financial control. Where an agency has its own vote, or is a trading fund, the Treasury appoints the chief executive as accounting officer; otherwise the departmental permanent secretary designates the chief executive as agency accounting officer (HM Treasury 1989, para. 5.5).

It is too early to say for sure whether, from the perspective of financial management, these arrangements have brought any enhancement or, alternatively, any loss in the system of control. There are, as noted in the last chapter, some concerns in connection with the broader vista of management control. The PAC has expressed its concerns about certain aspects of executive agencies and non-governmental bodies. These will be looked at from a slightly different angle in the final chapter. But whether the designation of agency chief executives as accounting officers is itself a contributory factor to any malfunctioning is much less certain. Indeed the PAC may derive certain advantage from the designation of chief executives as agency accounting officers – most obviously in having direct access to those with an immediate operational involvement. Of course, even before the creation of executive agencies officials with immediate charge of the operations in question would sometimes accompany the permanent secretary in appearances before the Committee. Their formal designation is nevertheless a move in the direction of calls for a greater number of accounting officers – calls which themselves long predated the widespread creation of agencies (Chapman 1979, pp. 125-34). But what about the perspective of the permanent secretary? Again, there are few detectable signs of anxiety, other than the general concerns noted in the last chapter. In one sense permanent secretaries have been relieved of a burden – or rather they have a responsibility now formally shared, since the permanent secretary retains a global remit for the financial affairs of the department of which agencies are a constituent element. Problems could arise were a chief executive to plead in self-defence that a particular shortcoming within his or her agency was the result of faulty financial management in the core department. The semi-independent status granted to chief executives by virtue of their status as accounting officers may increase the potential for such conflict. It has further been claimed that the retention of the permanent secretary's general oversight robs the agencies of the real independence they need for their proper functioning (Kemp 1993, p. 22). For the permanent secretary the opposite may seem nearer the mark: responsibility for global financial management without the lines of authority necessary to exercise control.

All this underlines the potential conflict of roles, not least within the office of permanent secretary itself. Former permanent secretaries have alluded to these conflicts. It has been suggested that there may be conflict between the permanent secretary's role as accounting officer and the other two roles of policy advice and departmental management (Nairne 1983, p. 254). It has been said that power and responsibility are never easy bedfellows – if they are, something is wrong (Cubbon 1993, p. 8). It remains to be seen whether the power of permanent secretaries within their departments diminishes in relation to their overall responsibilities. Whatever the case there is as yet no evidence that with the advent of agency accounting officers they are any less frequently called before the PAC. This can be seen in Table 4.1 below.

Table 4.1
Appearances before the Committee of Public Accounts

	Number of appearances			
	1961-62 and 1962-63	1971-72 and 1972-73	1981-82 and 1982-83	1991-92 and 1992-93
Permanent secretaries	56 (44%)	79 (36%)	62 (38%)	79 (32%)
Accounting officers (not permanent secretaries)	16 (13%)	11 (5%)	18 (11%)	14 (6%)
Other departmental officials	40 (32%)	109 (50%)	70 (42%)	83 (33%)
Next Steps agency staff	—	—	—	23 (9%)
Other witnesses	14 (11%)	20 (9%)	15 (9%)	50 (20%)
Total	126 (100%)	219 (100%)	165 (100%)	249 (100%)
Permanent secretaries as sole witnesses (proportion of appearances)	(43%)	(16%)	(21%)	(17%)

Notes: i. Figures in parentheses are percentages of the relevant totals for each period
ii. All calculations exclude the comptroller and auditor general and the Treasury officer of accounts

The figures in Table 4.1 show the number and distribution of PAC appearances at intervals over thirty years. Two consecutive Parliamentary sessions provide the basis for calculation in each of four periods. General elections in 1983 and 1992 interrupted the respective sessions, so figures for the last two of the four periods may represent a slight understatement. It is clear nevertheless that permanent secretaries remain as heavily involved and more so in making PAC appearances, albeit they are less likely (than in the early 1960s) to appear alone. There seems also to be a heavier emphasis upon outside witnesses in the 1990s. Agency staff – mainly but not exclusively chief executives – are only beginning to make their presence felt. This is almost certain to develop. It is notable, though, that on only four occasions did an agency chief executive appear without an accompanying permanent secretary. Two of these were in connection with Northern Ireland, one involved the Insolvency Agency of the DTI and the other concerned the Export Credits Guarantee Department (ECGD). The ECGD has long enjoyed a semi-independent status as a department in its own right.

The implication is clear: for the time being permanent secretaries retain top billing with the PAC. A rather different set of considerations is involved, however, in connection with the other select committees.

The modern select committees

The framework for the present Parliamentary select committee system was established during 1979-80. This followed procrastination, first, by the Callaghan administration and then, briefly, by the Thatcher government. These committees built, in part, upon the much paler experiments introduced by Richard Crossman as Leader of the House of Commons in the 1960s. It is unlikely that the mandarins were enamoured with the intrusions threatened by such experiments. Nor is it known to what extent, if at all, official recalcitrance ensured their feebleness. Certainly an earlier generation of mandarins had manoeuvred to thwart a proposal for the creation of supervisory committees. At a private meeting chaired by Richard Hopkins in November 1942 a group of thirteen permanent secretaries shared their objections and indeed their contempt for any such idea (Davie 1977).

Select committees are not of course a modern invention. As shown above, the PAC dates back to the early 1860s. Moreover, both houses of Parliament have been in the habit during this and during the last century of creating special select committees to investigate particular matters. Civil servants have long been accustomed to appearing before such committees. But the 1979-80 reforms involved for the first time a phalanx of committees with a potential to cover the length and breadth of Whitehall's activities. Each major department would be shadowed by a select committee. Each committee would be empowered to send for papers, persons and records – including the summoning of named officials. The committees would set their own agenda. Government departments were expected to co-operate.

Much has been written about the efficacy of these select committees as an instrument of Parliamentary scrutiny. Such considerations lie outside the scope of this book. Concerns – quite proper concerns – have been expressed about the possible implications for the constitutional position of civil servants. More general comment about this will be made in the final chapter. For the moment the focus is upon the relationship between select committees and the office of permanent secretary – in particular the permanent secretary's responsibility for running the department.

In contrast to the PAC, permanent secretaries are less in evidence as witnesses to other select committees. They tended to be called rather more frequently during the early days of the new select committee system. They still appear from time-to-time, especially where a committee needs an overall perspective from the official level, perhaps when considering the annual reports that are now presented by most departments. Otherwise select committees tend to go either for the broad, high profile policy issues, in which case they will call upon the minister; or for the more detailed aspects with which other senior or mid-ranking officials will have a deeper familiarity.

Select committees have nevertheless had a considerable effect upon the office of permanent secretary as well as upon other officials. A code of conduct, *Memorandum of Guidance for Officials Appearing before Select Committees*, was issued in 1980 to all senior civil servants. Based upon an earlier general notice, it was drafted by Edward Osmotherly, then an assistant secretary in the CSD. Thus known as the Osmotherly Rules, the memorandum was further redrafted and issued in 1994 as *Departmental Evidence and Response to Select Committees*. While encouraging civil servants to be as helpful as possible to select committees, the document retains a number of parameters (many of them quite reasonable ones) beyond which officials are warned against disclosure of information. Critics have therefore objected to the Osmotherly Rules as inhibiting officials from engaging in open exchanges with Parliamentary committees (Davies and Willman 1991, p. 37). Some have seen the select committees as reinforcing a safety-first preoccupation, making civil servants more concerned with 'political management' (Ross 1984, p. 19). This observation highlights the dilemma of the permanent secretary. For the permanent secretary is responsible to the minister for the conduct of the department. This, as has been seen, means getting the department behind the minister. The permanent secretary must ensure, so far as possible, that no official from the department publicly contradicts or in any way compromises the minister or the policies with which the minister and the government is associated. To an extent greater than ever before the fate of the permanent secretary is in the hands of other officials. This is not something over which permanent secretaries lose sleep. On the contrary, they will normally have confidence in their colleagues. It is nevertheless the job of the select committees to probe. They do not always have as their first consideration the constitutional dilemma of the civil servant. They may have genuine respect for the conflicts of loyalty that can arise but they may unwittingly draw the civil servant into areas of political sensitivity. Civil servants – even experienced ones and in spite of the Osmotherly Rules – may in innocence say something which, for the committee, is or turns out to be political dynamite, rather like 'discovered check' in a game of chess. The sheer scale, collectively, of select committees' activities ensures that this is at all times a real not an ethereal possibility, even though their proceedings still assume a relatively small part of the permanent secretary's vista. Between 1983-84 and 1987-88 no fewer than 1,653 civil servants appeared as witnesses before select committees (Select Committee on Procedure 1990b, p. 265). They constituted some 27 per cent of all witnesses, the remainder being ministers (4 per cent) and others mainly on the fringes or outside the orbit of Whitehall (69 per cent).

While critics may bemoan the negative caution sometimes exhibited by civil servants when making select committee appearances, permanent secretaries will be conscious of the hostages to fortune. Not surprisingly, there have been instances in which the Whitehall hierarchy has taken steps deliberately to thwart select committees in their probings. During the Westland Affair in the mid-1980s, Robert Armstrong prevented certain officials from giving evidence which might have incriminated not only themselves but also their ministers and the prime minister. The initial issue of policy which underpinned the whole affair had seemed innocuous enough – which of two contenders, one American and the other a nascent European consortium, should be given a contract to build helicopters for the British government. Quickly the issue became embroiled in questions of broader ideology, party manoeuvrings and, ultimately, personal reputations (Linklater and Leigh 1986). Two departmental ministers had already resigned. One (Michael Heseltine) had chosen to go; the other (Leon Brittan) stood down honourably but unwillingly, in effect on behalf of the government, hoping thereby to draw a line under the whole affair. The next stop would have been the prime minister. Whatever the niceties, whatever the conflicting perspectives, Armstrong had reason enough to play a dead bat. He himself faced the bowling and managed to smother the spin.

More recently, the government refused to permit the TCSC to conduct a survey of officials at various levels in the service. In so deciding, the government was prompted by the topmost mandarins. The TCSC had wanted to elicit officials' perceptions on matters such as values, loyalties, career development, promotion and the quality of management in Whitehall – all within the context of recent developments including the creation of agencies, privatization and market testing. In oral evidence to the Committee Robin Butler had undertaken to present his impressions as to how civil servants felt. With this the Committee was not satisfied. It wanted to take soundings from the rank and file themselves. This was too close to the knuckle for the government, fearing as it said it did for the principle of civil service impartiality. Whether this was simply a piece of disingenuity and whether indeed there would have ensued any breach of the principle are open questions. At any rate the government contended that impartiality could be jeopardized if the results of any such survey, even presented in aggregate form, were to be given public circulation as reflecting (among other things) the views of civil servants on aspects of current government policies. To the TCSC this was defensive stonewalling in the extreme. In its exasperation, and unusually, it published immediately the correspondence that had passed between itself and the government during February-May 1994.

These instances illustrate the fears, not only of government ministers but also of most permanent secretaries. When faced with possible Armageddon, they are apt to pull down the shutters. Perhaps, from their perspective, there is ample justification, bearing in mind all the attendant risks. Still, these are the exceptions and quite untypical cases. Less newsworthy but more noteworthy is the fact that almost every day when Parliament is in session civil servants are giving evidence to select committees. The information they impart is wide-ranging, detailed and usually helpful to the committees. For all the critics' banter, Parliament's own review expressed general satisfaction. It found no evidence that the Osmotherly Rules had placed 'unacceptable constraints' on select committees (Select Committee on Procedure 1990a, para. 157). It has been said that: 'Contrary to popular view, civil servants often actually rather enjoy appearing in front of select committees' (Kemp 1984, pp. 56-7). It is difficult to know how widely this joy is experienced among officials, especially since the broadcasting of committee proceedings. No doubt dispositions vary. So, too, do the perspectives of select committee members – even among those with previous ministerial experience in the same government. John Golding, former Labour minister and later chairman of the Employment Committee, said he found civil servants to be too timid for fear of embarrassing their ministers. He said he would 'rather have the organ grinder appear before the select committee and leave the monkeys back in Whitehall!' (Englefield 1984, p. 34). In contrast Charles Morris, a former minister for the civil service, argued that by no means all officials were so timid (Ibid. p. 43). From a ministerial and a permanent secretary perspective this clearly has its risks, especially if, as has been claimed (Hawes 1993, p. 174), some departmental officials have seized the opportunity to reopen lost battles or to push for changes 'on the back' of a committee report. To this extent the select committees have placed an additional management burden upon permanent secretaries. In any event permanent secretaries, while themselves seldom appearing before select committees, are often involved in the internal discussions about the nature and presentation of evidence to be given by other officials 'where politics, policies and facts may require some harmonization' (Cooper 1987, p. 17).

This notion of harmonization is central to much that today's permanent secretaries do. The previous two chapters have shown how they perform this role in their advisory and in their general departmental management roles. The trick is to maintain control and coherence without stifling the creative energies and initiatives of others. If greater delegation and a certain fragmentation of structure and of process have in certain respects removed permanent secretaries from the front line of policy, these same tendencies have presented other problems and potential hazards that are no less engaging. The sheer effort involved in being a permanent secretary has not diminished, as will be seen in the next chapter.

5 A day in the life: permanent secretaries at work

Introduction

Previous chapters have examined different aspects of the permanent secretary's changing roles. This one brings things together by looking at what permanent secretaries do with their time. This it does not by describing a typical day, or even a week, as exemplified in the engagements inscribed in a particular permanent secretary's diary. In this sense there is no one typical day. Experiences are simply too varied. Rather, this chapter proceeds, first, by looking at more general patterns of work, now and in the past. Second, it links these observations with the changing roles as analyzed in the last three chapters. Finally, this chapter considers some of the recent calls for reform, including those which prognosticize the diminution and even the demise of the office of permanent secretary.

Working patterns

The demands made upon permanent secretaries have often been considerable. The burdens assumed, sometimes self-induced, by certain of their number have occasionally been as much or more than could be borne by any one individual. The public are usually unaware of this and always have been. Comparisons over long periods are difficult. The virulent if progressively inhibited departmentalism of the nineteenth century yielded a variety of patterns. A sample of the numerous available accounts conveys the differing, sometimes conflicting, impressions upon contemporaries as they ascended the hierarchy.

'Why are the government clerks like the fountains in Trafalgar Square? Because they play all day from ten until four'. So ran the famous nineteenth century jibe about civil servants. Rumour gave it credit to a permanent secretary, Thomas Farrer – at least according to another permanent secretary, Algernon West (1920, p. 23). Farrer was Permanent Secretary to the Board of Trade between 1865-86. He was one of the most accomplished figures of his day, giving almost fatherly encouragement and advice on economic matters to Joseph Chamberlain in his first cabinet post as President of the Board of Trade during the early 1880s. West had been Chairman of the Board of Inland Revenue between 1881-92. He had begun his career as a young clerk in the Admiralty, having cut short his studies at Christ Church College, Oxford. He served in the India Office and in the Treasury, including as private secretary to Prime Minister Gladstone. West took a certain pleasure in the Trafalgar Square parody, though less so in *Punch*'s declamation of officials refusing coffee after lunch lest it keep them awake in the afternoon! Still, many civil servants did work from ten to four. They enjoyed the privilege of a Derby Day holiday.

Within and between departments during the nineteenth century the pace varied – in hard reality as also in the eyes of the beholder. In the Home Office, for example, business fluctuated according to the state of civil unrest in the country (Donajgrodzki 1972, p. 93). Laurence Guillemard (1937, p. 14) described the Home Office as 'the sleepiest of sleepy hollows'. He began his career there in 1886, his transfer two years later to the Treasury being 'like coming out of a mausoleum into a busy workshop' (Ibid., p. 19). Yet Henry Primrose recalled life in the Treasury during the 1870s and 1880s where he and his colleagues 'regaled themselves with sherry and betted whether the vehicles going down the street would outnumber the vehicles going down Whitehall, until it was time to adjourn to their clubs for luncheon' (Leith-Ross 1968, pp. 20-1). Primrose later headed the Office of Works (1886-95), the Board of Customs (1895-99) and Inland Revenue (1899-1907). Of the Admiralty around the turn of the century Arthur Salter (1961, p. 39) said: 'everything was... unbelievably static, the future calculable with terrifying precision'. The higher grade clerks in the Admiralty nevertheless had only alternate Saturday afternoons off. On other days they began work at 10.30am and were unable to get away before six (Murray 1940, p. 31).

Two allowances need to be made when considering accounts such as these. First, there is the inevitable element of nostalgia when individuals, civil servants no less, look back upon long careers. This may be so especially where careers have been spent almost entirely in the embrace of a distinct culture such as that of Whitehall. In all organizations there is a near obligatory tendency to assume that life is getting tougher. This seems to have been no less so a hundred years ago than it is today. Second, the amount of work falling directly upon permanent secretaries cannot necessarily be deduced from the impressions gained by civil servants, even future permanent secretaries, then operating at junior and middle-rank levels. The accounts noted above betray not simply the variability between departments at any one time, not only the slow but steady acceleration across the board down to 1914 but more, much more, the extent to which matters rested in the hands of the permanent secretaries and other luminaries of the day. This, at least, was so for the more heroic among them – those who chose and acted out the big roles. James Stephen's industry at the Colonial Office in the 1830s and 1840s was phenomenal. As his duties increased he had 'virtually no holidays, taking work with him while nominally on vacation' (Knaplund 1953, p. 17). He retired on grounds of ill-health. Chadwick proved more durable, physically. But upon his departure in 1854 he complained that for twenty-two years he had worked 'unintermittently for ten or twelve hours a day, with little recess or holiday except on the occasion of ill-health' (Lewis 1952, p. 358). Trevelyan claimed in 1848 that he habitually put in three hours before breakfast to read papers and reports and worked at the Treasury until late in the evening, returning home too tired for anything but sleep (Select Committee on Miscellaneous Expenditure 1848, p. 151). In his letter of resignation to Lord John Russell in 1849, Kay-Shuttleworth, after ten years heading the Education Department, referred to a twelve hour day which, while formerly a reflection of early zeal, had become a matter of necessity (Smith 1923, pp. 216-7).

By no means all permanent secretaries of the nineteenth century were as active or so hard pressed in their jobs as titans such as Chadwick or Kay-Shuttleworth. The likes of Charles Greville provide a contrast. Greville was Joint Secretary then Secretary to the Privy Council between 1821-59. He kept a detailed, colourful and sometimes revealing diary (Strachey and Fulford 1938) at least comparable in importance to that of Richard Crossman some one hundred years later. The keeping of the diary and its contents betray Greville's active participation in high society. There is little hint of his being tethered by the demands of office. His was a permanent secretaryship untypical even of its own age. It is unlikely, though, that his many other and lesser contemporaries worked at the same pitch as, say, James Stephen. Yet the observations, noted above, made both about Stephen and about Kay-Shuttleworth suggest a gathering momentum quite distinct from the inclinations of the individual incumbent.

Bureaucracy, then, began to take its hold during the second half of the nineteenth century. Some of the factors mentioned in chapters 2 and 3 were responsible. These include the advance of the regulatory state, the administration and often discretionary implementation of statute and other authorities within a context of ministerial responsibility which required permanent secretaries, as ministers' agents, to exercise quite careful control within their departments. As argued in Chapter 3, the early and middle decades of the twentieth century marked the closest proximity to a Weberian-type classical bureaucracy in Whitehall. These years were the zenith of permanent secretary authority. Preceding as they did the era of extensive delegation, they were therefore also years in which many permanent secretaries absorbed enormous workloads.

During the early decades of this century it was just possible for the permanent secretary to hold these forces at bay. Vansittart worked from ten to five, insisting on a two hour lunch break. He normally spent a quarter of his time in interviews and meetings, the rest on paper work. He often composed in ornate prose memoranda for ministers who did not always appreciate the style any more than they did the contents. Still, he took his boxes home in the evenings and at week-ends (Rose 1978, p. 72). John Anderson (Viscount Waverley) was PUS at the Home Office, 1922-32. He, too, ran his department in magisterial, Olympian style. When he and his Labour Home Secretary J.R. Clynes were summoned to a meeting beginning at 6.15pm and presided over by Prime Minister Ramsay MacDonald, the reply was received: 'Mr Clynes will attend the meeting. Sir John Anderson does not attend meetings beginning after six o'clock' (Kent 1979, p. 114).

Others of the Vansittart-Anderson generation were perhaps either less fortunate, less forceful or were willing victims of long hours. Beatrice Webb complained that she had seen nothing of her former Fabian colleague Sydney Olivier after he had been eight months into his permanent secretaryship at the Board of Agriculture (Mackenzie and Mackenzie 1984, p. 190). Olivier had taken the post in 1913 upon returning from his position as Governor of Jamaica. Sheer pressure of work was almost certainly the reason, rather than any proprietorial qualm or loss of friendship. Hankey, as Cabinet Secretary between the wars, rarely left his office before 8.00pm. He spent much time reading – mainly memoranda, letters, telegrams. Ensconced in Whitehall's nerve-centre he was in effect on call not only for officials but also for cabinet and other ministers who would constantly drop in 'to confer about some difficult point, or some great point of policy' (Naylor 1984, pp. 53-4). More generally, Dale (1941, p. 135) talked about permanent secretaries of this period routinely working an eight hour day five days of the week, with another four or five hours on the sixth day. They still took papers home in the evenings and at week-ends. Moreover, in times of crisis and then for weeks together it would be necessary for the permanent secretary personally to work 'the whole twenty-four hours with no intervals save those absolutely necessary for food and sleep' (Ibid.).

The advancing role of the state in the 1940s, '50s and '60s kept the pressure upon all senior mandarins. The war years were the high point. People like Edward Bridges literally had a bed in Whitehall. This was exceptional. But both during and after the Second World War the burdens of office remained considerable. Archibald Rowlands was Permanent Secretary of the Ministry of Aircraft Production (1940-43) and of the Ministry of Supply (1946-52). He used to claim that getting through all his work necessitated his sleeping only on six nights of the week. He never went to bed on Saturday, working through the night until Sunday morning so that by Monday he had cleared the paper that had accumulated on his desk (Musgrave, NOA Tr., p. 14). He died only several months after his retirement from the civil service. Cyril Musgrave, himself one of Rowlands's successors, felt so overworked that he jumped at the chance of leaving Whitehall when it was offered to him late in 1958. He took the chairmanship of the Iron and Steel Board. This, by comparison, he found to be 'a very light job', though the salary was appreciably greater (Ibid., p.32).

Permanent secretaries, like any other group of human beings, have and always have had varying thresholds of tolerance. Frederick Hoyer Millar, PUS at the Foreign Office 1957-61, said he never felt overworked (Inchyra, NOA Tr., p. 16). But he admitted to being exasperated with what he called 'silly sort of administrative things'. These included removing someone from a position for which they had proven themselves unsuited, or persuading a member of the diplomatic service to take an unattractive posting. These kinds of things were, to him, as much trouble as the major political problems. He reckoned to spend a third of his time on administration, in addition having quite a lot to do with the Cabinet Office, especially Cabinet Secretary Norman Brook. Hoyer Millar worked in his office from 9.30am to 7.30pm, going in one Saturday in three and quite often on Sunday mornings. He would lunch at one of his clubs. Here he would meet some of his Whitehall colleagues, including fellow permanent secretaries. But 'only under some grave compulsion would one "talk shop" out of the office' (Ibid., p. 13). At the Home Office, Charles Cunningham, a near contemporary of Hoyer Millar's, also worked from 9.30am to 7.30pm. If there was Parliamentary business he would often not return home until the small hours (Cunningham NOA Tr., p. 27). On major issues it was and still is common for permanent secretaries to attend Parliamentary debates observing, albeit helplessly, the fate of policy measures they have shaped. Cunningham, as was seen in Chapter 2, maintained a tight rein. This must have compounded the natural burdens of office. Arthur Peterson, a successor of Cunningham's in the 1970s, seems to have made for himself a lighter load. Peterson was usually away by seven in the evening and rarely worked at week-ends. By comparison with his previous post as Chief Executive of the Greater London Council he was struck by there being fewer social engagements in the evenings (Peterson NOA Tr., p. 37).

Peterson was one of the new managerialists, or semi-managerialists. He delegated extensively, bearing little comparison with Cunningham. His was more the model for the modern permanent secretaryship. Greater delegation has become the norm throughout Whitehall, quite irrespective of the creation of executive agencies which undoubtedly have and will further augment this trend. But there are limits. As Nairne (1982, p. 73) says, the permanent secretary is 'like a batsman who is always at the crease and can never take his eye off the ball'. The office of permanent secretary is more than that of deputy secretary or under secretary writ large. For one thing, the buck stops with the permanent secretary, as it does with the head of any organization. Permanent secretaries are acutely aware of this. One of the present incumbents said:

> I mean, what has struck me is that there's a world of difference even between being number two and number one... the peak is much more windswept than the next ledge down... there's no one to appeal to. You've got to sort it out yourself... The problems that land on my desk are by definition the ones nobody else has been able to solve. There is a sense of exposure and, if you like, loneliness about the job which isn't apparent at the lower level.

Another expressed similar sentiments:

> I then came here and I would be having meetings with my people – officials, you know. They were coming up with these really complicated things to be decided. And from day one I realized they were looking to me – you know, I was supposed to be in charge of all this.

It is not that permanent secretaries necessarily always handle a higher level of, say, policy work than do other senior officials. As shown in Chapter 2, their roles in policy formulation tend to be more the ones of broker or orchestrator than of initiator or handler, though sometimes they do get 'stuck-in'. The permanent secretary is the fulcrum around which much in the department revolves; the apex at which different dimensions come together. This business of pulling things together has, within the framework of wider change in Whitehall, brought a shift of emphasis in the way permanent secretaries spend their time. It has afforded little relief from the sheer volume of work, though now as always individuals have some influence in the precise roles they play, hence in the exact allocation of time.

Making time, shaping a role

The way in which different permanent secretaries operate clearly varies. In particular, as has been seen in Chapter 2, some spend more time with their ministers than do others. And, for any one permanent secretary, this itself will vary as ministers come and go. It is part of the permanent secretary's craft to dovetail with the talents and tendencies of different ministers in succession. This is not always easy. Sometimes personalities are an obstacle to reciprocation. Evelyn Sharp responded with vigour in anticipation of the published diaries of Richard Crossman, stung with the belief, among other things, that they betrayed confidences to which she had entrusted her former minister. Her ire was in no way quelled by the fact of Crossman's death eighteen months earlier. Yet she regretted not being able to establish a better, more stable relationship. She reflected: 'Perhaps it would have been better if I hadn't been so tempestuous and quick-tempered. He needed a steadier and wiser person than I' (Jenkins 1975). Usually the best relationships are the ones where the permanent secretary and the minister play to each other's strengths. If it is in the minister's best interests to learn how to handle the department, then the permanent secretary can help the minister to be the kind of minister he or she wants to be. As one permanent secretary said: 'Where the minister knows what he is doing, the permanent secretary keeps in the background. When the minister gets stuck the permanent secretary steps forward and says "I think, minister, what you need is this"'. All this inevitably has a bearing upon what permanent secretaries do and the way they spend their time.

Individually permanent secretaries, too, have their relative strengths and weaknesses. There are some areas, some aspects of the job, that appeal more to certain people than to others. Permanent secretaries will naturally try to play to their strengths and, where possible, will develop those aspects that most interest them. There remains a fair scope for individuals to shape the roles they play. Some, an increasing number, willingly lay more emphasis on management. Others like to keep a stronger grip on policy – or at least on certain areas over and above the staple fare of brokerage, or orchestration. Different permanent secretaries have different styles. Some operate very much through the medium of systems, while others adopt a more personalized approach. All now delegate quite extensively, though some more so than others and with different mechanisms for monitoring to ensure the necessary 'follow through'.

The proclivities of the individual permanent secretary (and minister) have a bearing upon the precise role played and therefore upon the way in which time is spent. So, too, do other variables, notably the size, complexity and nature of the department. Certain of these factors were noted in Chapter 3. Some departments have a higher ratio of policy to management work. In others there is much policy work and also a heavy management factor. Others again have structures that are more explicitly federal.

When all has been said there are nevertheless certain broad and indeed more specific aspects of the job that will demand the permanent secretary's attention, willingly or otherwise – a kind of core curriculum. These are the miscellaneous component parts within the tripartism of policy/political advice, running the department and accounting to Parliament. Some of these more specific tasks have been mentioned in the last three chapters. Added together they account for a good deal of the average permanent secretary's time. For example, all permanent secretaries hold regular meetings with other senior officials in addition to the formal (not to mention informal) meetings at which ministers will be in attendance. Some will hold such meetings ('morning prayers') each day, all at least once per week. Meetings may last no more than half an hour, perhaps longer in some cases. There will usually be meetings within the department at which the permanent secretary's presence is helpful and sometimes indispensable. This may be to establish strategic parameters, to unblock an impasse or simply to consolidate the smooth progress of an initiative already in train. Rarely, for most permanent secretaries, will a week pass without spending some time in at least one interdepartmental committee meeting. Occasionally, when their political masters fall out, it is civil servants who keep open the lines of communication (MacDougall 1987, p. 174). Interdepartmental activity is not exclusive to permanent secretaries. Nor are all permanent secretaries equally involved. Some, by the nature of their departments, remain more on the periphery. Moreover, interdepartmental committees are less pervasive within Whitehall than they were during the 1960s and '70s. Certainly there are fewer of the major official committees that 'shadow' those at the political level. But among those who are involved the level and sheer extent of such activity constitutes for the permanent secretary a dimension over and above that experienced by most departmental deputy or under secretaries. The select few are also members of the Senior Appointments Selection Committee (SASC – see Chapter 7), though this meets only when there is a vacancy to be filled.

Two further aspects of the external relations role are contacts with the media and contacts with pressure groups. Contacts with the media were mentioned in Chapter 3. This has been a growth area in recent years. Again, permanent secretaries are not the only senior mandarins to be in contact with media representatives and some have very little such contact. But at certain moments they can become heavily involved, especially where a global input is needed from the official level. It varies considerably from department to department, as do contacts with pressure groups. Here the permanent secretary will not normally be the immediate point of contact, though there may be a subsequent involvement.

The accounting officer function, still almost exclusive to the permanent secretary among mandarins in the core departments, is a considerable responsibility. During the course of a normal year it can absorb anything from five to twenty per cent of the permanent secretary's time. It may be extremely time-consuming when the heat is on, as we saw in the last chapter. With the growth of management accounting and value for money it is much more closely related to the general task of managing a department. This management function is seen by most (not quite all) as the obvious growth area, certainly over the last decade or two. One permanent secretary, head of a large spending department, estimated the breakdown of his time as follows: policy (30 per cent); management (30 per cent); accounting officer (20 per cent); senior personnel (10 per cent); and visits (10 per cent). This he compared with the time spent by one of his predecessors to whom, thirty years earlier, he had been private secretary. The proportions then he estimated to be: policy (70 per cent); accounting officer (20 per cent); senior personnel (10 per cent). Management did not feature – a characteristic of some if not all permanent secretaries of the period.

It is unlikely today that any permanent secretary would be able to devote much less than a quarter of the total available time to the task of managing the department. Much, of course, turns upon what exactly is meant by the weasel word 'management'. What to one may be a management task may, to another, be an aspect of something else.

Whether strictly policy or management related, there are vast amounts of material to be read and absorbed. Permanent secretaries also process vast quantities of paper, if only by way of adding an assenting signature. This is the ballast of the workload. It impinges well beyond the normal office hours. So, too, do the outside evening dinners – and sometimes lunch engagements – to which permanent secretaries are invited in a representative capacity at least once and typically twice, three or more times a week. Such events may involve the preparation (with help from other officials) and delivery of after-dinner speeches to professional bodies, business organizations, conferences or prize giving ceremonies. They keep permanent secretaries in touch with a wide range of people. They can be useful information gathering exercises.

Mention should be made of the regular Wednesday morning meetings of permanent secretaries. These seem to have become a feature during the 1970s (Greenhill 1993, p. 181). Such meetings were initially looked upon with disfavour by politicians, especially Labour ones. This was nothing new. At a more general level Hugh Dalton (1957, p. 407) once described high level interdepartmental committees as 'an irresponsible sub-ministerial underworld'. Meetings of permanent secretaries were seen as symbols, indeed as the very incarnation, of mandarin conspiracy. Prior to the 1970s permanent secretaries, or groups of them, were in the habit of meeting.

Barbara Castle (1984, p. 544) got wind of such a gathering in 1968. Indeed Edward Bridges inaugurated a dining club in 1946 in which ten or twelve permanent secretaries (not always the same ones) came together each month (Chapman 1988, pp. 55-6). Today the conspiratorial tones, never with accuracy so described, are much more muted. Mandarins are less equivocal about the existence and nature of these weekly meetings. There are rarely specific items on the agenda. It is a note-swapping rather than a policy co-ordinating exercise. As one permanent secretary put it: '... it creates a feeling of the college'. This collegiality is something that permanent secretaries continue to value and from which many derive strength.

If the weekly meetings have their lighter turn – as seemingly they do – there is no doubt that the weight of work falling upon the contemporary permanent secretary is as great as ever. An average eighteen hour day, excluding weekends, has been reported in one case – that of the Foreign Office (Edwards 1994, p. 52). This may be on the topside for the generality, but not by much. All permanent secretaries are kept at full stretch with workloads that are the equal and with anxieties that are at least as acute as those of their predecessors. They operate behind a much thinner veil of seclusion, relatively exposed as they are to the intrusions of a more feverish media network. As one said:

> The pressure is just extraordinary. I get in the office at 7.30am. If I'm not going out to a dinner – and I have quite a few of those – I get out by 7 or 7.30pm and there will be a box or two to do in the evening. It's just the pressure of so much paper....

Another confirmed: 'You've got to be very quick with your response times... life generally moves very fast'. And without any indication of intended humour or parody, the same permanent secretary went on: '... you're never asking yourself what to do. You always, unless you have arranged something else specifically, you work while you're cleaning your teeth, while you're shaving – just all the time. No, not just thinking, but processing paper.' He added that he found it necessary deliberately to arrange some specific recreation simply to stop himself from working.

In spite of – perhaps because of – all this some of the critics remain unconvinced about the utility of the office of permanent secretary. There have been calls for reform, even for the abolition of the office.

Calls for reform

Calls for reform are nothing new. The Fulton Committee received a proposal from Nevil Johnson for the abolition of permanent secretaryships and for their replacement by a management board system (Fry 1993, pp. 113-6). Fulton (1968, pp. 59-60) rejected this proposal, preferring instead the idea of groups of special policy advisers.

Other and similar proposals have surfaced again from time-to-time in recent years. A Fabian Society machinery of government committee in the early 1980s briefly considered the possibility of proposing abolition of the office of permanent secretary (Theakston 1992, p. 193). The idea, not pursued, was to redress a perceived imbalance in power between ministers and civil servants. The Thatcher government achieved this without abolishing permanent secretaries. While rejecting calls for French-style ministerial cabinets, a working party of the now defunct Royal Institute of Public Administration argued for an extended ministerial private office (RIPA 1987, pp. 56-60). This, it acknowledged, would have implications for the permanent secretary, though it considered a reconciliation of roles to be perfectly possible. Others have gone further. Williams (1989, p. 260) has suggested the replacement of permanent secretaries by 'a layer of top departmental executives'. This was before the new executive agencies really got under way and before the launching of market testing. With these developments now well established (agencies) or making their mark (market testing), the position of the permanent secretary is, in some eyes, increasingly precarious. A former incumbent has written:

> The permanent secretary is a prime example of the sort of ambiguous position which leads to poor policy advice. No one is ever quite clear what he, rarely she, is actually there for. They advise the minister, but are not politically accountable for the quality of that advice. They are supposed to manage the department, but the creation of executive agencies is fast making that role redundant... The question is how to break through the culture of lofty detachment, seen at its purest and most depressing at Wednesday morning meetings of permanent secretaries. (Kemp 1993, p.27).

Kemp is not averse to offering a helping hand in the process of diminution. 'In empowering the chief executives of agencies, we have forgotten to disempower the permanent secretary...', he has been reported as saying (*The Times*, 26 August 1993).

Plowden is less disparaging but no more encouraging. With the spread of executive agencies and contracting out he says (1994, pp. 68-9): '... it is not obvious that a permanent secretary will be able to do anything that could not be done by a small number of deputy secretaries'. In any event he questions (Ibid., p. 85) whether permanent secretaries are not now overpaid, having lost the bulk of their management responsibilities. This does not accord with the thinking of the Major government. The indications are that top salaries will increase above the rate of inflation (see Chapter 1).

Onslaughts upon the office of permanent secretary contain nuggets of truth but are ultimately misplaced. It is clear that, in a number of ways, the office has changed in character. Change is nothing new but has been more perceptible during the last two decades. It is easy to specify some of the senses in which change has been manifest. Permanent secretaries are now more the orchestrators of policy. They are sometimes but less likely to be the 'hands on' activists and rarely the semi-independent proselytizers of policy. There are many more policy and advisory inputs. No longer does the permanent secretary have a near monopoly or always even the close personal control over all the channels of advice going to the minister. A corresponding fragmentation of structure has reduced the capacity of the permanent secretary to maintain detailed, day-to-day, control in all except the smallest departments. Whitehall has always been more fragmented than is often supposed. It has never borne the tidy patterns of the classical Weberian 'ideal type'. But this did not prevent the permanent secretaries of yesteryear from exercising the kind of tight control that would be inappropriate and indeed impossible today. It would be inappropriate because there is today a different conception of running a department – one which emphasizes strategic management, target setting, financial control systems and so forth rather than a more personalized interventionism. It would be impossible because, among other things, there has been a deliberate attempt in the shape of executive agencies to insulate operational functions from day-to-day supervision by core departments. Some permanent secretaries have initiated or given additional momentum to this development. It is as yet unclear what will be the full implications. Already, though, some of the agency chief executives have a higher public profile than their permanent secretaries. They are accounting officers for their agencies, though the permanent secretary retains a general responsibility as departmental accounting officer. Agency chief executives appear before other select committees, as do other departmental civil servants. Only occasionally do permanent secretaries appear before select committees other than the PAC.

It would be easy to conflate these elements to give an overall impression of diminution in the office of permanent secretary. Yet it is these same elements that continue to make the permanent secretary indispensable – if for slightly different reasons today than twenty or thirty years ago. If the permanent secretary now has nothing like a monopoly over advice to the minister the orchestration role is no less vital. The sheer number and variety of inputs may enhance the utility of the permanent secretary, in the eyes of the minister, as the one, perhaps the only one, who can pull everything together. Probably more minister-permanent secretary relationships today are of the strictly professional than of the personal friendship variety. Still, the two will usually work closely together by the very nature of their respective roles. However much the critics may deride the 'propping up' role and even if their efforts are not always fully appreciated by the recipients, the permanent secretary remains on hand to help the minister out of tight corners. No doubt someone else could assist if permanent secretaries were not there. But there are certain specific things for which the minister will necessarily look and continue to look to the permanent secretary over and above even the most favoured special adviser or other departmental official. In particular, no one can swing a whole department behind a major policy initiative as can the permanent secretary. And if the fragmentation of which agencies and contracting out are manifestations brings its problems, then it is a challenge to be met by the permanent secretary. Whether they like it or not, permanent secretaries are bound up with the new management.

This new managerialism places a greater emphasis upon the strategic rather than upon the detailed control of operations – regulating outcomes rather than inputs and processes, steering rather than rowing, to borrow from the new gurus of contemporary management (Osborne and Gaebler 1992, pp. 25-48). Steering is less overtly active than rowing. It is less noticeable. To the extent that the office of permanent secretary is developing in this way its alleged dispensability is understandable. To some it evidently approximates more to the dignified than to the efficient parts of the constitution. No doubt it could, by act of will, be abolished. But the sheer utility of permanent secretaries to ministers – the vast majority of ministers – makes such a course of action as unlikely as it would be unwise. The strategic management function is equally important, if less easy to specify. Properly done it is no easier a role to play than that played by permanent secretaries of yesteryear. In some respects it may be more difficult. There are more fault-lines in the chain of things for which the permanent secretary retains a general oversight. The permanent secretary may not have a personal responsibility in the sense of 'taking it on the chin' if something goes wrong within an executive agency on a particular operational matter. But the permanent secretary remains responsible to the minister for the overall shape and general functioning of the department and for all activities within the department's embrace. The permanent secretary is expected to pull things together, to maintain an overall coherence in the face of mounting centrifugal tendencies – and all within the context of closer public scrutiny. This is not to deny that permanent secretaries may have been less influential in recent years. Assertions to this effect, and their implications, will be considered in the final section of this book. But such loss of influence, if such there has been, is not the same as a loss of responsibility or an amelioration of the pressures and cross-pressures that bear upon individual incumbents.

In its own way, then, steering can be as demanding as rowing. In any case, permanent secretaries do occasionally take the oars – especially at moments of crisis. They work no less hard than do their predecessors, though their efforts are given a rather different inflection. One could question whether their energies are always put to best advantage. Visits to various departmental outposts may give the permanent secretary a feeling of keeping in touch, but how are they perceived by the 'minions' they meet? Perhaps people at the top are too sensitive to the charge of remoteness. Is it sensible, it has been asked, for permanent secretaries to remain the sole accounting officers for their departments? Could not other senior officials be given a status similar to that of agency chief executives? This, of course, would require the PAC to adopt a different view about the responsibilities of the departmental (as distinct from the agency) accounting officer. It may be argued, *pace* Fulton and others, that permanent secretaries still spend too much time 'wet-nursing' their ministers. But by performing a function which most ministers apparently find valuable they continue to make a positive contribution to democratic government.

Within a different system, or within a similar system in which the civil service as an institution had a different role, other considerations could come into play. Some of these broader constitutional issues will be considered in the final chapter. It may well be that permanent secretaries must take a share of the blame for policy failures. This, again, is a separate matter and will be considered in Chapter 11. But for the time being and in the foreseeable future, the office of permanent secretary seems secure. With this in mind the next two sections of this book will analyze the backgrounds and career patterns of incumbents over the last century and a half.

PART II

PERMANENT SECRETARIES PAST AND PRESENT – A PROFILE

6 A changing social and educational elite

Introduction

To describe any group of people as an elite is to invite responses of various kinds. For some the word is linked inextricably with the notion of a ruling class and the exercise of power (Mosca 1939; Mills 1956). The existence in particular of a capitalist ruling class – not always a conspiratorial one – has been alleged by Marxists and others of the left (Miliband 1969; 1982; Scott 1991). Top civil servants have been seen as prominent and active members of such a class. For others, an elite is indicative in a more general way of mechanisms at work systematically to favour some at the expense of others. This need not imply a cohesive ruling class. For others again significance lies simply in the empirical fact that certain types of people tend to predominate – though the types may vary over time and as between different elite groups at any one time. Patterns of ascendancy may be the product of superior ability, expertise, preparation or the possession of a certain disposition. This makes for compatibility with the idea of meritocracy – the top people are top because they are the best performers in top positions. This is no doubt what most incumbents would like to believe. It is one reason why many recoil at their being described as an elite, especially where there is the further connotation of a ruling class. It is perhaps natural for those who have proven themselves in top posts to resent any suggestion that they enjoyed unfair advantage or that they owe their positions chiefly to a privileged education or a favoured social background. Equally, when things go wrong, it is natural for the critics to consider whether the particular reservoir from which top post-holders are typically drawn has some bearing upon the apparent shortcomings in performance.

The alleged connections between permanent secretaries' backgrounds and the performance of government is dealt with in Chapter 11. The present chapter provides a descriptive analysis of those backgrounds. As explained in the introductory chapter, permanent secretaries are the elite of an elite in that they hold the top positions within a group (the higher civil service) that is itself an elite – an institution which plays a central role in the running of the country. It is not axiomatic that permanent secretaries are a social or an educational elite, still less that they belong to any ruling class. The latter, notoriously difficult either to verify or to disprove, will not be the concern here. Nor, on the other hand, is it sufficient simply to confirm that top civil servants are not and never have been a microcosm of society at large. Other studies have shown that they are drawn disproportionately from relatively privileged backgrounds and tend to have attended the more prestigious schools and universities (Kelsall 1955; 1974; Guttsman 1963; Armstrong 1973; Boyd 1973; Rubinstein 1986).

Of course, no analysis of permanent secretaries' backgrounds can fail to note this manifest characteristic. But this chapter attempts above all to pinpoint some of the more significant changes in the pattern of educational and social backgrounds over the last century and a half. It tries to relate these changing patterns to some of the more notable long term developments, such as those emanating from the introduction in 1870 of open competition. Education is examined first – the universities attended, the subjects studied; and the schools, betraying a very British preoccupation with status. For both university and school education comparisons are drawn between permanent secretaries and their peers – that is, those who entered alongside them through open competition into the administrative grades. The social backgrounds of permanent secretaries are then examined with a focus upon the decline of connections, especially those of the political and aristocratic classes. The chapter concludes with a broad assessment of the extent to which permanent secretaryships have been increasingly held by self-made men and women.

One point should be cleared up at the outset. Fathers rather than fathers and mothers are the point of reference for the analysis of family backgrounds. To some this will seem odd, even inequitable. It is justified on three strictly practical grounds. First, until fairly recent times, fathers were much the more likely to have pursued a paid occupation or to have held public position. This applies to the generations of most of the permanent secretaries' parents covered by this book. Second, it is much easier to trace not only the occupations but also the education of fathers. Again, this is critical in a longitudinal study. Third, paternal backgrounds have usually been the focus in studies of other elite groups with which the data here presented may be compared.

Permanent secretaries and their peers: educational profiles

University education

Fig. 6.1 shows the proportion who had a university education among those becoming permanent secretaries in each of seven periods. The seven periods are those described in the introduction (pp. xvii-xviii).

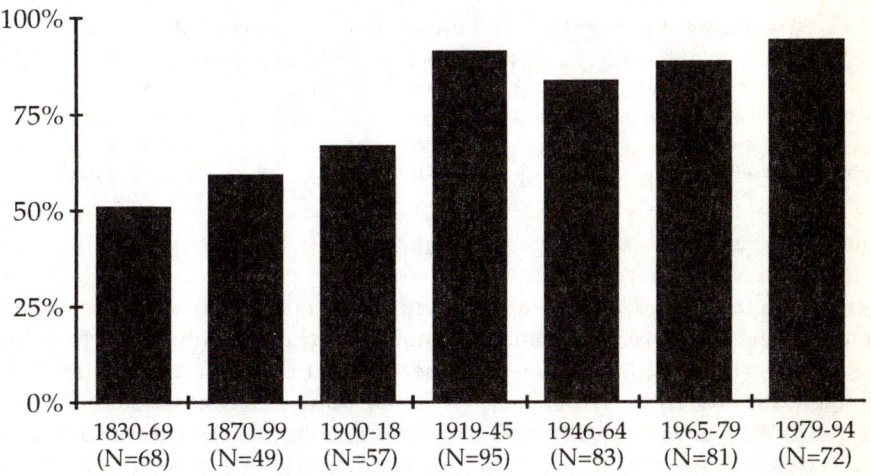

N= All who became permanent secretaries during each period.

Fig. 6.1   Percentage of permanent secretaries who attended a university

A number of points emerge. During the mid-nineteenth century, those with a university education barely outnumbered those without. In part this reflects the method of entry to the civil service – predominantly by patronage. It reflects also the fact that, save for certain professions such as law, medicine and the clergy, attendance at the unreformed English universities of the first half of the nineteenth century was by no means the exclusive gateway to success. Oxford in particular was heavily geared to the education of (Anglican) clerics (Reader 1966, pp 128-9). By the inter-war years a university education had become more closely – if by no means universally – associated with leadership in many walks of life. The slight decline among those appointed between 1946-64 is the consequence of two factors.

Primarily it is due to the Great War which deprived some permanent secretaries of a university education – more than were deprived by the 1939-45 war. It is also a function of the slight decline in the proportion who entered the administrative class through open competition. Those who entered in this way were more likely to have had a university education than were other permanent secretaries. This is not surprising since, by the turn of the century, university education was the characteristic of the overwhelming majority of candidates who were successful in competitive examinations for Class 1 clerkships (the forerunner of the Administrative Class). It is easy to overlook the significance of open competitive entry which can be seen more clearly (Table 6.1) during the important transitional period of 1870-1918.

Table 6.1
Percentage of permanent secretaries, 1870-1918, who had attended a university, by method of entry to the civil service

Method of entry		
Open competition %	Limited competition %	Other (incl. patronage) %
82	70	55
(N=27)	(N=10)	(N=69)

It is true that nearly all the open competition entrants rose to permanent secretary level after 1900. On the other hand, for those who entered by other routes the proportion of university educated permanent secretaries actually declined slightly from 59 per cent (1870-99) to 52 per cent (1900-18). Open competition was and continued to be responsible for a greater number of graduates among the higher echelons than otherwise there would have been. The transition was gradual – partly because open competition gathered its momentum only gradually. Although the first competitions for Class 1 clerkships were held in 1872, it was not until the mid-1890s that significant numbers began to be recruited annually as a matter of course.

With a steadily increasing national graduate population during the second half of the twentieth century there is unlikely to be any diminution in the present high levels of university educated permanent secretaries. This may serve to sharpen any residual stigma for the few non-graduates who do get to the top – perhaps more so now than in the past. It is difficult in any case to know precisely what significance it has or has had in Whitehall, either for those who have and for those who have not been to a university. Denis Greenhill (1993, p. 16) says that four years spent on the railway were more important to his education than were his three years at Oxford. Conversely, Richard Way said that, from the perspective of life in general, he felt a university education would have been an asset. But within

Whitehall he never felt conscious of his non-graduate status (NOA Tr., p. 13). It did not prevent him from reaching the top, heading first the War Office and then the Ministry of Aviation during the 1960s. Nor did it stop him from being among the best of twenty or so permanent secretaries to have served cabinet minister and future Chancellor of Oxford University, Roy Jenkins (1991, p. 158). Nor, for that matter, was it an obstacle to Way's later becoming Principal of King's College, London.

Non-attendance at a university need not imply under-privilege. Only three of the fourteen non-graduate post-holders since the mid-1960s went to state schools. At the Foreign Office between 1920-57, six of the nine PUSs were non-university men. All six entered through competitive examinations for the diplomatic service. Five of the six went to leading public schools: Ronald Lindsay (PUS, 1928-30) to Winchester; Robert Vansittart (1930-38) to Eton; Orme Sargent (1946-49) to Radley; Donald Gainer (1950-51) to Charterhouse; and Ivone Kirkpatrick (1949 and 1953-57) to Downside. The other one, Eyre Crowe, (PUS, 1920-25), went to the Dusseldorf Gymnasium. In contrast to the home civil service, the diplomatic service did not create an aristocracy of almost exclusively university educated talent, though its intake was usually drawn from higher social circles. But in Crowe and Vansittart it could claim two of the most notable of Whitehall's twentieth century luminaries. Sargent and Kirkpatrick were also among the most capable PUSs. Elsewhere in Whitehall, there has at no time been any similar succession of non-graduate heads.

It is less the question of a university education, more the particular university attended that has usually been the cause of controversy. Table 6.2 shows the universities that permanent secretaries have attended.

Table 6.2
Universities attended by permanent secretaries

	1830-69 %	1870-99 %	1900-18 %	1919-45 %	1946-64 %	1965-79 %	1979-94 %
Oxford	28	35	37	48	31	35	30
Cambridge	17	13	15	22	30	34	26
London	-	2	7	8	6	7	13
Civic	-	-	-	3	3	2	12
Scottish	6	6	8	6	10	7	8
Irish	3	2	2	1	1	-	1
Welsh	-	-	-	1	1	-	-
Other	-	4	3	3	3	3	5
None	46	38	28	8	15	12	5
Total %	100	100	100	100	100	100	100
N=	(71)	(52)	(60)	(100)	(91)	(86)	(77)

Note: Where someone attended more than one university both (or all) are included. Calculations therefore do not quite equate with those for Fig. 1. 'Other' includes universities abroad.

These figures speak for themselves, requiring only brief commentary. Oxford and Cambridge have been dominant among the universities. During the present century at least half and sometimes two-thirds of all post-holders have attended one of these universities. Not until after 1945, though, did Cambridge begin to match Oxford's claim on permanent secretaryships. There are two main reasons for this. First, Oxford's *Literae Humaniores* school was idealized by the civil service commissioners for many years down to the First World War. This leaning was endorsed by the Royal Commission on the Civil Service (MacDonnell 1914, p. 42, para. 47). The really outstanding candidates would probably succeed in the civil service examinations, whatever. But those slightly less gifted from the *Lit. Hum.* school could also succeed where their Cambridge equivalents might falter. Among all *Lit. Hum.* candidates successful in the examinations for Class 1 between 1870-1913, 40 per cent graduated with first class honours, compared with 70 per cent of Cambridge's classics men. Not surprisingly, *Lit. Hum.* candidates accounted for half the elite intake to the civil service during these years. But a second factor was also at work. Oxford almost certainly had a deeper and more widespread disposition towards the civil service. Down to and during the inter-war years, Oxford graduates were drawn more regularly from a wider range of colleges. Most of the Cambridge entrants to the civil service before 1914 came from one of two colleges, Trinity or St. John's. These colleges were matched by several from Oxford, though none had the claim upon top positions in Whitehall enjoyed by Balliol. Only for brief periods between 1870-1945 did the Balliol presence at permanent secretary level fall below 10 per cent. The ethos inculcated by Benjamin Jowatt, Master of Balliol during the 1860s and '70s, is legendary (Faber 1958). So too is that of other Balliol tutors such as T.H. Green and R.C. Nettleship (Richter 1964; Birch 1964, pp. 98-104). There may be reason to question the extent to which this ethos was decisive in the affairs of the nation. There can be little doubt that it reflected a strong public service tradition – stronger than existed in Cambridge.

For all this, it is important to remember that even at the turn of the present century there were more permanent secretaries who had been to no university than there were those who had been to Oxford. By this time, the civic universities were beginning very slowly to make their mark. The first civic graduate to become a permanent secretary was Edward Forber. He went to University College, Liverpool and was placed twenty-seventh among the forty-six successful candidates from the examinations held in 1900. He rose to head first the Board of Customs and Excise (1930-34) and then the Inland Revenue (1934-38). But Forber also received a supplementary 'Oxbridge' education. This was a characteristic of nearly half of all the redbrick graduates who entered the civil service before 1939. Edward Troup, PUS at the Home Office between 1908-22, had graduated from

Aberdeen University back in the late-1870s. He, too, had an Oxford 'top up'. He acknowledged no technical superiority in the education he received at Oxford, but did grant that it had given him some 'polish' (MacDonnell 1913, Q. 5053). The first permanent secretary graduate from an English civic university (excluding London) not to have had an Oxbridge 'top up' was William Hildred. He went to Sheffield and entered through the special reconstruction examinations held in 1919. He headed the Ministry of Civil Aviation between 1941-46.

Since 1945 and especially among those appointed from 1979 London and the provincial civic universities have tempered the Oxbridge dominance. This trend may be expected further to develop if recruitment patterns of the 1980s and early '90s are any guide and if there is a sustained move to bring in greater numbers of non-career civil servants. Two recent appointees to the top Treasury post were products of civic universities. Peter Middleton, Permanent Secretary 1983-91, studied at Sheffield and at Bristol. Terence Burns, who succeeded Middleton, went to Manchester. Neither entered into the Administrative Class immediately upon graduation. This prompts a further observation. Eighteen provincial civic university graduates have held permanent secretaryships since 1919 – five per cent of the total. Only ten of these entered the elite corps upon entry by open competition. Of these, three came through the reconstruction examinations. Five of the remaining eight have become permanent secretaries in the 1990s.

All this is to suggest that permanent secretaries who entered the civil service directly into the administrative grades by competitive examination have been drawn from a narrower range than the entire community of permanent secretaries. Confirmation can be found in the figures shown in Table 6.3. It can be explained largely, though not entirely, by the incidence of non-graduates among those who joined the civil service either later in life having established themselves elsewhere, or by initial entry into an executive, clerical or specialist grade. The table makes a further comparison – between all who entered the administrative grades by open competition and those among them who became permanent secretaries. In this sense permanent secretaries are not the elite of an elite. They very much reflect the broader entry cohorts from which the majority of them have been drawn. This close association has been maintained consistently over a long period. It suggests that, in the past, there has been little attempt to filter out the non-Oxbridge element once initial entry to the elite corps (i.e. the administrative grades) has been secured. It further enhances the expectation that, in the light of more recent recruitment trends, the Oxbridge presence among permanent secretaries should decline somewhat in the future.

There have been two broad critiques of the university education of Whitehall's upper echelons. One is that they have tended to be the products of prestigious institutions to which access has been denied or heavily

Table 6.3
Universities attended by permanent secretaries and by their peers

	Open comp. 1894-1936	All perm. secs. 1919-64		Open comp. 1937-1968	All perm. secs. 1965-94	
	A %	B %	C %	A %	B %	C %
Oxbridge	77	76	65	75	79	63
Other	21	22	23	24	20	29
None	2	2	12	1	1	8
Total %	100	100	100	100	100	100
N=	(1147)	(122)	(191)	(1519)	(87)	(163)

Col. A All candidates successful in open competition for the home civil service, excluding limited competition and post-1945 reconstruction examinations for principals
Col. B Those from Col. A who became permanent secretaries
Col. C All permanent secretaries of a generation with those in col. A and including those in col. B

Where an individual attended more than one university, both are counted.

restricted in respect of those from underprivileged backgrounds. This is the egalitarian critique. The other critique is founded upon considerations of efficacy. It has been asserted that Whitehall recruits people predominantly from academic disciplines that are inappropriate to the needs of modern government. Such critiques were a feature of the Fulton Report and of the Fulton era (Fulton 1968, pp. 27-32; Balogh 1959). They continue to find expression from time-to-time (Sedgemore 1980, pp. 148-53; Ham 1981, pp. 32-3; Ponting 1989, p. 10). In particular it has been asserted that too many top administrators have been educated in what may loosely be described as the humanities and too few in the more applied social sciences and in technical subjects. This, it is widely believed, is the characteristic of those whom the civil service has sought to attract from the universities.

The evidence presented in Fig. 6.2 supports some of these observations – at least at the descriptive level. Recruits to the Administrative Class down to the late-1960s continued to betray a heavy humanities emphasis. And, as with the different universities attended, permanent secretaries who entered through open competition directly from university have been pretty much a microcosm of their peers. Indeed there seems to have been a slight advantage to social science graduates among those who have risen to the top over the last thirty years. If there has been a humanities bias, it has been at the stage of initial recruitment rather than in subsequent promotion through the hierarchy.

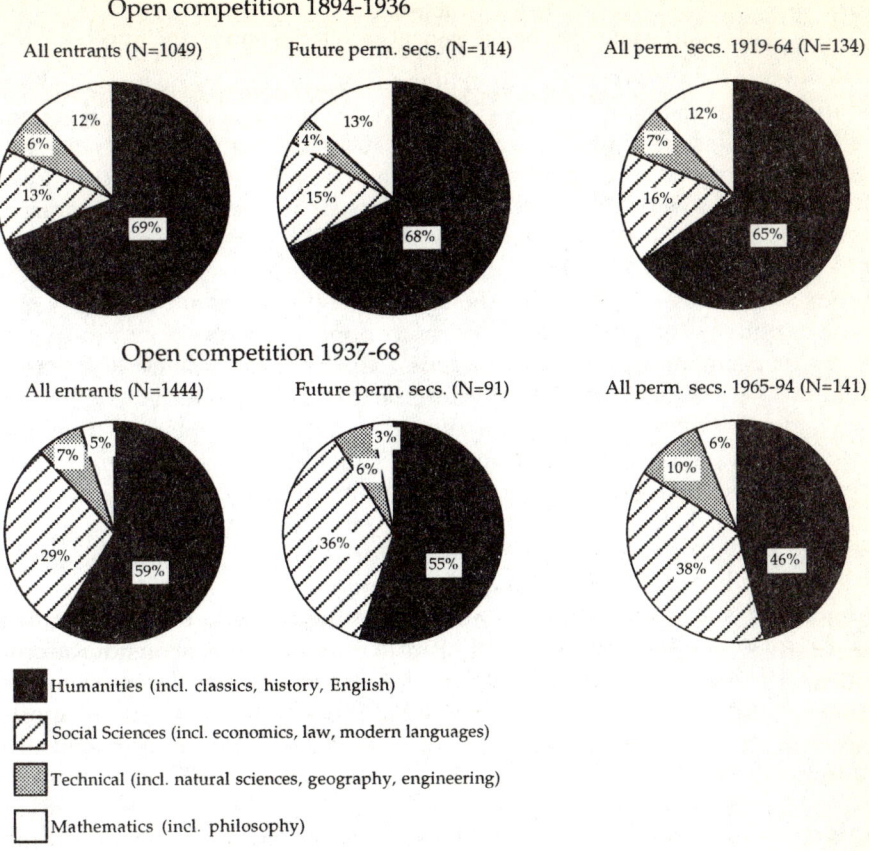

Fig. 6.2 University subjects studied by permanent secretaries and by their peers

Again, there is evidence of dilution occasioned by the appointment to permanent secretaryships of non-career civil servants and of those who entered Whitehall other than through the administrative grades. The stronger tendency to have studied a subject of relevance to the civil service, if such there is, has usually come from these groups. During the late-nineteenth century a succession of PUSs at the Home Office were legally qualified. During the present century the best example was the Department of Scientific and Industrial Research (DSIR), the forerunner of Mintech and thus of a part of the present DTI. During its existence between 1916-65 the DSIR was served by six permanent heads. All except one (Frank Heath,

1916-27) were graduates in the physical sciences. None of the six entered the administrative grades of the civil service directly from university.

A subject for which particular claims to relevance have been made is economics. In fact as many post-1945 permanent secretaries have read economics as read classics. But whereas nearly all the classics trained permanent secretaries entered directly into the administrative grades, more than half of the economists were recruited to other classes, or entered at comparatively senior levels from outside the service. Whitehall has, then, been prepared to look beyond its own ranks, not only recently but for some time past. Its imports have been brought to the heart of Whitehall, not merely kept at arm's length as temporary advisers or cocooned in a specialist group. Such post-war permanent secretaries include Laurence Helsby, Eric Roll, Samuel Goldman, William Nield, Peter Middleton and Terence Burns. On the other hand, few permanent secretaries have studied technical subjects. If the presence of such people in larger numbers is thought desirable at senior levels, then they, too, will have to be brought in from outside the fast stream track.

None of this is to assent automatically to the view that the broad humanities emphasis is or has been responsible for Whitehall's shortcomings. Nor is it to say that the appointment of permanent secretaries versed in other disciplines is any sort of panacea. The arguments and counter-arguments will be given more air in Chapter 11. But without doubt these characteristics are in part the product of Whitehall's recruitment arrangements over a long period. They are also in part the product of the schools.

School backgrounds

Any meaningful analysis of school education requires a classification of different types of school. A finely calibrated, hierarchical ranking is necessary to identify trends over a lengthy period. Table 6.4 embraces nine categories ranging upwards from the maintained, or state, sector (group I) to the Clarendon schools (group A). The latter, the leading and most famous elite schools are: Charterhouse; Eton; Harrow; Merchant Taylors' (Northwood); Rugby; St Paul's; Shrewsbury; Westminster; and Winchester. High status schools (group B) are those which appear in the lists of both Jenkins and Jones (1950) and of Honey (1977, pp. 252-82). These are: Cheltenham; Clifton; Haileybury; Malvern; Marlborough; Radley; Repton; Rossall; Sherborne; Uppingham; and Wellington. Together with the Clarendons they constitute the top twenty status schools. Middle status schools (group C) – some fifty of them – broadly follow Honey's long list with the addition of a few which achieved their renown or were founded during the present century, such as Bedales, Stowe and Gordonstoun. The other categories are largely self-explanatory. The distinction between independent and direct grant schools – groups D and E respectively – did not exist until 1919 and disappeared in the late-1970s. It nevertheless corresponds to a recognized distinction in the status of the schools involved, both before and after specific use of the term direct grant. Both groups D and E cover schools the headmasters of which are (or were) in membership of the Headmasters' Conference (HMC). This sets them apart from group F, in effect a residual category of other, minor, public schools. One further point is worthy of note. Attendance at a fee-paying grammar school pre-1944 is registered in group H, even though attendance at the same school in later years would qualify for the maintained sector (group I). In this way, the classification is sensitive to changes over time.

Table 6.4
Schools attended by permanent secretaries

	1830-69 %	1870-99 %	1900-18 %	1919-45 %	1946-64 %	1965-79 %	1979-94 %
A Clarendon	43	55	30	29	20	14	14
B High status	3	2	14	12	8	6	6
C Middle status	2	6	7	14	14	11	16
D Independent (HMC)	2	2	-	5	10	11	15
E Direct grant (HMC)	-	-	9	13	13	19	15
F Other public	6	4	4	10	11	12	11
G Private tutor	6	11	10	3	-	-	-
H Other non-maint'd	7	2	10	7	10	10	3
I Maintained	-	-	2	3	14	17	20
Unknown	31	18	14	4	-	-	-
Total %	100	100	100	100	100	100	100
N=	(68)	(49)	(57)	(95)	(83)	(81)	(72)

Note: where a permanent secretary attended more than one school the higher status one only is counted.
Other non-maintained (group H) includes abroad.

Table 6.4 confirms that the majority of permanent secretaries have at all times been the products of public schools. This was so even for those of the mid-nineteenth century whose school days would have preceded the era of educational reforms. For with education in a state of decay in some of the 'great schools' and in some of the foundation grammar schools, many who received their education in the early nineteenth century did so from private tutors. This was almost certainly so for many among the significant minority for whom details are unknown.

Three further broad points are evident from these figures. First, that the Clarendon schools have continued to hold their place, albeit with some diminution. Second, that there has been a progressive broadening of the public school base from which permanent secretaries are drawn. Third, there has been little significant shift in the balance between public schools and the maintained sector.

Among the Clarendon schools Eton has usually received the closest attention from commentators. This is well justified – especially for the nineteenth and early twentieth centuries. During the nineteenth century Etonians filled nearly a quarter of all permanent secretaryships. This, it must be said, is lower than the figure of 50 per cent for all senior posts in the highly elitist Foreign Office in 1919 (Tilley and Gaselee 1933, p. 88). Apart from the Foreign Office, Etonians did not entirely colonize any particular department. Rather, they semi-colonized almost the whole of Whitehall. Fifteen departments were headed by an Etonian at one time or another during the nineteenth century, nine of them on more than one occasion. It is, however, easy to overstate its significance. The Treasury is a case in point and warrants special comment.

It has been claimed that the Clarendon schools – Eton in particular – were crucial to the development of the dominant British financial, economic and political structures. These structures worked through the City-Bank of England-Treasury nexus (Ingham 1984, p. 141). In fact Reginald Welby was the only Etonian to head the Treasury during the nineteenth century. Prior to the appointment of Edward Bridges in 1945 there was only one other – Edward Hamilton, 1902-07. Thus, of the twenty who served the Treasury at permanent secretary level between 1870-1945 only three were Etonians. At the same time, some two-fifths were Clarendon school products – a proportion much in line with the rest of Whitehall for that period. And since 1945, only two among some forty who have operated at this level in the Treasury have been Etonians – Anthony Rawlinson (1977-83) and Nick Monck (1990-93).

Mention may be made of the fact that the two most recent heads of the home civil service – Robert Armstrong and Robin Butler – have been an Etonian and an Harrovian respectively. Harrow has never matched Eton as a reservoir for future top civil servants. Since 1945, Eton has had eight permanent secretaries, three of them at the FCO. Among the other Clarendon schools, there have during this period been five from Westminster; four each from Charterhouse, Rugby, St Paul's and Winchester; three each from Harrow and Merchant Taylors'; and two from Shrewsbury. Even since 1979, the presence of permanent secretaries from these and the other high status schools (i.e. the top twenty) has been equal to that of the entire maintained sector. There has nevertheless been a slow but steadily rising proportion of state school educated permanent secretaries. This trend may be expected to continue. To what extent it is difficult to say since the civil service commissioners no longer publish information about the school education of candidates who are successful in the 'fast stream' examinations. By the late-1970s some 45 per cent of the administrative trainees came from state schools (CSC 1979, p. 13).

Projections of this sort assume some correspondence between entrants to the elite corps and those among them who become permanent secretaries. As with university education, this assumption can be tested, at least retrospectively. The figures are shown in Table 6.5.

Table 6.5
School education of permanent secretaries and of their peers

	Open comp. 1894-1936		All perm. secs. 1919-64	Open comp. 1937-1968		All perm. secs 1965-1994
	A %	B %	C %	A %	B %	C %
Top 20	34	34	35	16	25	20
Other HMC	37	41	34	35	44	43
Public non-HMC	12	9	11	20	8	12
Rest	16	16	18	29	23	25
Unknown	1	-	2	-	-	-
Total %	100	100	100	100	100	100
N=	(1053)	(118)	(178)	(1430)	(87)	(153)

Col. A All candidates successful in open competition for home civil service, excluding limited competition and post-1945 reconstruction examinations for principals
Col. B Those from col. A who became permanent secretaries
Col. C All permanent secretaries of a generation with those in col. A and including those in col. B

Where an individual attended more than one school, only the higher (or highest) status one is counted.
Rest includes voluntary and other non-maintained as well as state schools.

The figures in Table 6.5 indicate a stronger elitism among permanent secretaries – not only among all post-holders but also and in particular among those who entered through open competition. This is certainly so for the more recent cohorts. It stands in contrast with the findings for university education. The differences are not overwhelming, but they are clear and consistent. In itself this proves nothing. It *may* be indicative of a slight leaning towards the 'old school tie network'. Equally, those from the high prestige schools may have been more capable – or more capable of accommodating to the mores of Whitehall. It cannot be said that the minority of non-public school educated (not quite synonymous with state educated) entrants have had an equal chance, statistically, of becoming permanent secretaries. This was so among those recruited during the early decades of the century, but not for the recent cohorts. Again there is a leavening effect among all permanent secretaries with the presence of those who entered Whitehall either at a later stage in their careers or in a clerical, executive or specialist grade.

There has always been uncertainty as to the precise implications of educational backgrounds. What inferences may be drawn from the knowledge that someone, or a group of people, went to a certain type of school? Moreover, the classification employed in the foregoing analysis takes no account of distinctions between boarders and day pupils. Nor does it allow for scholarships or other forms of assistance which have facilitated the access of limited numbers of less privileged pupils to the higher prestige schools. There are no reliable longitudinal data about the take up of scholarships, either to schools or to universities. What can be said is that permanent secretaries of recent decades are far more likely to have been the first within their families to have had access to an elite educational institution. Less than one in six of those appointed since 1964 and who had been either to 'Oxbridge' or to a top twenty school had fathers who went to one of these institutions. This compares with nearly two-thirds for those in post between 1870-1918 and two-fifths between 1919-64. It is necessary therefore to examine the family backgrounds of permanent secretaries. The picture that will emerge is one of gradual but steadily increasing heterogeneity – more so during the present century than is immediately apparent from the patterns of education. In short, it is a story about the decline of 'connections'.

Social origins and the decline of 'connections'

There are two specific senses in which the decline of connections may be considered so far as permanent secretaries are concerned – political connections; and the aristocracy. In examining each in turn of these phenomena the critical period of transition, 1870-1918, will claim a good deal of attention. This is followed by a sketch of the occupational backgrounds of permanent secretaries' fathers, highlighting also some of the more recent trends.

Political connections

In the nineteenth century there was much more overlap in the membership of the political and administrative elites in Britain than there is today. As will be seen in Chapter 8, some MPs became permanent secretaries, while some permanent secretaries left the civil service to go into politics. Even where permanent secretaries were not at any stage of their careers involved in party politics, they sometimes came from political families.

The late-nineteenth century was the heyday of permanent secretaries who were the sons of MPs. Nearly a third of all post-holders between 1870-99 had such connections. Six of them were the sons of government ministers. It would be easy to suppose that some form of nepotism was at work. All of the fifteen permanent secretaries involved entered Whitehall either before open competition had got under way or by direct appointment at a higher level. Only two submitted to limited competition. Yet closer examination suggests a more sophisticated and less direct form of patronage. Only three of these fifteen individuals seem to have entered Whitehall directly on account of their fathers' positions. Henry Goulburn was a former Conservative Chancellor of the Exchequer turned free trade advocate representing Cambridge University when, in 1845, his son Frederick became a commissioner (later Chairman) of the Board of Customs. Spencer Walpole was nearing the end of his second spell as Home Secretary when, in 1867, his son Spencer Jnr. was appointed Inspector of Fisheries, at that time a Home Office responsibility. He was the only one of the four early fisheries inspectors not to be qualified by experience for his task (Pellew 1982, p. 143). He went on to become Secretary of the Post Office between 1893-99. Samuel Kekewich was the Conservative MP for South Devon when his son, George, entered the Education Department in 1868. We have George Kekewich's own testimony (1920, pp. 5-6) to the fact that his father enlisted the support of Sir Stafford Northcote who effectively fixed the appointment. There is an obvious irony here. Northcote had been the joint author, with Charles Trevelyan, of the famous report which is seen as having done so much to undermine the practice of patronage as a means of recruitment to the civil service. Kekewich went on to head the Education Department between 1890-1903.

Paternal intervention, then, was decisive in the entry to Whitehall of Goulburn, Walpole and Kekewich. It did not ensure that they became permanent secretaries. And for the other twelve permanent secretaries who were the sons of MPs, the evidence of any direct leverage is either minimal or non-existent. In most cases the fathers were either dead or had ceased to be MPs long before the sons entered Whitehall. In some cases, the sons had already proven themselves in other walks of life before moving into the civil service.

None of this is to deny that family political affiliations could and sometimes did secure entry into Whitehall. Favours were almost equally divided, numerically, between Liberal and Conservative connections. It is an inescapable fact that all save two of these fifteen permanent secretaries entered Whitehall when 'their' party was in office. If their fathers rarely engineered their appointments personally, party colours played some part in the process. Only in one instance, though, did this have a clear bearing upon an appointment at permanent secretary level. In 1874 Disraeli promoted Algernon Mitford to head the Office of Works.

It is significant that, with one exception, these sons of politicians entered Whitehall prior to 1870. To what extent the subsequent mode of entry by open competition actively changed things is difficult to say. Certainly its introduction and gathering momentum coincided with a sharp decline in the intrusion of party connections. Only four twentieth century post-holders have had fathers who sat in Parliament. All four fathers assumed peerages, though two had previously represented constituencies, and another held a cabinet post. All four sons became permanent secretaries before 1945. Three

– Charles Hardinge, Robert Lindsay and Alexander Cadogan – headed the Foreign Office; the Earl of Drogheda was Director-General of the Ministry of Economic Warfare between 1940-45.

There therefore emerged early in the twentieth century a much sharper separation between the families of the two elite groups, politics and the salaried public service. Of course, close contact was maintained by the very nature of their respective roles, especially those of government ministers and senior civil servants. A certain amount of intermarriage continued to take place, though with declining frequency. The sons and (later) the daughters of some politicians occasionally sought and achieved entry into the civil service. But they were few in number, dissipated within a fast expanding bureaucracy and were absent from top posts in the home civil service. There was a similar though more gradual decline in another type of permanent secretary – the one with aristocratic connections.

Decline of the aristocracy

Much has been written about the decline of the British aristocracy from the second half of the nineteenth century and about the rise of the professional classes (Cannadine 1990; Reader 1966; Perkin 1989). The senses, the extent and the precise chronology of decline have been matters of contention (Adonis 1993). Table 6.6 shows both the height and the subsequent decline of aristocratic connections among permanent secretaries. The table measures connections of three types: those who themselves succeeded to an hereditary title, be it a peerage or a baronetcy; those who had other family connections by birth; and those who married into the aristocracy.

Table 6.6
Aristocratic connections of permanent secretaries, 1830-1994

	1830-69 %	1870-99 %	1900-18 %	1919-45 %	1946-94 %
Succeeded to title	4	4	2	4	-
Parental connections	9	41	14	1	1
Total blood ties (%)	13	45	16	5	1
By marriage	6	12	4	3	3
Total connections (%)	19	57	20	8	4
N=	(68)	(49)	(57)	(95)	(236)

Permanent secretaries of the mid-nineteenth century were not generally conspicuous in their connections with the aristocracy. They were, as a social group, more disparate than may be supposed. There were the big names such as Chadwick, Kay-Shuttleworth and Hill who represented the rising middle and professional classes. There were a few from the more established circles, including the minority of aristocrats. And there was a larger, miscellaneous group comprising the local lower gentry, military, merchant and even artisan classes. For nearly one in nine of these mid-century permanent secretaries there is little or no family information available. This almost certainly reflects their lack of social standing. As with political connections, then, it was the late-nineteenth century which marked the high-tide of the aristocracy among the top echelons of Whitehall. Over half the permanent secretaries of this period had some sort of aristocratic connection. These were mostly blood ties, though only five permanent secretaries of the nineteenth century succeeded to a title. Two of the five did so after leaving Whitehall.

The sheer extent of these connections must have had a bearing upon the way some of these permanent secretaries discharged their office. Exactly what kind of bearing is much more difficult to establish. It should not be thought that they took their permanent secretaryships lightly – certainly not the aristocrats of the late-nineteenth century. Those who were active in the bureaucracy were, like those in politics, increasingly businesslike in their approach: they were 'players' as well as being 'gentlemen' (Adonis 1993, p. 177). This, as much as the fact that they were aristocrats, may have been significant for their relationships with ministers. It has been said that top civil servants of the period spoke to politicians as social equals (Cannadine 1990, pp. 239-40). This they certainly did – and not only those civil servants who had aristocratic connections. More specifically, it has also been claimed that permanent secretaries of the period were sometimes of a higher social standing than their ministers (Dale 1941, pp. 117-8). Evidence to test this view is set out in Table 6.7. It uses the three levels, or strengths, of aristocratic connections employed in Table 6.6, with the residual status of no connection. It is possible to establish which, for each minister and permanent secretary who worked together, had the higher social standing. Figures are presented in aggregate form for each of four Liberal and three Conservative governments between 1868-1915.

The figures show, first, that even when aristocratic connections were at their height among permanent secretaries, they were never as strong, collectively, as among the ministers they served. Second, they show that the political colours of the party in office had little bearing, overall, upon the relative social standing of top civil servants and ministers. This says as much and more about the respective characteristics of the two parties as it does about the civil service. It confirms the continued strength of the aristocratic involvement in politics during this period. A significant minority of permanent secretaries were of higher social background than their ministers, especially in the Liberal government of 1892-95 and in the Conservative governments of 1895-1905. But they were always outnumbered by others who were of lower station than their political chiefs.

It can safely be assumed that at no time since have the higher echelons of

Table 6.7
Relative social standing of ministers and their permanent secretaries during select periods of office between 1868-1915

Government	Proportion who were of higher social background			
	Ministers %	Permanent Secretaries %	Equal %	
Liberal				
Gladstone 1868-74	52	11	37	(N=27)
Gladstone 1880-85	76	5	19	(N=21)
Gladstone/ Rosebery 1892-95	60	25	15	(N=20)
Campbell-Bannerman/ Asquith 1905-15	39	7	54	(N=54)
All Liberal governments 1868-1915	51	11	38	(N=122)
Conservative				
Disraeli 1874-80	48	9	43	(N=21)
Salisbury 1886-92	68	4	28	(N=25)
Salisbury/ Balfour 1895-1905	59	17	24	(N=46)
All Conservative governments 1874-1905	59	12	29	(N=92)

N= number of minister-permanent secretary relationships

the bureaucracy had stronger aristocratic connections than the governments they served – even Labour governments. After 1919, there was a marked decline in aristocratic origins among permanent secretaries. Since 1945, they have been minimal. Very few permanent secretaries of the last fifty years have come from the really high prestige families.

As with marriage into political families, so also marriage into the aristocracy has been rare in recent decades. That of Goronwy Daniel (Permanent Secretary at the Welsh Office, 1964-69) to Lady Valerie, daughter of the 2nd Earl Lloyd George and granddaughter of the illustrious premier, was the last marriage simultaneously to bring a permanent secretary into an aristocratic and a political family. Daniel's father was a colliery manager.

These facts are of wider significance. Marriage is derivative of social cohesion, rather than its major cause (Lisle-Williams 1984, p. 334). What these figures reflect is the changing relationship between the administrative elite and other elite networks. In the nineteenth and early twentieth centuries there was a greater degree of social intercourse between top civil servants and 'society' figures. Interaction was more pervasive and more intense. This cannot be quantified. But the diaries and memoirs of contemporaries give an impression of the natural and regular associations that carried on outside the workplace (Kriegel 1977; West 1908; Fitzroy 1925; Brett 1934, 1938; Bahlman 1972). Such associations probably declined after 1918, certainly after 1945 – but never to the point of extinction. A certain amount of socializing continued and still does, within the bounds of propriety. Occasionally, ministers and top civil servants have known each other at school or, more likely, university. Nowadays it is much more likely either that prior acquaintanceships (rather than close friendships) have been established in the course of official and associated business, or else not at all. This, as suggested in Chapter 2, need not imply any detriment to the working relationship between minister and permanent secretary. Nor need there be detriment even where the latter comes from a decidedly modest background. As Permanent Secretary of the Ministry of Labour in the late-1950s Harold Emmerson served Iain Macleod. The ambitious and highly capable Macleod did not suffer fools. A non-graduate, elementary school educated son of a Warrington wiredriller may not have seemed the most natural pairing. But Macleod soon developed a special affection and respect for Emmerson's expertise, common sense and unflappability (Fisher 1973, p. 138).

The modern permanent secretary is less the part of a cloistered elite network – certainly in terms of social origin and background. This reflects a progressive decomposition and heterogeneity in the fabric of the administrative elite. Further manifestations of this heterogeneity – and in contrast with the relative homogeneity of earlier periods – are to be found in a sketch of the occupations of permanent secretaries' fathers.

Fathers' occupations

A minority (approximately one-fifth) of all nineteenth century permanent secretaries whose backgrounds can be traced had fathers who had no specific occupation and who were landed proprietors. Nearly half had fathers in one of three professions: the military; the church; and the non-military paid public service. The latter two groups call for further comment.

Among the clergy, the Revd. George Murray, Bishop of Rochester, fathered two permanent secretaries. Herbert Murray became Chairman of the Board of Customs between 1890-94; George Jnr., twenty years younger than Herbert, entered the Foreign Office in 1873 and later headed the Board of the Inland Revenue (1897-99), the Post Office (1899-1903) and the Treasury (1903-11). The Revd. Kenhelm Digby, Canon of Norwich, was the father of Kenhelm Jnr., PUS at the Home Office between 1895-1903. William Baillie Hamilton, Deputy (Permanent) Secretary at the Admiralty 1845-55, and Charles Trevelyan also had fathers who occupied positions of modest authority in the established church. Otherwise, the clergy fathers were ordinary parish priests, or ministers. There was an almost equal numerical division between the Anglican and the various non-conformist denominations.

Twelve nineteenth century post-holders were the sons of men of the cloth – a figure that was to double among those who became permanent secretaries between 1900-45. This is the nearest Whitehall has been at any time this century to 'colonization' by a specific group, accounting – as they did – for one in every six permanent secretaries.

Nearly a fifth of all nineteenth century permanent secretaries' fathers held paid public appointments of one sort or another (excluding political office). Some held positions of considerable responsibility in Whitehall and in adjacent circles. George Hammond held the permanent under-secretaryship at the Foreign Office later held by his son, Edmund. John Godley, father of Arthur (future PUS at the India Office), was an assistant under-secretary for war. Others made their mark abroad. These included Richard Meade, British Ambassador in Berlin. His son, Robert, became PUS at the Colonial Office between 1892-97. Henry Mitford was an attaché in Florence. His son Algernon entered the Foreign Office in 1858 and later (1874-86) headed the Office of Works. Others had fathers whose public service was in the administration of justice. James Stephen's father was Master in Chancery. The 1st Viscount Esher was Master of the Rolls from 1883 until his death in 1897. By this time his son and heir, Reginald Brett, was Secretary of the Office of Works. There were two high court judges among the fathers of nineteenth century permanent secretaries. One of them, Stephen Lushington, was the father of twins both of whom became permanent secretaries. Vernon Lushington headed the Admiralty (1869-77), Godfrey the Home Office between 1885-92. Additionally, there were three county sheriffs, three commissioners of bankruptcy and two other court judges among the fathers of nineteenth century permanent secretaries.

This public service tradition has remained quite strong during the present century, though with a progressively weaker emphasis upon anything that could be described as the 'governing classes'. Evelyn Murray, for example, headed the Post Office (1914-34) and the Board of Customs (1934-40). He was the son of George Jnr. and nephew of Herbert, therefore becoming the third permanent secretary from one immediate family. The fathers of others appointed during the same era also held important public positions, such as Sir James Monteath. He was Secretary to the Political Department in the India Office, of which his son, David, was to become the last PUS between 1941-47. Edward Bridges was the son of the Poet Laureate, Robert Bridges. Indeed, among all who became permanent secretaries between 1900-45 forty-four (29 per cent) had fathers who could be deemed men of eminence. While comparisons over time can never be precise, this may be set against the twenty-one (8.9 per cent) since 1945 whose fathers had entries in *Who's Who*. Of these, six have occupied permanent secretaryships since 1979, the best known being Robert Armstrong whose father, Sir Thomas, was formerly Principal of the Royal Academy of Music.

Some idea about the changing character of Britain's administrative elite can be had from the sketch provided in Table 6.8. This shows the occupational backgrounds (where reliable data exist) of the fathers of approximately two-thirds of all post-1945 permanent secretaries, excluding present incumbents. The classification of occupations is notoriously difficult, especially when it carries implications about social class. The headings and sub-headings used in Table 6.8 lay no claim to originality, sophistication or to methodological purity. The purpose is no more than to provide a broad impression and overview.

Table 6.8
Fathers' occupations of post-1945 permanent secretaries

Public service		Misc. professional	
higher public service	13	church	14
other	17	military	7
Total	30	law	5
Business		engineering	5
top management/director	5	accountancy	3
middle management	6	medicine	1
commerce	12	other	7
finance/banking	8	Total	42
small business/			
entrepreneur	9	Non-professional	
Total	40	clerical (excl. public service)	3
Education		craft/supervisory	5
higher academic	4	manual/operative	6
teaching	10	Total	14
Total	14		

A number of points are worth making. First and above all there is the variety, the heterogeneity – perhaps even more so than the table shows. Some of the categories cover a greater range than is apparent on the surface. The predominant mode is nevertheless middle and upper middle class, for want of a better expression. But there is also a lower middle class presence with a small working class element, too. The public service tradition remains quite strong, including some holders of higher positions. So, too, is the church, though with only two bishops among the fathers of permanent secretaries of the last fifty years. The presence of those with fathers in business marks one of the more notable contrasts with post-holders of earlier generations. Their presence is far from being a dominant one, but it exceeds those from public service backgrounds, if education, the church and the military are excluded from the latter category. Opinions may differ as to Whitehall's ability fully to understand the needs of business. But it cannot be said to have been totally bereft in recent times of top people from business families. Again, from within the business community itself there are many and varied sections, only partly reflected in the sub-headings in Table 6.8. This further emphasizes the multifarious origins from which individuals enter Whitehall and become permanent secretaries.

Prestige bequeathed or self-attained?

Being a permanent secretary is itself a mark of prestige. Whether quite as much so today as a hundred, fifty or even thirty years ago is difficult to say. Still, the logic is inescapable. Few permanent secretaries of recent times have come from the really well connected families: yet being a permanent secretary remains a high prestige position. For the great majority, becoming a permanent secretary has therefore constituted a significant upward shift in social mobility – more so than for many of those appointed during the last century and in the early decades of the present century.

To what extent, then, are permanent secretaries a social and educational elite? Can it be said that these top people owe their positions to the accident of privilege? Can permanent secretaries themselves claim that they reached the top primarily by their own efforts?

If permanent secretaries are, ex officio, an elite group it does not follow that they are drawn exclusively from a tightly drawn network within society. Such was more or less the case during the nineteenth and early twentieth centuries. The present century, though, has seen a steadily increasing decomposition. This is not to say that contemporary permanent secretaries are a microcosm of the nation, or even of those in white collar occupations. Far from it. Although few over the last fifty years have had aristocratic connections, the majority have had a public school education. A good many of them may have been granted this privilege by means of scholarship and financial assistance; and the majority, unlike earlier generations of permanent secretaries, have not followed a family tradition of access to the high prestige schools and universities. But they have enjoyed a privilege nonetheless. It is a privilege not available to the vast majority of members of society or, for that matter, of civil servants outside the elite corps (i.e. the administrative grades). Those, the majority of permanent secretaries since 1918, who entered this elite corps directly from university did so in the knowledge that some among their number would fill the top positions.

Competitive entry from the late-nineteenth century ensured that members of the administrative elite should demonstrate at least their intellectual capacity. The higher civil service of the first half of the present century and perhaps even of today can be reckoned an intellectual aristocracy, even if the social aristocracy has long since declined. Not that the aristocrats of the late-nineteenth century treated Whitehall simply as their plaything. They were usually capable, hard-working men who made their contribution to the nation's affairs and to the office of permanent secretary. It is easy to forget how many people from privileged backgrounds fall by the wayside, often because of sheer lack of ability (Perkin 1989, p. 360). Permanent secretaries can therefore claim that they have proven themselves in competition with others, both upon entry to the civil service and during the course of their subsequent careers. There is only slight and certainly no compelling evidence that the more privileged among the initial entrants to the elite corps have been any more likely to rise to the top. What determines which of them do reach the top is the subject of the next chapter.

7 Reaching the summit – many are called, few are chosen

Introduction

There are various routes to the summit. Some permanent secretaries have spent most or a good part of their careers outside Whitehall. They will be considered in the next chapter. For most incumbents, at least during the present century, the route to the top has been within Whitehall. Here there are various ways in which future permanent secretaries get noticed and by which Whitehall bestows its imprimatur upon those who have proven themselves to be capable of higher things. Some, an increasing number, serve in the private offices of ministers. Others serve time in one of the powerful central departments. Most of these individuals will have entered the civil service directly into the elite corps of the administrative grades, though by no means all of them. There are and always have been different routes to the top.

This chapter examines what it takes to become a permanent secretary – why some civil servants rather than others reach the top. It begins with an account of the changing procedures for making appointments and of the relative influence at various times of politicians and of the bureaucracy itself in each of three periods: prior to 1920; the inter-war years; and post-1945. There follows an analysis of certain career characteristics thought to be significant - most notably service in a ministerial private office and employment in a central department. It would be easy simply to describe such characteristics, inferring that they are the keys to success. This chapter attempts the more complex task of establishing the precise extent and nature of their importance. This it does partly by comparing permanent secretaries with those who failed to reach the top and in the light of notions about meritocracy. The chapter concludes with a sketch of the qualities needed to become a permanent secretary. It analyzes the interplay of factors by which some are deemed to have what it takes and are afforded the more ample opportunities to demonstrate the requisite qualities. It is a theme of this chapter that Whitehall has usually been quite good at recognizing and exploiting talent within its midst; that in so doing it has, in more recent times, accommodated a variety of factors, including ministerial interventions, without undue jeopardy to the principles of meritocracy. But there is evidence also that in recent years certain groups, most notably women, have failed to advance such claim upon top posts as might have been expected; and that others, especially those who began their careers in clerical or executive grades, have been less conspicuous at permanent secretary level than in years gone by.

Appointing permanent secretaries: formal arrangements and illustrative examples

The following discussion considers not only the formal arrangements for making appointments but also the various influences brought to bear in practice. Particular attention is paid to the relative leverage of the bureaucracy itself and of ministerial interventions in the process of appointment. At both the official and the political levels a further distinction has often been evident - the tension between departmental and central forces.

Prior to 1920

In the nineteenth century there were no formal procedures for the appointment of permanent secretaries. Instead, working practices evolved from experience, shaped by the tensions between centralism and departmentalism. For the most part the former had to accommodate the latter. In 1850, Robert Peel told the Select Committee on Official Salaries that:

> The First Lord of the Treasury would not make an appointment in any department but his own; officially and formally it would be made by the Minister who presided over the department; but there would probably be communication between that Minister and the First Lord of the Treasury in respect of important appointments.
> (Select Committee on Official Salaries, 1850, p. 35, para 278)

Lord John Russell told the same committee that in the making of very important appointments: 'the Prime Minister is always consulted, and he concurs' (Q. 1264). This evaded the question as to what would happen should a prime minister disagree with one of his colleagues. Such a dispute arose in 1869 between Gladstone and his Chancellor, Robert Lowe. They clashed about whose responsibility it was to appoint a new permanent secretary to the Treasury. The matter was discussed in cabinet and Gladstone had to give way. Ralph Lingen was thus appointed, having worked with Lowe in the Education Department (Preston-Thomas 1909, p. 54; Lambert 1963 p. 519). This rebuff did not deter Gladstone. Nor did it prevent him from securing a permanent secretaryship for his protégé, John Lambert. But he had to wait another two years, and in a newly created and less prestigious department. Even then, Gladstone was unable entirely to overcome the newly appointed President of the Local Government Board, who favoured Henry Fleming. So Lambert and Fleming were appointed as joint secretaries.

Where a vacancy arose in a subordinate department of the Treasury, and where the chancellor concurred, there was greater scope for prime ministerial disposition. In recognition of political services, Disraeli in 1874 appointed Mitford as Secretary to the Office of Works, honouring an undertaking to place him in the first important post which fell within his gift (Redesdale 1915, vol.II p. 661). Reginald Brett's appointment to the same post twenty-one years later was bestowed, again as a political reward, by Lord Rosebery, though this time not without some embarrassment to the appointee and to the chief whip. On this occasion, Francis Mowatt, Permanent Secretary to the Treasury, asserted himself to the extent of seeking certain assurances about Brett's political activities (Rhodes James 1963, p. 354; Fraser 1973, p. 72). There was some irony here in the light of Mowatt's own subsequent excursion into the controversy over protectionism (see Chapter 1).

This and other examples illustrate the subtleties with which the prerogatives of some departmental ministers, while apparently inviolable, came to be more heavily circumscribed. In 1892, Lord Knutsford, Secretary of State for the Colonies, appointed Robert Meade as PUS. But this was in the context of a promise made to the Treasury, for financial reasons, not to appoint from outside the department. With this established, Lord Knutsford was virtually bound to accept that Meade could not be passed over (Blakeley 1972, p. 56). The emergence of a career service was beginning to reduce the latitude of ministers.

Another factor in the growing bureaucratization was the role of permanent secretaries in determining their own successors. Thus Thomas Farrer was instrumental in blocking Robert Griffin at the Board of Trade in 1886, and again in 1893. This kind of intervention was not novel, but could carry greater weight in an inbred career service. Moreover, careerists could usually be counted on to accept an offer of appointment, unlike the independent outsider. Thus Brett, a non-careerist, refused an offer in 1899 from Joseph Chamberlain to head the Colonial Office. He simply did not fancy Chamberlain as a political chief (Brett 1934 vol.1, p. 247). Instead, Montagu Ommanney was appointed.

The appointment of Ommanney's successor is a rare example before 1914 of prime ministerial assertion in a straight battle with a leading minister. In 1907, Lord Elgin wanted to appoint John Anderson, a Colonial Office careerist, but Campbell-Bannerman preferred Francis Hopwood from the Board of Trade (Snelling and Barron 1972, p. 161). But usually, where a minister insisted he would prevail. Thus, in 1902, Wyndham, the Chief Secretary for Ireland, appointed Antony MacDonnell as his under secretary despite Balfour's warning that this would cause 'violent suspicion' (Young 1963, pp. 244-6). MacDonnell was an Irish Catholic known to support Home Rule. In the Foreign Office and the Home Office, the authority of the minister remained more or less unbreached down to the First World War. Successive appointments at the FO were made by the secretary of state (Steiner 1969). At the Home Office, too, the secretary of state seems to have had the final say, though over the appointment of Edward Troup in 1908 Herbert Gladstone sought the permission of the prime minister (Pellew 1982, p. 71).

Where new ministries were created, as many were in the years immediately before and during the First World War, so there increased the scope for manoeuvre – not only for departmental ministers but also for an interventionist chancellor or premier. As Chancellor, Lloyd George appointed Robert Morant to head the National Insurance Commission in 1911, having formed a personal acquaintanceship earlier in the decade as an opposition member with a close involvement in education (Grigg 1978, pp. 49-52). In 1918, Bonar Law, as Chancellor, intervened to appoint John Beale as permanent secretary of the recently established Ministry of Food (Harris 1982, p. 146).

It is, of course, easy to overstate the influence of a prime minister or chancellor and difficult sometimes to determine to what extent their intervention was decisive. Daniel Hall's appointment in 1917 as Permanent Secretary at the Board of Agriculture undoubtedly owed something to the fact that Lloyd George knew him and recognized his ability. It was of greater account that an old friend of Hall's, Rowland Prothero, had succeeded as President of the Board Lords Selborne and Crawford with whom Hall was unpopular and under whose leadership he would not have been appointed (Dale 1956, pp. 104-5).

This survey shows that, in the normal course of events, ministers retained their powers of appointment down to the end of the First World War. Only exceptionally were they overridden where there was a clash with an interventionist premier. There existed greater scope for prime ministers in appointing to departments under the supervision of the Treasury and also to departments where there was no powerful minister. Similarly, the creation of new departments often allowed the exercise of such disposition without offending powerful interests. At the same time there was the emergence of a career civil service. This may have strengthened the hand of the bureaucracy, especially where it had probably long been legitimate for permanent secretaries to express opinion as to who should be their successors. A career service would also give potential to the Treasury, enabling it to mobilize knowledge across the board. It may well have prompted some of the prime ministerial interventions. It certainly began to make felt its influence on appointments in subtle and indirect ways, mainly financial. But there is little evidence during this period of systematic central direction or control over appointments.

The Inter-War Years

A Treasury Circular dated 12 March 1920 established that all appointments at permanent and deputy secretary level would require the approval of the prime minister. The prime minister would act upon the advice of the permanent secretary to the Treasury and head of the civil service. This was by no means a subterranean Treasury coup. The MacDonnell Commission (1914, p. 86) had recommended stronger Treasury control over establishments. So too had the Haldane Committee (Min. Reconstruction 1918, pp. 17-21); the Bradbury Committee (HM Treasury 1919, pp. 4-6); and the Committee on National Expenditure (1918, pp. 14-5). While none of these committees recommended specific procedures for top appointments, they reflected a climate favourable to greater centralization.

When in 1926 Parliament debated the role of the Treasury in the management of the civil service, it was mainly the filling of top positions about which misgivings were expressed. There was some truth in Lloyd George's claim that the new arrangements were merely a reformulation of what had existed before 1920 (HC Debs. 3rd series vol. 194, cols. 331-2). What was now at issue was the role of the head of the civil service, and the nexus between him and the prime minister. Whatever Fisher's constitutional rights to give advice there remained deep suspicions about the way in which he enacted his role. Fisher described to the Tomlin Commission how he and his colleagues in the departments held discussions, from which there would usually emerge: 'a trend of opinion...as to the suitability of people, either potentially or generally, for this class of post' (Tomlin Evidence 1930-31, Q. 18, 693). This implied only a secondary role for the departmental minister. An examination of some of the appointments made during the inter-war years gives a rather different picture.

In an early trial of strength, Fisher failed to prevent Herbert Creedy's appointment in April 1920 as PUS at the War Office. Churchill, Secretary of

State for War, proceeded without consulting either Fisher or the premier. This may have been the breach which allowed Fisher to legitimize the new protocol (O'Halpin 1989, pp. 67-71). Thus, in 1922, he overcame both the Home Secretary and the outgoing incumbent (Troup) to secure the appointment of John Anderson (Viscount Waverley). Of equal significance was the Home Secretary's acknowledgement that the entire service should be the field of choice in filling such important positions (Ibid., pp. 71-3).

The implication of this should not be underestimated. The practice of filling such posts by transfer from other departments, and in the context of a career service, was bound to strengthen the position of the Treasury. For, unless there had been an earlier association with the appointee, then the minister would know little, compared with the Treasury, of the range of potential candidates. Again, in new or fledgling ministries the Treasury was likely to meet less resistance. At the Ministry of Labour, James Masterton-Smith was appointed in 1920 with the task of assessing the administrative need for the Ministry. This brief was given to him by the Treasury without the knowledge of the minister (Lowe 1982, p. 131). The previous year Horace Wilson had been sent to the Ministry of Labour where he became permanent secretary in 1921. Wilson's successor, Francis Floud, was transferred in 1930 from the chairmanship of the Board of Customs and Excise. To this extent, it was a triumph for Fisher, Floud being a generalist in the image that he wanted to promote. But it also demonstrated the difficulties. Floud was unable to master the work and had eventually to be replaced by a departmental specialist, Thomas Phillips (Lowe 1986, p. 66).

In these and in other instances Fisher was able to appoint men of his choice, especially those who had served in the Treasury or in one of its satellite departments. He replaced, at very short notice, Charles Howell Thomas with Donald Fergusson to head the Ministry of Agriculture in 1936. A contemporary has described this as: 'an exercise of power, designed to appear as such' (Kent 1979, p. 53). But even at his height, Fisher did not always get his way, especially when pitched against a powerful minister. In 1925 he recommended Hugh Clifford to head the Colonial Office, but Leo Amery wanted someone with direct experience of the colonies (Amery 1953, p. 337). He appointed Samuel Wilson, recently retired as Governor of Jamaica, who Fisher thought 'not at all conspicuously qualified for the permanent headship' (O'Halpin 1989, p. 149).

The Foreign Office remained independent, as ever. In 1920, Lord Curzon fought successfully to protect it not only from Fisher but also from the prime minister. He appointed Eyre Crowe, to whom Lloyd George had taken most violent objection (Roskill 1972, pp. 138-9). Fisher's greatest triumph in FO appointments came with that of Robert Vansittart in 1930. There is no doubt that this was Fisher's recommendation. He is said to have persuaded MacDonald against the wishes of the Foreign Secretary, Henderson (Carlton

1970, p. 23). MacDonald can have needed little persuading. For Vansittart was already his official adviser on foreign affairs; and he (MacDonald) had an intense dislike of the only serious rival, Sir Eric Drummond. But Fisher was powerless to prevent Anthony Eden appointing Alexander Cadogan to succeed Vansittart eight years later (Avon 1962, p. 521).

By this time, Fisher's judgement was increasingly regarded as suspect. He had to proceed with ever greater caution. In 1938 the Home Secretary, Sir Samuel Hoare, appointed Alexander Maxwell despite fierce opposition from Fisher (Cross 1977, p. 281). In the same year, Fisher took the initiative in pressing the claims of Bridges to succeed Hankey as Cabinet Secretary. Hankey's preference was for a military man. But Fisher was careful to work in conjunction with Horace Wilson who, on this occasion, shared the same view and whose opinions by now carried greater weight with the Prime Minister, Chamberlain. Now Fisher's authority and, temporarily, that of his office was beginning to wane. This undoubtedly fuelled the clamour for ministerial independence in the early 1940s (Lee 1980a, pp. 94-5).

With whatever misgivings Churchill had as premier, ministers enjoyed during the war a freedom probably greater than at any time since 1919. Herbert Morrison brought George Gater from the Ministry of Supply to the Ministry of Home Security. The two men had worked together previously in the London County Council. On becoming Minister of Reconstruction in 1943, Lord Woolton was given freedom by Churchill to choose his officials. Churchill honoured this undertaking, even though it was greatly to his inconvenience to lose the services of Norman Brook (Woolton 1959, p. 263). Gilbert Ince's appointment in 1944 as Permanent Secretary of the Ministry of Labour crowned a rapid rise within that department under Ernest Bevin. As a trade union leader, Bevin had been impressed by Ince, with whom he now combined to form one of the most effective ministerial - civil servant relationships of the war (Bullock 1967, pp. 120-1). Dalton took with him his permanent secretary Frederick Leith-Ross when he moved from the Ministry of Economic Warfare to the Board of Trade in 1942 (Leith-Ross 1968 p. 292). Dalton was constantly making direct approaches to entice civil servants from other departments. By no means did he always succeed. But there was more than a hint of dissolution about wartime arrangements in the movement of senior personnel. The Treasury itself was less powerful. Ministers were able temporarily to recover some of the autonomy they felt they had lost.

Since 1945

Edward Bridges therefore inherited a position weaker in authority than that of Fisher at its zenith. His methods of working, if not his personal manner, nevertheless resembled those of Fisher. He held informal meetings with colleagues in the departments, from which the name of a candidate would emerge. He then sought the approval of the minister. Above all, he resisted calls for the creation of a formal board to advise the prime minister, so retaining his role as the sole pivot. The appointment of permanent secretaries he likened to the placing of a cricket eleven in the field, so as to give the strongest result for the team as a whole (Bridges 1964, pp. 176-7). He clearly saw himself as the captain.

Bridges proceeded with caution. He was able to prevent Dalton drawing Oliver Franks from the Ministry of Supply to the Board of Trade. He stalled a proposal from Duncan Sandys to take Franks to the Ministry of Works. But he shrank from the political crossfire in 1951 between Chancellor Gaitskell and the President of the Board of Trade, Sir Hartley Shawcross, about who should be the latter's permanent secretary in succession to John Woods (Williams 1983, pp. 272-3). Senior ministers continued on occasion to assert themselves. Arthur Creech Jones, Colonial Secretary 1945-50, secured the appointment of Thomas Lloyd in preference to a more senior candidate (Goldsworthy 1971, p. 51). In 1945 Aneurin Bevan was given three names from which to choose a permanent secretary at the Ministry of Health. Making his own independent enquiries, he chose William Douglas, upon word that the qualities Douglas possessed were the opposite of his own. 'We can't have two ministers of health', Bevan declared (Foot 1973, pp. 42-3). It is significant that Bevan was given a choice of candidates; equally significant that he chose from the list put up by Bridges.

There is little evidence about the roles played during Bridges's time by successive premiers. Churchill in 1951 blocked a proposal for Thomas Padmore to succeed Brook as Cabinet Secretary. He was simply not prepared to release Brook to the Treasury (Seldon, 1981, p. 112). Otherwise Churchill, like Attlee, seems to have taken little regular interest in civil service appointments. He did not reject a Bridges recommendation (Ibid., p. 113). There is evidence of only one occasion when a recommendation from Bridges was overturned by a prime minister. This was the proposal that Richard Way should succeed George Turner in 1956 as PUS at the War Office. In rejecting this proposal Anthony Eden overrode not only Bridges but also the Secretary of State, Antony Head. Eden objected that Way was too young and inexperienced (Way, NOA Tr., pp 13-7 and letter to author, 31st March 1989). Way was forty-one and had been a deputy secretary for only six months. Eden evidently discounted or considered irrelevant the fact that, aged thirty-eight, he had become the youngest foreign secretary this century. Eventually, Edward Playfair, aged forty-seven, succeeded Turner. Way got the post when again it became vacant four years later.

The Way episode was the exception during the 1950s and 1960s. Rarer still was the appointment of an individual civil servant at the behest of a politician – and then usually within the tolerance of the bureaucracy. The surprise move of Roger Makins from the Foreign Office to succeed Bridges in 1956 was initiated at the political level. Chancellor Macmillan knew Makins. He was given his head by a surprised Anthony Eden, though R.A. Butler, the then Lord Privy Seal, may also have played a part (Williams 1983, pp. 554-5; Seldon 1981, p. 162). With Labour now in office, Roy Jenkins insisted on having Philip Allen brought from the Treasury in 1966 to succeed Charles Cunningham as PUS at the Home Office. Allen had in any case spent much of his career in the Home Office and was almost certainly on the short list put up by Laurence Helsby. Jenkins's influence may have upset some of his cabinet colleagues, but not the bureaucracy. When ministers did assert themselves against the bureaucracy, it was usually in a negative way. Richard Crossman, having failed to secure the transfer first of Philip Allen, then of Douglas Allen (no relation to Philip), was able to block a proposal that Antony Part should replace Evelyn Sharp at the MHLG. In so doing he was then obliged to accept Matthew Stevenson, clearly the 'civil service man' (Crossman 1975, pp. 419-20 and 469-70). Frank Cousins flatly refused to take Bruce Fraser as his permanent secretary at Mintech. Approached by Cabinet Secretary Burke Trend he gave his reasons: 'one, he doesn't like me. Two, I don't like him' (Goodman 1984, p. 409). He accepted the alternative candidate, Maurice Dean. It was much more difficult for ministers to secure a particular appointee where this completely upset the plans of the bureaucracy or of other ministers, or both. Barbara Castle wanted Douglas Allen to replace Thomas Padmore at the Ministry of Transport in the mid-1960s. But the civil service had plans to promote Allen within the DEA (Castle 1984, pp. 94-126).

By this time there were growing calls for reform. In 1968 the Fulton Committee (1968, paras.120 and 260) recommended the creation of a small committee to replace the informal arrangements favoured by Bridges and maintained by his successors. In July 1968 a committee was established, though without the outsiders recommended by Fulton. This still exists and is known as the Senior Appointments Selection Committee (SASC). Recommendations continued to require the approval of the prime minister 'to whom the Head of the Civil Service tenders his advice' (CSD 1969, p. 40). Though no longer also the head of the Treasury, the head of the home civil service remained and remains the pivot. William Armstrong's account of the way appointments were made suggested little substantive change from the days of Fisher and Bridges. Much of it, he admitted, he did personally. He tried to match particular vacancies to the likely candidates (Kellner and Crowther-Hunt 1980, pp. 174-5). The reality may well have been an increase in centralization and of bureaucratic power. Harold Wilson complained that SASC had reduced his power (Crossman 1977, p. 882). James Callaghan assumed the premiership from Wilson in 1976. He said later that he had never overruled SASC, though he implied a great care, even tentativeness, by the bureaucracy in putting up recommendations where he had indicated an interest (TCSC 1986b, Qs. 728-9). Whether or not there was increased centralization from the late-1960s, William Armstrong, Douglas Allen and Ian Bancroft as successive heads of the civil service continued to take ministers into their confidence. They tried to take account of ministers' wishes, at least to the point at which they came into conflict with the plans of the bureaucracy.

It was widely believed that, during her premiership (1979-90), Margaret Thatcher was more interventionist in the making of top appointments than were most of her predecessors. This was true. But associated implications of politicization were unfounded - if by politicization is meant the packing of top posts by officials known or assumed to share Conservative Party sympathies (RIPA 1987, pp 41-4; Richards 1993). The appointment in 1983 of Peter Middleton as Permanent Secretary of the Treasury is a case in point. At forty-eight and a deputy secretary, Middleton may not have seemed in pole position for what is one of the top three jobs in the civil service. His involvement with monetary policy and his having headed (under Labour) the Treasury's Monetary Policy Division was seen by some as betraying a political dimension to the appointment. In a sense it did. Nigel Lawson (1992, p. 67) describes Middleton as the closest the Treasury could produce in the early 1980s to a monetarist. It was in fact Geoffrey Howe who had secured Middleton's appointment towards the end of his chancellorship. He did so against Thatcher's initial equivocation. Lawson (p. 268) observes that Middleton had in particularly large measure the civil servant's ability to be in some sense all things to all people - the classic quality necessary to serve effectively masters of different political persuasion. Denis Healey (1989, p. 442), Labour's chancellor during the 1970s, has confirmed Middleton's wider acceptability. Middleton got the top job because he was considered to be the best among those under consideration.

Ministers during the Thatcher years seem to have asserted themselves more vigorously and with greater success than previously. One such was Patrick (now Lord) Jenkin. He was closely involved in appointing permanent secretaries to replace first Patrick Nairne (at the DHSS), then Peter Carey (Department of Industry) and then George Moseley (DoE). In each case the person eventually appointed was not on the list submitted by the civil service (TCSC 1986b, Qs. 486-7). Jenkin has described his battle to bring Kenneth Stowe to the DHSS as involving a three month ordeal in which the central bureaucracy employed various manoeuvres to place alternative candidates (interview with author). Brian Hayes, appointed to succeed Peter Carey, had impressed Jenkin ten years earlier. Jenkin was then Chief Secretary to the Treasury, Hayes an under secretary in MAFF with responsibility for milk and poultry. Hayes's ingenuity had been vital during negotiations for an EEC price review in 1973 - the first one following Britain's entry into Europe. He played his role in a settlement which earned Agriculture Minister Joseph Godber a standing ovation from his own back-benchers in the Commons. Jenkin had been present at the meetings and had seen Hayes in action. His appointment at the Department of Industry and that of Terence Heiser at the DoE involved skirmishes with the bureaucracy. One of the objections raised about Heiser was that he had not been a direct entrant to the Administrative Class (author interview with Lord Jenkin). But the battle was not so protracted as the one which brought Stowe to the DHSS. In all three cases, prime ministerial backing was the key to Jenkin's success.

During the Thatcher years, then, ministerial intervention secured the appointment of a number of individuals who might otherwise not have been promoted. The opposite also happened. In particular Thatcher herself is known to have vetoed certain recommendations put to her. Moreover, she made known her dislike of certain otherwise potential candidates whose careers were thus blighted. One such was Donald Derx. As a deputy secretary in the Department of Employment he had clashed with Thatcher early in her premiership during a visit she made to meet officials in the Department. According to the Employment Secretary Jim Prior (1986, p. 136) Thatcher 'insisted on picking an argument without knowing the facts on secondary industrial action'. Derx pressed his point in trying to apprise her of the facts. In so doing he was simply 'displaying qualities which a civil servant must have if he is to serve his Minister properly' (Ibid.). Derx was one of the best and most able officials. But he was passed over for promotion. It was an untypical but by no means isolated case of its kind. Exactly how many careers were blighted in this way during the 1980s – or for that matter before or since the 1980s – is difficult to say.

It is difficult indeed to know exactly what has been happening during the Major premiership or the extent to which the Thatcher years of greater ministerial assertion have left a lasting legacy in the disposition of top appointments. At one level there has been no radical change. SASC remains to assist the head of the civil service in making recommendations to the prime minister. It comprises a small number of the more senior departmental permanent secretaries who, together now with one outsider, work under the chairmanship of the head of the civil service. It continues to help the head of the home civil service to make recommendations about the filling of deputy as well as permanent secretaryships. SASC is therefore able to feed in information about a range of potential candidates. Up to a dozen or more names may sometimes be tossed about en route to a short list of three or four front runners. The outgoing permanent secretary will usually offer a view, even if he or she is not a member of SASC. The head of the civil service always consults the departmental minister. This normally happens following SASC's initial deliberations. More than one name will normally be offered to the minister, often with a stated preference. The minister may already have been briefed, perhaps by the outgoing permanent secretary. If the minister is happy, the head of the civil service puts the recommendation to the prime minister. The premier's ratification is virtually assured. If the minister demurs, then either the bureaucracy must relent, or the minister must yield; or a mutually acceptable accommodation be contrived. As will be seen in Chapter 9, the mobility of senior officials within and between departments has long been a feature of Whitehall. If nothing else, it has given greater flexibility in the deployment of personnel, especially where top mandarins are sent out from the central departments (see below). Here there may be less immediate dislocation in the functional ministries, though still some as the Treasury and (especially) the Cabinet Office replenish their staffing levels by drawing from elsewhere. At any rate, this fluidity has allowed Whitehall to accommodate a certain amount of ministerial intervention. In this way, and personalities aside, Bridges and his successors have been able to manage top appointments with fewer of the head-on, zero-sum conflicts characteristic of the Fisher era. Such accommodation may not always be possible. Increasingly, SASC is attempting to give greater weight to the specific requirements of the vacancy in question - a job-centred approach, rather than identifying those 'ready' for the next vacancy, wheresoever it may arise. Other considerations will also conflict with ministerial inclinations and always have done. A ministerial reshuffle or a general election may be imminent. Thus it was rumoured that Michael Heseltine wanted Richard Mottram as his permanent secretary at the DoE to succeed Terence Heiser. Heiser would reach the normal age for retirement in May 1992. Mottram had spent most of his career in the MoD where, some years earlier, he had been Heseltine's PPS. In other circumstances, the bureaucracy might have acceded to the wishes of such a senior minister. But with a general election looming, it stalled. In the event, Heseltine was moved to the DTI after the election of April 1992. Within months Richard Mottram had taken the reconstituted permanent secretaryship at the OMCS following the unexpected departure of Peter Kemp. Richard Wilson was moved from the Treasury to fill the impending vacancy at the DoE. In these, as in all top appointments, the head of the civil service (and the prime minister) must reconcile the legitimate demands of different perspectives where these do not coalesce naturally. There are the immediate and future needs of the particular department and of the wider Whitehall scene. There are the needs of the minister in situ who must be able to work with the new permanent secretary but who may soon be replaced by another minister of different inclination if not also of different political persuasion. If a transfer is involved, other ministers may be unwilling to lose a trusted lieutenant.

Heseltine's attempt to bring Richard Mottram to the DoE was understandable. Ministers often find it helpful and reassuring to have as permanent secretary one with whom they have previously worked or come into contact and in whom they have confidence (Young and Sloman 1982, p. 96).

The next section looks at the significance of getting noticed, both by politicians and by the bureaucracy itself.

Getting noticed

Whatever the ability of the individual civil servant, advancement through the hierarchy depends upon attracting the attention of those who bestow or influence promotions. As shown above, getting noticed by a minister can sometimes be crucial: at all times recognition by the bureaucracy itself is a necessary ingredient. Service in a private office is the best-known though by no means the only way of coming to the attention of a minister. A spell in one of the central departments has also often been a sign of recognition by the bureaucracy - though, again, not the only sign.

Service in a private office

As noted in Chapter 2, the private secretary usually works closer to the minister than does the permanent secretary. From at least the middle of the nineteenth century the position of private secretary to a minister has been an important and coveted one. Not until after the First World War, though, did it become the exclusive preserve of the career civil servant (Jones, 1976, pp. 30-1). It has been seen as one of the more significant stepping stones to a permanent secretaryship. Among those who spent their careers in Whitehall and who became permanent secretaries between 1900-1945, nearly half had served in the private office of a cabinet minister. This has risen to almost two-thirds among those appointed since 1945, three quarters since the mid-1960s. There are, of course, more private secretaryships nowadays, especially with the expansion of the PM's private office.

There have been some clear examples of ministerial sponsorship of individuals' careers. Otherwise, closer examination suggests a more complex picture. During the first half of the present century nine private secretaries advanced immediately to permanent secretaryships, a further eight doing so within four years. These seventeen constituted over 10 per cent of all permanent secretaries appointed during the period. Their average age upon reaching the top (forty-two years) was markedly lower than that of their peers (just under fifty). In its obituary for one of them, John Woods, *The Times* (13 December 1968) described the 1930s in particular as 'the heroic age of the private secretary'. There is little doubt that these seventeen cases represented some sort of sponsored promotion to permanent secretary level - but sponsorship within certain parameters. Six were promotions within a department. Another five were placed to head departments directly or indirectly subordinate to the Treasury. A further three took new departments where there was no heir apparent. Elsewhere it would have been more difficult to place an able and trusted private secretary. Even so, Henry Babington Smith was imposed upon the Post Office in 1903, James Masterton-Smith upon the Ministry of Labour (1920) and Donald Fergusson upon the Ministry of Agriculture (1936). So, during the first half of the twentieth century private secretaries - especially those to prime ministers and chancellors of the exchequer - could and did advance more quickly than their peers.

Since 1945, there have been few promotions quite so sensational or rapid as some of those in earlier decades. Six post-war PPSs - all to prime ministers - have become permanent secretaries either directly or within four years of leaving the private office. They are: Leslie Rowan (Office of the Minister for Economic Affairs, 1947); Kenneth Stowe (Northern Ireland Office, 1979); Clive Whitmore (MoD, 1983); Robin Butler (1985); Nigel Wicks (1989); and Andrew Turnbull (1993). The latter three all took second permanent secretaryships in the Treasury. Rowan, aged thirty-nine, was the youngest of his generation. Of the others, all except Stowe were under fifty - certainly below the average age for becoming a permanent secretary.

It would be easy to overstate or to misinterpret the significance of these more recent examples. The PPS to the prime minister is nowadays a deputy secretary post. Promotion to a permanent secretaryship - either directly or within a few years - can be considered neither exceptional nor any cause for allegations of undue favouritism. At this level and to this special PPS post only the best are appointed - those who have not only the potential but who have already proven themselves, at quite senior levels, as having what it takes to be a permanent secretary. Service as the prime minister's PPS is therefore strongly indicative of a future permanent secretaryship. So, too, though less strongly, is that of PPS to a chancellor of the exchequer.

Service in other private offices has also been associated with promotion. Here, though, the connections are weaker and there is no guarantee of becoming a permanent secretary. This is demonstrated by a comparison of permanent secretaries with those who failed to reach the top. Table 7.1 covers all those who entered the administrative grades by open competition and who stayed long enough to have reached the top. It excludes all those who died in post, or who left the civil service while still having a realistic possibility of becoming a permanent secretary. It excludes those who were still in Whitehall in 1994 and who may, therefore, still become permanent secretaries. The table shows service in different types of private office according to the various grades reached by civil servants recruited between 1914-36 and between 1937-58. These periods correspond roughly to incumbents of the post-war years from 1945 to the mid-1960s and from the mid-1960s onwards, excluding current post-holders.

The general pattern is quite consistent: the higher the destination in the civil service the greater the likelihood of having served in a private office. In

Table 7.1
Proportion of civil servants, by final grade reached, who served in a private office

	Recruited 1914-1936				Recruited 1937-1958			
	Terminal Grade				Terminal Grade			
Type of Office	Assist Sec %	Under Sec %	Dep Sec %	Perm Sec %	Assist Sec %	Under Sec %	Dep Sec %	Perm Sec %
PM/Chanc excheq	–	3	4	12	–	2	5	21
Other cab. minister	29	32	28	39	20	46	47	42
Junior min/perm sec	33	37	41	38	17	21	15	23
None	38	28	27	11	63	31	33	14
Total %	100	100	100	100	100	100	100	100
N =	(86)	(122)	(73)	(65)	(82)	(138)	(71)	(64)

The figures include only those recruited through open competition for direct entry into the administrative grades. Where an individual served in more than one type of private office, only that in the more or most prestigious is counted. The figures exclude post-1945 reconstruction examinations for entry at principal level.

particular, the distinction between permanent secretaries and others has become more clearly drawn. Put simply, service in a private office increases the chances of becoming a permanent secretary. It appears to have become almost - not quite - a necessary condition among those who have spent their careers in Whitehall. But it does not guarantee a future permanent secretaryship. As Table 7.1 shows, many mandarins have served cabinet and other ministers without having advanced beyond under secretary or even assistant secretary level. Nor do these figures alone establish what exactly is the career significance of service in a private office. It is not clear to what extent such experience is the prime mover in the ascent through the hierarchy or, as with being PPS to a prime minister or chancellor, a reflection of talent already demonstrated and recognized. Here an analysis of ages upon promotion is more revealing. It gives rather a differentiated picture. Those who were private secretaries (or PPSs) to cabinet and other ministers rose to the top no more quickly than the small minority of permanent secretaries who never served in a private office. Their private secretaryships provided no accelerated advancement. Those who served prime ministers or chancellors have, however, reached the top with distinct rapidity - five years earlier than other permanent secretaries among those recruited between 1914-36, two years earlier among those recruited between 1937-58. Yet the average ages upon promotion to assistant secretary level were almost identical. Acceleration through the hierarchy therefore came after and probably as a result of having served in these two highly prestigious private offices - even those (the majority) who served as a private secretary but not as PPS.

These relatively privileged people clearly benefited from their time at No. 10 or No. 11 Downing Street. They have constituted nearly a quarter of all Whitehall's careerist permanent secretaries over the last thirty years. But the significance of this piece of career development should not be misunderstood. For sure, they got noticed - not only during but prior to and as a necessity for their being placed in these important private offices. There they were placed because they were considered to be among the best of the likely prospects, having proven themselves at relatively junior levels. Service in No. 10 or No. 11 gave them a special opportunity to parade their talents on the widest stages. In a few cases the premier who ratified their appointment as permanent secretary was the one they had served earlier as private secretary. The familiarity can only have helped. Three prime ministers in particular were involved in a number of such appointments - Margaret Thatcher, Harold Wilson and James Callaghan. Thatcher's was the longest unbroken premiership this century. Wilson's, although interrupted, spanned a period almost as great as the Thatcher era. Callaghan, whose premiership was comparatively brief, had been Foreign Secretary, Home Secretary and Chancellor of the Exchequer in a front bench ministerial career spanning almost fifteen years. By dint of longevity either in No. 10 or in other high office these three were bound to have had put to them the names of those by whom previously they had been served. But for the most part, individuals who served in No. 10 or No. 11 have risen to permanent secretary level under a prime minister other than the one they served as private secretary. This suggests an institutionalized tendency, rather than naked personal association.

Even if institutionalized rather than personalized, private secretaryships remain significant en route to the top. There is some indication that this significance may be declining (Efficiency Unit 1993, p. 25). But this involves the projection of trends that are far from clear. It has not yet become evident in the careers of those who are permanent secretaries. Moreover, officials at assistant secretary level and above still perceive service in a private office as having a significant bearing on their careers (Ibid., p. 106).

There are other ways in which officials can come to the attention of ministers. As noted in Chapter 2, it has become increasingly common in recent times for ministers to have access to officials well down the hierarchy. A minister who has been in post for any length of time will certainly know and will have seen quite a lot of any candidate in line for promotion to permanent secretary level from within the department. This may not always work to the advantage of the candidate in question. For one thing, the minister may have developed a dislike. For another, the minister may have been more impressed by someone with whom he or she has worked in another department. Quite often permanent secretaryships are filled by promotion and/or transfer from another department. In a third of all such cases since 1945 this has re-established an earlier association between minister and civil servant - at least to the extent of their having previously worked in the same department at the same time. Furthermore, as in the case of Patrick Jenkin and Brian Hayes, an earlier association may have been established without their having worked together in the same department. On the other hand, the intersection of careers may be pure coincidence. It does not in itself imply ministerial initiative in the appointment of permanent secretaries, though this has been so in some cases. It is certainly unlikely that a civil servant would move simultaneously with the minister into a senior position, still less into the permanent secretaryship of another department. This used to happen sometimes, especially before 1914. It is rare nowadays, certainly at permanent secretary level. Ministers have reasserted themselves in recent years. The bureaucracy has had to modify but not to abandon the principle that it (usually) shapes the field from which the choice is made. In this way ministerial sensibilities have been etched into the Whitehall psyche. For some, this has been a worrying development (Wass, 1985, p. 236). The bureaucracy may also determine the final choice, though this is now far from automatic. But even where civil servants are known to ministers, it is usually because the bureaucracy has put them where they will get noticed. Richard Way (NOA Tr., p. 7) has said that the key event in his career was his promotion within the War Office to become an assistant secretary in 1946. As one of the more junior principals he was picked out from the pack by the PUS, Eric Speed. Now, his talents would be given some air. He never looked back, though he never served in a private office. Such sponsorship by a more senior official, or group of officials, is equally if not more typical of those who do come to serve in private offices. It is true also of those who serve in one of the central departments.

Service in Central Departments

The Treasury has long been the most important central department. Perhaps it still is. The planned reduction in staffing levels there during the second half of the 1990s may change its relationship with other departments. It is yet far from certain as to what extent, if at all, this will threaten its special position in Whitehall. In recent times the Cabinet Office has also been a considerable powerhouse, though in rather a different way. These two remain supreme even if, as noted in Chapter 1, other central departments have also enjoyed transitory moments of glory. The number of future permanent secretaries in a department gives some indication of its position in the pecking order. George Brown (1972, p. 110) claimed that the DEA's decline in status during the late-1960s was reflected in the return of high-flying civil servants to their former departments. No fewer than nine future permanent secretaries worked in the DEA during its relatively brief existence. Thirteen moved in and out of the CSD during its somewhat longer life. Neither of these two departments, though, could match the Treasury or the Cabinet Office as a stable for those on the way to the top.

As will be seen in Chapter 9, it was Warren Fisher's policy to move senior personnel around Whitehall. Critics further held that he used the Treasury as a kind of academy to attract, nurture and send out the best people to infuse other departments with its (and his) values. This he always denied. Whatever the case, the Treasury was and is still widely perceived as attracting the crème de la crème. Such implications of superiority can sometimes excite the strongest loyalties and counter-loyalties, even among permanent secretaries. One, interviewed for this book, was quite certain that the average Treasury mandarin was a cut above the rest. Another, who had never worked in the Treasury, was equally emphatic: 'They think they're better than anyone else. I've yet to see any evidence of that'. Similar claims and counter-claims may have been made about the Cabinet Office, though with much less ferocity. For Norman Brook established the tradition of using people on secondment from the departments - the high flyers - rather than retaining a resident Cabinet Office staff (Seldon 1981, p. 115). Fig 7.1 shows how the two central departments have claimed a goodly share of Whitehall's most promising talent.

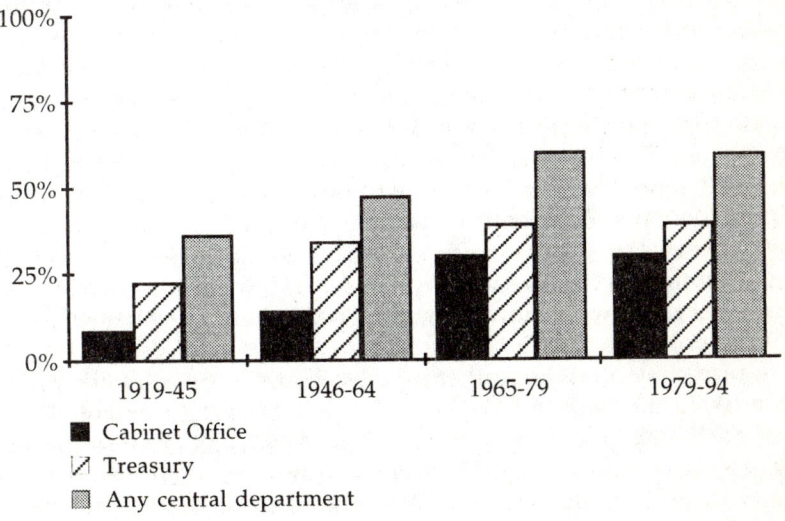

Fig. 7.1 Proportion of permanent secretaries who have served in a central department

Numerically, the Treasury remains more significant than the Cabinet Office as a nursery for permanent secretaries. Its supremacy is also of much longer standing. During the second half of the nineteenth century nearly one in every five permanent secretaries had spent some time in the Treasury. But two even more important factors lie hidden behind the figures in Fig.7.1. When both are brought into the reckoning, the Cabinet Office seems to have become almost equally as significant in the career development of future permanent secretaries - though in a different way from the Treasury. First, Fig.7.1 includes some who were promoted to permanent secretaryships within one or other of the central departments in question. There have been many more such promotions within the Treasury than within the Cabinet Office. We get a rather different picture, then, by excluding all internal promotions. With this adjustment the Treasury contributed a steady 30 per cent of post-holders elsewhere between 1945-79, rising to almost a half since 1979. That of the Cabinet Office jumps dramatically from 15 per cent among those appointed between 1946-64 to nearly two-fifths (1965-79), rising also to nearly a half since 1979. It has now joined the Treasury as a prolific provider of permanent secretaries for other departments, having indeed overtaken it during the 1970s. Second, there is a distinction in the levels at which the future permanent secretaries of other departments have tended to serve in the Cabinet Office as against the Treasury. Two-thirds of all such permanent secretaries since 1945 who had served in the Treasury first did so at principal (grade 7) level or below. Less than a quarter made their Treasury debut as either under secretaries or deputy secretaries. By contrast, nearly a half of those with service in the Cabinet Office moved there at one or other of these two more senior grades: only a quarter did so at grade 7 or below. The Cabinet Office has therefore tended to be served by future permanent secretaries who had made their mark in Whitehall - those already well on their way to the top. The Treasury, on the other hand, has also given more of an early boost to those who go on to head other departments, albeit only a minority of these people actually began their careers in the Treasury.

As with service in a private office, further insight can be gained by comparing permanent secretaries' service in central departments with that of other civil servants who did not become permanent secretaries. Table 7.2 presents the broad picture.

The figures show that the further up the hierarchy civil servants progress, the more likely they are to have served in a central department. The incidence of such service among permanent secretaries is stronger here than was indicated in Fig. 7.1 This is because Table 7.2 includes only those recruited directly into the administrative grades through open competition. There is nevertheless a clear distinction between permanent secretaries and their peers. Over two-thirds had served in a central department prior to becoming a permanent secretary - at least among those recruited between 1937-58. Most of them reached the top between the mid-1960s and the mid-1980s. As with service as a private secretary, it cannot be said to have been imperative, but it is worth noting that over 90 per cent of all who have

Table 7.2
Proportion of civil servants, by final grade reached,
who served in central departments

Department	Recruited 1914-1936 Terminal Grade				Recruited 1937-1958 Terminal Grade			
	Assist Sec %	Under Sec %	Dep Sec %	Perm Sec %	Assist Sec %	Under Sec %	Dep Sec %	Perm Sec %
Any central dept	17	21	23	52	18	41	56	70
None	83	79	77	48	82	59	44	30
Total %	100	100	100	100	100	100	100	100
N =	(86)	(122)	(73)	(65)	(82)	(138)	(71)	(64)
Treasury	13	14	24	38	12	15	20	41
Cabinet Office	5	9	6	17	7	16	32	37
Other	–	3	3	11	4	16	12	24

Some individuals served in more than one central department. The percentage figures for service in the Treasury, the Cabinet Office and for other central departments are therefore given separately and do not, in total, correspond with the figures for 'any central department'.

become permanent secretaries since the mid-1960s after a career spent in Whitehall have served either in a private office or in a central department. And among the small minority who have not worked in a central department or in a private office, all except three entered the civil service in either an executive, clerical or specialist grade.

All this suggests if not a predestination to reach the top, then a deliberate nurturing of those within the elite corps who are considered to have the potential. As one permanent secretary said: 'I was lucky. I had a lot of attention. Not everyone gets that amount of attention'. How, then does this square with the notion of a meritocracy?

A Whitehall meritocracy?

Promotion by merit was one of the cornerstones of the Northcote-Trevelyan Report. This was closely allied to the notion of recruitment by competitive examination. It remained the intention of the civil service commissioners to attract the best available intellects. Few doubt that in this they have consistently succeeded. Indeed they have on occasion been attacked for bagging too many of the best brains, to the privation of industry, commerce and other walks of life. But what has Whitehall done with such talent as it has attracted and retained? There is positive evidence that the best academic minds have tended to rise to the top. Over half the graduates who have become permanent secretaries since 1945 achieved first class honours – just under half among those appointed since 1979. This is nearly half as great again as the proportion among all Administrative Class entrants. Differences of such magnitude are unlikely to have arisen by chance. Of course, degree classification is only one fairly tenuous indication of merit. Critics would see in these facts confirmation that those who rise to the top are often intellectually brilliant but not necessarily the best equipped to meet the changing needs of modern government, especially the increasingly important managerial function. Such arguments can be more than a mite perverse. Senior civil servants may well be lacking in certain aptitudes – but evidence of high intellect scarcely constitutes proof.

Similarly, those who have become permanent secretaries have tended to be the more highly placed in open competition examinations. Over two-fifths of those appointed since 1945 were placed in the top quarter among the successful candidates and nearly three quarters in the top half. This gives further crude support – no more – to the proposition that those who reach the top are among the most able, intellectually, of those initially recruited. Again, this can be a two-edged sword. What it really shows is that open competitive examinations have been tolerably good at predicting future career destinations within Whitehall. This begs a number of questions. Are there any identifiable types from among the initial entrants who seem not to have had a fair crack of the whip? Has there been undue emphasis upon the elite corps (i.e. the administrative grades)? Do these facts reveal more about Whitehall than about the capacity of senior civil servants adequately to serve the country?

One group noticeably underrepresented at permanent secretary level is women. There have been only five women permanent secretaries. The first and best known was Evelyn Sharp. She headed the MHLG between 1955-66. The others are: Mary Smieton (Ministry of Education, 1959-63); Mildred Riddlesdell (2nd Perm. Sec., DHSS 1971-3); Anne Mueller (2nd Perm. Sec., Cabinet Office/Treasury, 1984-90); and Valerie Strachan (Chairman, Board of Customs and Excise since 1993). Women were first admitted in 1925 as candidates for competitive entry into the administrative grades (Meynell 1988, pp. 79-101). Between 1925-39 some seven per cent of all successful candidates were women – exactly the same as the proportion of women among those entrants who became permanent secretaries. Between 1948-68, women took 14 per cent of the places upon initial entry. But among those who became permanent secretaries only two (3.5 per cent) were women. The reasons are complex and no doubt partly extraneous to the civil service. They evoke all sorts of considerations, some of them highly emotive, which lie beyond the purview of this study. At the very least one may question whether Whitehall has been able fully to exploit the talent it recruits.

In another sense critics have questioned whether Whitehall has deployed its human resources to full effect. Its emphasis on developing talent within the administrative grades is a long standing bone of contention. Has not this emphasis been to the exclusion of those from other grades? Such was one of the Fulton Committee's major objections. Whitehall's response in the 1970s was to create the open structure. Senior posts, including permanent secretaryships, were no longer by definition exclusive to the Administrative Class. But how many of those who initially entered the civil service in other grades have become permanent secretaries? Administrative Class entrants have never completely monopolized the top positions. One in eight of all the permanent secretaries appointed between 1919-64 rose from an executive or clerical grade. The best known was Horace Wilson who, despite public opprobrium over appeasement, went on to be head of the civil service between 1939-42. Since 1964, such upward mobility has been less apparent. And since 1979 only two have come up through these particular ranks – Gordon Manzie from a clerical grade and Terence Heiser from the Executive Class. Manzie succeeded Montague Alfred in 1984 as Chief Executive of the PSA. Heiser headed the DoE between 1985-92. There may have been a more abstract factor at work here. The middle decades of the twentieth century were ones of substantial and sustained growth in government. The number of senior posts expanded too, though to a lesser extent. To fill these posts it may have been necessary to draw into the higher echelons greater numbers of those who had initially entered the service other than into the administrative grades. But since the 1970s there has been a contraction in the bureaucracy. There has been a near sufficiency of people who entered directly into the Administrative Class, mainly during the 1950s and '60s. At the same time, a steady one in eight permanent secretaryships have since 1945 been held by those who initially entered the civil service in one of the specialist classes. This shows no sign of decline. To this extent the 'top doors' in Whitehall have remained open – less so than critics would like but more than they are usually prepared to acknowledge. In this sense and in contrast to women Whitehall has recognized talent within its midst even when such talent has lain outside the privileged elite corps.

Critics may still claim that progress beyond the less favoured groups and certainly to the level of permanent secretary is confined to those prepared to 'play the game', to conform to Whitehall's values. There are two points of contention here. First, what should be the qualities sought in a top civil servant. This turns, in part, upon what is seen as being the proper role of the civil service itself. Second, one may question whether Whitehall has succeeded in attracting and promoting those with such qualities as are thought desirable. Both questions are pregnant with prescription and subjectivity. What this chapter has shown so far is that, by and large, Whitehall has recognized those who have possessed and demonstrated the qualities it has thought necessary. Exactly what are these qualities? And what brings one rather than another possessor of such qualities to the level of permanent secretary? In concluding this chapter some attempt is made to answer these questions.

Reaching the summit – the qualities sought

It is possible to identify the general qualities necessary to operate as a permanent secretary. There are personal, intellectual and technical attributes. At the personal level all permanent secretaries must be resilient, mentally and physically. They must be good team players, yet able when necessary to rise above the tide of consensus. This includes the ability to work with ministers of almost any hue or persuasion though without sacrificing their own integrity or that of the office of permanent secretary. An equable temperament will help, though a bit of 'fizz' is sometimes needed to push things through or to knock heads together. Charisma is a further asset, or at any rate a leadership style that inspires others. Intellectually, permanent secretaries must be able quickly to assimilate and analyze vast amounts of material; to seize upon the central issues and see the way forward. They must be good at problem-solving. They must also be sound in their judgement – quick to spot trouble while maintaining a sense of proportion. Intellectual rigour remains essential, even if the policy role with which in the past it was often associated is no longer quite so dominant. It is less dominant because the policy role of permanent secretaries has changed and because management has become increasingly important. This calls for certain technical qualities. It demands a more deliberate, systematic approach. This includes a broad familiarity with techniques such as management accounting, operational monitoring and strategic planning. Permanent secretaries do not, cannot and need not know all that is going on in their departments. But they must have or acquire the technique of semi-disengagement without losing control. They can and do imprint their personalities. They develop their own styles, emphasizing particular areas of work. The good permanent secretary, though, is one whose legacy to the department is more than just happy memories followed by uncertainty and chaos. In managerial terms, the lasting achievements are often more impersonal – new methods, new systems, sometimes new structures.

Clearly, no one individual can possess all these qualities in full abundance. Not all departments require all such qualities in their fullest measure. But effective operation requires all of these qualities in some measure. As one permanent secretary put it:

> You can afford to have some unsafe deputy secretaries but you can't have an unsafe permanent secretary. You can't afford to

make mistakes as a permanent secretary....you've got to be much more rounded and much safer. None of your abilities may quite reach the heights of some deputy secretaries, but taken overall you must have a fairly high marking on most things. You must have a sort of 70 per cent rating across the board with perhaps the occasional dip down....

Other officials, then, may be better equipped in certain respects than the permanent secretary. They may have a more powerful intellect, or a better grasp of policy. But if, for example, they are poor at conducting human relationships they will be unsatisfactory as permanent secretaries. They may be excellent with people, but if they have no head for managerial command then, again, they are unlikely to reach the top – certainly not nowadays. This raises a further point. As mentioned above, SASC tries to marry candidates to particular permanent secretaryships. This has not yet gone so far as the preparation of detailed job descriptions or job specifications. This may come and some think it should. It is, however, less likely nowadays – as it certainly was sometimes in the past – that someone comes to head a department primarily because they happen to be deemed 'ready' and next in line to take a permanent secretaryship, wherever a vacancy may occur. This is a change of emphasis rather than a reversal of Whitehall's time-honoured practices. The evidence of this chapter is that certain civil servants are marked out for potentially great things. They get the opportunities to succeed, or to fail. This marking out is not primarily a matter of personal favouritism, though both ministers and top civil servants have been instrumental in enhancing the prospects of those with whom they have worked.

There is no precise inevitability in the process. Peter Hennessy (1989, p. 671) has written of Robin Butler that, a decade or so before the event, it was possible to foresee that he would fill one or other of the 'super' permanent secretaryships. As a tribute to Butler, this is no doubt justified. But this kind of ex post facto observation can be misleading. Some high-flyers give every appearance of having what it takes and, like Butler, duly go on to confirm their promise. Others flatter to deceive. To borrow a racing expression, not all will 'train on'. They will have their limitations exposed; or go off the boil; or simply burn themselves out. Conversely, others who seem no more than adequate may, if given the opportunity, develop as they are given more responsibility. One thing seems fairly clear. Promotions to under secretary and certainly to deputy secretary level have been made by the bureaucracy with at least one eye upon the potential of the individual eventually to become a permanent secretary. This is confirmed by more than one former principal establishments officer (interviews with the author). It is difficult to know to what extent it will be possible to combine this perspective with the more job-specific approach to the filling of vacancies in an increasingly fragmented civil service. The candidate who fits the needs of the moment for a particular post may not be the one best equipped to rise to the top. It will be interesting to see whether this has any bearing upon the career patterns of future permanent secretaries.

The jump to assistant secretary level has long been seen as a critical one in ascending the hierarchy. Objectively, it marks a qualitative change. It often brings the civil servant more regularly within the horizon of the minister and certainly of the permanent secretary. It is normally the first time the official assumes responsibility for a specific area of work. This demands certain organizational as well as policy skills. More specifically it calls for the ability to delegate. The significance of an assistant secretaryship should not be misunderstood. It is not the promotion to but the performance at assistant secretary level that is critical to further advancement. Most fast stream entrants – or Administrative Class entrants in years gone by – could expect to become assistant secretaries. There is little difference in average ages upon promotion to this level among permanent secretaries as against those who finish as deputy secretaries or under secretaries. Even those who are to remain as assistant secretaries are usually there by forty or approaching forty, as against mid-thirties for the rest. But those who are going to be permanent secretaries have normally become under secretaries at forty or in their early forties and deputy secretaries by their mid to late-forties. This is five years earlier than under secretaries who will remain under secretaries and deputy secretaries who will remain deputy secretaries. It should be stressed that these are average ages: they belie a certain amount of overlap as between those who do and those who do not go on to become permanent secretaries. Realities are often less clear cut, less orderly, than cold figures are apt to suggest. Nevertheless, those who are unable for whatever reason to prove themselves by a certain stage in their careers are unlikely to become permanent secretaries. As we have seen, it is not always necessary to enter Whitehall with a silver spoon, though that helps. Again to use a racing analogy, it is not always necessary to be up with the pace from the start. Equally, as mid-career approaches, one cannot afford to lose touch with the leaders. There is the danger of getting tailed off.

For some, then, promotion to an under or a deputy secretaryship can come simply too late. Beyond this, some deputy secretaries will be too lopsided in their talents. Others may be permanent secretary material yet fail to reach the summit by sheer bad luck, simply being in the wrong place at the wrong time. They may be beaten to it by a slightly better candidate. Their candidature may have met resistance from a strong minister, or else the minister was already fixed upon someone else. The minister may soon be gone – but so too is that particular vacancy. The hapless deputy secretary may get another chance, but not necessarily. Things can move quickly – perhaps more so now than ever before.

Of course, if some are unlucky then others are more fortunate to reach the top. A bit of good luck in the running is a necessary ingredient in the civil service as it is in most organizations. This is not to imply any undue element of hit and miss. Nor is it to impugn the vast majority who have worked their way up to become permanent secretaries. There may be a small minority of 'frauds' who are unworthy of the office they hold – probably around 10 per cent according to one former permanent secretary (interview with the author). Still, Whitehall has for the most part been quite effective at recognizing, cultivating and promoting its own talent – at least within certain parameters and according to its own values. Critics may object that these values are self-serving and inappropriate to the needs of the country. An equally profound and consistently resonant jibe is that Whitehall has failed sufficiently to engage talented individuals from outside the civil service. This alleged insularity is the subject of the next chapter.

PART III

PERMANENT SECRETARIES IN WHITEHALL – CAREER PATTERNS

8 An insular order? Permanent secretaries and the outside world

Introduction

The previous chapter showed that Whitehall has been fairly adept at recognizing and promoting to the highest levels talent within its own ranks. Its attentions have been confined by no means exclusively to those who entered directly into the elite administrative corps. It has to some extent drawn from other constituencies within the civil service – at least more so than critics are apt to acknowledge. Yet it has still been asserted that the mandarin elite is an insular order in two other senses. First, that Whitehall has failed to draw widely enough at senior levels upon the reservoir of talent outside the civil service. Second, that too little has been done to broaden the experience of the majority who do spend most of their careers in Whitehall.

These two further criticisms provide the focus for this chapter. In different though closely related ways both allegations would, if substantiated, support the wider claim that the administrative elite is an insular order detached from the society it serves. Of course, a certain detachment may have its own virtues. It may at any rate be a price worth paying for some of the benefits it may bring. In particular, the notion of a career civil service has long been upheld as a supposed foundation for the maintenance of neutrality and impartiality. This chapter therefore begins with an account of the notion of a career service as understood by contemporaries over the last hundred years and more. There then follows an empirical analysis of the rise of the career civil servant. This is done by examining the career characteristics of permanent secretaries. The spotlight is also thrown upon outsiders – that is those who have been drawn into Whitehall having pursued a career in another walk of life. This includes a survey of the professions from which they have been recruited and the ways in which they have been used in Whitehall. The final section of the chapter examines the extent to which permanent secretaries collectively have had experience of the outside world. This includes periods of secondment. In this way it is possible to establish the extent to which Whitehall has been comparatively open or insular at various times from the 1830s down to the present day.

A career civil service – adherence to a principle

The mid-nineteenth century reformers saw a career civil service together with competitive entry as a step towards greater efficiency. It was to be a counterweight to the prevailing practice of patronage. As such it was a cornerstone in the blueprint provided by Northcote-Trevelyan (1854, pp. 12-3). As Peter Hennessy (1989, p. 40) puts it: 'Whitehall was to be a life-long finishing school for the class of Charles Trevelyan'. As events unfolded it came also to be associated with a politically non-partisan, anonymous civil service (Greenaway 1985).

The idea of careerism was therefore part of a set of broader moral, constitutional and practical objectives. It became an important element in the transformation of the civil service. Yet surprisingly, while other elements with which it was associated remained the centre of controversy, the notion of a career service seems to have gained silent but fairly widespread acceptance. Disraeli, although suspicious of open competition, favoured reserving the more important posts for career officials (Monypenny and Buckle 1929, vol. 1, p. 1434). As will be seen below, there continued the practice of appointing outsiders to top posts. Not until the early and middle decades of the twentieth century did careerists gain anything like a stranglehold on permanent secretaryships. Yet by the second half of the nineteenth century the principle, if not the practice, of careerism seems already to have taken root.

There was sometimes an acute sensitivity when outsiders were appointed. The appointment in 1870 of Patrick Cumin as an assistant secretary in the Education Department was a case in point. It upset the existing staff (Kekewich 1920, p. 20). His promotion fourteen years later to the permanent secretaryship briefly threatened the resignation of one of his political chiefs, A.J. Mundella. Gladstone, above all the leading figures of the day, was sensitive to charges of favouritism and patronage, particularly where this involved the promotion of some of his closest confidants. As noted in the last chapter, private secretaryships were at that time by no means exclusively filled by civil servants. Yet a number of those whom Gladstone brought into Whitehall in this capacity went on to take very senior positions, including permanent secretaryships. One such was Arthur Godley. Having been Gladstone's private secretary he became, in 1882, one of the commissioners of customs. The following year, with Gladstone still as premier, he became PUS at the India Office where he remained until 1909. It was the question of patronage that stirred public controversy rather than the relative merits of outsiders and careerists *per se*.

It would be a mistake to assume that the period down to 1914 was one entirely free from adverse comment about the notion of a career civil service. In the 1850s the Administrative Reform Association had canvassed for the greater involvement of businessmen and the use of business methods in public offices (Anderson 1967, p. 122). Such ideas made little headway but gathered new momentum at the turn of the century as part of the 'efficiency movement' (Searle 1972, pp. 86-92). The MacDonnell Commission, 1912-15, felt obliged to respond to similar notes of discord. But the majority of the Commission were satisfied that there was little scope for business methods in Whitehall, the purposes of public and private administration being quite different (MacDonnell 1914, pp. 82-3). It noted the continued use of patronage, against which a career service remained the most obvious bulwark. In particular it bemoaned the use of outsiders brought in to help staff the Health Insurance Commission. In fact this had been accomplished with little internal hostility, partly because the venture also brought promotions for many career officials (Bunbury and Titmuss 1957, pp. 259-98). But the rapid acceleration of functions that accompanied the reforms of the Liberal governments between 1906-14 and those which were consequential upon the Great War put increasing strain upon the machinery of government and its personnel. There was a growing irritation at the alleged shortcomings of the bureaucracy and of permanent career officials. In a rare outpouring, Asquith (1928, vol. II, pp. 241-2) described one of his former officials as 'a highly cultivated man with a vast knowledge of literature, but with all the characteristic limitations of the civil service type, amongst which is excessive caution and non-committal-ness'. During the war Lloyd George had already taken up Rosebery's earlier and more muted call for the introduction of business methods. As Minister of Munitions Lloyd George developed a deliberate policy of bringing in men with business experience (Jones 1951, p. 66). In her diary for 22 February 1917 Beatrice Webb noted that permanent officials were 'fighting desperately for the control of their departments, against intruding "interests" and interloping amateurs' (Mackenzie and Mackenzie 1984, p. 276). William Beveridge expressed similar concerns (Harris 1977, p. 235). Both Webb and Beveridge were overreacting, as things turned out. They were nevertheless expressing a perceived threat to what was still the widely accepted principle that the majority of top jobs should be held by career officials.

During both the world wars substantial numbers of business people, academics and outsiders of all types were drawn into Whitehall. Business people were more evident during the first than the second war, academics vice versa. The significance of their presence, immediate and longer term, has been the subject of fierce controversy. One participant and former businessman claimed that the permanent bureaucracy failed to capitalize upon the ideas brought in by outsiders between 1914-18 (Demetriadi 1921, p. 31). Certainly there developed during the inter-war years a greater gulf between insiders and outsiders (Chapman and Greenaway 1980, p. 72). Any attempt to invade the territory of the careerists brought a sharp response. Such was the case with the appointment in 1939 of George Gater as PUS at the Colonial Office. Gater's career had been in local government. As noted in the last chapter, he had worked alongside Herbert Morrison in the London County Council. Of more immediate significance, he had also been associated with Prime Minister Neville Chamberlain. The appointment precipitated an exchange in the House of Commons. One member declared that any deviation from the practice of appointing career civil servants was to be regretted and should be resisted (HC Debs 1938-39, 5th series (vol. 350), cols. 1242-3). But this was by no means the universally accepted wisdom. Harold Laski thought that cases like Gater's should be normal, not exceptional (Mallalieu 1942, p. 11). He believed that improvements had usually been accomplished by 'the impact of external reality rather than by internal introspection' (Ibid. p. 15).

The Laski thesis has retained a certain attraction. Thomas Balogh (1959, pp. 119-20), one of the best-known and distinguished exemplars of this view, wrote:

> Whenever any effort had to be organised, indeed palpably threatening disaster averted, outsiders had to be recruited to take charge... In conditions where the nation's will to live awakens and demands positive action the mandarins must be displaced. They are a hindrance to policy making, though, when properly supervised, they are often superb in its execution.

The temporary appointment of large numbers of outsiders was a generally accepted necessity without which Whitehall could not have met the challenge of war, especially between 1939-45. Hennessy (1989, p. 88) considers the interaction of the outsiders with existing careerists to have been 'the high point of achievement in the history of the British civil service'. Conversely he believes the failure after 1945 to maintain the presence of outsiders to have been '...probably *the* greatest lost opportunity in the history of British public administration' (Ibid., p. 120). What is notable is the relative ease with which large number of outsiders were assimilated and the flexibility with which career officials responded between 1939-45 (Strauss 1961, p. 273; Hancock and Gowing 1949, p. 89). Hilton Poynton has testified to the harmonious relations that existed between career civil servants and business people (NOA Tr., p. 7). Poynton, a career official, served in the Ministry of Supply and in the Ministry of Reconstruction during the war. He later became PUS at the Colonial Office. Yet the contributions of the irregulars were often facilitated by careerists – men such as Norman Brook and Edward Bridges (Hennessy and Hague 1985, p. 40). It has further been argued, at least with reference to the 1914-18 war, that much of the direct initiative for 'experiments in state control' came from within the permanent bureaucracy (Marwick 1973, p. 252).

More recent calls for the modification or abandonment of a career civil service have failed to shake the prevailing faith in the principle. There have been calls for greater flexibility, including the importation of outsiders at levels below that of permanent secretary (RIPA 1987, pp. 52 and 62). Others have gone further. Hoskyns (1983, pp. 145-6) believes that 'the present system of career politicians supported by career officials is a failed system'. He sees no reason why the permanent secretary should not be an outsider, perhaps supported by a career official as the second permanent secretary responsible for day-to-day matters. Similar arrangements would be implicit in any proposal to politicize the civil service along American lines.

Whether on technical or on political grounds, proposals to throw the higher civil service open to outsiders have not, on the whole, found widespread favour. And from where would Whitehall draw the large numbers sometimes advocated? The most common answer given by advocates is the world of business. But many would judge that business needs to keep all its best talent. It has been pointed out that the performance of British industry inspires little confidence that the contribution of business people to government would be beneficial (Fry 1986, p. 549). A former permanent secretary has objected, with specific reference to Hoskyns, that any large scale infusion of outsiders would be a threat to competitive entry and promotion by merit (Pliatzky 1984, p. 25). Further difficulties can arise when, in order to attract outsiders, they are paid substantially more than career officials for doing the same job. This was a bone of contention following the appointment of Montague Alfred as Chief Executive of the PSA in 1982 and, in 1984, of Peter Levene as a temporary adviser to the Secretary of Sate for Defence. Both were remunerated well above permanent secretary level. In Levene's case there was also a possible conflict of interest. For he continued as Chairman of United Scientific Holdings and as Deputy Chairman of the Defence Manufacturers' Association. These positions he relinquished the following year when he was formally appointed as Chief Executive (PUS) for Defence Procurement. He was then assimilated with little further public outcry. Nor were the appointments of John Cuckney or Derek Rayner in the early 1970s the occasion for any great controversy. Cuckney was appointed to the post later held by Montague Alfred, Rayner to the one to which Levene was subsequently appointed. There was mild surprise but no expression of outrage when in 1991 Terence Burns was appointed to head the Treasury. But Burns had already spent over ten years in Whitehall as Chief Economic Adviser, remunerated at permanent secretary level. Such appointments have not generally been seen as placing in jeopardy the notion of a career civil service.

The principle of a career service is no longer held with quite the same nervous tenacity as once it was. Many who uphold the principle are prepared to tolerate the presence of a few outsiders, especially in the more specialist posts. Yet the daggers can still be drawn when the principle is seen as being under threat. The Ibbs Report concluded that 'the concept of a career in a unified civil service has little relevance for most civil servants, whose horizons are bounded by their department' (Efficiency Unit 1988, para. 12). This seemed to signal a deliberate break with the Fulton Committee's endorsement of a career service (Fulton 1968, p. 46, para. 134). Subsequent flirtations by the government with ideas about fixed contracts and variegated pay schemes have heightened fears for the notion of careerism. A significant minority of agency chief executives have been drawn from outside the civil service. All these things have been seen by some as a threat to the principle of a career civil service. Lord Callaghan told a Commons select committee that the new breed of officials were less likely to view the civil service as a career for life (TCSC 1993, Q. 621). This, he thought, could undermine the service ethos. Such criticisms clearly touched a nerve within Whitehall. The government was quick to allay fears that whole tranches of top jobs were going to be filled by outsiders. It stated that 'most of the top Civil Service posts will continue to be filled by those with substantial previous experience within the Service' (Cabinet Office 1994, p. 3). At the same time it upheld the values of 'integrity, political impartiality, objectivity, selection and promotion on merit and accountability through Ministers to Parliament' (p. 1, para. 1.3). In this way the government was acknowledging some sort of link between those values and the existence of a predominantly career civil service. Two questions arise. First, in what numbers could outsiders be accommodated at very senior levels without sacrifice to such values? Second, if beyond a certain point the sacrifice becomes too high a price to pay, are there not other ways in which the advantages associated with outsiders can be had while retaining a predominantly career civil service? Definitive answers to such questions are liable to prove elusive. But a number of clues can be gathered from an analysis of trends in the filling of permanent secretaryships. The next section therefore charts both the rise and the slight recent recession of the career civil servant.

The rise of the career civil servant

In classifying the career backgrounds of permanent secretaries we may identify three categories: careerists; semi-careerists; and outsiders. A careerist is one who entered the civil service under the age of twenty-seven, remaining there until becoming a permanent secretary. Due allowances are made for delayed entry on account of wartime military service, and for subsequent breaks in service of under three years. A semi-careerist is one who entered the civil service aged twenty-seven or over; or who had previously followed another career for at least five but less than fifteen years; or whose civil service career was broken by at least three years (excluding secondment). An outsider is defined as one who worked in Whitehall for less than seven years prior to becoming a permanent secretary or who had a total of at least fifteen years' experience in another career – unless he or she had also had at least fifteen years in the civil service in which case they are classified as semi-careerists.

With these definitions Table 8.1 shows the proportions of careerists, semi-careerists and outsiders among all permanent secretaries appointed in each of the seven periods between 1830-1994.

Table 8.1
Proportion of careerists, semi-careerists and outsiders appointed as permanent secretaries between 1830-1994

	1830-69 %	1870-99 %	1900-18 %	1919-45 %	1946-64 %	1965-79 %	1979-94 %
Careerists	27	52	65	86	87	84	82
Semi-careerists	25	21	21	7	8	10	11
Outsiders	48	27	14	7	5	6	7
Total %	100	100	100	100	100	100	100
N=	(60)	(48)	(57)	(95)	(83)	(81)	(72)

The broad trend is clear. Careerists struggled to establish supremacy during the nineteenth century. Only towards the closing years of the century did they fill the majority of top posts. By this time a politically neutral bureaucracy was well established. So, too, was the idea of a career civil service. Not until the inter-war years did the careerists achieve numerical supremacy – a supremacy they have since retained. Why did it take so long to achieve? Three main factors account for the time-lag: patterns of recruitment to the civil service; the growth of government; and the characteristics of individual departments. The following paragraphs deal briefly with each in turn of these three factors.

The first and perhaps most powerful factor is the pattern of recruitment. During the first half of the nineteenth century patronage remained virtually unchallenged as the means by which people entered the civil service. Many who were appointed in this way were of average ability, sometimes worse. Careerists nevertheless constituted the majority of permanent secretaries in post in 1830. But with the growth in volume and the importance of government activity it became necessary to look outside. Even Northcote and Trevelyan acknowledged the need to fill many of the top posts from outside until the more highly qualified recruits they proposed to attract had worked their way through the hierarchy. In the meantime those who came from outside were better qualified than their careerist colleagues. Two-thirds of the outsiders as against nearly one-third of the careerists appointed between 1830-69 had had a university education. Furthermore, the pace of reform in methods of recruitment was slower than proponents wished. Open competition was not introduced until 1870. As we saw in Chapter 6, early competitions were spasmodic, yielding relatively few recruits. Moreover, a number of departments were able to circumvent the new procedures for a time. Allowing for these delays and for a generation or so until the new recruits had had time to rise to the senior levels, a predominantly careerist profile could not have been expected much before the turn of the century.

As already suggested, patterns of recruitment, as they affected the relative presence of careerists and outsiders, worked in tandem with a second and almost equally telling factor – the growth of government. Relatively rapid and unplanned growth requires manpower levels greater than those for which recruitment in an antecedent period was intended to meet. As noted in the last chapter, the growth of government in the twentieth century may have facilitated a certain amount of upward mobility from the lower grades. In the nineteenth century and with fewer really able careerists, growth necessitated recourse to ready-made talent from outside. It is instructive to compare the career backgrounds of those appointed to departments newly created between 1870-1918 with those appointed during the same period to departments established before 1870. New departments were, upon their creation, notably more likely than were the established departments to appoint either an outsider or a semi-careerist – 60 per cent as against 36 per cent. The inference is clear: without the expansion of business and the creation of new departments the trend towards careerism would have advanced more rapidly than it did. Equally notable, though, is the speed with which the new departments came into line. In filling permanent secretaryships upon the third and fourth vacancies they were neither more nor less likely than were the older departments to appoint non-careerists. This well illustrates Whitehall's capacity to assimilate and then regularize irregular tendencies.

It must be remembered that some of these third and fourth vacancies were filled after 1918 when the trend towards careerism was stronger throughout Whitehall. By this time the more rampant impulses of departmentalism had been brought to heel. Before then, though, it continued to enjoy considerable rein. This, then, is the third factor explaining the gradual shift to careerism. In some departments the nature of the work was held to require certain qualities or qualifications that were less likely to be found among careerists. At the Home Office the qualification sought was a legal background. In the Education Department it was an academic standing beyond simply that of graduate status. For example, both Robert Morant (Permanent Secretary, 1903-11) and Amherst Selby-Bigge (1911-25) were distinguished scholars. Even where there were no special requirements or characteristics, departmental traditions sometimes prevailed. Between 1870-1918, the period of transition towards a career service, the Treasury, the India Office and the Customs (and Excise) Office consistently appointed careerists. This can have had little to do with the nature of the work. The Treasury may have tried to set an example. It would have had a strong hand in appointments at the Customs Office, one of its subordinate departments. But it would have had an equally strong hand with the Inland Revenue, another of its subordinate departments, where there was nevertheless a quite different pattern of top appointments. The nature of the work at the India Office may be thought similar to that at the Colonial Office. But there were different organizational cultures. That these examples betray no overall pattern is little surprise. The strong ministerial and departmental autonomy of the period entailed an inevitable fragmentation. This was to change with the setting up in 1920 of the more centralized procedures for top appointments described in the last chapter. These changes were accompanied by a deliberate drive to consolidate the reality of a career civil service. In 1919 Maurice Hankey wrote of the need 'sooner or later (to) revert to the employment generally of civil servants' (Middlemas 1969, pp. 90-1).

The figures in Table 8.1 show just how successful Hankey, Fisher and others were in realizing their wishes. Since 1919, careerists have consistently filled more than four out of every five permanent secretaryships. Semi-careerists and, even more so, outsiders have remained a fairly small minority. They tend to have been drawn from rather different walks of life than were the outsiders of the nineteenth century. This partly reflects changing economic and social factors. It reflects also changing dispositions within Whitehall. This can be seen in the professions from which non-careerists have been drawn and from the way in which they have been deployed as permanent secretaries.

Non-careerists in Whitehall

Although they have been only a fairly small minority in recent decades it is nevertheless worth examining the backgrounds of those non-careerists who have become permanent secretaries. They provide interesting comparison with the non-careerists of the nineteenth and early twentieth centuries. Then they were a prominent feature on the Whitehall landscape. In particular there were those who came to the civil service from politics. One of the most notable aspects is the apparent ease with which they moved between politics and the bureaucracy. This warrants closer attention as a prelude to the more general analysis of their professional backgrounds and of their deployment within Whitehall.

As noted in Chapter 1, the boundary between politics and administration was pretty clearly established by the 1830s. It was easy to tell who were the politicians and who were the civil servants. Their respective roles were coming into sharper relief, even if some of the higher profile officials were unable to disengage from public controversy. Yet if the boundary was well established, there continued throughout the nineteenth century a conspicuous two way traffic across the boundary. Between 1830-99 one in seven of all permanent secretaries and nearly two-fifths of the outsiders had been MPs. Rather fewer left their permanent secretaryships for politics – a little over six per cent among all post-holders. Among the latter group was Alfred Milner. He was Chairman of the Board of Inland Revenue between 1892-97. Before that he had been Under Secretary for Finance in Egypt, having earlier been Private Secretary to Chancellor of the Exchequer George Goschen. He had already tried unsuccessfully to enter Parliament. Upon leaving the Inland Revenue he took on a number of important colonial governorships. He was one of the most noted imperialist administrators of his day. As High Commissioner for South Africa he played a vital role in the prosecution of the Boer War. Perhaps not surprisingly, he considered his Inland Revenue sojourn to have been comparatively small beer. He wrote to a friend: 'the solemn joys of a well rendered estimate are tame compared with empire building' (Marlowe 1976, p. 23). Yet for most of those who moved from politics to take permanent secretaryships the attractions were positive ones. Only two of the eighteen permanent secretaries who had been MPs returned or made any attempt to return to politics. Nor was their gravitation towards the civil service a facile response to involuntary loss of political office or of a Parliamentary seat. In no sense were permanent secretaryships of the nineteenth century conferred as consolation prizes for failed politicians. This is not to obscure the fact that certain posts were used as gifts of patronage in one way or another. The Irish Office, the Office of Works, the Board of Trade and the Poor Law Board were all so used to a greater or lesser extent at one time or another during the nineteenth and early twentieth centuries. Only three of the fourteen (permanent) under secretaries for Ireland between 1840-1914 were career civil servants. Three successive incumbents were appointed immediately following a Parliamentary career – Edward Lucas (Under Secretary, 1841-45), Thomas Redington (1846-52) and John Wynne (1852). Others were overt partisans, such as James Dougherty, a Presbyterian minister appointed in 1908 by the Chief Secretary for Ireland, Augustine Birrell. Known publicly to favour home rule, Dougherty fell foul of the Ulster Unionists. He resigned in 1914 and became MP for Londonderry City.

The Irish Office was untypical and provides little basis for generalization. Still, less spectacularly the Office of Works was headed by three men with manifest political connections – Algernon Mitford (1874-86), Reginald Brett (1895-1902) and Schomberg McDonnell (1902-12). At the Board of Trade, three of the permanent secretaries appointed during the mid-nineteenth century had been, or were to become, active in politics as also were three at the Poor Law Board.

It is notable that, among those who came to Whitehall from politics, there were almost equal numbers of Conservatives and Liberals. A similar balance was noted in Chapter 6 in the party colours of those who came from political families but who did not themselves engage in politics. It is difficult to know to what extent this balance allowed the two way traffic between the civil service and politics to continue without controversy. Many who crossed the boundary did so with the modern notion of an impartial constitutional bureaucracy still in its infancy. Although with declining frequency, these passages continued without apparent threat to the neutrality of the civil service. Needless to say, it was of critical importance that nearly all of these politicians-turned-permanent secretaries played the constitutional role of civil servants once they began their careers as officials.

The kind of movements that were fairly common during the nineteenth century have virtually ceased during the present century. Two post-holders of the 1960s and '70s had formal political connections prior to joining the civil service and many years before they became permanent secretaries. William Nield worked in the Labour Party Research and Policy Department, Leo Pliatzky in the Fabian Society – both during the 1940s. Andrew Cohen had considered looking for a Labour constituency in the 1950s (Theakston 1988, p. 12). Instead he remained in the civil service. He went on in 1964 to become Permanent Secretary of the Ministry of Overseas Development, having previously headed its progenitor, the Department of Technical Co-operation.

The last MP to become a permanent secretary was David Shackleton. He was appointed in 1916 to head the newly created Ministry of Labour. He had been MP for Clitheroe, a president of the TUC and, in effect, deputy leader of the Labour Party. Since 1919, only four permanent secretaries have gone on to become active in national politics. In 1924 Sydney Olivier became Secretary of State for India in Ramsay MacDonald's first Labour government. The other three entered Parliament and held ministerial office in the context of war, or impending war. They were Maurice Hankey, John Anderson (Viscount Waverley) and James Grigg. Hankey had already been raised to the peerage upon his retirement in 1938. His two brief spells in Churchill's war cabinet were in an administrative/military capacity rather

158   The Elite of the Elite

than in a political role. Anderson became an Independent (Conservative) MP and was Lord Privy Seal (1938-39), Home Secretary (1939-40), Lord President of the Council (1940-43) and Chancellor of the Exchequer (1943-45). James Grigg's entire time in Parliament was spent as Secretary of State for War, having previously been PUS at the War Office. The transposition in 1939 was accomplished 'without anyone's noticing the difference' (Taylor 1965, p. 479). This says more about the special circumstances of war than about the boundary between politics and the bureaucracy. For most of the present century this boundary has assumed almost Berlin Wall proportions, though with no visible prospect of similar dismantlement. To some this is a source of regret and frustration. There have been calls for the relaxation of what one observer describes as the 'neurotically tight boundaries between the Civil Service and politics' (Walden 1983). Certainly the British practice is at odds with the relative freedom of movement that takes place in some other European countries (Aberbach et al. 1981).

A similar though less profound rigidity is apparent in the movement of permanent secretaries into Whitehall from other walks of life – at least among those appointed since 1919. As already noted, there has been much less such movement than during the nineteenth century. And where people have been brought in from outside they tend to have come from different professions. This is evident from Table 8.2.

Table 8.2
Professional backgrounds of non-careerist permanent secretaries

	1830-99 %	1900-45 %	1946-94 %
Academic	9	33	30
Business	7	8	30
Government	7	3	-
Other public service	4	14	10
Law	33	14	3
Military/naval	30	14	3
Journalism	3	6	19
Other	7	8	5
Total %	100	100	100
N=	(61)	(36)	(37)

Note: Government includes ministerial office – otherwise MPs are excluded.

During the nineteenth century, the heyday of the non-careerist, law and the military were the main professions from which permanent secretaries were drawn. This reflected both the spirit of the age and the nature of the business in certain departments. It was common during the last century for public figures to have been called to the bar, even if they did not practise.

Over two-fifths of all the permanent secretaries appointed between 1830-69 had been called, though this proportion was halved among post-holders over the next fifty years. The figures in Table 8.2 show only those who practised or who held formal appointments. Such individuals went on to take permanent secretaryships throughout Whitehall. In some departments, though, the work was especially appropriate to a legal mind. Thus at the Home Office, the appointment in 1848 of Horatio Waddington began an unbroken sequence of five non-careerists over the next sixty years. All had practised or held public legal appointments. Military men were quite widespread though, again, more naturally drawn to some departments in particular. From its reorganization in 1855 down to 1918 the War Office had five permanent under-secretaries. Four of them were professional soldiers. This connection does not seem surprising, though it contrasts with the Admiralty. Here, following the retirement of William Baillie Hamilton in 1855, the permanent secretaryship fell only once to a naval man. This was in the exceptional circumstances of the early 1880s which brought the appointment of George Tryon (see Chapter 1).

Lawyers and military men constituted nearly two-thirds of all the nineteenth century non-careerists. By contrast there was only a minor presence of businessmen, as indeed there were among the fathers of all nineteenth century permanent secretaries (see Chapter 6). This probably reflects the limited involvement of government in the affairs of privately owned businesses. It may also signal a general concord between the interests of business and government – what has been called the triumph of the entrepreneurial ideal (Perkin 1969, pp. 271-339). On this interpretation business people may have felt no greater need to become involved in the world of Whitehall than they did in Westminster, at least during mid-Victorian Britain (Searle 1993, pp. 9-10). Whether in larger numbers they would have been any more warmly welcomed is another matter. Be this as it may, it is only since 1945 and indeed from the 1970s that those with experience of private business have assumed any significant presence in Whitehall at permanent secretary level. Among businessmen, Derek Rayner, John Cuckney, Laurence Tindale, Montague Alfred and Peter Levene are the most notable. Among the more recently appointed semi-careerists, Nigel Wicks, David Fell, David Gillmore and Patrick Brown all held positions in privately owned companies before joining the civil service. Interestingly, not one permanent secretary has been drawn from the world of banking and finance, although quite a number have moved into this sector upon leaving Whitehall.

A sense of proportion must be adopted when interpreting these figures. Those from the world of business have assumed a much higher proportion of non-careerists since 1945 than they did during the nineteenth century. But non-careerists have, in recent decades, assumed a much lower proportion of all permanent secretaryships. In fact the proportion of post-holders with previous experience in the private sector has been consistent over the long term at approximately five per cent.

Much the same can be said about those from the world of academia and, in a slightly different way, of journalism. The presence of ex-journalists is mainly, though not exclusively, to do with the Central Office of Information (COI). Created in 1946, the COI was headed by five directors-general with experience in journalism or publicity, until the post was downgraded in the 1980s. In this it compares with lawyers at the Home Office during the nineteenth century as an example of a profession virtually colonizing a permanent secretaryship. More than this, it substantiates the thesis that, while there has been much less recourse to non-careerists since 1919, such call as has been made has tended to be more selective. It has been more selective in two closely related senses – and more so in connection with outsiders than with semi-careerists. First, they have tended to be deployed in permanent secretaryships appropriate to their professions. This links with the question of subject-related qualifications, dealt with in Chapter 6. Second, they tend to have been placed in the more singular, or specialist, permanent secretaryships – for example in the PSA (DoE) or the Procurement Executive (MoD). A further and more general point may be made. Non-careerists have rarely been strangers to Whitehall upon becoming permanent secretaries. This, of course, is so as a matter of definition for semi-careerists. It is true as a matter of fact among many outsiders. Even where they have held no formal civil service appointment before becoming permanent secretary, they have often been involved informally or in some advisory capacity. This was more so among outsiders of the last century than those of recent years. Two-thirds of the outsiders who became permanent secretaries up to 1918 had had a previous involvement in Whitehall. If backbench MPs are included, then nearly 80 per cent could be said to have had some sort of professional connection. This illustrates the caution with which outsiders were used even when Whitehall was supposedly at its most open. It is therefore necessary to examine more broadly the extent to which Whitehall has become allegedly less or arguably more open.

Mandarins and the outside world

It has often been said that civil servants in Whitehall are isolated from the world outside. Mandarins, it is claimed, have too little experience of and lack any deep personal familiarity with the broader society they serve. Such criticisms are directed primarily at careerists – those who, for much of the present century, have held most of the top positions. The appointment of more outsiders and semi-careerists is one obvious corrective. Another is to ensure that career civil servants get some experience outside Whitehall. The idea is hardly novel. It has been suggested by numerous critics throughout the present century (Wallas 1908, p. 263; Greaves 1947, p. 79; Skelsey 1957, p. 85; Plowden 1994, p. 74). Various official reports, too, have called for a broadening of careerists' horizons (Assheton 1944, paras. 108-17; Estimates Committee 1965, Q. 758; Fulton 1968, paras. 124-33; TCSC 1986a, paras. 5.17-5.18). The most recent broad policy statement endorses the importance of 'giving civil servants more experience of work in outside organisations' (Cabinet Office 1994, p. 39).There are two main ways in which such experience can be gained. One is where individuals move in and out of an organization (i.e. Whitehall) in response to advertized vacancies or the blandishments of a headhunter. The mechanism of exchange is the employment market. It involves formal resignation from the one organization in order to join the other. Many officials have left the civil service in this way never to return. Only two individuals since 1945 left and returned to become permanent secretaries - Dennis Proctor and Arthur Peterson. Proctor was a third (i.e. deputy) secretary in the Treasury when he left in 1950 to take an appointment in the private sector. He returned three years later to head the Ministry of Power. Peterson was also a deputy secretary when in 1968 he left the DEA to become Director-General and Clerk to the Greater London Council. He returned as PUS at the Home Office.

It has usually been through the other route that permanent secretaries have gained their outside experience – secondment, sometimes as part of a two way exchange. Here movement is directed by the sponsoring organization(s). Even so, it is not always possible to retain control, especially if differential reward systems and other conditions apply. During the 1980s the civil service was often the nett loser in exchange schemes. Some of its brightest people went on secondment never to return, having allegedly experienced greater freedom and the prospect of more favourable rewards. Even among critics, such as Peter Hennessy, who want a more open civil service there is scepticism as to the value of secondments, especially when they amount to 'perhaps one or two really quite pleasing secondments to a merchant bank' (TCSC 1993, Q. 335). On this view secondments are no substitute for the import of greater numbers of outsiders. Even where mutual benefits do accrue, the systematic management of secondments has proved elusive (Gosling and Netley 1990).

In spite of these difficulties, Whitehall has remained sensitive to the need to enlarge the horizons of its *corps d'élite*. In 1968 an industrial interchange scheme was introduced to facilitate secondments to and from industry. This was supplemented by the Whitehall and Industry Trust, established in 1990. The number of outward secondments has increased in recent years (TCSC 1994a, para. 280). But are those who have risen to the top any more likely to have had experience outside Whitehall? Fig. 8.1 shows the proportion of careerist permanent secretaries who spent at least one continuous year away

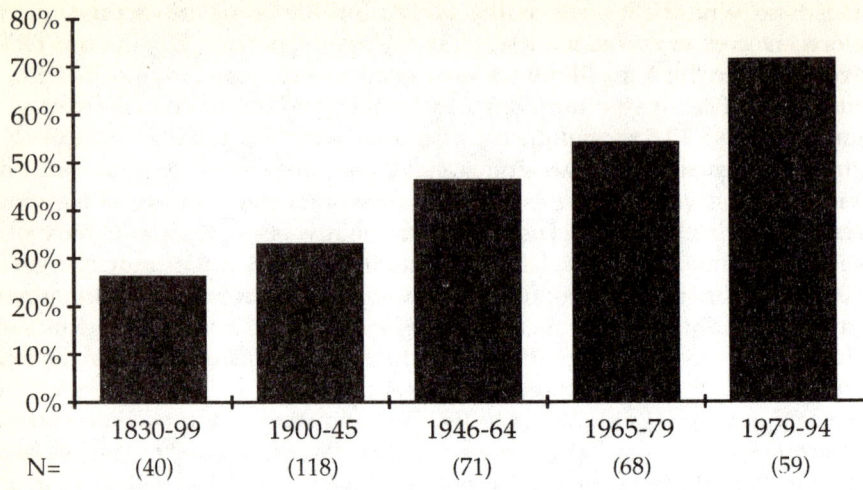

Fig. 8.1 Careerist permanent secretaries with at least one year's absence from Whitehall after entry to the civil service

from Whitehall after entering the civil service.

The trend is unmistakably an upward one, accelerating steadily since 1945 and especially among those appointed from 1979. Periods spent abroad are and have throughout the present century been the most common types of experience away from Whitehall. This is partly accounted for by the careers of those in the diplomatic service. Even with the exclusion of this group, service abroad has accounted for a broad average throughout this century of some two-thirds of all absences from Whitehall. Two things have changed over the years in connection with periods spent abroad. First, they now constitute a higher proportion of a greater number of secondments. Many more permanent secretaries of recent decades have therefore done a stint abroad. Second, there has been a changing emphasis in the nature of such stints. Prior to 1945, postings were normally to a British base abroad, though a number of permanent secretaries also served for periods of less than a year during the era of international conferences – especially those held between the wars (e.g. in Paris, Geneva, Ottawa). Since 1945, and particularly from the 1960s, there has been a tendency to serve in the bureaucracies of one of the international organizations. Britain's membership of the European Union has obviously been a major factor here. Other organizations such as NATO, the UN, the World Bank, the International Monetary Fund (IMF) and the OECD have also featured in the careers of permanent secretaries. One-third of all post-1979 careerist incumbents have served at least one twelve month spell in the offices of one of these organizations. A smaller proportion – one in six since 1945 – have served in public bodies adjacent to Whitehall, such as the NEDC, NBPI. Few have served in the regions – fewer in fact since 1945 than between the wars. This is a type of movement for which it is hoped to create enhanced opportunities (Efficiency Unit 1993, p. 9). But secondment to regional offices has often been seen as a career cul-de-sac. Most members of the elite corps have been sent out to a region only in exceptional circumstances or in moments of crisis, such as during the last world war. A rare example among recent post-holders is Peter Harrop. He was Chairman, and for a while also Regional Director, of the Yorkshire and Humberside Economic Planning Board during the early 1970s. He was at that time an under secretary, later becoming second permanent secretary within the same department, the DoE. Few also have been seconded to private industry – only three among careerists who have become permanent secretaries since 1979. One of them, David Fell, also spent a year as a sales manager with Rank Hovis McDougal Ltd, three years before he entered the civil service. This raises two further questions about the experience gained by careerist permanent secretaries outside Whitehall. First, what is the duration of such experience? Second, how fresh is it by the time they become permanent secretaries?

The outside experience of most careerist permanent secretaries has been of relatively brief duration – at least in the context of their life long association with Whitehall. This cannot be said of those who have headed the FCO and who spent most if not the whole of their careers in the diplomatic service. But among the others, the vast majority (90 per cent) of all permanent secretaries since 1945 have spent a total of less than five years away from Whitehall. Five years is the minimum period spent in other activities prior to joining the civil service in order to qualify as a semi-careerist by the definition employed in this chapter. Even since 1979, fewer than one in five of the careerists have had sufficiently long periods of secondment to equate in this respect with semi-careerists. Moreover, relatively few, excluding those in the diplomatic service, have had experience outside Whitehall in the years immediately prior to becoming permanent secretary. There are, of course, different schools of thought as to when in the duration of a career a secondment or posting is most beneficial. Some would say that the formative years are best. Others prefer mid-career. Few would insist upon a break from Whitehall immediately prior to a permanent secretaryship. On the other hand, an experience that is too dim and distant may have lost much of its utility if the main value is the freshness of a different environment. During the inter-war and early post-war years spells away from Whitehall tended to take place at more senior levels: the higher the grade the greater the incidence of secondments. Since the mid-1960s, there has been a more even spread. Only one in seven reached the top within five years of their return to Whitehall. Conversely, for approximately half of them, secondment was followed by at least ten years back in Whitehall prior to becoming permanent secretary.

This brief survey has shown that, in recent times, career servants have had less the appearance of cloistered mandarins than did their predecessors. Moreover, the above calculations ignore the greater extent to which the modern mandarin gets out of Whitehall for shorter periods. For example, Antony Part had only one formal twelve month absence from Whitehall – that on a civil service commonwealth fellowship to the USA. Yet his career took him to twenty-seven different countries (Part 1990, p. 17). Do the wider horizons of the modern careerist compensate for the broader experience brought to bear by the stronger presence of outsiders and semi-careerists of the last century and down to 1914? Qualitatively it is impossible to say. It bears repeating, though, that many of the outsiders of the last century were drawn from the wider orbit of government and the public service. Few were completely unknown within Whitehall.

If a qualitative assessment remains elusive, it is possible crudely to calculate the proportion among all permanent secretaries who have had 'open' careers. Within this category can be included all outsiders and semi-careerists. We may also include those careerists who spent at least five years outside Whitehall, or three years where the most recent such experience was within ten years of becoming a permanent secretary. With these definitions, Fig. 8.2 estimates Whitehall's changing proximity to the extremes of open (all permanent secretaries having open careers) and closed states (all having closed careers).

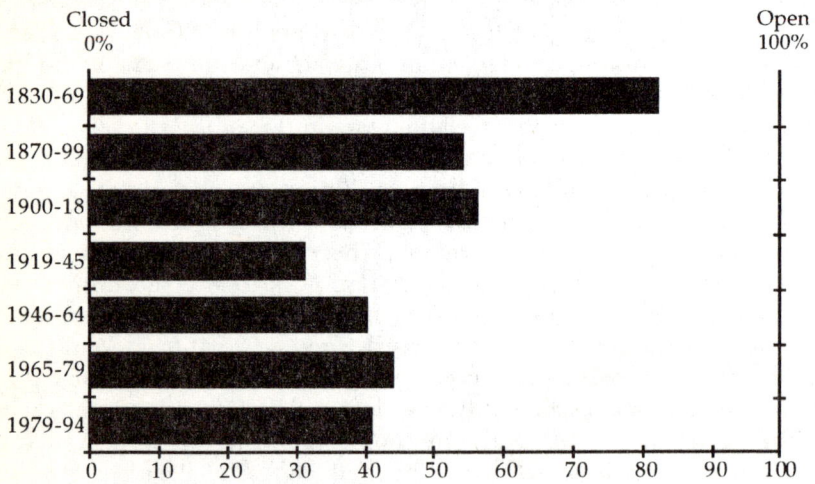

Fig. 8.2   Whitehall's openness, as measured by the proportion of permanent secretaries with open or closed careers

On this aggregate basis and employing the above definitions of open and closed careers, Whitehall has never recaptured the relative openness of the mid-nineteenth century, or even of the decades around the turn of the present century – at least not among its permanent secretaries. The inter-war years marked the height of Whitehall's insularity. It has been less insular since 1945. But the wider experience enjoyed by careerists in recent years has not been sufficient to effect substantially greater openness. This vindicates Peter Hennessy's point that unless there is to be a change in career patterns, greater openness is likely to come only from the import of more outsiders and semi-careerists. This may be facilitated by the higher salaries to be paid to permanent secretaries and to other senior mandarins (see Chapter 1). Time only will tell whether greater financial rewards will induce greater numbers of outsiders into Whitehall. For some, this remains an imperative. For others, it carries the risk of jeopardy to the virtues of impartiality, neutrality and objectivity. Much would depend upon the way in which outsiders were used. The historical analysis of this chapter shows that outsiders were used in the nineteenth century entirely without threat to the constitutional role of the civil service. Their roles as civil servants were well understood and, in the vast majority of cases, adhered to with punctiliousness. This was then a vital condition for the successful assimilation of outsiders, especially those from the world of politics. It would be nothing less than vital today. The same strictures of propriety apply to careerists, too. Moreover, it is not only a question of constitutional propriety but also of the efficient conduct of government. Both constitutional propriety and efficiency have been implicit and often explicit in much of this chapter. In the next chapter, the discussion is fixed more firmly upon operational efficiency and upon the conduciveness to efficiency of one particular aspect of many permanent secretaries' careers – the interdepartmental transfer.

9 The dance of the mandarins: interdepartmental mobility within Whitehall

Introduction

The last chapter focused upon civil servants and the outside world. This one turns the spotlight back within Whitehall. It examines a particular feature of permanent secretaries' careers: transfers between different departments. Since the nineteenth century there has been debate about the desirability or otherwise of staff mobility between departments in Whitehall. For some, interdepartmental transfers are a valuable ingredient in the mandarin's career development. Others, however, either see little virtue in the principle or are critical of the way in which transfers have been handled. The first section of this chapter therefore outlines the main arguments and counter-arguments as they have been advanced from the Northcote-Trevelyan Report onwards. The second section examines the extent of interdepartmental mobility. It shows the number of departments served by permanent secretaries in different periods. It measures the incidence of transfers year by year over a span of some one hundred years. In this way it is possible to pinpoint trends and to link them with specific events and developments. It will be seen, for example, that the effects upon mobility of the two world wars were greater than the conscious efforts of Warren Fisher during the 1920s and '30s.

In the third and final section, attention is turned to the nature of interdepartmental mobility. It will be shown that, despite intentions to the contrary, transfers over the last quarter of a century have been only slightly more frequently contained within areas of related activity. This further confirms one of the broad themes of this chapter – the triumph of events over ideas and designs.

Mobility within Whitehall: a century of debate

The ability to move between departments implies the philosophy of the all-rounder, the adaptable generalist. That Charles Trevelyan and Stafford Northcote upheld these Macaulayan ideals is not in doubt. Nor is the fact that they envisaged a common service, one whose homogeneity at senior levels would facilitate transfers between departments (Northcote-Trevelyan 1854, p. 18; p. 23). These broad principles they nevertheless tempered with an important caveat. In answering some of their critics they declared: 'We have nowhere suggested or even hinted at the idea of transferring men from one office to another in cases where the business is not of a cognate character' (Re-organisation Papers 1855, p. 421). This was essentially a statement about the extent of departmental mobility compatible with efficiency. A similarly cautious approach was expressed twenty years later by the Playfair Commission. Playfair saw value in transfers, especially during early career and provided they were made judiciously. It counselled against frequent transfers, recognizing the special character of much of the work in Whitehall (Playfair 1875, p. 29). Such sentiments were echoed by the Ridley Commission (1888, para. 31, p. xiii). As the Great War approached, views seem to have become more polarized. The majority of the MacDonnell Commission (1914, p. 60) were adamant that: 'Promotion to the higher grades should be determined by the selection of the most competent officers, to whatever class or department they belong, subject to the approval of the Treasury'. The minority members of the Commission took a different view. They held that 'for all but a few of the higher situations, promotions must run in the departments, and not on a service basis' (Ibid., p. 150).

These differences notwithstanding, Warren Fisher had in mind something more far-reaching than anything previously countenanced. He told the Tomlin Commission (Evidence 1930-31, Q. 18, 695) that the best man may be serving in the department in which the vacancy occurred, but that there was a good deal to be said for 'musical chairs'. This view was explicitly predicated upon his conception of permanent secretaries as 'general managers', not experts (Ibid., Q. 18, 697). He was aware of the potential damage to morale in appointing from outside a department but thought that this was outweighed by the benefits to the civil service as a whole.

Fisher's design is widely assumed to have become the reality. It has been claimed that, under his influence, the transferring of senior officials gained general acceptance soon after the First World War (O'Halpin 1989, p. 75). He is thought to have effected a rapid acceleration in the incidence of mobility within Whitehall. It is thereby assumed that he transformed a position in which transfers were rare into one in which they became common, perhaps to the point of excess (Hamilton 1951, pp. 25-6; Fry 1969, pp. 56-8; Greenaway 1983, pp. 133-4). He is said to have succeeded by 1932 in his broader aim of fostering a corporate spirit among the higher echelons (O'Halpin 1989, p. 182). Greater mobility between departments may be presumed to be both a manifestation of and an underpinning for the enhancement of such a corporate spirit.

Undoubtedly Fisher inspired a generation and more of senior officials – perhaps more the up and coming mandarins of the inter-war years than his own contemporaries. John Woods, one of Fisher's protégés, was adamant that the vision of a single *corps d'élite* was both right in principle and had proven its worth in practice. Central to this was frequent movement from one department to another, especially in and out of the Treasury (Woods 1954, p.376). Wilfred Morton, like Woods weaned on the Fisher tradition, put the argument as eloquently and unequivocally as had ever his mentor:

> A completely different environment on work very largely different, and with colleagues who are for a time comparative strangers, provides a test and a challenge of very considerable order… disturbance and discomfort can induce extra growth in the right kind of human plant. The special effort of adaptation and application to unfamiliar work help to bring out full power… (also) the different experience adds to the knowledge, to the store of reference of the individual… so, in suitable cases and where circumstances are found favourable, we aim to provide the shock treatment – the object is greater stretch through wider experience. (Morton 1963, p. 32).

This was certainly a claim for mobility more ambitious than that made by Edward Bridges who, as Head of the Home Civil Service between 1945-56, bore the principal custodianship of the Fisher tradition (Bridges 1950, p. 25). Morton's confidence was no doubt fortified by the Plowden Report. Plowden had endorsed the practice of 'a careful system of selection and interchange between departments in order that the best individuals may ultimately emerge in the most senior posts' (HM Treasury 1961, para. 48). The Report stated with satisfaction 'a growing realization… that in place of single departments dealing with individual problems in comparative isolation, the public interest requires a team pursuing its common objectives with a single purpose' (Ibid., p. 3). This implied an achievement more recent than the Fisher era. Indeed neither among his own contemporaries nor among the generation that followed did Fisher's notion of 'musical chairs' prevail without challenge. The FDA complained to the Tomlin Commission that transfers – at least those involving promotions – were inimical to the principle of promotion by merit. The FDA believed that it was not possible to equate relative merits in different parts of the service (Tomlin Evidence 1930-31, Q. 12, 986). Others, weighing up the pros and cons, gave more credence to the latter (Dale 1941, pp. 224-7). Even as Plowden was extolling the virtues of common objectives and a single purpose, one of the permanent secretaries of the day observed that : 'When one looks from department to department, or even inside one department, one finds very considerable differences' (Dunnett 1961, p. 227). This reflects an emphasis clearly different from that of John Woods or Wilfred Morton and the spirit of Fisherism. It is perhaps more compatible with that of Northcote-Trevelyan a century earlier. Much turns upon the extent to which movement takes place between departments whose activities are considered to be of a cognate character.

There have been two main bones of contention over the last thirty years. One is that civil servants are moved too frequently between too many departments. The other is that movements have been capricious rather than carefully directed; that they have had little apparent regard to the nature of the work. The Fulton Committee acknowledged many of the virtues claimed for mobility so long as transfers were at less frequent intervals and between more closely related areas of activity. They should also take greater account of the wishes and aptitudes of the individual civil servant (Fulton 1968, para. 115). This was part of Fulton's wider strategy of 'preference for relevance'. It was an echo of Northcote-Trevelyan's plea for transfers to be kept within areas of cognate character.

Fulton had received evidence that the frequent and seemingly capricious mobility of senior personnel had been detrimental to the efficient conduct of business. It had been claimed that movements took place from one post to another with 'no necessary relationship between them' (Plowden, Deakin and Mayall 1968, para. 5, p. 999). These critics observed tartly: 'the more one learns about the probation service or restrictive practices legislation, the nearer one comes to the moment of transfer to deal with the problems of Ulster' (Ibid., p. 1000). Another remarked that Whitehall seemed to take 'a positively malicious pleasure in putting square pegs into round holes' (Jay 1968, para. 20, p. 933). Such observations were not novel. Similar anxieties had been voiced long before Fulton (Chorley 1944, p. 122). But the Fulton era was more receptive to Whitehall's transparent absurdities. Few now were prepared to embrace unreconstructed Fisherism. In its evidence to the English Committee, the CSD was highly apologetic about the 'practical difficulties of achieving more stable and better planned careers for senior civil servants' (Expenditure Committee 1977b, vol. II (part I), para. 86). Douglas Allen, Head of the Home Civil Service, was similarly cautious. He was at pains to bury the caricature of the all-rounder so squarely condemned by

Fulton. He denied that there existed 'a type of mind which is relatively untutored and which can adapt to everything' (Ibid., Q. 30). Ian Bancroft, later to succeed Allen, acknowledged that assistant and under secretaries were often moved too frequently. In Whitehall's defence he pleaded the intrusion of 'organizational and policy turbulence' (Ibid., Q. 733).

The implications of all this are clear. The most genuine intentions have often run aground when pitched against the immediate necessities and practical implications of running a large, complex organization in an uncertain world. Career planning is a tricky business. Nor is there by any means complete agreement as to where the balance lies between the supposed virtues and the alleged drawbacks of interdepartmental mobility. Some continue to emphasize the virtues of regular postings. According to Chapman (1988, p. 303) these include:

> ... an effective check against influence in some areas of government activity (especially areas like the Tax Inspectorate); they moderate the perfectly understandable enthusiasms of officials; they minimise demoralisation in the civil service when policies are reversed; and they help to maintain common standards of professional conduct in the civil service as a whole.

These virtues are, it will be noted, quite different in emphasis from those identified by Wilfred Morton. They reflect a different era and a different context. Few if any today would support the wilful 'musical chairs' approach. Yet others continue to complain that career patterns are eclectic; that there is too much rapid mobility between posts which have little in common (Plowden 1994, p. 33). Others again have seen such mobility as a contributory factor in the underperformance of Whitehall, hence of Britain's economy (Pollard 1984, pp. 154-5). Pollard does not condemn the practice out of hand. Rather he claims that 'both its virtues and its failings work in the wrong directions' (Ibid., p. 156). In its interim report on the role of the civil service the Treasury and Civil Service Committee received complaints about the frequency of movement from post to post. In the language but certainly not in the spirit of Warren Fisher such movements were now condemned, by Professor Eric Caines, as 'a musical chairs style of managing' (TCSC 1993, p. 186).

Whitehall remains sensitive to many of these criticisms. An independent study commissioned in 1992 for the Efficiency Unit found that some 60 per cent of respondents in grades 1 - 3 had been two years or less in their current posts (Efficiency Unit 1993, p. 49). The Oughton Report itself acknowledged the existence of a culture which has 'sometimes confused job rotation with career development' (Ibid., p. 49, para. 6.22). It called for 'career anchors' – the delineation of one or two areas of work around which mobility would revolve (Ibid., p. 50, para. 6.24). This was a reincarnation of Fulton's 'preference for relevance' and of Northcote-Trevelyan's 'cognate' areas of work. The government endorsed these ideas to the extent that it wanted greater interchange of staff between departments, and between departments and executive agencies, but with Oughton-style career anchors (Cabinet Office 1994, p. 39). It wanted the OPSS to play a role in 'promoting movements between departments in the context of the annual succession planning bilaterals' (Ibid., p. 39). Mobility therefore continues to be seen as a virtue – especially mobility between the central departments and the spending departments (TCSC 1994b, Qs. 1436-7). It is also the intention to encourage individual civil servants to assume greater responsibility for their own careers – a deliberate further move away from centrally planned career management (Efficiency Unit 1993, p. 39, para. 5.7). It remains to be seen whether it will prove possible to reconcile individual preferences with the corporate needs of the service; and whether, in the absence of strong central direction, it will be possible to control both the frequency and the nature of staff mobility. We can nevertheless examine more carefully the trends as reflected in the careers of permanent secretaries, the focus for the rest of this chapter.

The extent of mobility, the chronology of change

One simple measure of mobility is the number of departments in which permanent secretaries have served during their careers in Whitehall. Table 9.1 shows the figures for permanent secretaries appointed in each of seven periods between 1830-1994. The table includes only those who spent their entire careers in Whitehall – that is those defined as careerists in the last chapter. Outsiders and semi-careerists are excluded. So too are those who spent their careers in the diplomatic service and who went on to head the FCO. Their careers are untypical in that they involve movements between the FCO and various postings abroad rather than transfers between departments in Whitehall. Table 9.1 incorporates a further refinement. So far as possible, movements directly consequential upon departmental reorganizations are excluded from the calculations. The purpose is to measure genuine interdepartmental mobility rather than the restructuring that has taken place from time-to-time by the creation of new departments, the merging of existing ones or the transfer of functions between departments. On this basis the table shows the number of departments in which individuals served both throughout their careers (or careers to date) and also prior to their becoming permanent secretaries.

   A few comments may be made about the figures. The heyday of the one department permanent secretary was the mid-nineteenth century. Even then nearly one-third of these careerists served in more than one department,

Table 9.1
Number of departments served by careerist permanent secretaries, 1830-1994

No. Depts.	1830-69 A %	1830-69 B %	1870-99 A %	1870-99 B %	1900-18 A %	1900-18 B %	1919-45 A %	1919-45 B %	1946-64 A %	1946-64 B %	1965-79 A %	1965-79 B %	1979-94 A %	1979-94 B %
1	94	69	44	36	57	40	45	26	20	16	20	14	18	13
2	6	25	44	30	23	23	29	22	32	18	26	20	24	20
3	-	6	6	18	17	16	17	26	28	23	28	28	36	34
4	-	-	6	9	3	9	5	16	14	23	11	17	16	16
5	-	-	-	4	-	9	1	3	3	9	11	15	4	13
6 or over	-	-	-	3	-	3	3	7	3	11	4	6	2	4
Total %	100	100	100	100	100	100	100	100	100	100	100	100	100	100
Av. no. depts.	1.1	1.4	1.8	2.4	1.7	2.4	2.0	2.7	2.6	3.4	2.8	3.2	2.7	3.1
N=	(16)		(23)		(35)		(76)		(64)		(65)		(55)	

A = before becoming permanent secretary
B = entire careers

often transferring at permanent secretary level. And by the late-nineteenth century, the majority had seen the inside of two or more departments by the time they became permanent secretaries. Any simplistic notion about senior civil servants of the nineteenth century never having transferred between departments is clearly misplaced. They did transfer, though not so frequently as did later generations. Moreover, some of the transfers were of a highly personal nature, at the behest of ministers who wanted to retain the services of a trusted aide. It is difficult to say exactly what proportion of the transfers were of this type: at least a third of those taking place between the 1830s and the 1870s would not be an over-estimate. This type of mobility probably began to decline towards the end of the nineteenth century. There was as yet neither the formal machinery nor any compelling impulse to establish the more routine, institutionalized type of transfer which was to emerge as the twentieth century unfolded. This may explain the partial reversion in the trend among those appointed between 1900-18.

The one department permanent secretary has not become extinct but has been comparatively rare since 1945. Centralized arrangements for the filling of top posts have prevented departments from sustaining any tradition of in-house promotions. The nearest to any such tradition has been in the Ministry of Agriculture, Fisheries and Food (MAFF). Five of MAFF's ten post-1945 permanent secretaries had never previously served in any other Whitehall department. This includes the one second permanent secretary, Frederick Kearns (1973-78). In addition, Derek Andrews (1987-93) was on secondment from MAFF when he was a private secretary to Harold Wilson in the 1960s. On the other hand, MAFF has been headed by three post-war permanent secretaries who were completely new to the department – Alan Hitchman (1952-59), John Winnifrith (1959-67) and Alan Neale (1973-78). Four successive heads of the Post Office spent their entire careers there. The last of these, Ronald German, was succeeded in 1966 by an outsider, John Wall. But the Post Office was set to become a public corporation in 1968. It was quite untypical, an exception to the rule.

Most post-war incumbents have served in at least three departments. Usually they have done so by the time they become permanent secretaries. But the hyper-mobility of the mid-twentieth century seems to have been curbed somewhat. There has been no recent repetition of the careers of Henry Self or Henry Hardman. Both served in nine departments, reaching permanent secretary level in 1942 and 1949 respectively. Nor since John Anderson (Viscount Waverley) has anyone held permanent secretaryships in five different departments. This he did between 1917-32, though his brief tenure at the Irish Office in 1920 was facilitated by secondment from his chairmanship of the Board of Inland Revenue. On the other hand, Table 9.1 understates the general upward trend in mobility during the second half of the twentieth century. This is because some civil servants – an increasing number – have made several moves to and fro between the same two, or perhaps three, departments. Approximately a quarter of all post-1945 careerist permanent secretaries made at least five transfers during their careers. This is double the proportion among permanent secretaries of the inter-war years. There is little doubt that some sort of acceleration was in train before 1945.

The precise chronology of the trends in mobility may be seen more clearly from the graph in Fig. 9.1. The graph is an index of mobility based upon the number of transfers year by year over a one hundred year period from the late-nineteenth to the late-twentieth century. Calculations rest upon the number of transfers per year for every permanent secretary and future permanent secretary in post. The mobility index for any given year is:

$$\frac{\text{no. of transfers}}{\text{no. perm. secs. and future perm. secs.}} \times 1000$$

Fig 9.1 incorporates five year moving averages. The figure for, say, 1955 is therefore an average for the years 1953-57 inclusive; that for 1956 is the average for 1954-58, and so on. This allows both for temporary aberrations and for imperfections in some of the raw data (e.g. the exact date a particular transfer took place). At senior levels, especially, one transfer can set off a chain reaction, so exaggerating the levels of mobility in any one year. In any case, no importance should be attached to the absolute values: the sole purpose of Fig. 9.1 is to show the chronology of the trends. It is not possible, however, to chart a reliable trend beyond the late-1960s, certainly not

174 *The Elite of the Elite*

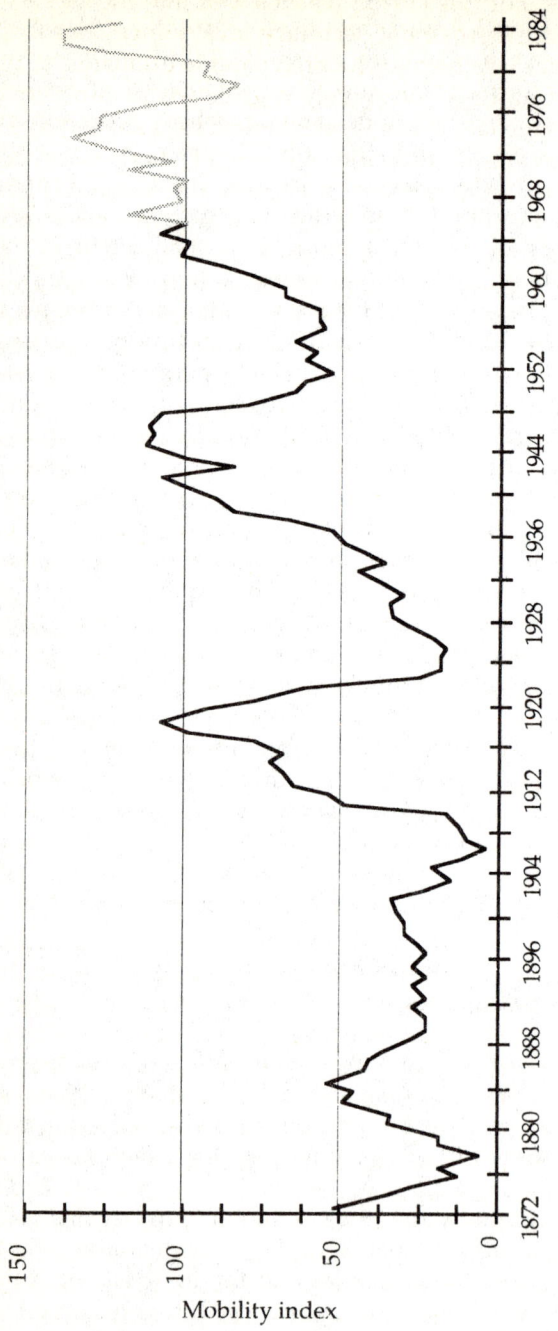

Fig. 9.1 Interdepartmental transfers: mobility index, 1872–1984

beyond the mid-1980s. For this period reaches well into the careers of many who are as yet to reach permanent secretary level. Since transfers are less common in early career (see below) the unavoidable exclusion of this group leaves the figures registering deceptively high levels of mobility. For this reason the trend from the late-1960s is represented by a shaded line.

As noted in the previous section, it was Warren Fisher's policy to encourage mobility among the mandarinate. It is generally assumed that he succeeded. But it is clear from Fig. 9.1 that this view requires substantial modification. Much of the first decade of Fisher's headship of the civil service was marked by falling levels of mobility – levels that were no greater than they had been during the 1880s and for much of the 1890s. Not until the late-1930s did mobility reach the peacetime peak of the pre-1914 period, stimulated then by the Liberals' social welfare reforms and in particular by the establishment in 1912 of the Health Insurance Commission. The Commission was largely staffed by civil servants brought in at short notice from other departments. It became known in Whitehall as the 'loan collection' (Bridges 1950, p. 12). This, followed by the exigencies of the 1914-18 war, elevated the levels of mobility to new heights that were unlikely to be sustained. Nevertheless, it was not until the late-1930s that Fisher began to achieve mobility on the scale of the 1880s or the immediate pre-First World War era. And not until the early 1940s was there any return to the peaks experienced during the Great War.

Unlike the peaks of mobility achieved during the Great War, those of the Second World War were sustained for a time after 1945. The comparative trough of the 1950s was considerably higher than it had been almost throughout the inter-war period. No doubt the abstract philosophy of interdepartmental transfers had become imprinted in the Whitehall psyche. But the hard practicalities of war were clearly a major factor in stimulating higher levels of mobility between 1939-45 than had existed previously. These practicalities did not necessarily imply centralized direction. Rather they involved a multiplicity of ad hoc solutions to meet specific staffing requirements. There was greater flexibility but little planned career management. This is partly reflected in the proportion of transfers involving the Treasury and other central economic departments (Inland Revenue, Customs and Excise, but not the Cabinet Office). These departments accounted for nearly a third of all transfers below permanent secretary level between the wars. During the Second World War they assumed no more than a quarter, as interdepartmental transfers broadened their embrace out of sheer necessity. But during the first post-war decade (1946-55 inclusive) the proportion doubled to around half of all transfers. The managed economy – of which the Treasury was the main pivot within Whitehall – now played its role in sustaining these quite high levels of mobility. All in all, then, the exigencies of the two world wars and of the managed economy had greater purchase than did either Warren Fisher's abstract vision or the immediate effects of his policies.

None of this is completely to deny Fisher's achievement. Two points may be made on his behalf. First, as already noted, many of the transfers of the late-nineteenth century were of a personalized nature. What Fisher did was to nurture a more institutionalized type of transfer as part of the Whitehall routine. That he presided over a period of declining mobility says as much about the exceptional circumstances of the war years that preceded his headship of the civil service as it does about the limits of his achievements. Second, Fisher's importance lies perhaps more in the legacy he bequeathed than in the sheer number of transfers he was able to effect during his own day. He may be accorded some indirect credit (or blame) for the levels of mobility approaching and sometimes exceeding those of wartime which became part of the landscape after 1945. Exactly how much is impossible to say. Obviously other factors were making their mark by the 1960s and '70s, arguably the high-tide of peacetime planning, interventionism and institutional reform. For reasons already mentioned, the mobility index from the late-1960s must be interpreted with the greatest care. It almost certainly overstates the levels of mobility by its emphasis on the higher grades. It is in fact worth examining the levels of seniority at which transfers have taken place as part of a broader analysis of the nature of mobility.

The nature of mobility

Comment has already been made about the tendency in the nineteenth century for some permanent secretaries to move laterally, taking a permanent secretaryship in another department. In the mid-nineteenth century the majority of transfers were at permanent secretary level. As Table 9.2 shows, transfers at and to this level have, since 1919, continued to be more common in the careers of permanent secretaries than transfers within or promotions to any other grade.

For permanent secretaries of the inter-war years top level transfers were considerably more common than those in the lower grades. This provides a further insight into the Fisher years. Fisher was able to achieve greater mobility at the most senior levels where, through the appointments procedures described in Chapter 7, he had a direct influence upon matters. But he was less successful in infusing the spirit of musical chairs at the middle and lower levels where he had no formal authority. Indeed it seems to have been the general practice during the inter-war years to leave the more junior graded officials long enough in post to become familiar with the work (Russell-Smith 1974, p. 83). Even in the careers of post-holders of the last thirty years half the transfers have been at permanent and deputy secretary level – the appoint-

Table 9.2
Incidence of transfers, by grade, among careerist permanent secretaries appointed between 1919-94

Grade (Transfer within or promotion to)	1919-45 %	1946-64 %	1965-79 %	1979-94 %
Perm. Sec.	42	33	26	25
Dep. Sec.	10	25	25	24
Under Sec.*	11	11	17	15
Assist. Sec.	13	8	10	12
Principal/Assist Principal	20	19	17	22
Other/not known	4	4	5	2
Total %	100	100	100	100
No. transfers	(150)	(204)	(189)	(178)

* incl. principal assistant secretary

ments in which SASC is involved. There have been comparatively fewer transfers in the lower and middle grades, especially at assistant secretary level.

It is a moot point as to what the figures in Table 9.2 betray about the nature of interdepartmental transfers. What is striking is the broad consistency of the patterns, especially since 1945. As with the secondments described in the last chapter, opinions vary as to the best stage at which to make a transfer. One permanent secretary interviewed for this book made his first transfer when he was a deputy secretary. This, he said, was too late in his career, If this is so then the figures in Table 9.2 suggest that Whitehall has failed to capitalize on the potential benefits that may accrue from earlier interdepartmental mobility.

There is a further indication both of the nature and of the utility of interdepartmental transfers. As noted in the earlier discussion, importance has often been attached to the areas of work between which transfers take place. It is possible to identify a number of areas each of which have a recognizable integrity. Each area will embrace a number of cognate departments. We may then establish whether mobility has been confined within any one such area; or whether it has been spread across different areas. For this purpose six areas are identified. They are listed below together with the main departments in each area.

Economic and central services: Cabinet Office (incl. MPO, OMCS/OPSS); CPRS; CSO; Civil Service Commission; CSD; Board of Customs and Excise; DEA; Ministry of Economic Warfare; Board of Inland Revenue; Privy Council Office (incl. Lord President's Office); HM Treasury.

Defence and technical: Admiralty; Air Ministry; Ministry of

Blockade; Ministry of Civil Aviation; MoD; Ministry of Munitions; Ministry of Supply; Mintech; DSIR; War Office.

External and territorial: Colonial Office; CRO (Dominions Office); FCO; India Office; Irish Office; Northern Ireland Office; ODA; Scottish Office (incl. Scottish departments); Welsh Office.

Regulatory: MAFF; Charity Commission; General Registry Office; DoE (MHLG); Local Government Board; Home Office; Ministry of Home Security; Department of Prices and Consumer Protection; Ministry of Shipping; DTI; Department of Transport.

Social and other services: DFE (DES/Ministry of Education); Department of Employment (Ministry of Labour); Department of Health (DHSS); DSS; National Assistance Board (Unemployment Assistance); MPNI (incl. National Insurance Commission); Post Office.

Physical resources: Central Land Board; Department of Energy; MFP; Ministry of Materials; Mines Department; Ministry of Production; MPBW.

Needless to say these six areas by no means constitute definitive categories. Other areas of activity could be delineated with equal justification. A more refined classification would increase the number of areas or categories – but more categories would increase the chances of a transfer traversing into a non-cognate area. Conversely, there could be fewer and broader categories, in which case there would be a higher ratio of intra to inter-area transfers. But this would involve placing within one category departments whose work was quite dissimilar. In any case, the placing within any one category of a particular department will be contentious. The disparate activities of some departments could justify their inclusion in more than one of the specified categories. Moreover, some departments have changed their character over time. Others have either merged or been broken up into separate entities. Sometimes these changes in the Whitehall landscape have themselves violated the boundaries between the six areas identified above. These niceties are only partly offset by the exclusion from the calculations of movements consequent upon the creation of new departments and the merger, fission or reallocation of functions between existing departments.

With these methodological complexities in mind, the overall trends are again perhaps more telling than the absolute figures. Nevertheless, Table 9.3 shows the number of areas in which permanent secretaries have served.

The picture that emerges is rather a mixed one. The majority have at all times remained within no more than two areas – approximately two-thirds except for those who became permanent secretaries between 1965-79. Fewer among the post-1979 group than at any other time spent their entire careers within one area. But fewer of these recent incumbents have experienced the more wide-ranging transfers embracing four or more areas. To this extent

Table 9.3
Number of cognate areas served by careerist permanent secretaries
appointed between 1919-94

No. areas	1919-45 %	1946-64 %	1965-79 %	1979-94 %
1	40	22	28	20
2	32	40	30	45
3	18	22	32	31
4	7	11	10	4
5	3	3	-	-
6	-	2	-	-
Total %	100	100	100	100
N=	(76)	(64)	(65)	(55)

Whitehall has made some gesture to Fulton's preference for relevance and Northcote-Trevelyan's cognate mobility. Levels of mobility have been maintained and indeed increased, while avoiding the extremities which, during the middle decades of the century, took a minority of individuals to many and disparate quarters of Whitehall. This provides some support to the testimony given to the English Committee in 1976 by Douglas Allen that efforts had been made from the late-1960s to keep movements within 'defined areas'. On the other hand, there has been little change since the First World War in the proportion of transfers which have taken place within rather than between cognate areas. For those who became permanent secretaries between 1919-79 the ratio of cognate to non-cognate transfers remained remarkably constant at almost exactly one to two. Among those appointed since 1979 the proportion of cognate transfers has risen slightly to 38 per cent of all transfers. If mobility had been perfectly random, then cognate transfers would account for a ratio of approximately one to five, or just under 17 per cent of all transfers. It is therefore important to maintain a sense of proportion in the analysis of mobility. Whitehall has succeeded only partially over the last couple of decades in establishing more coherent patterns of transfers between departments. The evidence of this chapter is that events have usually had a greater bearing than conscious design or desire upon both the frequency and the nature of transfers. But patterns of mobility are not and never have been quite so capricious as some of the fiercer critics allege.

Two other observations give further support to this conclusion. First, mobility between non-cognate departments is not always synonymous with migration to an area of work completely new to the individual civil servant. The main focus of the work in two departments may be quite different: but there may be specific points of intersection, to say nothing of common activities such as finance, staffing, procurement and so forth. Second, a good deal of career mobility takes place within departments. This is not reflected in the foregoing analysis. Such mobility is, by the definition used in this chapter, within a cognate area. On the other hand, this means that the sheer extent of mobility from post to post is greater than the figures suggest. By how much it is difficult to say since there are no reliable and comprehensive data for intradepartmental movements. It is nevertheless possible to combine the focus of this chapter with that of the previous chapter – that is to say conflating transfers between departments with periods of secondment from Whitehall. It may be that spells away from Whitehall are in themselves beneficial but become detrimental when augmented by more frequent movements within Whitehall. Here there has emerged a significant trend since 1945. Among permanent secretaries of the first two post-war decades, one in five made at least five career moves, either interdepartmental transfers or secondments outside Whitehall. This proportion almost doubled for those appointed between 1965-79 and has edged up to 45 per cent among the post-1979 group.

It is clear that more recently appointed post-holders have experienced greater career mobility of one sort or another even if this has incurred less likelihood of transfers between non-cognate areas of work. Whether this is a good thing or a bad thing is less clear. As we saw in the discussion with which this chapter opened, there has never been universal agreement as to what exactly constitutes the ideal career pattern for an aspiring permanent secretary. The notion of an ideal is in one sense perhaps an illusion: variations upon a theme would seem a more credible prospect. Whatever the case, the evidence of this chapter suggests that the force of events would make difficult the realization of any ideal that did receive universal or near universal acclaim. Moreover, the proposed variegated salary levels for different permanent secretaryships (see Chapter 1) will introduce a further complication. Much will depend upon the magnitude of the disparities that begin to emerge. If there were to be, say, two or three clear bands within the hierarchy of remuneration but with some overlap, then transfers at permanent secretary level could, in principle, continue with little hindrance. Otherwise, mobility may be concentrated more heavily upon groups of posts carrying commensurate salaries. Whether commensurate salaries will correspond to cognate areas of activity is, again, another matter. This, together with a more job-specific approach to the filling of senior posts, may have a bearing both upon the extent and upon the nature of future patterns of mobility. For it is at senior levels, including that of permanent secretary itself, that mobility has been greatest. And at these levels it has often in the past been between non-cognate departments. This may have had a bearing upon the capacity of permanent secretaries to run their departments – or at least upon the way that they run their departments. It may also have a bearing upon their roles relative to ministers. The next chapter therefore looks, among other things, at the degrees of familiarity that both permanent secretaries and their ministers have had with their departments.

10 Strangers in paradise? Permanent secretaries, ministers and their departments

Introduction

This chapter completes the profile of permanent secretaries' careers. It builds upon some of the findings of previous chapters. It also provides a platform for the next chapter which will examine the contribution of permanent secretaries to the performance of government.

The first section of this chapter looks briefly at the ages at which people have become permanent secretaries. This links in with the length of time they spend in the civil service both before reaching the top and while remaining permanent secretaries. As noted in the last chapter, most modern permanent secretaries have transferred between departments. Some transfers have been between cognate, or connected, areas of work. Many have been between departments whose work is not of cognate character. This increases the chances of permanent secretaries coming to head departments of which they have had little or no previous experience. The second section of this chapter therefore examines the extent to which permanent secretaries have had previous experience in their departments. The third and final section focuses upon the respective experience of permanent secretaries and of cabinet ministers. This will include an analysis of turnover in particular departments.

Age, previous service and tenure as permanent secretary

Table 10.1 shows the ages of individuals upon becoming permanent secretaries. It shows average ages, the distribution of ages and the standard deviation (SD). The latter is simply an expression of the variation around the average – the higher the SD the greater are the variations above and below the average; the lower the SD the greater the concentration around the average.

Table 10.1
Age upon appointment as permanent secretary

Age (years)	1830-69 %	1870-99 %	1900-18 %	1919-45 %	1946-64 %	1965-79 %	1979-94 %
Under 40	22	8	10	6	1	-	-
40-44	21	8	16	20	4	-	1
45-49	26	29	18	19	18	9	25
50-54	22	27	23	32	47	53	43
55-59	6	13	21	20	26	38	28
60 and over	3	15	12	3	4	-	3
Total %	100	100	100	100	100	100	100
Av. years	44.9	50.9	50.2	49.5	52.2	53.5	52.4
SD	8.3	7.3	7.8	6.2	4.5	2.9	3.5
N=	(55)	(47)	(57)	(95)	(83)	(81)	(72)

During the nineteenth century and down to 1914 average ages were lower than they have been in more recent times. There were also greater variations. This reflects the less systematic, more departmentally driven and therefore relatively uneven pattern of appointments. The majority were under fifty upon appointment as permanent secretary during the nineteenth century, over a quarter being under forty-five. The youngest, Ralph Lingen, was thirty when in 1849 he succeeded Kay-Shuttleworth at the Education Department. The under forties have been a rare breed since 1919, becoming almost extinct after 1945. The one such case and therefore the youngest post-war permanent secretary was Leslie Rowan. He was thirty-nine when, in 1947, he became Permanent Secretary of the short-lived Office of the Minister for Economic Affairs. Later that year he became a second (i.e. permanent) secretary at the Treasury.

The so called bureaucratic phenomenon has been largely responsible for the higher averages and for the more consistent patterns since 1945. The appointment of careerist permanent secretaries has not, in itself, been a significant factor. At any rate during the nineteenth century careerists tended to be younger than their fellow non-careerist permanent secretaries. Of greater import has been the routinization – in particular the greater central control and the tendency to look across the service rather than within one department when filling a vacancy. It is also a function of the more rigid and finely calibrated hierarchical structures that have existed in most departments over the last sixty or seventy years. These structures may often be by-passed in day-to-day operations (see Chapter 3) but the formal hierarchy is a mountain that all must climb en route to the top.

The trend towards a more concentrated pattern of older permanent secretaries reached its apogee in the 1970s. Since then the average age has declined slightly. Over a quarter of the post-1979 group were under fifty upon appointment, a higher proportion than at any time since the war. It is difficult to know to what extent this is the product of conscious policy. Margaret Thatcher was keen to appoint younger people (Peters 1986, p. 91). In fact the average age of permanent secretaries upon appointment under Thatcher was just over fifty-three years, only slightly less than the average during the 1960s and '70s. It is under John Major that younger people have come to the fore. Eight of the sixteen top jobs filled so far during his premiership have gone to people under fifty. The overall average is 50.4 years.

Why is age important? It betrays the character of an institution – for example the routinization and central control mentioned above. But for most observers it has more to do with the capacity of the post-holder. Politicians of different parties have expressed support for younger people – or at least for a system that allows talented younger people to come through the hierarchy more quickly (Young and Sloman 1982, pp. 55-7). A more radical proposal is the removal of all over the age of fifty. This has been advocated by Sir John Hoskyns (*The Times*, 7 December 1982). Others have suggested a less brutal and more selective pruning of officials between the ages of forty-five to sixty (Plowden 1994, p. 78). Permanent secretaries themselves have entered the fray. Edward Playfair (1968, p. 997) believed that the characteristics of a good top official were to be found in the comparatively young. He called for the compulsory retirement of deputy secretaries who, after seven and a half years in that grade, had not become permanent secretaries; and for the retirement of all after five years as permanent secretary. The implication is that older individuals have lost some of their vitality, ingenuity and flexibility. On the other hand Leo Pliatzky (1982) believes that he was a better civil servant when he was in his late-fifties, having the benefit of accumulated experience.

These arguments are difficult to resolve. Much depends upon the individual permanent secretary. Certainly some potential candidates have been ruled out because they were too young, as in the case of Richard Way in the 1950s (see Chapter 7). Others may have been considered too old. But the point is not simply one about age. It is also about the long haul through the hierarchy. Since 1945 it has taken an average of around thirty years for a career official to reach permanent secretary level. The appointment of rather younger people since 1979 has reduced this only slightly, though one in eight has reached the top in less than twenty-five years from first joining the civil service. This is a higher proportion than at any time since 1945 but it still means that the vast majority have had more than a quarter of a century in Whitehall by the time they reach the top.

What critics allege is that a long, slow haul through the hierarchy tends to sap the enterprise and initiative if not also the intellect of even the most able individuals. Such objections are nothing new (Beveridge 1920, p. 41). On the other hand, as noted in the last chapter, the justification for mobility between departments is that it keeps the highly tuned intellect at full stretch. But this may mean overstretch if it involves a succession of high pressure jobs. According to William Plowden: 'the best people are used again and again in the key jobs, the places where the jobs are under pressure and they can... generally lose the capacity for thought in the fullest sense of the term' (Young and Sloman 1982, p. 56). If this were true, it could mean that many civil servants' powers are already diminishing just as they reach the most demanding positions. One minister during the 1980s complained to a cabinet colleague about a certain individual who, he claimed, had retired in spirit the day he became permanent secretary (private information). There are two separate points here. One is the possible relaxation, conscious or otherwise, upon reaching the pinnacle of a career. The other is the sheer exhaustion consequent upon the long and demanding haul necessary to get there.

It is doubtful if more than a small minority are either consciously complacent or exhausted upon reaching permanent secretary level. The sheer momentum of life at the top makes it difficult to soft-pedal. Allied to this is the notion of 'energy elasticity' – the sheer exhilaration of being in a top job inducing extra reserves of vitality not evident earlier in an individual's career. This is true of some very senior politicians (Searing 1994, pp. 341-2). It may also be true among civil servants. In any case, if civil servants reach the top only toward the end of their careers then they are going to stay there for only a few years. Most permanent secretaries retire at sixty. Only a few stay on, though quite a number have left early, for various reasons. Retirement is compulsory at sixty-five under provisions initially introduced by an Order in Council issued in 1890. This was in part a response to the appointment the previous year of George Leach to head the newly created Board of Agriculture. Aged sixty-nine upon appointment, he is the oldest permanent secretary. He retired three years later.

The majority of modern incumbents have operated as permanent secretaries for five years or less before retiring or resigning from the civil service. This was true of approximately a third of those who were appointed between 1919 and the mid-1960s when the average span at permanent secretary level was a little over seven years. Since the mid-1960s, the average has been around five years. Over half (56 per cent) remained permanent secretary for five years or less and just over 20 per cent for less than three years. During this period only four individuals have served more than ten years at permanent secretary level – Antony Part (1965-76), Douglas Allen (1966-77), Brian Cubbon (1976-88) and Clive Whitmore (1983-94). None remained in the same post: all held more than one consecutive permanent secretaryship. There is unlikely to be any repeat of the pattern of the mid-nineteenth century when a quarter of all post-holders operated in Whitehall at permanent secretary level for over fifteen years. Even then, long spells at the top often involved heading two or more departments in succession. The most notable exception was Arthur Godley who, despite the initial controversy surrounding his appointment (see last chapter), spent twenty-six years as PUS at the India Office between 1883-1909. He turned down opportunities to head the War Office, the Colonial Office and the FO, hence his uncommonly long stay at the India Office (Kaminsky 1986, p. 230). Horace Hamilton is the longest serving among the six twentieth century permanent secretaries to have lasted twenty years or more. He held three permanent secretaryships in twenty-seven years between 1919-46. The last of the six to be appointed was Richard Hopkins in 1922. He, like the others, held more than one permanent secretaryship.

It is a characteristic already noted in the last chapter that some individuals move from one permanent secretaryship to another. This means that average periods spent in one post are lower than those spent at permanent secretary level. It is to the implications of this that we must now turn our attention.

Permanent secretaries and their departments

Table 10.2 below shows how long individuals have remained in any one permanent secretaryship. It illustrates even more clearly the trend towards briefer incumbencies.

Table 10.2
Tenure of permanent secretaryships

Tenure (years)	1830-69 %	1870-99 %	1900-18 %	1919-45 %	1945-64 %	1965-79 %	1979-94 %
Over 25	10	2	2	-	-	-	-
16-25	19	12	3	4	1	-	-
11-15	23	16	10	6	4	-	-
6-10	19	32	23	32	39	24	21
3-5	14	28	36	31	32	43	41
Under 3	15	10	26	27	24	33	38
Total %	100	100	100	100	100	100	100
Av. years	12.3	8.9	5.8	5.5	5.2	3.9	3.7
N=	(59)	(44)	(55)	(89)	(80)	(111)	(66)

N = number of permanent secretaryships excluding deaths in post and excluding current permanent secretaryships.

For much of the present century the average tenure remained at a little over five years. Over the last thirty years it has fallen to less than four years. There is little indication of any reversal of this trend. Whereas during the early and middle decades of the century upwards of two-fifths stayed at least six years in one post and sometimes much longer, little more than one-fifth have done so since the mid-1960s. Over a third of all incumbents during this period have spent less than three years in any one permanent secretaryship. It should be borne in mind that changes of departmental nomenclature, mergers and the like are counted as a continuation of the same permanent secretaryship. So, too, are promotions within the same department from the level of second permanent secretary. The brevity of tenure portrayed in Table 10.2 is therefore a reflection of reality, not simply an illusion created by some quirk of definition or statistical sleight of hand.

It is clear from these figures that the vast majority of modern permanent secretaryships have been held for less than five years. This, as noted earlier, is the maximum that Edward Playfair thought any individual should remain in a top job. More recent and current post-holders have also expressed doubts about the utility of long stays. A former permanent secretary explained:

> I always reckoned that seven years would be the most I would remain in that particular job and then I would have to move to another department; or retire early... I could get stale if I remained for the duration. It also becomes very disheartening for all the ambitious young officials if the top post is blocked for many years.

He decided to ask the head of the civil service for a move and was duly transferred to another department when a suitable vacancy arose.

Taking the reins in another department or transferring upon promotion is a challenge to anyone. The pace of activity in Whitehall now and perhaps even in the past prevents any formal handing over period or running-in time. As a current permanent secretary explained: 'I simply spent an hour and a half with my predecessor over a drink in the Reform Club'. How long, then, does it take for a permanent secretary to acclimatize, especially when new to a department? Patrick Nairne was appointed in the mid-1970s as Permanent Secretary at the DHSS. He had spent nearly all his career in defence administration. He admitted to the English Committee that it was taking time to become effective, although his former political chief seems to have had complete confidence in him (Expenditure Committee 1977b, vol. II (part I), Q. 896; Castle 1980, p. 467 and 733). He later referred to a period (of unspecified duration) necessary for a permanent secretary fully to master a new department (Nairne 1983, p. 253). Others have endorsed this, indicating periods of up to three years as the minimum to achieve full utility in a top job (Peterson, NOA Tr., p. 22). If this is so then a significant minority of incumbents never reach a full head of steam as permanent secretaries. On the other hand, some would see shorter periods as sufficing. As one of the present permanent secretaries said: 'In a sense one is contributing almost from the word go simply because you have to. If you are asked to make a judgement you have to make it as best you can'. Another gave a more equivocal view:

> It does mean that for a period a new permanent secretary is not contributing a great deal, particularly in the policy area... I suppose you're talking about three to six months – something like that. Of course you have your knowledge of Whitehall and your knowledge of the public scene (and) the ability to ask the obvious question that sometimes gets overlooked. But I don't think you really make a full contribution until you've understood the origins of the present policies, until you've got to understand what sort of ethos there is in the department.

Much turns upon what exactly is meant by operating to full effect. There is also the question of whether or not a permanent secretary has had some previous experience in the department. There are three categories of circumstance. First, there is promotion from within the department. Here there is a natural lead-in and presumably little problem of acclimatization. Second, a permanent secretary may return from elsewhere to head a department. According to Richard Way, there is nothing quite like returning to one's 'own' department after an absence of a few years (NOA Tr., p. 32). This implies that the best of both worlds may be possible: familiarity with the department together with a wider vision. The third category is the one in which the individual makes his or her first inside contact with the department upon becoming its permanent head. This is where running-in time and duration of tenure will have their most powerful bearing upon performance.

The majority of immediate promotions to permanent secretary level take place within a department – some 58 per cent since 1945, excluding newly created departments. The proportion has varied somewhat over this period, but not substantially. There is no discernible trend. But in nearly all cases any subsequent move at permanent secretary level, other than from the second permanent secretaryship, will by definition involve a departmental transfer. So when all permanent secretaryships are taken into account there is a stronger tendency for vacancies to have been filled by transfer. Here there has been both a greater variation and a distinct trend since 1945. During the first two post-war decades, only a little more than a third of all permanent secretaryships were filled by appointment from within a department. Since the mid-1960s this has risen to almost exactly a half and has remained remarkably steady at that level.

As noted above, to fill a vacancy by transfer is not necessarily to imply that the incumbent has had no previous service in the department he or she is about to head. With the higher levels of mobility analyzed in the last chapter – especially the toing and froing – there is increasing likelihood of returning to head one's 'own' department. In fact most permanent secretaryships, though never more than two-thirds, have been filled by people who had at least some previous experience in the department. A notable minority have spent at least fifteen years at some stage previously in the departments they head. This has fluctuated between a third and two-fifths throughout most of the present century. There were fewer (approximately a quarter) with such long service during the mid-nineteenth century when the majority of appointments fell to non-career civil servants. It is a moot point as to what, if any, minimum length of service in a department is necessary to be an effective permanent secretary. Devout adherents to the musical chairs philosophy may well say 'none', or at any rate very little. Others, too, have seen virtue in a fresh mind brought to bear upon the work and problems of a department, uninhibited by long and close association (Wass 1984, p. 49). Nevertheless at least three years' previous service in a department may be considered to be the minimum for a permanent secretary to make an early and decisive contribution based upon personal knowledge of the business in hand. A significant minority of posts have fallen to individuals who had less than three years and in many cases no previous service in their departments. Some of these people have not stayed long in their posts, either. A little over 15 per cent of all top posts since 1945 have been held by individuals who had had less than three years' previous service in a department and who remained there for less than three years as permanent secretary. The proportion has remained remarkably constant throughout the post-war period. It may therefore be said that more than one in every seven of the top posts in the British civil service have been held by incumbents who had little or no previous service in their departments and who left before having had time to gain any deep familiarity. It is interesting to note how this particular characteristic of the Whitehall scene has borne upon particular departments.

Table 10.3 covers the main departments that have existed in more or less recognizable form since 1945. It includes second permanent secretaryships and shows both the average tenure and the average previous departmental experience of all incumbents. It also shows the incidence of brief incumbencies (under three years), of minimal previous experience (again, under three years) and of both these factors working together.

For the purposes of broad analysis, a crude line of demarcation may be drawn at an average of five years' previous service and five years' tenure as

Table 10.3
Previous service and tenure of permanent secretaryships
in certain departments, 1945-94

Department	No. Perm. Secs.	Av. Service	Av. Tenure	< 3 yrs Service	< 3 yrs Tenure	< 3 yrs Service and < 3 yrs Tenure
Agriculture (MAFF)	10	20	5.6	3	-	-
Cabinet Office	16	2	5	11	5	3
Customs and Excise	11	7	5.3	7	-	-
MoD (incl. Procurement)	31	14	3.8	9	9	4
Education (DFE)	12	4	4.6	10	3	3
Employment	10	17	4.9	4	-	-
FCO (excl. ODA)	17	29	3.8	1	4	1
Home Office	9	14	7.3	4	1	1
Inland Revenue	9	9	5.4	6	-	-
Scottish Office	7	7	8.3	2	-	-
DTI (incl. Dept. Industry, 1974-83)	16	5	4.4	11	5	4
Treasury	44	16	4.4	6	9	1

Note: includes permanent secretaries in post in 1945. Excludes deaths in post and retirements on medical grounds from calculations of average tenure.

marking a minimum of sufficiency. Bearing in mind the wide variations that can be obscured by averages it may be said that five of the twelve departments listed in the table have enjoyed a sufficiency in terms both of previous experience and tenure among their permanent secretaries – MAFF, Customs and Excise, the Home Office, Inland Revenue and the Scottish Office. The FCO almost qualifies for 'dual sufficiency'. Most of its incumbents have spent their entire careers in the diplomatic service and have usually been older upon becoming PUS. Being nearer retirement they have therefore tended to have rather shorter terms in the top job. The Department of Employment also nearly qualifies on both counts. It has had four permanent secretaries with little or no previous service. They all stayed to head the department for at least three years. Of these four, Laurence Helsby's was the briefest tenure. He stayed three years en route to the headship of the civil service. But the other six permanent secretaries had between them an average of twenty-nine years' previous service in the department. The Treasury, the Cabinet Office, the MoD, the DTI and the DFE also warrant a few brief words.

Most of the forty-four Treasury people operated there as second secretaries or second permanent secretaries. Only one, Maurice Dean, had less than three years' previous service and stayed in post for less than three years. Dean was a second secretary between 1963-64. He took this post after an eight year spell as Permanent Secretary at the Air Ministry. He had earlier spent a year in the Treasury as a third (i.e. deputy) secretary. But Dean is an exception. In fact twenty-eight of the Treasury's permanent secretaries had had at least fifteen years' previous service there. The slightly briefer than average tenure is accounted for by the second (permanent) secretaries, many of whom went on to head one or other of the big spending departments. This has been so for ten of the sixteen second permanent secretaries since the early 1970s. Overall, then, there has been a reasonable depth of experience and a fair degree of stability in the top echelons of the Treasury. There has been no repeat of the 1950s when, following the retirement of Edward Bridges, Norman Brook and Roger Makins became joint permanent secretaries. Neither had previously served in the Treasury, though they were supported by the three second secretaries Herbert Brittain, Thomas Padmore and Leslie Rowan, all of whom were well versed in the ways of Great George Street.

The Cabinet Office is a different case. As noted in an earlier chapter, it draws most of its personnel by loan from other departments. Not surprisingly, the majority of its top people have had less than three years there. Moreover, it is mainly its second permanent secretaries that have moved on quickly. By contrast, successive cabinet secretaries have had notably long tenures. Upon taking post in January 1988 Robin Butler became only the fifth post-war appointee and the seventh incumbent since the creation of the Secretariat in 1916.

Permanent secretaries at the MoD have had a fairly high average level of previous service. They have been a disparate bunch, partly because of the nature and the changing nature of the department. Further variety is given by the inclusion in Table 10.3 of the eight heads of procurement in addition to the eleven second permanent secretaries, only one of whom (Michael Cary) was subsequently promoted to the top job within the Ministry. Five of the first six appointees following the creation of the MoD in 1947 arrived there without previous service in the department. Only one of them stayed three or more years. All this was before 1964 when the MoD became a major department with the absorption of the Admiralty, the Air Ministry and the War Office. Since then it has usually had the benefit, if such it is, of longer serving permanent secretaries who have had fairly extensive previous experience there. Only one arrived without any previous service whatsoever and left after only a year – Derek Rayner, who was Chief of Procurement between 1971-72.

The DTI and the DFE seem to have been stricken with a number of short-stay permanent secretaries who had had little previous departmental experience. The figures for the DTI include the separate Departments of Trade and of Industry between 1974-83. But this cannot disguise the fact that eleven of the sixteen incumbents took up post having served in the department for less than three years, nine of them with no previous experience at all. Indeed in this important area of government only four of the post-war permanent secretaries had had extensive previous experience – Max Brown,

Peter Carey and Peter Thornton from the 1960s and 1970s; and the present incumbent, Peter Gregson, appointed in 1989.

There has been even greater turbulence and generally less previous experience among post-holders at the DFE. Gilbert Flemming retired in 1959, completing over forty years in the then Ministry of Education. Since then only two of the ten permanent secretaries have taken over with previous service to their credit. One of the two, Herbert Andrew, had been there just one year prior to his appointment in 1963. The other, William Pile, had spent fifteen years at the ministry earlier in his career when, in 1970, he was brought back from his position as Director-General of the Prison Service (which he had held for one year). None of Pile's five successors had ever served in the department before assuming the permanent secretaryship. There has been nothing quite to match the turbulence of 1964 when two successive joint permanent secretaries (Maurice Dean and Bruce Fraser) arrived and departed within a few months. But the events of 1993-94 were almost as frantic. John Caines had retired after four years as permanent secretary. He was succeeded in January 1993 by Geoffrey Holland who moved over from the permanent secretaryship of the Department of Employment. Within a year Holland had announced his resignation. Even during his short stay he had made some impact, mainly through his influence upon a number of key appointments in the education world. But he didn't stay long enough to fight for his preferred and controversial option of merging education and employment to form a new Department of Education and Training. On this and almost certainly on other issues he is said to have clashed with his Secretary of State, John Patten. He is reported to have told colleagues 'either he (Patten) goes or I do' (*Times Education Supplement*, 19 November 1993). He was not pushed out by Patten. The vice-chancellorship of the University of Exeter which he took may well have been a positive attraction. But his brief spell at the DFE was an unhappy and an uncomfortable one. Ironically, within months of Holland's departure, Patten had been removed from the DFE and dropped from the cabinet. His inability to handle the department and the constant public controversies over policies, some of which he had inherited, were factors in his political demise.

All this raises a broader issue – the departmental experience and tenure of permanent secretaries in relation to their ministers. This is the focus of the next and final section of this chapter.

Permanent secretaries, ministers and departments

The analysis so far has shown that most permanent secretaries have had some prior experience in the departments they head – sometimes quite substantial experience. A minority, however, have had little or no previous service. Moreover, a small minority have taken the reins with little previous service and then moved on before they could have gained much familiarity with their departments. To this extent it is necessary to modify any crude notion about the permanence of the Whitehall bureaucracy – a permanence which is often contrasted with the transitory nature of the political executive. Yet, as noted in Chapter 2, ministers are birds of passage. They move even more rapidly than permanent secretaries. The average tenure of any one ministerial portfolio since 1945 is approximately two and a half years. This is rather more than half that for permanent secretaryships. It is briefer than has been common for ministers in many countries of Europe (Rose 1991, p. 53). It is not that Britain experiences more frequent changes of government; rather that there are more ministerial reshuffles. On the other hand, most serve in some junior ministerial capacity before reaching cabinet level. This was a practice initiated by Robert Peel and reaffirmed by Gladstone in the last century (Keith 1939, p. 175). During the present century it has become a common feature (Willson 1959; Willson 1970, p. 238; Riddell 1993, pp. 178-85). It increases the chances that cabinet members will assume responsibility for ministries in which they previously held more junior office. It is doubtful whether there has been any deliberate and sustained planning to ensure the accumulation of ministerial experience in specific areas of work. Previous experience in a department is only one factor in the disposition of portfolios. But it is a dimension worthy of consideration when comparing the relative experience of ministers and their permanent secretaries.

Fig. 10.1 shows the amount of accumulated departmental experience, in months, of ministers and their permanent secretaries from 1830 onwards. It develops the earlier work of Alt (1975, pp. 35-9) over a shorter period and for ministers only. Periods of tenure as shown by Alt are lower than those in Fig. 10.1 since they do not include previous junior ministerial experience in a particular department. The calculations for Fig. 10.1 are based upon average periods of service at six monthly intervals – i.e. at 30 June and 31 December for each year. Departments included are those with a life of at least seven years; and which have normally been headed by a minister of cabinet rank. Only 'principal' and joint permanent secretaries directly serving those ministers are included in the calculations: second and other permanent secretaries are excluded.

During the mid-nineteenth century ministers, collectively, reached peaks of experience rarely since equalled. This despite eleven changes of government between 1832-68. In fact during this period the pool of ministers changed only slowly. The formation of a new government was often a case of one set of old hands replacing another. As often as not the old hands went back to their former departments, especially when their absence in opposition had been comparatively brief. There was a partial upturn during the 1890s, but for most of the twentieth century average levels of depart-

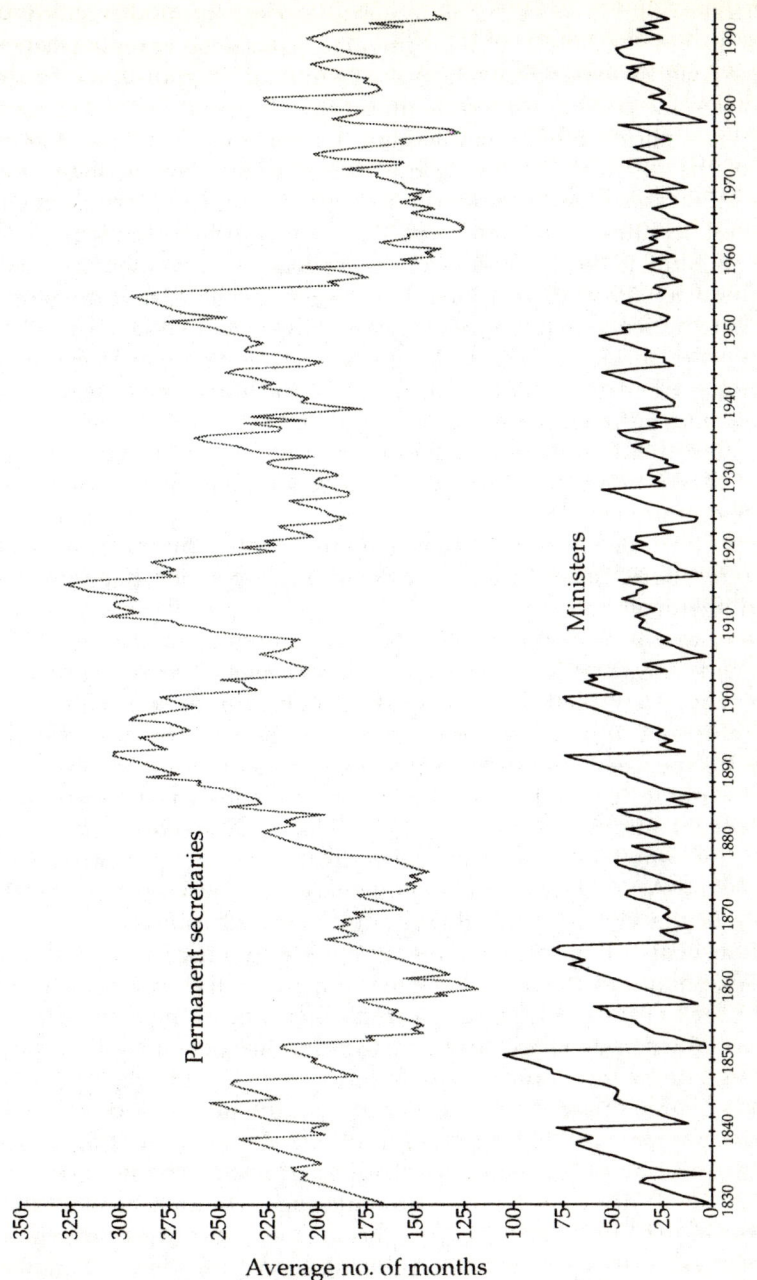

Fig. 10.1 Departmental service of permanent secretaries and ministers, 1830-1994 (av. no. of months, calculated at six monthly intervals)

mental experience have been lower. The penchant for reshuffles, as much as changes of party in office, has been responsible for this. The uninterrupted period of Conservative government between 1951-64 did not bring any sustained increase in the levels of departmental experience among ministers. The average level of experience was not substantially higher in 1964 than it had been when the party returned to office thirteen years earlier. Indeed the departmental experience of Macmillan and his ministers was lower in consequence of the reshuffle following the 1959 general election than at any time since 1830 other than that occasioned by a change of party in government. A similar pattern followed John Major's reshuffle in the wake of the 1992 election. Similar though less extensive reshuffles prevented the Liberal ministers between 1905-16 and Labour between 1964-70 from developing the depth of experience that would otherwise have been possible during relatively extensive periods in office. The greatest levels of departmental experience among twentieth century ministers were accumulated during Baldwin's Conservative government of 1924-29, Churchill's Coalition 1940-45 and, to a lesser extent, Attlee's Labour governments of 1945-51. This was also true of the Thatcher era, 1979-90. All these were periods uninterrupted by a change of premier.

Margaret Thatcher's was the longest uninterrupted premiership in the period covered here. Reshuffles and resignations prevented her from leading a team of ministers having longer associations with their departments than those of any other cabinet. Yet she did sometimes appoint at senior level ministers with previous service in a department. Over a third of the senior cabinet appointments at her disposal involved internal promotions or ministers returning to their former departments. During the post-war period this has been exceeded only by Attlee, two-fifths of whose ministers had previous experience of the departments they headed; and by the Wilson/Callaghan administrations of 1974-79 in which nearly half took the helm with the benefit of prior experience in the same department. Many members of the Attlee governments had served in the wartime coalition; while those of the Wilson/Callaghan period were returning to office after less than four years in opposition. Nevertheless what characterizes both the Wilson/Callaghan and the Thatcher governments is the proclivity to promote within or to return former junior ministers to head their departments. This has partially compensated for the discontinuities occasioned by reshuffles and resignations from office.

So far as permanent secretaries are concerned, the fluctuations are, again, greater than may be expected from assumptions about bureaucratic stability. This reflects some of the features noted earlier in this chapter and in the last chapter - mobility between departments together with the fact that a consistent minority have had little experience of their departments and briefer tenure as permanent secretaries during recent decades. The graph in

Fig. 10.1 shows sustained linear (or near linear) ascents which signify steadily accumulating collective experience. Yet such a pattern has been rarer during the present century. It has become more common for one or more permanent secretaries with extensive experience to be replaced by another, or others, with less or no previous service in a department. Alternatively, the reverse has sometimes happened – that is to say, the replacement of a relatively inexperienced permanent secretary by one who has had extensive previous service in a department. This can produce abnormally sharp increases in the average levels of experience.

For an eighty year period from the 1870s to the late-1950s, average levels of experience remained high among permanent secretaries. Never did they fall below 180 months, or fifteen years. From the mid-1880s until just after the turn of the century, and again from 1909-1919, very high average levels were maintained, peaking at twenty-seven years in 1915. The late-nineteenth and early twentieth centuries may fairly be described as the climax of bureaucratic stability and depth of experience. Never since have departments been served by permanent secretaries so familiar with their work, though there was an upturn in the early 1950s.

From the late-1950s, average levels have fallen. Indeed the pattern since then broadly resembles that of the 1850s, '60s and '70s. Quantitatively, mobility in Whitehall has had the same effect on collective levels of departmental experience among permanent secretaries as did the use of outsiders in the last century. But the lower levels of experience among permanent secretaries of the nineteenth century were accompanied by levels that were relatively high among ministers. The general depression of the last thirty-odd years has been matched by a similar downturn at the political level. This vindicates the arguments of critics who object that the career characteristics of top civil servants reflect and reinforce those of ministers, rather than offering a complement or a counterweight.

It would be unwise to draw any firm conclusions from aggregate data of this sort. In particular it would be foolish to accord to such figures alone any decisive explanatory power in terms of the relationships between ministers and permanent secretaries, or as to the achievements of different governments over such a period of time. It may be at the level of the individual department and in terms of the frequency of turnover that personnel changes have had their greatest purchase. Table 10.4 shows the number of ministers and permanent secretaries in certain departments since the coming to office of the Liberals in 1905. Second and certain other permanent secretaries are excluded. The post-1945 figures for permanent secretaries are therefore not comparable with those shown above in Table 10.3.

The figures in the table are presented to highlight the broad contrast between the two halves of the century. During the first half there was a higher ratio of ministers to permanent secretaries, approximately 3:1. Since

Table 10.4
Turnover of ministers and permanent secretaries in certain departments, 1905-94

	Dec. 1905-July 1945		July 1945-July 1994	
	No. Ministers	No. Perm. Secs.	No. Ministers	No. Perm. Secs.
Admiralty (to 1964)	20	6	8*	3*
Agriculture	19	7	17	9
Cabinet Office (from 1916)	11*	2*	11	6
MoD (from 1947)	-	-	23	12
Education	20	5	24	10
Employment (from 1916)	13*	6*	24	10
FCO	12	9	20	14
Home Office	18	5	19	9
Scottish Office	21	6	17	7
DTI (excl. Dept. Industry)	22	6	28	14
Treasury	15	7	19	10
War Office (to 1964)	22	5	10*	5*
Total	193	64	220	109

Notes: where there have been joint permanent secretaries, only the one longer (or longest) in post is counted.
Figures for 1945-94 include those (permanent secretaries) already in post in July 1945.
Ministers are counted twice where they returned to the same portfolio.
* means not included in calculations for rank correlation (see text below).

1945 there have been fewer ministers in relation to permanent heads, approximately 2:1. This is not because ministers have stayed longer but because permanent secretaries have held their posts for shorter periods. During the first half of the century there was an inverse relationship between the turnover of ministers and the turnover of permanent secretaries in particular departments. This is reflected in a negative statistical rank correlation of -0.49. This means that departments which had a high turnover of ministers were more likely to have had a lower turnover of permanent secretaries, and vice versa. Since 1945 there has been a strong positive association (+0.82) – low turnover among ministers has usually been linked with low turnover among permanent secretaries. Conversely, departments which have had a more rapid turnover of ministers have also had a higher turnover of permanent secretaries. This is probably coincidental. Certainly there is no reason to suppose that one has been the consequence of the other. Nevertheless, some of the departmental patterns are quite distinct. Three departments have had lower levels of turnover among both ministers and permanent secretaries – the Cabinet Office, the Scottish Office and MAFF. The Cabinet Office is a special case. The figures in Table 10.4 for the Cabinet Office relate to prime ministers and cabinet secretaries. Neither are quite typical of their peers. Nor is the relationship between prime minister and cabinet secretary usually quite the same as that between departmental minister and permanent secretary (see Chapter 1). At the other end of the scale the DTI, the DFE and the MoD have had during the post-war period higher than average levels of turnover both among ministers and permanent secretaries. As noted earlier in this chapter, a good number of the permanent secretaries at the DTI and the DFE also had precious little previous departmental experience. It is difficult to escape the conclusion that this must have had some bearing upon the conduct of business and ultimately upon the performance of government – especially in combination with a high turnover of ministers most of whom had no previous working experience in their respective departments. It is true that five of the last eight secretaries of state at the DTI did have previous experience – Cecil Parkinson (1983), Norman Tebbit (1983-85), Paul Channon (1986-87), Nicholas Ridley (1989-90) and Michael Heseltine (1992-). But they are a minority overall during the post-war period.

It is worth looking more closely at the levels of experience among particular ministers and particular permanent secretaries as they have come together in their departments. Since 1945 approximately two-thirds of the senior cabinet ministers have come to their departments never having previously worked there. Just over half of these (34 per cent of all ministers) had as permanent secretary one who had been less than three years in post and of whom half had also spent less than three years in the department before becoming permanent secretary. Among the remaining third of all ministers – those with previous experience in the department – less than a quarter (that is, 8 per cent of all ministers) returned with longer service than the incumbent permanent secretary had in post. In only four instances has this also meant greater experience in the department than the permanent secretary.

The position of the minister looks rather stronger when the alternative 'snap-shot' is taken – the appointment of the permanent secretary. If a minister stays he or she will see in a new permanent secretary, perhaps one with comparatively little experience of the department. Yet less than one in every nine permanent secretaries new to a department have found themselves in harness with a minister whose total service in the department exceeds three years. In terms of combined experience, nearly a quarter of permanent secretary appointments in the main departments since 1945 have brought together a civil servant and a minister neither of whom had more than three years' service in the department. At the highest levels of British government some of the most important departments have therefore operated at least for a time with ministers and permanent secretaries neither of whom had a deep familiarity with the work.

It would certainly be possible to mobilize these figures in support of various and more general observations about short termism in public policy; about the lack of subject specific competence at the highest levels; and indeed about the way in which top civil servants, collectively, have handled or been handled by their ministers. Needless to say, the evidence presented in this chapter provides no more than a foundation for any such expatiation. Inevitably, data are capable of alternative and conflicting interpretation. There is, as we have seen, continued debate about the relative virtues of deep familiarity as against a fresh mind uninhibited by past association with an area of work or a set of problems. Moreover, in the tight network of the Whitehall village, lack of previous service in a department does not always imply ignorance about the area of work. Such ignorance could, however, become a feature of Whitehall's increasing fragmentation and of the more job specific nature of modern permanent secretaryships. Again, interdepartmental mobility at senior levels need not be an impediment even if it means that a permanent secretary is unable immediately to make a full contribution. But it is likely to shape the way the permanent secretary runs the department and relates with other senior officials. It is likely also to bear upon relationships with ministers. Ministers are birds of passage – more so than permanent secretaries. Exactly how their respective career characteristics bear upon the relationship is difficult to know. As stated in Chapter 2, there are at least two basic abstract models of the relationship. On the one hand there is the adversarial model. This assumes a zero-sum game in which an advance for one is a retreat for the other. Here high levels of departmental experience among permanent secretaries relative to ministers may help the bureaucracy to assert itself. On the other hand, the roles of permanent secretaries may be seen as complementary to those of ministers. What is good (or bad) for one is also good (or bad) for the other. This is the formal constitutional position. The minister and permanent secretary work in harness, sharing a common interest in good or at least better government, albeit from differing perspectives and perhaps for different reasons. Higher levels of combined or aggregate experience among permanent secretaries and ministers may assist them in their mutual pursuits.

All this comes back to the roles played by permanent secretaries, both now and in the past. It connects with the contributions they have made at various times to the formulation of policies and to the running of the Whitehall machine – in short to the performance of government and in the context of their constitutional position as civil servants. These will be the themes of the next and final section of this book.

PART IV

PERMANENT SECRETARIES AND THE STATE

11 Permanent secretaries and the performance of government

Introduction

In this final part of the book a more synoptic approach is adopted. It draws upon and summarizes material presented in the earlier sections and chapters. This chapter deals with the contribution of permanent secretaries to the performance of government. The next and final chapter considers permanent secretaries in the wider context of the constitution.

To assess permanent secretaries in terms of the overall performance of government is, in a sense, to embark upon mission impossible. At one level this would involve the painstaking accumulation of case-study material highlighting the roles played by individuals, or small groups of individuals, in particular areas of activity at particular times. There is some such evidence, but much is still unknown and may well remain so. Nor is there likely to be any universally accepted evaluation of the performance of successive governments – that is to say, the product to which permanent secretaries have contributed. On the other hand, these obstacles have not inhibited Whitehall's stouter critics – those who, in a flurry of rhetoric, have been ready to dismiss or to deprecate the contribution of top officials and of the bureaucracy in which they have plied their trade. One of the more trenchant and widely quoted critics has complained that Whitehall's top mandarins have proved themselves 'able at a touch to transmute life into paper and turn action into stone' (Barnett 1986, p. 215). With specific reference to the

Treasury, another has observed: 'Give them a problem and they will turn it into a crisis' (Haines 1977, p. 41). Nor are such broadsides of recent origin. According to Mallalieu (1942, p. 27) the Whitehall bureaucracy 'looks long before it leaps, and then lands in the most obvious pitfalls'. Even one of the more friendly critics from yesteryear described the prevailing character as a Casaubon-like 'humanism with the sap dried out' (Sadler 1932, pp. 28-9).

This kind of intellectual slap-stick is often elegant, amusing and not without nuggets of truth. But it cannot pretend to be either the rounded picture or the definitive judgement. How, then, can one develop an analysis based upon observation grounded in evidence – a broad view which avoids crass simplicity and which at the very least offers a viable foundation for further enquiry about the changing role and contribution of Britain's administrative elite? The discussion which follows tries to do this in four stages. First, it analyzes the nature of the 'bureaucratic phenomenon', the foundation of official influence and the way in which it has embedded itself in the governmental process. Specifically, it reassesses some of the arguments introduced or alluded to in chapters 1 and 2 about the nature of mandarin power. Second, it considers whether, and if so in what senses, permanent secretaries are a flawed elite. This mobilizes some of the evidence presented in the two middle sections of this book concerning permanent secretaries' backgrounds, the way they are appointed and their careers as civil servants. Of course, such evidence can at best be indicative and never conclusive. We need to take a broad view as to how permanent secretaries have performed their roles in Whitehall. Third, then, it assesses their contribution to the processes of government. It poses the question 'do permanent secretaries have a case to answer?' If so, then we must assess also the burden of responsibility that permanent secretaries should bear. One view is that things would have been much better if they had played a less forceful hand, at least in the past. Another is that their contributions have not always been for the good but that they had thrust upon them a more commanding role than they were equipped to discharge. Yet another is that things would be better if permanent secretaries played, or re-established, a more powerful role. This is one of the subtexts for the fourth stage of the discussion. This examines the view, expressed by a former incumbent, that in recent years permanent secretaries have been reduced from princes to pawns.

The foundations of mandarin power

For reasons outlined in Chapter 1, mandarin power in the mid-nineteenth century differed from that of subsequent periods. It differed in three ways. First, the titans of the 1830s, '40s and '50s were unabashed proselytizers. They made little attempt to steer a middle course or to 'temper the wind to the shorn lamb'. They never regarded themselves as dispassionate brokers. Second, theirs was a highly personalized approach to public affairs. They made little pretence at representing any wider constituency. By no means always did they purport to speak on behalf of their departments. Third, they did speak out – and in the open when necessary. This proclivity for public engagement was the first of these three characteristics to be curbed by the demands of constitutional propriety. But the other two – the proselytizing (in private and now tempered by the winds of mass party democracy) and the more personalized approach – remained, albeit with steadily declining force, well into the second half of the twentieth century. This did not imply any loss of bureaucratic influence. It may, in a more general sense, have brought an accretion of mandarin power. Lord Robert Montague explained how anonymity enhanced the influence of officials:

> Chief clerks are now the real rulers of England, they have already a power too despotic. The ministers above them when first appointed are always ignorant of their subject, and trust to those chief clerks and so commit themselves, and are subsequently too vain to change.
> (Sanitary Commission, 1869, vol. II, p. 345).

This gives a clue both as to the chronology and the nature of mandarin power. Of course, the very notion of power in this context invites controversies of definition as well as of interpretation. For some, power is the ability of one person or group of persons to assert themselves over the manifest will of others. This is a definition derived from the writings of Max Weber (Gerth and Mills 1948, p. 180). It implies an observable conflict as the medium through which power is exercised. This assumption is challenged by those who see power as the ability to shape the broad values which in turn shape specific outcomes (Lukes 1974). Indeed little effort may be required from those whose interests are nourished by society's prevailing values. Such values usually coalesce naturally with the interests of those who hold strategic positions. On fundamental issues a power relationship may therefore exist, from this perspective, even in the absence of observable conflict and sometimes in the presence of apparent consensus. These different approaches to the notoriously slippery concept of power may have some, limited, applicability to relationships between ministers and mandarins. Overt conflicts have been apparent from time-to-time, usually between individual ministers and individual civil servants or groups of civil servants. The invisible mechanism of power may provide the model for those who believe that certain ministers have been happily ensnared in Whitehall's disarming embrace, mistakenly believing that they 'rule the roost'; or for those who allege that officials have developed an unconscious mind-set in consequence of sustained service to one party in office. Further complications can arise when one pitches alongside the notion of power other concepts such as 'influence' and 'manipulation' (Dahl 1970, pp. 14-34; Ware 1981). Such concerns lie beyond the scope of this volume. But much of the 'power' literature, as applied to Whitehall, would assume the adversarial paradigm in analyzing relationships between ministers and the bureaucracy. The alternative of a genuinely (as distinct from artificially) co-operative mutual perspective among ministers and mandarins is certainly closer to the constitutional ideal and may often have been closer to the reality. This is not to deny that the Whitehall bureaucracy is a powerful instrument; or that it can and sometimes has been carried by a momentum of its own. To identify the main features by which this power may be characterized is simply to adopt the strongest hypothetical construction. It is not to assume that the bureaucracy has at all times or indeed at any one time fully asserted itself. Nor is it to imply any inevitable or irreversible trend. What, then, have been the main foundations of mandarin power? And what is the broad chronology?

The regulatory state of the nineteenth and early twentieth centuries begot a legalistic approach to the functions of government, at least in domestic affairs. The ethos of the Local Government Board, for example, reflected 'the values appropriate to an essentially quasi-judicial and bureaucratic business, heavily tempered by a pragmatism derived from its political constraints' (Bellamy 1988, pp. 111-2). Similar observations have been made about the Home Office and, in a slightly different way, about the Labour Department of the Board of Trade (Pellew 1982; Davidson 1985). An increasingly legalistic, systematic and data-gathering approach placed a premium on the contribution of officials. It was a premium underscored by the accumulated experience of a permanent bureaucracy. But the source of mandarin power in Britain was not and never became a purely technocratic phenomenon. On the contrary, as explained in Chapter 2, senior officials operate within the crucible of ministerial sensibilities. H.E. Dale (1941, p. 102) ascribed mandarin power to a general temper of mind 'created by, and therefore adapted to, the inevitable facts of life and government in a great and closely organized community'. If mandarins have left their mark on the political scene from off-stage, it is because they are themselves politicians of a sort. They have usually known what the traffic will bear. They are or used to be as good and sometimes better than their political chiefs at trading ideas, at least in the context of conflicting perspectives and considerations. Inasmuch as politics is the art of the possible, this is a considerable asset. Inasmuch as politics is the incarnation of a given ideology, it may be less of an asset.

Another source of mandarin power has been co-ordination. Co-ordination often implies centralization, though not always. Whitehall has usually been as adept as any state bureaucracy in ensuring that its personnel are singing from the same hymn-sheet. In part this is a function of an homogeneous elite though, as noted in Chapter 6, this homogeneity is far less evident now than in the past. It is also in part the product of the fairly wide experience that many top officials have had in Whitehall, facilitated by the interdepartmental mobility examined in Chapter 9. More specifically, it is a reflection of Whitehall's relative centralization, in the shape mainly of the Cabinet Office and the Treasury. Authority for this relative centralization resides ultimately at the political level but it has its day-to-day manifestation in the official machine. It has sometimes been a source of frustration for ministers to find that they have been 'stitched-up'; that their cabinet colleagues have been 'squared' in a process of careful orchestration that can sometimes appear as conspiracy. Much depends upon the nature of the signals coming from No. 10 Downing Street. But co-ordination is the administrator's forté (Self 1972, p. 175). It is a potential source of mandarin power. This potential is enhanced when there is a conscious emphasis upon planning and even more so when this involves spending proposals. It has been claimed that the greater credence given to the planning of public spending in the 1960s placed ministers more firmly within the embrace of policies devised by officials (Lowe 1993, p. 43). Conversely, while there have been equal and greater efforts to control public expenditure in the 1980s and 1990s, there has been less emphasis upon long term, co-ordinated planning. Whitehall's penchant for co-ordination may not be quite what it used to be. As noted in Chapter 5, there seem to be fewer high level interdepartmental committees. This may have something to do with the more capricious approach to policy that now allegedly prevails (see below), though whether as cause or consequence is even more difficult to determine. At the time of writing we still await the report of the Scott Inquiry into the sale of arms to Iraq. It would therefore be unwise to advance any firm conclusions. But, if nothing else, the report seems almost certain to call into question Whitehall's capacity effectively to co-ordinate high and highly sensitive policy.

Be this as it may, a more carefully planned, co-ordinated approach does not imply a monolith. It is consistent with and may even give greater focus to the development of the so-called departmental view. Different departments may have different views, different cultures, even when interdepartmental co-ordination is working sweetly. As noted in Chapter 3, the phenomenon of the departmental view has been variously described. It is something of which ministers and even some permanent secretaries are wary. It may be a source of mandarin power, though it may also be a source of stability and coherence provided it is properly harnessed. The worry is that it may become detached from the political (i.e. democratic) impulse, giving forth its own agenda.

Mandarin power and the Whitehall machine may be a powerful instrument in the service of democratically elected government; or it may seem insensitive, if not obstructive. In the past, Whitehall has usually responded positively where there has been a clear signal for reform. This can be said of the three most notable waves of reform during the present century – those of 1906-14; the 1940s and the 1980s. The Liberals before the First World War seemed to have encountered little orchestrated resistance. Some officials, such as Robert Morant and Hubert Llewellyn Smith, were as progressive as their political chiefs (Judge 1984; Davidson 1972). As Roseveare remarks (1969, p. 224), even the Treasury 'did its duty to a united government with an overwhelming mandate'. As noted in Chapter 8, even the more severe critics acknowledge that Whitehall met the challenge of the two world wars. On both occasions it benefited from an infusion of outsiders deployed to good effect. In 1945 more than in 1918 top officials were favourably inclined towards interventionism (Lee 1980b). The Attlee governments of 1945-51 were served by an official machine in which there were many radical impulses (Morgan 1984, pp. 85-9). The Thatcher era is discussed more fully below. There were some uneasy and occasionally unseemly skirmishes, especially during the early 1980s. But many of Thatcher's ministers have testified to the loyalty with which they were served by their senior officials (Carrington 1989, p. 371; Heseltine 1990, p. 44; Fowler 1991, pp. 112-3; Lawson 1992, p. 589).

These three waves of reform were accompanied by a coherent political impulse and clear popular signals, at least as mediated through the British electoral system. Where the political climate has been uncertain, officialdom tends to appear stronger. This may happen where the position of a government is precarious, or where it lacks push or determination, or seems simply to be overwhelmed by the problems with which it is confronted. This may have happened during the inter-war years, allegedly the peak of bureaucratic power (Beloff 1975). It may also have happened during the 1960s and 1970s when ministers expressed more forcefully than ever before (or since) feelings of frustration with the 'iron grip' of the Whitehall embrace (Benn 1980; Castle 1973; Crossman 1974; Meacher 1979; Sedgemore 1980). As often as not, these more radical ministers were also expressing the frustrations of containment by the political centre and a lack of direction by their own colleagues. The bureaucracy has often come to the fore when there is a vacuum. Occasionally, individuals such as Horace Wilson in the 1930s and William Armstrong in the 1970s have, in moments of crisis, assumed a role and a position of prominence that has caused widespread resentment. Hindsight suggests that they were less influential and certainly less powerful than they seemed to their contemporaries. Neither Wilson nor Armstrong forced themselves upon unwilling political chiefs: they were encouraged by their respective premiers, Neville Chamberlain and Edward Heath. This is not to deny that, by its nature, mandarin power in a well functioning liberal democracy usually works best when it is operating in tandem with the prevailing political impulse. Equally politicians, in Britain and in other countries, are usually more effective when they take permanent officials fully into their confidence

(Plowden 1987, p. 172). This is not a ransom to bureaucracy but an anthem for good government. So how well equipped has been the British administrative elite to help pursue the cause of good government?

A flawed elite?

As explained at the beginning of this book, permanent secretaries are the elite of an elite by virtue of the positions they hold. They are at the apex of the state bureaucracy. Yet much more than this is often implied by the term elite, having regard to their backgrounds, career patterns and modes of behaviour. The two middle sections of this book examined permanent secretaries' backgrounds and careers in Whitehall. The evidence presented lends a certain credence to some of the alleged shortcomings in the constitution of top administrators as an elite group and of their capacity to help govern the country. Yet many of the more biting criticisms were seen to have been either exaggerated, unbalanced or misplaced. The Fulton-like image of the generalist all-rounder was never more than a caricature, though one with a good deal of plausibility. It is further from the truth today. At permanent secretary level there have been more specialists than is often supposed – people with 'relevant' qualifications and experience. Nor have these people – economists and social scientists in particular – simply been dissipated at random across Whitehall's farther horizons. On the contrary, they have often been drawn to the heart of government and used in areas appropriate to their talents. They have been the minority, though. And a corresponding minority have operated as permanent secretaries in departments in which they had had little or no previous experience. For this the Whitehall penchant for interdepartmental transfers is mainly responsible. This was consonant with the nineteenth century view which saw the talents of top officials as being transferable, at least between what Northcote and Trevelyan called 'cognate' areas of work. Under Warren Fisher and his disciples the principle of transferability became almost an unbound dogma. Faith in the efficacy of regular and varied postings within Whitehall remains, though with much greater circumspection. Critics continue to complain that top people move too quickly from job to job, both as they ascend the hierarchy and upon reaching the summit. There is at best only slight evidence of more carefully structured career patterns in recent years. There is still much movement between apparently unrelated or non-cognate areas of work, especially at deputy and permanent secretary levels. Permanent secretaries stay in their posts longer than their ministers – but not substantially longer. A minority (one in seven) since 1945 spent less than three years as permanent secretaries in departments of which they had had little or no previous experience. One must wonder what contribution this minority of people can have made to their departments and to the performance of government. There is no indication that this trend will abate in the immediate future.

If there has been fairly free mobility within Whitehall, movement between the civil service and other walks of life has been more inhibited. Permanent secretaries of recent times have been less cloistered than their predecessors of the early and middle decades of the present century. Many of them make a point of visiting the outposts of their own departments. Many of them have occasion to make visits abroad. They come into contact with a variety of people from organizations beyond Whitehall. The majority of incumbents over the last thirty years have been seconded outside Whitehall for periods of at least twelve months. Top mandarins can no longer with accuracy be described as an insular order. Yet few have had extensive experience in organizations beyond the orbit of government. The greater incidence of secondments has not compensated for the decline of the outsider, prevalent during the nineteenth century. Even then, when Whitehall was arguably at its most open, it drew from a limited range of outside professions. Usually the people who were attracted to permanent secretaryships were those who had had some informal connections in Whitehall prior to their becoming civil servants. Little was left to chance. Few individuals were drawn from business. This has changed only in fairly recent times, and even now as a greater proportion among the much smaller number of permanent secretaries who have had jobs outside the civil service.

In another sense, too, permanent secretaries can be portrayed as an insular order though, again, with less justification than in the past. Permanent secretaries are and have always been an educational and social elite. They tend to have gone to the more prestigious schools and universities and to have come predominantly from middle and upper middle class families. A large minority of post-holders during the late-nineteenth century had aristocratic connections though never, on the whole, matching those of their political chiefs. But these connections became far less significant as the twentieth century unfolded, certainly after 1918. Today the majority are nevertheless Oxbridge products many of whom went to a public school. The most prestigious schools are less heavily over-represented than they were before 1945. There is a much stronger presence from the minor public schools. Moreover, no longer does a public school education, still less an Oxbridge one, imply an upper middle class family background. Scholarships and the like have, to a limited extent, permitted access for those who would formerly have been denied such advantages. But state schools are less in evidence than might have been expected some fifty years on from the Butler Education Act of 1944. They are rather less in evidence among permanent secretaries than among the cohorts initially recruited into the elite corps – that is the Administration Group, formerly the Administrative Class and Class I before that. And in recent years those who entered the civil service directly into this elite group have had no less of a claim upon permanent secretaryships than before. At the same time there has been a notable increase in the number of permanent secretaries who were recruited initially into a specialist grade. This has been matched by a decline in the numbers drawn from the executive and clerical grades. Only two among over seventy post-1979 permanent secretaries initially entered the civil service in these grades. Where, one may ask, are the modern Richard 'Sam' Ways, the Harold Emmersons, the Cyril Musgraves or the Frederick Bishops – to name just a few who held permanent secretaryships in the first three post-Second World War decades? There seems to have been a decline in opportunities for long range upward mobility within the civil service. The halt to expansion may have had something to do with this (see Chapter 7). Moreover, the likes of those mentioned above may well have gone to a university and entered directly into the administrative elite had they been of a later generation. Extraneous factors may also be a partial explanation for the paucity of women at permanent secretary level. Women seem to have made no further headway in their claims upon top posts since the Evelyn Sharp generation which came to the fore during the 1950s and '60s.

In these various ways, then, it may be said that permanent secretaries are an imperfect if not a flawed elite. Yet they are also an intellectual elite of meritocrats. Whitehall has consistently attracted a good share of the best brains from the best educational institutions. And, once within Whitehall, those who get to the top have usually been among the best of those initially recruited to the elite corps. There have no doubt been exceptions. But all those who have got to the top after a career in Whitehall have done so by demonstrating their abilities. If they have been a group unrepresentative of society at large then this says at least as much about the wider society as it does about Whitehall. In particular, it reflects the complex interaction between educational and social institutions.

Much blame has been laid not only upon the elitist character of the schools and universities typically attended by many top mandarins but, more specifically, upon the type of education offered by these institutions. In a celebrated monograph, Martin Wiener (1981, pp. 16-24) has held the educational values associated with these institutions to have been responsible for the transmission, from the nineteenth century onwards, of an anti-industrial spirit. Civil servants, politicians and business people themselves are said to have absorbed and in turn perpetuated a set of ideals more conducive to cultural indulgence than to the pursuit of economic growth. Inevitably, and with some justification, there have been rebuttals. Certainly down to 1914, and perhaps after, the British manufacturing classes showed themselves to be capable of hard-headed expansionism (Pollard 1989). Some have questioned whether the British system of elite education was, or is, any more anti-industrial than that of its competitors (Rubinstein 1993, pp. 134-9). It has further been argued that the values imparted were only incidentally anti-industrial:

that much more important was the positive belief in education for the public service (Perkin 1989, p. 370). Private industry simply offered less scope for the activation of such values, fewer opportunities to change the world and to change it for the better. This has never been fully understood by those who have enjoined civil servants to get out into the real world and do something 'useful'. Such critics underestimate the attractions of the public service ethos. Even today, these attractions remain quite vivid for probably the majority of senior mandarins. This is not to deny that Whitehall could benefit from a greater infusion of outsiders, perhaps coming in at levels below that of permanent secretary and working their way upwards.

Permanent secretaries are now less of a closed, socially exclusive elite than formerly. This, in itself, is no cause for regret. As Hennessy says (1989, p. 130), the insularity of the earlier decades of the present century was a reflection not of timidity or fear of the outside world but of a smug self-confidence. The smugness has certainly gone. Many believe that some of the self-confidence has gone, too (Wass 1983). In part this is, again, the result of wider social changes. In part it may also be the result of a greater assertiveness by politicians. Warren Fisher saw salvation in the public schools as being more likely to produce people who would stand up to ministers and say: 'That is a damned swindle, sir, and you can't do it' (Chapman 1984, p. 170). Perhaps if he were alive today Fisher would have abandoned or at least qualified his faith in the public schools. Yet for some the public service principle flourishes best in an elite group – provided it is neither set too far apart from the rest of society nor assumes any misguided sense of superiority (Couzens 1985, p. 46).

Permanent secretaries are not and never have been the near-omnipotent philosopher kings. But nor are they by any means a substantially or fatally flawed elite. As an elite group they possess virtues which have usually outweighed their defects. And some of those defects have been the defects of the wider society. Conversely, one of the most consistently impressive virtues is the meritocracy through which most post-holders have risen to become permanent secretaries. Another is the spirit of public service, even though this has been under challenge in recent years (see the next chapter). With what effect has the permanent secretary elite applied its virtues and how serious have been its defects for the performance of government?

A case to answer?

It is inconceivable that, being at the centre of affairs, permanent secretaries have no case to answer for such policy and other failures of administration as there have been. At the micro level, they are responsible to their ministers for the running of their departments. If random mistakes are made lower down the line, then the permanent secretary is not personally culpable. But if a broader issue is at stake, then the permanent secretary will be drawn in. It is the permanent secretary's responsibility to provide the broad context within which more junior officials operate – or at least to see that someone within the department discharges the function of first-line gatekeeper. The advent of executive agencies has and will affect the way this role is performed but it does not disturb the basic principle.

At the other end of the scale, the macro issues, together with matters of day-to-day presentation, bring the permanent secretary into the ministerial orbit. There is nothing recent or novel about this. It is here that most permanent secretaries have made their most notable contributions. Much of even the most creative work has, of course, been done in the shadow of anonymity. Yet we know enough to understand that permanent secretaries in the past sometimes made highly significant and positive contributions. It is easy to assume that the gladiators of the mid-nineteenth century died with the passing of the Chadwick, Hill, Trevelyan generation. By contrast, permanent secretaries of the present century are easy targets for those who want to portray the dead hand of negativism. Whitehall has been described as a 'beautifully designed and effective braking mechanism' (Williams 1980, p. 81). Within this syndrome, permanent secretaries have been typified as providing merely the 'last redoubt of resistance in the consideration of new initiatives' (Hennessy 1989, p. 32).

In a sense it is part of the permanent secretary's job to counsel caution – at least to 'search the minefield' and to alert the minister to possible time-bombs. To an extent it is a role that reinforces caution in the already cautious. No doubt some have honed their craft to perfection. Yet even from behind the curtain of anonymity that descended from the late-nineteenth century positive, independent and sometimes inventive offerings have issued forth, albeit from the minority and probably less so of late in terms of high policy. At the Board of Trade in the late-nineteenth century, Thomas Farrer, an ardent free trader, shaped many of the commercial laws of the day. He was largely instrumental in curbing the monopoly excesses of the early gas companies (West 1920, pp. 67-8). He did so without any blemish to his constitutional role as a civil servant such as attended near contemporaries such as Francis Mowatt or Robert Morant (see Chapter 1). As head of the Western Department in the FO, future PUS Eyre Crowe submitted his now famous memorandum warning of German expansionism long before the First World War. His political chief, Campbell-Bannerman, chose not to act (Wilson 1973, pp. 538-9). During the inter-war years it was Robert Vansittart, Maurice Hankey and Warren Fisher who, despite disagreements among themselves, made the running on rearmament. They almost overstepped the mark, as indeed Vansittart did. But they served their country to good effect – so far as they were permitted by their political chiefs.

Other examples can be cited to show a greater flexibility and imagination than has often been acknowledged. Long before it became widely acceptable among the governing classes, Alexander Maxwell, PUS at the Home Office between 1938-48, was a firm believer in the abolition of capital punishment (Jones and Donoughue 1973, pp. 309-10). It was Maurice Holmes who, as permanent secretary, played a critical role in the foundation of the Education Act, 1944. His role did not eclipse that of his minister, R.A. Butler. But it was certainly more than that of a mere cypher, hand-holder or go-between. His contribution was essential to Butler's success. The Central African Federation (CAF) was an initiative of CRO officials in the 1950s, especially of its architect and future permanent secretary Andrew Cohen (Seldon 1981, pp. 360-1). The CAF was doomed eventually to failure, but only on account of the broader and deeper nationalistic complexities at work. Meanwhile, Frank Lee proved himself to be one of the most perceptive and effective top mandarins of the post-war period. Between 1949-62 he headed first the Ministry of Food, then the Board of Trade and finally (and jointly) the Treasury. He grasped quicker than almost anyone else the economic as well as the political attractions of joining the (European) Common Market, as it was then known (Roll 1985, pp. 105-6). By sheer force of intellect (and personality) he helped to sway the Macmillan government in the early 1960s to make Britain's first, albeit unsuccessful, application for membership. For a time Richard 'Otto' Clarke was a senior official working under Lee at the Treasury. A few years earlier, as an under secretary, Clarke had launched a paper pressing the case for a conditional floating of the pound and easier convertability outside the sterling area (MacDougall 1985, pp. 82-110). The plan was dropped only when other forces in Whitehall began to mobilize. It was Clarke, too, who devised the Public Expenditure Survey Committee (PESC) in the early 1960s (Hubbock 1988, p. 33). This was a system designed to provide a more structured, co-ordinated approach among ministers and officials from different quarters of Whitehall in the formulation of national spending plans. As such it was perhaps more typical of the modern mandarin's craft – a piece of administrative machinery, organic in nature, intended to systematize and routinize. But it suited the needs of the moment and of many years to come.

Taken together, the examples given above are sufficient at the very least to dispel the image of chronic negativism and universal lack of imagination. Other such examples could be cited. On the other hand, Whitehall has certainly had its darker moments. Even some of the cases mentioned above had their less happy sides. Eyre Crowe was in a small minority, if not a lone voice in the FO before 1914. By the late-1930s Vansittart, Fisher and even Hankey (who retired in 1938) had lost in influence to Horace Wilson. This was mainly because Wilson made the noises Premier Neville Chamberlain wanted to hear. The Suez fiasco of 1956 was not the fault of the civil service alone, but it sent profound shock-waves through the corridors of Whitehall. It made a number of senior officials, including one future PUS, think seriously about resigning (Gore-Booth 1984, p. 232). Yet the following year the PUS at the FO told Prime Minister Macmillan that Israeli consent would be forthcoming during a crisis in the Lebanon (Horne 1989, p. 95). This proved to be a disastrous misjudgement. Ministers have often complained about the efficacy of data provided by civil servants, especially in connection with trade and economic management (Healey 1989, pp. 379-82; Jenkins 1991, p. 279; Lawson 1992, pp. 643-6). In short, senior officials, permanent secretaries included, have on occasion made errors of judgement or given poor advice. They have presided over malfunctioning, apparently unable to spot or correct imperfections in the administrative system for which they are responsible to their ministers.

That such should happen from time-to-time need be cause neither for surprise nor for undue alarm, unless the benchmark for evaluation is perfection. Nor need it be any slight upon the office of permanent secretary to observe that many of the more positive and imaginative contributions were made by individuals before they reached the top. In recent decades it has become more the role of permanent secretaries to orchestrate the efforts of others than to have a 'hands-on' role themselves. Sometimes and for various reasons the permanent secretary may get personally involved. But a good deal of the work is not directly policy-orientated in any strict sense. It is nevertheless the skill of a good permanent secretary to know when to give others their head.

It is, of course, a matter for concern if mistakes occur too frequently, especially serious ones; or if the performance of government leaves a good deal to be desired. If these become consistent themes then something is almost certainly wrong and permanent secretaries, whether they like it or not, are in the thick of it. There are and always have been those who register dissatisfaction. This is the hallmark of a democracy. Over the last two decades or so there have been an uncommonly high number of former top officials who have gone public (usually after retirement) to vent their spleen. Some, having been the gatekeepers of secrecy, now proclaim their faith in more open government. Others, having advised ministers, no doubt to the best of their abilities, are now evidently unhappy with the way decisions are made. A former cabinet secretary has alluded to poor quality advice and the need if not for more advice then at least advice given 'earlier and in greater depth' (Hunt 1987, p. 69). A former PUS has put it more boldly: 'No one could claim, whatever their Party political position, that government decisions in the last 30 years have been of a high standard' (Cubbon 1994, p. 109). Current incumbents are naturally and quite properly more circumspect. Privately, some of them allude to faults in the system, even to the proclivity of certain ministers (in other departments) to make policy 'on the hoof'. This may always have been a temptation to those ministers anxious to assert themselves, though there seems now to be a greater scope for the exercise of their whims. It invites comparison with the way in which the policy machine operated twenty or thirty years ago. As one permanent secretary put it:

> In the old days... senior officials would get together in a cabal in the department and say "well, that's what we will present to ministers". That is much less prominent now, not least because in those days policy was a much more managed affair... ministers deliberated; it would go to an official committee shadowing a political sub-committee of the cabinet and then ministers went up, perhaps on a basis agreed by officials, and there were just a few things to settle.

These are not the words of men engaged in self-confession for their deeds or lack of deed; or in eulogy of the leading figures of yesteryear. Something deeper is implied. For the moment we may offer only a preliminary answer to the question 'do permanent secretaries have a case to answer?' Of course they do. But how much of a case and in what sense? Much turns upon the sheer extent of the alleged shortcomings or underperformance of government. If the likes of Brian Cubbon are right then there is a certain amount of guilt by association. They cannot completely absolve themselves nor can they be absolved. Yet nor can it be assumed that the end-product of the governmental processes is synonymous with the input of permanent secretaries or of their mandarin colleagues. The Whitehall bureaucracy may have become a more sensitive and transparent conduit for the transmission of the democratic impulse as reflected in the will of ministers. It is a moot point as to whether this has enhanced the quality of public policy. This raises two further issues. First, there is a question about the constitutional role of permanent secretaries and of the higher civil service. This will be the subject of the next chapter. Second, there is a question about the ability of permanent secretaries to carry the day in Whitehall, especially vis-à-vis ministers. This is the focus for the next and final section of this chapter.

From princes to pawns?

'Under Thatcher, permanent secretaries were reduced from princes to pawns'. Such are the words of one who was a permanent secretary during the 1970s (in conversation with the author). These words beg a number of questions. Has the influence of permanent secretaries been reduced to this extent? Was Margaret Thatcher alone responsible, or is there a secular trend at work? Is this trend, such as it may be, to the undoubted detriment of good government? Are permanent secretaries in any sense to blame for their own diminution, if such it is?

The changing role of permanent secretaries was analyzed in Chapter 5. It was argued that change did not necessarily imply a lesser role. Permanent secretaries today work at full stretch – as much as, though probably no more so than, their predecessors. The emphasis of their efforts has changed. They spend more time systematically running their departments. They spend less time on policy, acknowledging that much of the work they do and always did in harness with their ministers is not really policy work. Certainly they are less likely to spend a great deal of time personally carrying a particular policy initiative, though sometimes they do. They no longer monopolize channels of access to the minister. The sheer number and variety of inputs to the ministerial level is greater than ever before. Ministers may feel overwhelmed and sometimes isolated. Nowadays, they have more reason to feel overwhelmed than to feel isolated. The permanent secretary remains the best placed among all others to pull things together for the minister. This may be on a question of strategy, policy development, the presentation of policy, advice on a tricky or contentious issue, a complex matter requiring decision or simply the coherence of the work going on in the department.

For these reasons the office of permanent secretary is likely to remain at the apex of the bureaucracy, unless there is a deliberate and radical overhaul. It is tempting to say that if it did not exist or were done away with, some very similar institution would soon be re-established or would re-emerge naturally by dint of necessity. This is perhaps going too far, bearing in mind the historical context within which the modern office of permanent secretary emerged and developed. Nevertheless, a big job it still is and a difficult one, too. Yet this observation is consistent with another one: that permanent secretaries have less clout, less influence upon the sway of events. First, within their departments, permanent secretaries no longer 'lord it' in quite the way that many of them once did. In recent decades a more collegiate form has prevailed almost everywhere with, as ever, differences of personal style and of departmental ethos. Permanent secretaries no longer maintain and do not pretend to have the tight control exercised by some of their predecessors. Second, they may in recent years have held less sway with ministers. It is an exaggeration to describe them as pawns. Due allowance must be made for the fact that, as a rule though not always, the full extent of the contribution made by particular officials becomes apparent only some while after the event – and sometimes never. Historians may subsequently judge the roles of officials in recent years to have been far more significant than present indications (such as they are) would seem to warrant. Even so, top officials have probably been less adept at holding the line when ministers want to move in a direction they consider unwise and for reasons they judge to be unsound. The pivotal decade was the 1980s under Margaret Thatcher.

Few now subscribe to the view that permanent secretaries or other senior officials really run the country; that ministers, deluded with the trappings of office, are in reality the poodles of a manipulative bureaucracy. To an extent (no more) this is the product of a misleading contrast. The mandarins of the 1980s and '90s are considered relatively powerless against the supposed supremacy of the bureaucracy in the 1960s and the 1970s. This view of the bureaucracy of the 1960s and '70s was given air by the outpourings of a number of ministers, mainly Labour but some Conservative ones, too. Civil servants and permanent secretaries in particular almost certainly did carry more clout then than has been typical over the last fifteen years. But the 1960s and '70s were years of relative political instability. No government managed to get itself re-elected having completed a full or near full term in office. Politicians seemed at times unable to cope, uncertain of the way forward in dealing with problems such as inflation, incomes policy, industrial relations or macroeconomic policy. A series of international crises seemed for a time larger than life – the disintegration of the Bretton Woods system in the early 1970s; the oil crises of the mid and late-1970s; the IMF loan of 1976. The latter, of course, was more of a domestic than an international crisis. So, too, were the uncertainties that attended the direction of policy in the first few years following the renewed outbreak of troubles in Ulster from the late-1960s. In all these circumstances it is not surprising that ministers turned to their civil servants. If top civil servants seemed to be more firmly in the driving seat, it was partly because politicians looked to them to find solutions to some major and extremely tricky problems. Occasionally, this threw mandarins to the fore – more so than was good for them, the government of the day, or the civil service as an institution.

A further feature of the 1960s and '70s was the relative caution emanating from the centre of government in the shape of prime ministers Wilson, Callaghan and, to a lesser extent, Heath. When radical departmental ministers felt thwarted by their mandarins they often found that the latter enjoyed the support of No. 10 Downing Street. This was to change under Thatcher. In particular, the early Thatcher years were marked by some unseemly skirmishes with the bureaucracy. Thatcher made little effort to hide her contempt. It was a contempt rooted partly in the unsatisfactory relationship she had had in the early 1970s with William Pile, her permanent secretary at the DES (see above Chapter 2). In part it was simply a manifestation of her populism, her distrust of corporatist bureaucracy and of the reflective intellectualism which many permanent secretaries seemed to personify.

As noted earlier in this chapter, by no means all of Thatcher's ministers shared these antipathies – at least not to the same extent. But those who shared her radicalism knew that they had a powerful ally in a showdown. Officials came to know it, too. During the early years, the mandarins tried to hold the line – some with more tenacity than others. No one could have known that Thatcher was set to enjoy the longest uninterrupted premiership in modern times; that the Conservative Party had won the first of what have turned out (so far) to be four successive general election victories. By the mid-1980s nearly all the permanent secretaries had been appointed under her premiership. She took a particular interest in such appointments. She vetoed or effectively blocked certain potential candidates. She supported certain ministers who wanted to make their mark in the appointments process. Party colours played virtually no part in this process, even at the height of Thatcherism. Rather, she wanted a different type of mandarin – the doer not the thinker. This happened in the context of a government which was not only to enjoy an almost unparalleled spell in office but one which, more than any of its immediate predecessors, also maintained a consistent vision and sense of direction. Mandarins got the strong, purposeful government they have often said they prefer. It may not have been quite what they had in mind. Some felt uneasy. A few left, mainly at levels below permanent secretary. But as the Thatcher era unfolded, it became clear that those who stayed would have to toe the line – or at least make known their reservations in more muted and elliptical terms. They would not be rescued by a change of government which would allow lost battles to be fought again. They could not claim a political vacuum into which they must needs step for the sake of the country.

Undoubtedly the Thatcher phenomenon brought a certain redefinition of role and diminution of influence for top mandarins. But some of the factors associated with the Thatcher era – the long period in office, the strong political impulse and sustained sense of direction – might have brought similar advantage in Whitehall to any government possessing the same characteristics. Moreover, certain of the developments went with the grain of secular currents. For example, Thatcher's preference for the 'can do' type mingled in with a drift towards managerialism that was already in train. Already permanent secretaries were delegating more. From the 1960s temporary advisers of various kinds had been introduced in greater numbers and in a more systematic way than before. During the 1970s they were beginning to make their mark, though relationships with permanent officials were still strained, occasionally. Now, by the 1980s, they had found their niche.

Undercurrents had already begun to bring forth a tide of change that would have occurred even without Thatcher. But the hue of Thatcherism seems to have gotten into the timber of Whitehall. It has coloured the roles of permanent secretaries and their relationships with ministers under the Major governments. To what extent it is difficult to say. Of course, the chemistry of each minister-permanent secretary relationship is in a sense singular. Yet the one cry that has been heard above all others is that top mandarins are no longer able and perhaps less resolutely inclined to prevent their ministers from pursuing flawed policies.

Were the grandees of yesteryear so much more resolute? Were they really heavier characters? Mention of the likes of Anderson, Brook, Bridges, Fisher, Hurcomb, Lee, Sharp or Vansittart, to say nothing of those from the last century, is to invite a tentative 'yes'. Certainly they were more assured members of a more confident, more homogeneous elite group. The greater heterogeneity and decomposition chronicled in Chapter 6 may be a contributory factor to the partial loss of confidence that has probably occurred. This in turn may be loosely linked to a wider social and economic fragmentation that has been given expression in terms such as post-industrialism, post-structuralism, post-Fordism and so forth. In various walks of life the big figures of yesteryear seem to have little counterpart in the world of today. Film stars seem less exotic, bishops are made of softer clay, politicians are lesser mortals than before – with Thatcher the resounding exception. It is not surprising if permanent secretaries, too, seem less rarefied. There is greater exposure. What may once have passed unnoticed is now more likely to receive the attentions of a mass media driven by ever probing and increasingly well informed journalists. Parliamentary select committees have effected greater exposure. The doors of Whitehall have been forced ajar. Over the last two or three decades there has been a steady process of demystification. There is less deference, at least among the informed public. We should perhaps ask not whether the characters of today are as weighty as those of the past but how the permanent secretaries of yesteryear would have measured up to the challenges of the 1980s and 1990s.

There can, of course, be no definitive answer to such a question. One possible reply is that they would simply never have allowed the emergence of any threat to their influence. This is to imply that the modern breed of permanent secretaries has been partly to blame for such loss of influence as there may have been. It is a superficially attractive interpretation but not one which stands serious scrutiny. More to the point, recent incumbents have been left holding the parcel when the music stopped, so to speak. In the circumstances of the 1980s and the 1990s it is difficult to know what else either they or their predecessors could or would have done. In the past there were more men of independent means – but this is to go quite a long way back, before the First World War, to find them in reasonable numbers. Perhaps the Fisher, Bridges or Lee generations may nevertheless have left in disgust. They could still have got themselves fixed up with nice jobs in business or the City. But from there they would have had little influence in Whitehall. They might never have become permanent secretaries – they might have had their promotions withheld, like the hapless Donald Derx in the 1980s. This is quite likely. In any case they could not and, with the partial exception of Vansittart, did not attempt to carry their battles in public as did some of the firebrands of the nineteenth century. More likely still, they would have donned the mantle of a Robert Armstrong or a Robin Butler. Even in their own day – the inter-war and early post-war decades – they had sometimes to bite their lips as ministers faltered having rejected their advice; or else, like Evelyn Sharp (see Chapter 2), they put their shoulders to the wheel of policies contrary to those they had initially counselled. This may have happened more often in recent years. Certainly we cannot assume that decisions equate with the advice given. If the ensuing outcomes have been to the detriment of good government then civil servants, even permanent secretaries, cannot be held primarily to blame. It is the constitutional prerogative of ministers to reject advice. It may have been more the habit of certain ministers in recent years. If so, then good government has been a bigger and more immediate casualty than constitutional propriety. Yet some think that constitutional proprieties have been disturbed, too. So the next and final chapter reconsiders the constitutional position of permanent secretaries.

12 Permanent secretaries and the constitution

Introduction

As pointed out in Chapter 2, Britain has no unified written constitution. There are various documents, but much has the status of convention. The notion of ministerial responsibility is one of these conventions. It stems from the fact that ministers, not civil servants, are democratically elected. It means that ministers, not civil servants, should be both answerable and accountable to Parliament and the public. The only formal exception is the specific charge that is placed upon permanent secretaries, and upon certain other civil servants, as accounting officers. This is why, in a clash with civil servants, the will of ministers must ultimately prevail.

There has, however, been increasing dissatisfaction with the doctrine of ministerial responsibility. On the one hand, it can become a protective cloak behind which civil servants operate to their own agenda, safe in the knowledge that not they but their ministers will face the music. Ministers, publicly accountable and therefore unable easily to dissociate themselves from deeds done in their name, will be obliged in public to support their officials. At worst, it can become a fog of obscurity in which culpability, as distinct from constitutional formality, is difficult to locate. On the other hand, partly to extricate themselves from their dilemma, ministers have sought to shed some of the burdens previously associated with the convention in its full purity. This, too, has invited controversy. It is one thing for a minister to disclaim previous knowledge or to deny personal responsibility for an isolated calamity clearly not of his or her own making. It is another thing to deny responsibility when something more serious has gone wrong, especially when the malfunctioning has its roots in broad policy – though this can sometimes be difficult to establish. In recent years ministers have sought increasingly to disclaim responsibility for what have been described as operational matters. This was Home Secretary Michael Howard's defence following a number of escapes by prisoners from high security gaols in 1994 and 1995. In this he was assisted by the fact that the Prison Service had become an executive agency. And one of the proclaimed purposes of establishing executive agencies is to separate out the business of policy from that of administration, or day-to-day operations. In fact, Michael Howard denied this when he told the Commons that: '...there has always been a division between policy matters and operational matters. That has existed not only since the introduction of agencies – it has been recognised for years, and indeed for generations' (HC Debs, 10 January 1995, col. 40). The main questions, then, were whether this distinction should be reflected in a separation of responsibilities so that the minister was answerable and accountable for policy but not for operational matters; and, if so, whether the escapes were a knock-on effect of policy, or whether they were purely operational failures. Howard did not mollify his critics but nevertheless tried to offer some clarification when he went on to say:

> I am accountable to Parliament for the Prison Service. I am accountable to Parliament for all matters that are relevant to the Prison Service. I am responsible to Parliament for policy. The director general, according to the framework document, is responsible for operational matters. That is the distinction, but I am accountable to Parliament for the Prison Service generally (Ibid.).

Our concern here is with the general principles unearthed by the case, not with the particular case itself. Where does all this leave permanent secretaries? At one level, they retain an overall responsibility to their ministers for the entirety of their departments, even for the work of executive agencies. Yet agency chief executives have clearly defined areas of responsibility, set out in their own employment contracts and in the framework documents for their agencies. If within this context things go wrong, then few would expect to see the permanent secretary's blood on the carpet. The permanent secretary may be involved in the oversight of any general remedial action, such as the reformulation of the framework document or the appointment of a new agency chief executive. If greater fragmentation has given permanent secretaries a more complex managerial task, then they may also be less easily implicated when things go wrong.

This is not the whole story. The policy-operations divide is not watertight. The two are by no means synonymous but there is an overlap, an area of grey. If, rightly or wrongly, ministers deny responsibility for operations then are there not circumstances in which, with only a small further step, they could disclaim responsibility for what many may regard as policy? Some ministers have blamed officials for what they consider to have been poor quality advice. Usually this is implicit, occasionally explicit. To this there remains the standard riposte: if ministers have been led astray by officials then more fool the ministers. As more than one prime minister has said, if ministers cannot assert themselves in their own departments then they are not fit to be ministers.

What if the opposite has happened – if ministers have over-asserted themselves? Constitutionally, ministers cannot over-assert themselves. As argued in the last chapter, the performance of government is the more likely casualty than any constitutional principle. But what if this over – or at any rate greater – assertiveness has been accompanied by an undue obsequiousness among top civil servants? Three issues then arise. First, the constitutional question about the loyalties of senior officials and of permanent secretaries in particular. Second, there is the question about the public service ethos. And third, there is the neutrality of the administrative elite within the 'ship of state'. These three issues provide the agenda for the rest of this final chapter.

A wider loyalty?

The time-honoured working assumption is that the immediate loyalty of the top civil servant is to his or her minister. This was formally set out in the Armstrong Memorandum, issued in 1985 in the wake of the Ponting Affair and, since 1993, enshrined in the Civil Service Management Code. As noted in Chapter 2, the proposed new code will require civil servants to recognize the law, the administration of justice and the ethical standards of particular professions. It states that officials should not knowingly mislead ministers, Parliament or the public (Cabinet Office 1995, p. 49). The government acknowledges these as 'duties' which civil servants may have in addition to those they owe to ministers (Ibid., p. 48). But the code does not and is not intended to disturb the primary loyalty of civil servants to their ministers. Has this loyalty been abused and, if so, why? Are there circumstances in which civil servants in general and permanent secretaries in particular can look beyond their ministers to claim a wider loyalty? If so, to whom or to what?

The evidence is by no means clear, but there is a widespread belief that if top civil servants have any case to answer in recent years it is an excessive willingness to please ministers. A permanent secretary of the 1980s has written: 'A public service is not, in a proper sense, efficient, no matter how capable and well-tuned, if it is serving ends which are wrong by ministerial design or incompetence' (Stowe 1992, p. 392). Kenneth Stowe wonders whether even the well-tuned Whitehall instrument can any longer be relied upon to resist the entreatment of ministers to play 'bad music'. As mentioned in the last chapter, Warren Fisher might well have told his minister that a proposed course of action was plain wrong and that 'you can't get away with it'. Even then, ministers may not always have acted accordingly – notwithstanding the obvious element of value judgement as to what is right or wrong, or as to what constitutes good music or bad. Maybe some of the recent and current permanent secretaries have given equally strong advice, at least about the efficacy and even about the broader desirability of particular proposals. But what if the minister sticks to his or her guns? Only on a matter of financial regularity does the permanent secretary, as an accounting officer, have the formal authority to register a note of dissent. Otherwise, there may often be little left to say except: 'I have had my say and you have heard me. You know my reservations and I remain unhappy. You (and I) may live to regret it, but, if this is what you want, then this is what we will do'. Some of the factors mentioned in the last chapter provide the backdrop – a party long in office with ministers, individually and collectively, having a reasonably clear sense of direction. In this knowledge it becomes tempting for the civil servant to abandon the dire warnings that he or she knows will be or have been ignored and to offer instead only token qualms. If the permanent secretary takes an independent and more conspicuous position (within the department) which is overridden by the minister, will not his or her credibility suffer, especially if it happens on a few occasions? It will be wiser to keep close to the minister, or to lay off and loosen the reins. There may then be a loss of independence and even integrity.

In recent years critics have raised further and more specific concerns. It has been claimed that senior officials have played down known problems for fear of upsetting ministers and so damaging their own promotion prospects (MacDonald 1992, p. 95). The penchant for short term contracts may, it is claimed, make civil servants more anxious to please ministers (Greer 1994, p. 104). Of course permanent secretaries themselves are not in the hunt for promotions – they are already at the top. Nor, at the time of writing, are they to be placed on fixed term contracts. Moreover, a certain amount of trimming may well have gone on in the past – more so than is commonly supposed (Pliatzky 1989, p. 164). There has never been any point in offering options that are obviously beyond the political pale. Above and beyond all, though, it is the behaviour of ministers that is decisive. They set the tone. Some in recent years have allegedly shown an indifference, even a certain contempt, for the views of senior officials – more so than ministers in the past. The likes of Attlee, Bevin, Macmillan or R.A. Butler were no pushover. Nor were they saints. But they listened and took careful note when their officials demurred. While never losing the initiative they nevertheless welcomed and encouraged alternative perspectives, a function of their confidence, equanimity and indeed magnanimity. Such qualities are by no means entirely absent among ministers of today– though they are probably less common and more sparingly applied. At the same time, being a minister is now a more consistently difficult business. Politics has become much more of a career, ministerial office especially. If a minister falters, then a personal as well as a political future may be at stake. The pace of events is relentless. An ambitious minister may feel a stronger temptation to make his or her mark in the shape of some major new initiative (King 1981, pp. 279-80). Simply to keep things 'ticking over' is not enough. All this inevitably impounds upon the permanent secretary.

In one area, as mentioned above and as described in Chapter 4, permanent secretaries can and still do stand up to ministers – in connection with financial probity. Tim Lankester's note of dissent over the Pergau Dam project is one of the best known among recent exercises of this prerogative (see p. 70). He did not stop the project. But he laid down a marker which was instrumental in the subsequent rescheduling of British financial support. More than this, he re-established in some measure both his own independence and that of the office of permanent secretary.

It has been suggested that the procedures designed to ensure financial regularity could be adopted for other matters (Plowden 1994, p. 122). This would include the authority for permanent secretaries to issue similar notes of reservation about other forms of 'irregular behaviour'. As noted above, the new code to which the Major government has agreed requires civil servants to recognize the law, the administration of justice and the ethical standards of certain professions. Recognition of the law could raise some nice points of interpretation, especially laws and directives emanating from the European Union (EU). Strictly, this need present few problems. All member states are party to EU decisions: all are equally bound by those decisions. Inevitably, though, there are points of interpretation and matters of judgement as to the extent and the precise senses in which a member state is bound on a particular issue. Civil servants are doing no more than their duty if they draw their minister's attention to what they see as the imperatives of EU legislation or other regulations. To the minister, it may sometimes appear that the civil servant's loyalty lies with Brussels. As the minister's principal agent, the one who is expected to 'square' the department on behalf of the minister, the permanent secretary can be in a tricky position. At one level, there arises no new question of principle over and above that which would come into play were the minister to embark upon a collision course with some aspect of British law or other provision made by Parliament. At another level, the difficulties are much more acute. The fundamental question of the status of EU decisions is the subject of controversy – perhaps more so in Britain than in any other member state. If not in terms of EU legislation itself, then in the interpretation of such legislation and certainly in the application of regulations, directives, decisions, recommendations and opinions as ratified by the Council of Ministers there is considerable scope for dispute. Mid-ranking and other senior officials from Whitehall, if not so much permanent secretaries themselves, spend a fair amount of time with their counterparts in other member states and with officials of the Commission in Brussels. They are involved, however tentatively, in the business of harmonization. Questions of loyalty are bound to arise for many mandarins including, and perhaps in a slightly different way, permanent secretaries. Of course, quite apart from the EU dimension, there are serious questions about whether permanent secretaries should have any explicit loyalty other than to their own departmental ministers.

There is near universal acknowledgement that the immediate day-to-day loyalty of the civil servant, permanent secretaries included, should be to the departmental minister – in most cases and for most of the time. Debate has centred upon the residual categories – the untypical cases that arise from time-to-time. Some have been unwilling to admit any deviation from the principle of loyalty to the minister, save for the special role performed by permanent secretaries as accounting officers where there is a specific loyalty to Parliament (Part 1990, pp. 173-4). On another occasion, however, even Antony Part seemed to waver. He claimed that civil servants were justified in trying to influence ministers toward the common ground (Jessel 1980, p. 775). This, he said, was not to be confused with the centre ground or with some piece of ground which the civil service had constructed, but was ground 'on which, or to which, the majority of people can be persuaded to move' (Ibid.). It was something born of 'a sense of what can succeed for Britain'. But what if ministers have a different conception of this common ground, or of what will succeed for Britain? Are civil servants justified in retaining and acting upon their own (different) perceptions? And if there is a wider loyalty then, in more concrete terms, to whom or what should it be directed? Setting aside the European dimension discussed above, there are three main contenders: the government as a whole; Parliament; and the state.

It may be said that civil servants do have a loyalty not only to their departmental ministers but also to the government as a collective entity. Both the Armstrong Memorandum and the proposed new code specify a loyalty to ministers and to the duly elected government of the day. Neither document specifies any order of precedence for the proper discharge of a civil servant's loyalty in the event of a rift between a minister and the government as a whole. This is particularly pertinent to permanent secretaries. As noted in Chapter 5, it is they more than any other mandarins who operate interdepartmentally. The Wednesday morning meetings are merely the outer manifestation of this. Former ministers, such as Tony Benn, have complained that this betrays a corporate loyalty which overrides all other loyalties. One former head of the civil service has argued that permanent secretaries owe a loyalty to the prime minister through the head of the home civil service (Jay 1985, p. 81). There is a rationale for this. Cabinet government is supposed to rest upon the principle of collective responsibility. This implies a corporate, co-ordinated approach to the formulation and discharge of cabinet decisions. The prime minister is its chief custodian; the cabinet secretary the principal agent. It may make good practical sense for the permanent secretary to look beyond his or her minister when that minister looks set to confound the rest of the government. At the very least the permanent secretary will alert other relevant permanent secretaries as well as the cabinet secretary and head of the civil service. But the permanent secretary alone has no authority to put a brake on the errant minister. This must come from elsewhere, ultimately at the political level. Nor should there be any misunderstanding about the authority of the head of the home civil service vis-à-vis other permanent secretaries. The head of the home civil service has the final say in recommending to the prime minister the names of candidates (see Chapter 7). This is a very considerable influence. But it does not imply any formal authority once the appointee is in post. There is the power to persuade and a variety of informal manoeuvres that may be employed, but no formal command mechanism.

As noted earlier, permanent secretaries have a specific loyalty to Parliament in connection with the regularity of approved expenditure. Could not this loyalty be extended to other issues? The simple answer is that it would run counter to the notion of ministerial responsibility. There may be a case, in very particular circumstances, to extend the facility for permanent secretaries to issue notes of dissent in their capacity as accounting officers. Such circumstances may include the rare occasions where a minister wanted to take a course of action which, in the view of the permanent secretary, was contrary to the law or other regulation explicitly laid down by or under the authority of Parliament. This would be simply an extension of the principle which underlies notes of dissent on matters of financial regularity. But any further extension to embrace dissent on matters of policy or prescriptive judgement could only weaken the notion of ministerial responsibility. It would, in effect, invite permanent secretaries and other senior officials to appear before Parliament over the heads of their ministers rather than as representatives of their ministers. As such it would undermine the authority of ministers and, ultimately, of the democratic process – especially if it were to legitimize the offering of perspectives which were at variance with those of ministers. Perhaps ministers ought to ponder this point more carefully when redrawing the rules to get themselves off the hook in an immediate crisis. The longer term consequences may be less welcome for all and less favourable to ministers. Alternatively, maybe the entire edifice of ministerial responsibility needs to be reconsidered. The relationship between permanent secretaries and Parliament could then be on the agenda, though this does not presuppose a specific loyalty. In any case, such consideration would have wider implications. It would make sense only in the context of a fundamental review of Britain's entire system of government and of its representative institutions.

If not a loyalty to Parliament then could permanent secretaries have a loyalty to the state? The state is not synonymous either with Parliament or with any particular government of the day. This is implicit in the acknowledgement that 'the Civil Service is not the property of any single Administration' (Cabinet Office 1994, p. 4). By this the Major government meant simply that no one administration should render the civil service incapable of serving a future administration of different political colour – in other words that it should not impair the neutrality of the civil service. The specific question of neutrality will be addressed below. But if the civil service is not the property of any government then to whom does it belong? A former head of the civil service once said that it belonged neither to politicians nor to officials but to the Crown and the nation. Does this mean that, in the name of the Crown or of the nation, permanent secretaries could be justified in confounding their ministers or indeed the whole government? Such prescriptions about Crown and nation surely mean little unless there is some specified point, in principle at least, at which they come into play – some point at which loyalty to the minister (or the government) comes into conflict and is overridden by this greater loyalty. Given the high stakes involved, was not Robert Vansittart justified after all in trying to undermine his ministers over appeasement during the 1930s? In truth there can be no definitive answer. Yet even among those who doubt that he was justified there are those who believe that civil servants, permanent secretaries in particular, should have if not a higher formal loyalty then a set of higher ideals as their touchstone. For many, this is connected with the public service ethic.

Decline of the public service ethic?

There has in recent years been a growing belief that the public service ethic is less prescient in the minds of officials than formerly. This implies an earlier age, if not a golden age, when a more strenuous public service ethic prevailed (O'Toole 1990; Inglis 1993). Such observations are not novel (see Wheare 1954, p. 26). Nor has Whitehall itself been insensible to the more recent expressions of concern (Efficiency Unit 1993, p. 108). What is meant by a public service ethic? Has it declined? And what if it has declined?

It is not easy to define what exactly is meant by the public service ethic.

Most would accept that it has something to do with a sense of duty, for its own sake, to a broader public rather than for personal gratification; a sense of corporate endeavour; a concern for values such as fairness, justice and the rule of law; and a recognition that the civil service in particular possesses certain characteristics which set it apart from other (non-public) institutions. With reference to the latter, Robin Butler (1988, p. 15) has written about 'the requirements of equity, accountability, impartiality and a wide view of the public interest'. Has there been any deterioration in standards? The PAC (1994a, p. v, para. 1) has talked about 'a departure from the standards of public conduct which have mainly been established during the past 140 years... following publication of the Northcote and Trevelyan Report'. In saying this the PAC was referring to executive agencies and the greater number of non-departmental bodies 'intended to improve the provision of public services through delegation of responsibilities, streamlining and a more entrepreneurial approach to work' (Ibid., para. 2). It denied that these were the results of efforts to ensure economy and efficiency – objectives which, the PAC held, remain quite consistent with traditional standards. But it alluded to some of the potential problems of managerial control discussed above in Chapter 3. This diagnosis was broadly confirmed by the TCSC. The TCSC (1994a, p. xxi, para. 84) argued that 'the devolution of authority within the Civil Service and the disappearance of traditional structures of control reinforces the need for greater vigilance about standards... (and) reinforces the importance of the less tangible shared values'. But this, as the TCSC acknowledged, is not the same as saying that there has been a decline in standards. There is a distinction between lapses in performance and adherence to values such as equity, fairness and so forth.

Beyond this it is difficult to be more specific. This is one reason why it is difficult to know whether public service values are still held with the same widespread and heartfelt ardour as apparently they were held in days gone by. In truth we have no systematic and certainly no quantitative data from the past against which any contemporary survey could be compared. It is fairly clear, though, that the notion of a public service ethic has been less than wholeheartedly endorsed by certain individual ministers, especially of the Thatcher and, to a lesser extent, of the Major governments. Even this is difficult to pin down. It has nevertheless found indirect expression in facile notions about 'private good, public bad'; and in an equally simplistic faith in the indiscriminate application of business methods in Whitehall. In this context it has almost certainly been more difficult for senior civil servants, permanent secretaries no less, to follow the dictats of a public service ethic, even if their belief in such ideals has remained undiminished. There may have occurred a certain atrophy. The Major government has both given implicit acknowledgement to the fact and sought to prevent any further slippage. This it has done by spelling out its commitment to 'the maintenance of a permanent Civil Service, based on the values of integrity, political impartiality, objectivity, selection and promotion by merit and accountability through Ministers to Parliament' (Cabinet Office 1995, p. 3, para. 2.1).

Why should there be any cause to regret a decline in the public service ethic, if such there has been? For some it is a woolly notion anyway, perhaps carrying connotations of state socialism or intrusive interventionism. For some at least it is seen as a convenient camouflage for a self-serving bureaucracy. Against this it may be held that a public service ethic remains vital as a mainspring in the absence of any equivalent to the profit motive which drives the private sector. A public service ethic provides a sense of mission which transcends any immediate management objective or performance target. As many of Whitehall's more commercially-orientated functions and operations are removed from the state sector there may be a greater need to reassert the service ethic in that which remains public. Above all it may be essential to the neutrality of the higher civil service, a neutrality of which permanent secretaries are the chief custodians. But permanent secretaries, more than any other civil servants, operate within the orbit of ministers. Ministers, more than any other group, set the scene. It is they as much as anyone else who must uphold and sustain the essential values of public service. Calls for a code of conduct for civil servants may help officials to resist ministers' inducements to perpetrate acts of impropriety. The FDA has for many years pressed the case for such a code. The Treasury and Civil Service Committee accepted the idea as a formal recommendation (TCSC 1994a, paras. 103-7). The government, in turn, has accepted, with minor modifications, the TCSC's draft code (Cabinet Office 1995, pp. 46-53). This includes an endorsement of some of the clauses contained in *Questions of Procedure for Ministers*. The latter has been available for public inspection since 1992, though its status has been uncertain. A stronger and more detailed code for ministers may be necessary. More importantly, it should have, in order to be effective, the widespread and sincere endorsement of politicians at all levels. It is difficult for politicians sometimes to conceive that civil servants can be driven by a desire to do public good in a way that is detached from party preference. It is perhaps even more difficult for ministers (and others) to understand how officials are able to transfer their loyalty from one administration to another without loss of commitment. It requires a very special type of commitment and a certain type of detachment. This links with the question of neutrality.

A neutral elite?

For some the idea of neutrality is a myth (Ponting 1989, p. 35). It certainly is a myth in that, far from being above or detached from politics, the work of top officials is permeated by the rough and tumble of political life. As noted on more than one occasion in this book, whatever bears upon ministers bears also upon permanent secretaries. There are two caveats here. First, the permanent secretary should maintain a broader and longer term vision. It is the permanent secretary's job to try to impress this vision upon the minister and to bring it to bear upon decisions that are made. Second, the permanent secretary must not get too closely identified, in the public mind, with any one minister, government or particular policy. If this happens it may be difficult to win the confidence of another minister or another government. The implication is that what is unacceptable in public may be acceptable behind closed doors. Permanent secretaries can and do take positions – usually but not always in concert with their ministers. If a new minister comes in or a new government takes office the permanent secretary may be seen (within Whitehall) to be adopting a different position from the one adopted before. In this sense Ridley (1985, p. 37) has likened permanent secretaries to the mercenary generals who 'would advise whatever prince they served at the time on tactics of war and then lead his troops into battle'. Ridley distinguishes between two types of neutrality. On the one hand there is the giving of sane, impartial advice to governments of whatever hue. On the other hand, it may mean bending to the will of whoever happens to be in office – in other words a neutrality that begets a lack of independence. It is the first rather than the second of these versions of neutrality which has been the traditional assumption. But some people think that this has been impaired by a growing lack of independence.

Lord Callaghan has said that the senior civil service has become part of a ministerial 'private fiefdom' (TCSC 1993, Q. 586). The only remedy, he says, is a change of government. In this he claimed to be making not a party political point, simply an observation that a lengthy period in the service of one party reduces the capacity of the bureaucracy readily to transfer its allegiance to another government. In one sense he is right: the capacity of the civil service adequately to serve another party can only be proven or disproven in the event of a change of government. Perhaps the British bureaucracy, as it evolved, was never tooled up to maintain its neutrality (in the first of Ridley's two senses) in the context of sustained and uninterrupted rule by one party exclusively. But this cannot pass as evidence that the top mandarins of the 1990s are incapable of serving a government other than a Conservative one. Privately, permanent secretaries express their confidence in the ability of the official machine to serve a government of different political persuasion. This may be sheer disingenuity, but that is extremely doubtful. They probably relish the prospect of a change of government – not because they prefer a Labour to a Conservative government but because they enjoy the challenge, the excitement, the promise that comes with a new administration. To a lesser extent, the individual permanent secretary will often feel the same sense of exhilaration when a new minister takes the helm even if there is no change of government. This, together with their sheer professionalism, may be why permanent secretaries seem relatively phlegmatic about the high turnover among ministers, though it brings extra work and may upset proposals that have been long in careful preparation. This is probably closer to the truth than the alternative, conspiratorial, interpretation – that a new minister may be more malleable. Of course the promise of a new government may soon disappear with the momentum of events. A new minister may be more 'difficult' and occasionally near impossible. Nevertheless, the ability to work with and to serve different ministers and different governments has been one of the traditional hallmarks of the British mandarin elite. Proclamations about the decline of this tradition are premature and ill-founded. The TCSC (1994a, p. xxi, para. 85) had little doubt that civil servants would be able 'to demonstrate the same level of commitment to any incoming Government' and that 'the commitment of the overwhelming majority of civil servants to the principle and practice of a politically impartial Civil Service is undiminished'. If in recent years anything has been lost, it is the ability to get ministers to give sufficient consideration before launching new initiatives, not the loss of ability to serve those ministers faithfully or of the potential to transfer their allegiance in the event of a change of minister or a change of government.

The ability to serve to equal effect ministers and governments of different political colour or shade is not always fully acknowledged. Nor is it always admired even when it is the acknowledged fact. It implies what one writer considers to be a 'psychological nonsense' (Plowden 1985, p. 403). Yet no one supposes that private doubts about the innocence of a client need prevent the lawyer from presenting powerful advocacy in the courtroom. Similarly, what the permanent secretary is offering is a professional rather than a personal commitment. Ministers have sometimes observed that officials are over-scrupulous in avoiding party prejudices (Healey 1989, p. 107). But they are not party politicians. As Ian Bancroft once said: 'conviction politicians certainly: conviction civil servants, certainly not'. Bagehot (1974, pp. 130-1) was not referring specifically to civil servants when he championed the virtues of 'animated moderation'. But the phrase he coined perhaps describes the ideal modern permanent secretary.

This will not and manifestly has not silenced the calls for a (partial or semi-) politicization of the higher civil service. For some, this is a necessary corrective to an insidious form of politicization which is held already to have taken place (Plowden 1985). But there is, as we have seen, little evidence that politicization has taken place – certainly not among permanent secretaries. For others there is a need to redraw the boundary line between political and other specialist advisers (Ponting 1989, p. 47). This need not involve the politicization of the regular, permanent bureaucracy. Others again have called for a two-tier arrangement (Ridley 1985, pp. 39-42). At one level would be a group avowedly partisan, presumably on the US model. At another level there would be officials with a loyalty not only to the ministers of the day but also to the service of the state. But much would be lost if the office of permanent secretary were to be located other than firmly within the second category. They more than anyone else are the custodians of much that remains of value in the higher civil service – impartiality; integrity; objective analysis; a broad, long term vision; and the authority to mobilize a powerful but sometimes wayward administrative machine. Permanent secretaries are best placed to protect, nurture and apply these qualities not only by virtue of their seniority but also because they, uniquely, bring together policy advice, decision-making, strategic management and financial probity. This they could not do if they were political partisans, or if they were accorded simply the role of 'production engineers'. Despite recent changes of emphasis in the roles they play they are and should remain more than that. A good deal depends upon them. Collectively, they are an imperfect but by no means fundamentally flawed elite. Individually, there are some who have brought greater credit and honour to the office of permanent secretary than have others. Most have been among the best and ablest people of their respective generations, not only within Whitehall but in the country at large. Some have been quite outstanding. Few have been driven by anything other than a genuine desire to give to their country the best, as they have seen it. So two cheers for permanent secretaries – not three, they don't deserve that. Two cheers, yes; and two hearty cheers. It should never be forgotten that, in a democracy, even the most outstanding officials perform only as effectively as they are permitted by their political masters.

Appendix:
List of office-holders, 1830-1994

1. The list below contains the names, educational details and permanent secretaryships held by those in post in 1830 together with those appointed from 1830 until the summer of 1994.
2. Individuals are listed as they were known upon retirement or exit from the civil service. Peerages and other titles subsequently inherited or conferred are indicated in parenthesis. Where this involves a substantive change of name, entries are cross-referenced. Only civil and military decorations are included. Designatory letters in connection with academic qualifications or membership of professional bodies are excluded.
3. Except where otherwise stated, all posts are or were designated permanent secretary. This may not always be strictly correct. During the nineteenth century and in the early decades of the present century especially, there was some flexibility in usage. For example, the terms 'permanent secretary' and 'secretary' (Secy.) were sometimes used to describe the same post.

Abbreviations are used for certain departments, as follows:

BoT	Board of Trade
COI	Central Office of Information
CRO	Commonwealth Relations Office
CSD	Civil Service Department
DEA	Department of Economic Affairs
DES	Department of Education and Science
DFE	Department for Education
DHSS	Department of Health and Social Security
DoE	Department of the Environment
DSIR	Department of Scientific and Industrial Research

DSS	Department of Social Security
DTI	Department of Trade and Industry
FCO	Foreign and Commonwealth Office
FO	Foreign Office
LGB	Local Government Board
MAFF	Ministry of Agriculture, Fisheries and Food
MFP	Ministry of Fuel and Power
MHLG	Ministry of Housing and Local Government
MoD	Ministry of Defence
MPBW	Ministry of Public Buildings and Works
MPNI	Ministry of Pensions and National Insurance
MPO	(Cabinet Office) Management and Personnel Office
Mintech.	Ministry of Technology
MSC	Manpower Services Commission
MTCP	Ministry of Town and Country Planning
ODA	(FCO) Overseas Development Administration
OMCS	(Cabinet Office) Office of the Minister for the Civil Service
OPSS	(Cabinet Office) Office of the Minister of Public Service and Science
PSA	(DoE) Property Services Agency

Abbreviations for decorations

AFC	Air Force Cross
CB	Companion of the Bath
CBE	Commander of the British Empire
CIE	Companion of the Indian Empire
CMG	Companion of St. Michael and St. George
CSI	Companion of the Star of India
CVO	Commander, Royal Victorian Order
DBE	Dame Commander of the British Empire
DCB	Dame Commander of the Bath
DFC	Distinguished Flying Cross
GBE	Knight Grand Cross of the British Empire
GCB	Knight Grand Cross of the Bath
GCIE	Knight Grand Commander of the Indian Empire
GCMG	Knight Grand Cross of St. Michael and St. George
GCSI	Knight Grand Commander of the Star of India
GCVO	Knight Grand Cross, Royal Victorian Order
ISO	Imperial Service Order
KBE	Knight Commander of the British Empire
KCB	Knight Commander of the Bath
KCIE	Knight Commander of the Indian Empire
KCMG	Knight Commander of St. Michael and St. George
KCSI	Knight Commander of the Star of India
KCVO	Knight Commander, Royal Victorian Order
KG	Knight of the Garter
MBE	Member of the British Empire
MC	Military Cross
MVO	Member, Royal Victorian Order
OBE	Officer of the British Empire
OM	Order of Merit
PC	Privy Counsellor

ABBOT, Charles Stewart Aubrey – see TENTERDEN, Lord.
ACLAND, Sir Antony GCMG, GCVO (b. 1930). Educ. Eton; Ox., Christ Church. – PUS, FCO and Head of Diplomatic Service, 1982-86.
ADDINGTON, (Rt. Hon.) Henry Unwin (PC) (1790-1870). Educ. Winchester – PUS, FO, 1842-54.
AIREY, Sir Lawrence KCB (b. 1926). Educ. Newcastle Royal GS; Camb., Peterhouse – 2nd Perm. Sec., HM Treasury, 1977-79; Chm. Bd Inland Revenue, 1980-86.
ALFRED, A Montague (b. 1925). Educ. Central Foundation Sch.; Imperial Coll., Univ. London – Chief Exec., PSA (DoE), 1982-84.
ALLEN, Sir Douglas (Lord Croham) GCB (b. 1917). Educ. Wallington County GS; LSE – PUS, DEA, 1966-68 (2nd PUS, 1966); Perm. Sec., HM Treasury, 1968-74; CSD and Head of Home Civil Service, 1974-77.
ALLEN, Sir Philip (Lord Allen of Abbeydale) GCB (b.1912). Educ. King Edward VII Sch., Sheffield; Camb., Queens' – 2nd Secy., HM Treasury, 1963-66; PUS, Home Off., 1966-72.
ANDERSON, Sir John KCB, GCMG (1858-1918). Educ. Univ. Aberdeen – PUS, Colonial Off., 1911-16.
ANDERSON, Rt. Hon. Sir John (Viscount Waverley) GCB, OM, GCSI, GCIE, PC (1882-1958). Educ. George Watson's Coll. Edinburgh; Univs. Edinburgh, Leipzig – Secy., Min. Shipping, 1917-19; Additional Perm. Sec., LGB, 1919; 2nd Secy., Min. Health, 1919; Chm. Bd. Inland Revenue, 1919-22, (Jt. Under Sec., Irish Off., 1920); PUS, Home Off., 1922-32.
ANDERSON, Sir John KBE, CB (1908-65). Educ. Rugby; Camb., Christ's – Chm. Bd. Customs and Excise, 1963-65.
ANDREW, Revd. Sir Herbert KCMG, CB (1910-85). Educ. Manchester GS; Ox., Corpus Christi – Min. Education, 1963-70 (PUS, DES, 1964-70).
ANDREW, Sir Robert KCB (b. 1928). Educ. King's Coll. Sch., Wimbledon; Ox., Merton – PUS, Northern Ireland Off., 1984-88.
ANDREWS, Sir Derek KCB, CBE (b. 1933). Educ. Sloane Sch., Chelsea; LSE – MAFF, 1987-93.
ANSON, Sir John KCB (b. 1930). Educ. Winchester; Camb., Magdalene – 2nd Perm. Sec., HM Treasury, 1987-90.
APPLETON, Sir Edward GBE, KCB (1892-1965). Educ. Hanson Sch., Bradford; Camb., St. John's – Secy., DSIR, 1939-49.
ARMSTRONG, Sir Robert (Lord Armstrong of Ilminster) GCB, CVO (b.1927). Educ. Eton; Ox., Christ Church – PUS, Home Off., 1977-79; Cabinet Secy., 1979-87, and Head of Home Civil Service, 1981-87 (Jt Head 1981-83).
ARMSTRONG, Rt. Hon. Sir William (Lord Armstrong of Sanderstead) GCB, MVO, PC (1915-80). Educ. Bec Sch.; Ox., Exeter Coll. – Jt. Perm. Sec., HM Treasury, 1962-68; Perm. Sec., CSD and Head of Home Civil Service, 1968-74.
ATKINSON, Sir Alec KCB, DFC (b. 1919). Educ. Kingswood Sch.; Ox., Queen's – 2nd Perm. Sec., DHSS, 1977-79.
AUSTIN, Alfred CB (1805-1884) – Secy., Off. Works, 1854-68.

BABINGTON SMITH, Sir Henry GBE, KCB, CSI (1863-1923). Educ. Eton; Camb., Trinity – Secy., Post Off., 1903-09.
BACKHOUSE, John (1784-1845). Educ. Cartmel Sch.; Clitheroe Foundation Sch. – PUS, FO, 1827-42.
BAILEY, Sir Alan KCB (b. 1931). Educ. Bedford Sch.; Ox., St. John's; Merton – 2nd Perm. Sec., HM Treasury, 1983-86; Perm. Sec., Dept. Transport, 1986-91.
BAILLIE HAMILTON, William A. (1803-81) – Second (Perm.) Sec., Admiralty, 1845-55.

BALDWIN, Sir Peter KCB (b. 1922). Educ. City of London Sch.; Ox., Corpus Christi – 2nd Perm. Sec., DoE, 1976; Perm. Sec., Dept. Transport, 1976-82.

BAMFORD, Sir Eric KCB, KBE, CMG (1891-1957). Educ. Stonyhurst; Ox., Corpus Christi – Dir.-Gen. COI, 1946; Chm. Bd. Inland Revenue, 1948-55.

BANCROFT, Sir Ian (Lord Bancroft) GCB (b. 1922). Educ. Coatham Sch.; Ox., Balliol – 2nd Perm. Sec., CSD, 1973-75; Perm. Sec., DoE, 1975-77; CSD and Head of Home Civil Service, 1978-81.

BANKS, Sir Donald KCB (1891-1975). Educ. Elizabeth Coll., Guernsey – Dir.-Gen., Post Off., 1934-36; Perm. Sec., Air Ministry, 1936-39 (PUS, 1938-39).

BARLOW, Sir Alan, Bart., GCB, KBE (1881-1968). Educ. Marlborough; Ox., Corpus Christi – 2nd Secy., HM Treasury, 1938-48.

BARNES, Sir Denis KCB (1914-92). Educ. Hulme GS, Manchester; Ox., Merton – Min. Labour, 1966-73 (Dept. Employment and Productivity, 1968-70; Dept. Employment, 1970-73).

BARNES, Sir George KCB, KCSI, CB (1858-1946). Educ. Eton; Ox., Univ. Coll. – Jt. Perm. Sec., BoT, 1915 (2nd Secy., 1913-15).

BARNES, Sir James KCB, KBE (1891-1969). Educ. Manchester GS.; Ox., Merton – PUS, Air Ministry, 1947-55.

BARNES, Sir Kenneth KCB (b. 1922). Educ. Accrington GS.; Ox., Balliol – Dept. Employment, 1976-82.

BARROW, Sir John, Bart. (1764-1848). Educ. Town Bank GS, Ulverston – Second (Perm.) Sec., Admiralty, 1804-06, 1807-45.

BARSTOW, Sir George KCB (1874-1966). Educ. Clifton Coll.; Camb., Emmanuel – Controller of Supply, HM Treasury, 1919-27.

BATHURST, William Lennox (5th Earl Bathurst) (1791-1878). Educ. Eton; Ox., All Souls – Clerk, Privy Council, 1827-60 (Jt. Clerk, 1827-59).

BATTISHILL, Sir Anthony KCB (b. 1937). Educ. Taunton Sch.; LSE – Chm. Bd. Inland Revenue, 1986 – .

BEALE, Sir John KBE (1874-1935). Educ. Harrow; Camb., Trinity – Secy., Min. Food, 1918-19.

BEVERIDGE, Sir William (Lord Beveridge) KCB (1879-1963). Educ Charterhouse; Ox., Balliol – Secy., Min. Food, 1919.

BICKERTON, Frank D. CBE (b 1917). Educ. Liverpool Collegiate Sch. – Dir.-Gen. COI, 1971-74.

BIRCHALL, Sir Raymond KCB, KBE (1888-1968). Educ. Westminster; Camb., Trinity – Dir.-Gen., Post Off., 1946-49.

BISHOP, Sir Frederick CB, CVO (b. 1915). Educ. Colston's Hospital, Bristol; Univ. London – Min. Land and Natural Resources, 1964-65.

BLACHFORD, Lord – see ROGERS, Sir Frederic.

BLACK, Sir Frederick KCB (1863-1930). Educ. Newport GS; Univ. London – Dir.-Gen., Min. Munitions, 1915.

BLACKETT, Sir Basil KCB, KCSI (1882-1935). Educ. Marlborough; Ox., Univ. Coll. – Controller Finance, HM Treasury, 1919-22.

BLACKWOOD, Sir Stevenson KCB (1832-93). Educ. Eton; Camb., Trinity – Secy., Post Off., 1880-93.

BLELLOCH, Sir John KCB (b. 1930). Educ. Fettes; Camb., Gonville and Caius – 2nd PUS, MoD, 1984-88; PUS, Northern Ireland Off., 1988-90.

BLOOMFIELD, Sir Kenneth KCB (b. 1931). Educ. Royal Belfast Academical Inst.; Ox., St. Peter's – 2nd PUS, Northern Ireland Off. and Head of Northern Ireland Civil Service, 1984-91.

BOOTH, James (CB) (1796-1880). Educ. Camb., St. John's – Jt. Perm. Sec., BoT, 1850-65.

BOVENSCHEN, Sir Frederick KCB, KBE (1884-1977). Educ. King's Sch., Canterbury; Ox., Corpus Christi – Jt. PUS, War Off., 1942-45.

BOWYER, Sir Eric KCB, KBE (1902-64). Educ. Whitehill, Glasgow; Univ. Glasgow – Min. Materials, 1953-54; MPNI, 1955-64.

BOYLE, Sir Courtenay KCB (1845-1901). Educ. Charterhouse; Ox., Christ Church – BoT, 1893-1901.

BRADBURY, Sir John (Lord Bradbury) GCB (1872-1950). Educ. Manchester GS; Ox., Brasenose – Jt. Perm. Sec., HM Treasury, 1913-19.

BRADE, Sir Reginald GCB (1864-1933). Educ. St. Andrew's Coll., Bradfield – Secy., War Off., 1914-20.

BRETT, Reginald Balliol – see ESHER, 2nd Viscount.

BRIDGES, Rt. Hon. Sir Edward (Lord Bridges) KG, GCB, GCVO, PC (1892-1969). Educ. Eton; Ox., Magdalen – Cabinet Secy., 1938-46; Perm. Sec., HM Treasury and Head of Home Civil Service, 1945-56.

BRIETZEKE, R.B.D. – see DEAN, Richard.

BRIMELOW, Sir Thomas (Lord Brimelow) GCMG, OBE (b. 1915). Educ. New Mills County Sec. Sch.; Ox., Oriel – PUS, FCO and Head of Diplomatic Service, 1973-75.

BRITTAIN, Sir Herbert KCB, KBE (1894-1961). Educ. Rochdale Sec. Sch.; Univ. Manchester – 2nd Secy., HM Treasury, 1953-57.

BROADBENT, Sir Ewen KCB, CMG (1924-93). Educ. King Edward VI, Nuneaton; Camb., St. John's – 2nd PUS, MoD, 1982-84.

BROOK, Rt. Hon. Sir Norman (Lord Normanbrook) GCB, PC (1902-67). Educ. Wolverhampton Sch.; Ox., Wadham – Min. Reconstruction, 1943-45; Cabinet Secy., 1947-62 (Additional Secy., 1945-46) and Jt. Perm. Sec., HM Treasury and Head of Home Civil Service, 1956-62.

BROOKE, Sir John CB (1880-1937). Educ. Haileybury; Ox., Corpus Christi – Secy., Min. Transport, 1923-27.

BROWETT, Sir Leonard KCB, CBE (1884-1959). Educ. King Edward's Sch., Birmingham – Secy., Min. Transport, 1937-41.

BROWN, Sir Patrick KCB (b. 1940). Educ. Royal GS, Newcastle upon Tyne; Sch. of Slavonic and E. European Studies, Univ. London – 2nd Perm. Sec. and Chief Exec., PSA (DoE), 1990-91; Perm. Sec., Dept. Transport, 1991- .

BROWN, Sir Max KCB, CMG (b. 1914). Educ. Wanganui Coll., Victoria; Victoria Univ., New Zealand; Camb., Clare Coll. – 2nd Perm. Sec., BoT, 1968-70; (2nd) Secy., DTI, 1970-74; Perm. Sec., Dept. Trade, 1974.

BROWN, Sir William KCB, KCMG, CB, CBE (1893-1947). Educ. Royal GS, Newcastle upon Tyne; Camb., King's – BoT, 1937-40; Min. Supply, 1940-42; MFP (Petroleum), 1942-43; Secy., Min. Home Security, 1943-45; PUS, Air Ministry, 1945-47.

BULLER, Rt. Hon., Gen. Sir Redvers GCB, GCMG, PC (1839-1908). Educ. Eton – Under Sec., Irish Off., 1887.

BULLOCK, Sir Christopher KCB, CBE (1891-1972). Educ. Rugby; Camb., Trinity – Secy., Air Ministry, 1931-36.

BURNS, Sir Terence (b. 1944). Educ. Houghton-le-Spring GS; Univ. Manchester – HM Treasury, 1991- .

BURKE, Thomas H. (1829-82). Educ. Abroad – Under Sec., Irish Off., 1869-82.

BUTLER, Sir Robin GCB, CVO (b. 1938). Educ. Harrow; Ox., Univ. Coll. – 2nd Perm. Sec., HM Treasury, 1985-87; Cabinet Secy. and Head of Home Civil Service 1988- .

BYRNE, Rt. Hon. Sir William KCVO, CB, PC (1859-1935). Educ. St. Bede's Coll.,

238 The Elite of the Elite

Manchester – Under Sec., Irish Off., 1916-18.

CACCIA, Sir Harold (Lord Caccia) GCMG, GCVO (1905-90). Educ. Eton; Camb., Trinity – PUS, FO, 1962-65 (and Head Diplomatic Service, 1964-65).

CADOGAN, (Rt. Hon.) Sir Alexander OM, GCMG, KCB, (PC) (1884-1968). Educ. Eton; Ox., Balliol – PUS, FO, 1938-46.

CAINES, Sir John KCB (b. 1933). Educ. Westminster, Ox., Christ Church – ODA (FCO), 1987-89; DES/DFE, 1989-93.

CALCROFT, Sir Henry KCB (1836-96). – BoT, 1886-93.

CANNY, Sir Gerald KCB, KBE (1881-1954). Educ. Malvern Coll.; Camb., Queens' – Chm. Bd. Inland Revenue, 1938-42.

CARDWELL, Sir David KCB (1920-82). Educ. Dulwich Coll.; Univ. London – Chief Exec., (Procurement) MoD, 1980-82.

CAREY, Sir Peter GCB (b. 1923). Educ. Portsmouth GS; Ox., Oriel; School of Slavonic Studies, Univ. London – 2nd Perm. Sec., DTI, 1973-74; Perm. Sec., Dept. Industry, 1974-83 (2nd Perm. Sec., 1974-76).

CARNOCK, Lord – see NICOLSON, Sir Arthur.

CARTER, Sir Archibald GCMG, KCB, KCIE (1887-1958). Educ. Eton; Camb., Trinity – Admiralty, 1936-40; Chm. Bd. Customs and Excise, 1942-47; PUS, India Off., 1947; Jt. PUS, CRO, 1947-48.

CARY, Sir Michael GCB (1917-76). Educ. Eton; Ox., Trinity – 2nd PUS, MoD, 1964-68, Perm. Sec., MPBW, 1968-70; (2nd) Secy., DoE, 1970-72; Chief Exec. (Procurement), MoD, 1972-74; PUS, MoD, 1974-76.

CASSELS, (Sir) John CB (b. 1928). Educ. Sedbergh; Camb., Trinity – 2nd Perm. Sec., Cabinet Off., 1981-83 (MPO from Nov. 1981).

CHADWICK, (Sir) Edwin (KCB) (1800-90). Educ. Privately, Manchester and London – Secy., Poor Law Bd., 1834-47; General Bd. Health, 1848-54.

CHALMERS, Sir Mackenzie KCB, CSI (1847-1927). Educ. King's Coll., London; Ox., Trinity – PUS, Home Off., 1903-08.

CHALMERS, Sir Robert (Lord Chalmers) GCB (1858-1938). Educ. City of London Sch.; Ox., Oriel – Chm. Bd. Inland Revenue, 1907-11; Perm Sec., HM Treasury, 1911-13; Jt. Perm. Sec., HM Treasury, 1916-19; (Under Sec., Irish Off., 1916).

CHAPMAN, Sir Sydney KCB, CBE (1871-1951). Educ. Manchester GS; Owens Coll., Manchester; Camb., Trinity – BoT, 1919-27.

CHILCOT, Sir John KCB (b. 1939). Educ. Brighton Coll.; Camb., Pembroke – PUS, Northern Ireland Off., 1990- .

CHIPPERFIELD, Sir Geoffrey KCB (b. 1933). Educ. Cranleigh; Ox., New Coll. – PUS, Dept. Energy, 1989-91; 2nd Perm. Sec. (Grade 1) and Chief Exec., PSA (DoE), 1991-93.

CHRYSTAL, Sir George KCB (1880-1944). Educ. George Watson's Coll., Edinburgh; Univ. Edinburgh; Ox., Balliol – Min. Nat. Service and Min. Reconstruction, 1918-19; Min. Pensions, 1919-35; Min. Health, 1935-40.

CLARK, Sir Fife CBE (1907-85). Educ. Middlesbrough High – Dir-Gen., COI, 1954-71.

CLARKE, Sir Richard KCB, OBE (1910-75). Educ. Christ's Hospital; Camb., Clare Coll. – 2nd Secy., HM Treasury, 1962-66; Perm. Sec., Min. Aviation, 1966; Mintech, 1966-70.

CLERK, Sir George KCB, CSI (1800-89). Educ. Haileybury – PUS, India Off., 1858-60.

CLUCAS, Sir Kenneth KCB (b. 1921). Educ. Kingswood Sch.; Camb., Emmanuel – Dept. Prices and Consumer Protection, 1974-79; Dept. Trade, 1979-82.

CLUTTERBUCK, Sir Alexander GCMG (1897-1975). Educ. Malvern Coll.; Camb., Pembroke – PUS, CRO, 1959-61.

COCHRAN-PATRICK, Robert W. (1842-97). Educ. Univ. Edinburgh; Camb., Trinity Hall – PUS, Scottish Off., 1887-92.
COHEN, Sir Andrew KCMG, KCVO, OBE (1909-68). Educ. Malvern Coll.; Camb., Trinity – Dir.-Gen., Dept. Technical Co-operation, 1961-64; Perm. Sec., Min. Overseas Development, 1964-68.
COLES, Sir John KCMG (b. 1937). Educ. Magdalen Coll. Sch., Brackley; Ox. Magdalen – PUS, FCO and Head of Diplomatic Service, 1994-
COLLER, Frank, H. CB (1866-1938). Educ. Westminster; Ox., Christ Church – Secy., Min. Food, 1919-21.
COOPER, (Rt. Hon.) Sir Frank GCB, CMG (PC) (b. 1922). Educ. Manchester GS.; Ox., Pembroke – PUS, Northern Ireland Off., 1973-76; PUS, MoD, 1976-82.
CORNFORD, Sir Clifford KCB (b. 1918). Educ. Kimbolton Sch.; Camb., Jesus – Chief Exec. (Procurement), MoD, 1975-80 (Chief Exec. and Perm. Sec., Procurement Exec., 1975-77).
COTTESLOE, Lord – see FREMANTLE, Sir Thomas.
COURTENAY, William Visc. Courtenay – see DEVON, 11th Earl.
COUZENS, Sir Kenneth KCB (b. 1925). Educ. Portsmouth GS; Camb., Caius Coll.; Birkbeck Coll., London – 2nd Perm. Sec., HM Treasury, 1977-82; PUS, Dept. Energy, 1983-85.
COX, Sir Robert KCB (1922-81). Educ. Peter Symonds' Sch., Winchester; Camb., Christ's Coll. – Chief Exec., PSA (DoE), 1974-81.
CREEDY, Sir Herbert GCB, KCVO (1878-1973). Educ. Merchant Taylors'; Ox., St. John's – War Off., 1920-39 (Jt. Perm. Sec., 1920-24; PUS, 1924-39).
CROFT, Sir William KCB, KBE, CIE, CVO (1892-1964). Educ. Winchester; Ox., Trinity – Chm. Bd. Customs and Excise, 1947-55.
CROHAM, Lord – see ALLEN, Sir Douglas.
CROMBIE, Sir James KCB, KBE, CMG (1902-69). Educ. Aberdeen GS; Univ. Aberdeen; Camb., Gonville and Caius – Chm. Bd. Customs and Excise, 1955-62.
CROWE, Sir Eyre GCB, GCMG (1864-1925). Educ. Dusseldorf Gymnasium – PUS, FO, 1920-25.
CUBBON, Sir Brian GCB (b. 1928). Educ. Bury GS; Camb., Trinity – PUS, Northern Ireland Off., 1976-79; PUS, Home Off., 1979-88.
CUCKNEY, (Sir) John (b. 1924). Educ. Shrewsbury; Univ. St. Andrews – 2nd Perm. Sec. and Chief Exec., PSA (DoE), 1972-74.
CULPIN, Robert P. Educ. Bedford Sch.; Camb., Christ's Coll. – 2nd Perm. Sec., HM Treasury, 1994-.
CUMIN, Patrick CB (1823-90). Educ. Shrewsbury; Univ. Glasgow; Ox., Balliol – Secy., Educ. Dept., 1884-90.
CUNNINGHAM, Sir Charles GCB, KBE, CVO (b. 1906). Educ. Harris Academy, Dundee; Univ. St. Andrews – PUS, Home Off., 1957-66.
CUNNISON, Sir Alexander KBE, CB (1879-1959). Educ. George Watson's Coll.; Univ. Edinburgh; Ox., Oriel – Min. Pensions, 1941-45.
CURRIE, (Rt. Hon.) Sir Philip (Lord Currie) GCB, (PC) (1834-1906). Educ. Eton – PUS, FO, 1889-93.

DANIEL, Sir Goronwy KCVO, CB (b. 1914). Educ. Pontardawe Sec. Sch.; Amman Valley Sch.; Univ. Coll. Wales, Aberystwyth; Ox., Jesus – PUS, Welsh Off., 1964-69.
DANNREUTHER, Sir Sigmund CB (1874-1965). Educ. Eton; Camb., Trinity – Jt. Secy., Min. Munitions, 1920.

DAVIS, Sir Charles GCMG (1873-1938). Educ. Christ Coll., Brecon; Ox., Balliol – PUS, Dominions Off., 1925-30.
DEAN, Sir Maurice KCB, KCMG (1906-78). Educ. St. Olave's; Camb., Trinity – PUS, Air Ministry, 1955-63; 2nd Secy., HM Treasury, 1963-64; Jt. PUS, DES, 1964; Perm. Sec. Mintech, 1964-66.
DEAN, Richard B. (Formerly Brietzeke) (1773-1850). Educ. Ox., Christ Church – Chm. Bd. Customs, 1819-46.
DENMAN, Sir Roy KCB, CMG (b. 1924). Educ. Harrow GS; Camb., St. John's – 2nd Perm. Sec., Cabinet Off., 1975-77.
DEVON, 11th Earl, (Formerly Rt. Hon. William Visc. Courtenay) (1807-88). Educ. Westminster; Ox., Christ Church – Secy., Poor Law Bd., 1851-59.
DIGBY, Sir Kenhelm GCB (1836-1916). Educ. Harrow; Ox., Corpus Christi – PUS, Home Off., 1895-1903.
DODDS, Sir James KCB (1861-1935). Educ. Univ. Glasgow; Ox., Merton – PUS, Scottish Off., 1909-21.
DOUGHERTY, Rt. Hon. Sir James KCB, KCVO, PC (1844-1934). Educ. Queen's Coll., Belfast – Under Sec., Irish Off., 1908-14.
DOUGLAS, Sir William GCB, KBE (1890-1953). Educ. George Heriot's Sch., Edinburgh; Univ. Edinburgh – Min. Supply, 1942-45; Min. Health, 1945-51.
DOYLE, Sir Francis, Bart. – Chm. Bd. Excise, 1833-38.
DREW, Sir Arthur KCB (1912-93). Educ. Christ's Hospital; Camb., King's – PUS, War Off., 1963-64; MoD, 1964-72.
DROGHEDA, Rt. Hon. 10th Earl (Formerly Moore, Henry Ponsonby) KCMG, PC (1884-1957). Educ. Eton; Camb., Trinity – Dir-Gen., Min. Economic Warfare, 1940-45 (Jt. Dir-Gen., 1940-42).
DRUMMOND, Thomas (1797-1840). Educ. Univ. Edinburgh – Under Sec., Irish Off., 1835-40.
DU CANE, Sir Charles KCMG (1825-89). Educ. Charterhouse; Ox., Exeter – Chm. Bd. Customs, 1878-89.
DUFF, Sir Patrick KCB, KCVO (1889-1972). Educ. Blundell's Sch., Tiverton; Ox., Balliol – Secy., Off. Works 1933-41, (Perm. Sec., Min. Works, 1940-41).
DUKE, Sir William GCIE, KCSI (1863-1924). Educ. Arbroath High Sch.; Univ. Coll., London – PUS, India Off., 1919-24.
DUNNELL, Sir Francis, Bart. KCB (1868-1960). Educ. Rossall Sch. – Secy. and Solicitor, Min. Transport, 1919-21.
DUNNETT, Sir James GCB, CMG (b. 1914). Educ. Edinburgh Academy; Ox., Univ.Coll. – Min. Transport, 1959-62; Min. Labour, 1962-66; PUS, MoD, 1966-74.

EADY, Sir Wilfred GCMG, KCB, KBE (1890-1962). Educ. Clifton Coll.; Camb., Jesus – Chm. Bd. Customs and Excise, 1941-42; 2nd Secy., HM Treasury, 1942-52.
EARLE, Sir Lionel GCVO, KCB, CMG (1866-1948). Educ. Marlborough; Univs. Göttingen and Paris; Ox., Merton – Secy., Off. Works, 1912-33.
ELLIOTT, Sir Thomas, Bart. KCB (1854-1926). Educ. Privately – Bd. Agriculture and Fisheries, 1892-1913 (Bd. Agriculture, 1892-1903).
EMERSON TENNENT, Sir James, Bart. (1804-69). Educ. Dublin, Trinity – Secy., Poor Law Bd., 1852; Jt. Perm. Sec., BoT, 1852-67.
EMMERSON, Sir Harold GCB, KCVO (1896-1984). Educ. Warrington Sec. Sch. – Min. Works 1946-56; Min. Labour and Nat. Service, 1956-59.
ENGHOLM, Sir Basil KCB (1912-90). Educ. Tonbridge; Sorbonne, Paris; Camb., Sidney Sussex – MAFF, 1968-72.

ERRINGTON, Sir Lancelot KCB (b. 1917). Educ. Wellington Coll.; Camb., Trinity – 2nd Perm. Sec., DHSS, 1973-76.

ESHER, Rt. Hon. 2nd Viscount (Formerly Brett, Reginald Balliol) GCVO, KCB, PC (1852-1930). Educ. Eton; Camb., Trinity – Secy., Off. Works, 1895-1902.

EVANS, Sir Hywel KCB (1920-88). Educ. Liverpool Collegiate Sch.; Univ. Liverpool – Welsh Off., 1971-80.

FAULKNER, Sir Alfred CB, CBE (1882-1963). Educ. St. Alban's Sch.; King's Coll., Univ. London – PUS, Dept. Mines, 1927-42.

FARRER, Sir Thomas, Bart. (Lord Farrer of Abinger) (1819-99). Educ. Eton; Ox., Balliol – BoT, 1865-86 (Jt. Perm. Sec., 1865-67).

FAWCETT, E.A. Sandford CB (1868-1938). Educ. Private Schs. – Min. Nat. Service, 1917.

FELL, David CB (b. 1943). Educ. Royal Belfast Academical Instn.; Queen's Univ., Belfast – 2nd PUS, Northern Ireland Off. and Head of Northern Ireland Civil Service, 1991-.

FERGUSSON, Sir Donald GCB (1891-1963). Educ. Berkhamsted Sch.; Ox., Magdalen – Min. Agriculture and Fisheries, 1936-45; MFP, 1945-52.

FIDDES, Sir George GCMG, KCB (1858-1936). Educ. Dulwich Coll.; Ox., Brasenose – PUS, Colonial Off., 1916-21.

FIGGURES, Sir Frank KCB, CMG (1910-90). Educ. Rutlish Sch.; Ox., New Coll. – 2nd Perm. Sec., HM Treasury, 1968-71.

FISHER, Sir Warren GCB, GCVO (1879-1948). Educ. Winchester; Ox., Hertford – Chm. Bd. Inland Revenue, 1918-19; Perm. Sec., HM Treasury and Head of Civil Service, 1919-39.

FITZROY, Sir Almeric KCB, KCVO (1851-1935). Educ. Privately; Ox., Balliol – Clerk, Privy Council, 1898-1923.

FLEMING, Henry (d. 1876). Educ. Harrow – Secy., Poor Law Bd., 1859-71; Jt. Perm. Sec., LGB, 1871-76.

FLEMMING, Sir Gilbert KCB (1897-1981). Educ. Rugby; Ox., Trinity – Min. Education, 1952-59.

FLETT, Sir Martin KCB (1911-82). Educ. George Watson's Coll., Edinburgh; St. Paul's; Ox., St. John's – PUS, Air Ministry, 1963-68; PUS, MoD, 1968-71.

FLOUD, Sir Francis KCB, KCSI, KCMG (1875-1965). Educ. Cranleigh; King's Coll., Univ. London – Min. Agriculture and Fisheries, 1920-27; Chm. Bd. Customs and Excise, 1927-30; Secy., Min. Labour, 1930-34.

FLYNN, Sir Albert KCB (1863-1933). Educ. Private Schs.; King's Coll., Univ. London – Min. Pensions, 1918-19.

FORBER, Sir Edward KCB, CBE (1878-1960). Educ. Liverpool Coll.; Univ. Coll., Liverpool; Camb., Trinity – Chm. Bd. Customs and Excise, 1930-34; Chm. Bd. Inland Revenue, 1934-38.

FRANCE, Sir Arnold GCB (b. 1911). Educ. Bishop's Stortford Coll. – Min. Health, 1964-68; Chm. Bd. Inland Revenue, 1968-73.

FRANCE, Sir Christopher GCB (b. 1934). Educ. East Ham GS; Ox., New Coll. – DHSS, 1986-88 (2nd Perm. Sec., 1986-87); Dept. Health, 1988-92; PUS, MoD, 1992-95.

FRANKLIN, Sir Michael KCB, CMG (b. 1927). Educ. Taunton Sch.; Camb., Peterhouse – Dept. Trade, 1982-83; MAFF, 1983-87.

FRANKS, (Rt. Hon.) Sir Oliver (Lord Franks) GCMG, KCB, KCVO, CBE, (PC) (1905-92). Educ. Bristol GS; Ox., Queen's – Min. Supply and Aircraft Production, 1945-46.

FRASER, Sir Angus KCB, TD (b. 1928). Educ. Falkirk High; Univs. Glasgow and Bordeaux – Chm. Bd. Customs and Excise, 1983-87.

FRASER, Sir Bruce KCB (1910-93). Educ. Bedford Sch.; Camb., Trinity – Min. Health, 1960-64; Jt. PUS, DES, 1964-65; Perm. Sec., Min. Land and Natural Resources, 1965-66.

FRASER, Sir Robert OBE (1904-85). Educ. St. Peter's, Adelaide; Univs. Melbourne and London – Dir-Gen., COI, 1946-54.

FRASER, Sir W. Robert KCB, KBE (1891-1985). Educ. Christ's Hospital; Ox., Univ. Coll – Dep. Chm. and Perm. Sec., Central Land Board and War Damage Commission, 1947-59 (Secy., Central Land Bd., 1947-49).

FRASER, Sir William GCB (b. 1929). Educ. Eastwood Sch., Clarkston; Univ. Glasgow – PUS, Scottish Off., 1978-88.

FREELING, Sir Francis, Bart. (1764-1836) – Secy., Post Off., 1797-1836.

FREMANTLE, Rt. Hon. Sir Thomas F., Bart. (Lord Cottesloe) PC (1798-1890). Educ. Eton; Ox., Oriel – Chm. Bd. Customs, 1846-74.

FRENCH, Sir Henry GBE, KCB (1883-1966). Educ. Private Sch.; King's Coll., Univ. London – Min. Food, 1939-45.

GAINER, Sir Donald GBE, KCMG (1891-1966). Educ. Charterhouse; Abroad – PUS, FO (German Section), 1950-51.

GARDINER, Sir Thomas GCB, GBE (1883-1964). Educ. Lurgan Coll., Co. Armagh; Royal High, Edinburgh; Univ. Edinburgh – Dir.-Gen., Post Office 1936-45 (and Jt. Secy., Min. Home Security, 1939-40).

GARLICK, Sir John KCB (b. 1921). Educ. Westcliff High; Univ. London – 2nd Perm. Sec. Cabinet Off., 1974-78; Perm. Sec., DoE, 1978-81.

GARNER, Sir Saville (Lord Garner) GCMG (1908-84). Educ. Highgate; Camb., Jesus – PUS, CRO, 1962-68, (Commonwealth Off. and Head of Diplomatic Service, 1965-68).

GATER, Sir George GCMG, KCB (1886-1963). Educ. Winchester; Ox., New Coll. – PUS, Colonial Off., 1939-47 (Jt. Secy., Min. Home Security, 1939-40, 1940-42; and Jt. Secy., Min. Supply, 1940).

GERAGHTY, Sir William KCB (1917-77). Educ. Emanuel Sch.; Ox., Brasenose – 2nd PUS, MoD, 1975-76.

GERMAN, Sir Ronald KCB, CMG (1905-83). Educ. HM Dockyard Sch., Devonport – Dir.-Gen., Post Office, 1960-66.

GILBERT, Sir Bernard GCB, KBE (1891-1957). Educ. Nottingham High; Camb., St. John's – 2nd Secy., HM Treasury, 1944-56.

GILLMORE, Sir David GCMG (b. 1934). Educ. Trent Coll.; Camb., King's – PUS, FCO and Head of Diplomatic Service, 1991-94.

GIROUARD, Sir Percy KCMG (1867-1932). Educ. RMC, Kingston – Dir.-Gen., Munitions Supply, 1915.

GODLEY, Sir Arthur (Lord Kilbracken) GCB (1847-1932). Educ. Rugby; Ox., Balliol – PUS, India Off., 1883-1909.

GOLDMAN, Sir Samuel KCB (b. 1912). Educ. Davenant Foundation Sch.; Raine's Sch.; LSE – 2nd Perm. Sec., HM Treasury, 1968-72.

GORE-BOOTH, Sir Paul (Lord Gore-Booth) GCMG, KCVO (1909-84). Educ. Eton; Ox., Balliol – PUS, FO, 1965-69 (FCO and Head of Diplomatic Service, 1968-69).

GOSSET, Sir William (1782-1848) – Under Sec., Irish Off., 1831-35.

GOULBURN, Frederick CB (1818-78). Educ. Camb., Trinity – Chm. Bd. Customs, 1873-78.

GOWERS, Sir Ernest GCB, GBE (1880-1966). Educ. Rugby; Camb., Clare Coll. – PUS, Dept. Mines, 1920-27; Chm. Bd. Inland Revenue, 1927-30.
GREENE, Sir Graham KCB (1857-1950). Educ. Cheltenham Coll. – Admiralty, 1911-17; Min. Munitions, 1917-20.
GREENHILL, Sir Denis (Lord Greenhill of Harrow) GCMG, OBE (b. 1913). Educ. Bishop's Stortford Coll.; Ox., Christ Church – PUS, FCO, 1969-73.
GREGG, Sir Cornelius KCB, KBE (1888-1959). Educ. Christian Schools, Kilkenny; Blackrock; Univ. Coll., Dublin – Chm. Bd. Inland Revenue, 1942-48.
GREGSON, Sir Peter KCB (b. 1936). Educ. Nottingham High; Ox., Balliol – PUS, Dept. Energy, 1985-89; Perm. Sec. DTI, 1989-.
GREVILLE, Charles, C.F. (1794-1865). Educ. Eton; Ox., Christ Church – Jt. Clerk, Privy Council, 1821-59.
GRIGG, (Rt. Hon.) Sir James KCB, KCSI, (PC) (1890-1964). Educ. Bournemouth Sch.; Camb., St. John's – Chm. Bd. Customs and Excise, 1930; Chm. Bd. Inland Revenue, 1930-34; PUS, War Off., 1939-42.
GROVES, John D. CB, OBE (b. 1922). Educ. St. Paul's – Dir.-Gen., COI, 1979-82.
GUILLEMARD, Sir Laurence GCMG, KCB (1862-1951). Educ. Charterhouse; Camb., Trinity – Chm. Bd. Customs and Excise, 1909-19.
GUINNESS, John R.S. CB (b. 1935). Educ. Rugby; Camb., Trinity Hall – PUS, Dept. Energy, 1991-92.

HADDOW, Sir Douglas KCB (1913-86). Educ. George Watson's Coll., Edinburgh; Univ. Edinburgh; Camb., Trinity – PUS, Scottish Off., 1965-73.
HALIBURTON, Sir Arthur (Lord Haliburton) GCB (1832-1907). Educ. King's Coll. Sch., Nova Scotia – PUS, War Off., 1895-97.
HALL, Sir Daniel KCB (1864-1942). Educ. Manchester GS; Ox., Balliol – Bd. Agriculture and Fisheries, 1917-20.
HAMILTON, Sir Edward GCB, KCVO, ISO (1847-1908). Educ. Eton; Ox., Christ Church – Jt. Perm. Sec., HM Treasury, 1902-07.
HAMILTON, Rt. Hon. George Alexander, PC (1802-71). Educ. Rugby; Ox., Trinity – HM Treasury, 1859-70.
HAMILTON, Sir Horace GCB (1880-1971). Educ. Tonbridge Sch.; Ox., Hertford – Chm. Bd. Customs and Excise, 1919-27; Perm. Sec., BoT, 1927-37; PUS, Scottish Off., 1937-46.
HAMILTON, Sir James KCB, MBE (b. 1923). Educ. Penicuik Higher Grade Sch.; Lasswade Sec. Sch.; Univ. Edinburgh – PUS, DES, 1976-83.
HAMILTON, Sir Robert KCB (1836-95). Educ. Univ. Aberdeen – Admiralty, 1882; Under Sec., Irish Off., 1882-86; Chm. Bd. Customs, 1886-92.
HAMMOND, Rt. Hon. Edmund (Lord Hammond) PC (1802-90). Educ. Eton; Harrow; Ox., Univ. Coll. – PUS, FO, 1854-73.
HANCOCK, Sir David KCB (b. 1934). Educ. Whitgift Sch.; Ox., Balliol – DES, 1983-89.
HANCOCK, Sir Henry GCB, KBE, CMG (1895-1965). Educ. Haileybury; Ox., Exeter Coll. – Min. Nat. Insurance, 1949-51; Min. Food, 1951-55; Chm. Bd. Inland Revenue, 1955-58.
HANKEY, (Rt. Hon.) Sir Maurice (Lord Hankey) GCB, GCMG, GCVO, (PC) (1877-1963). Educ. Rugby – Cabinet Secy., 1916-38 (Secy., Imperial Defence Cttee., 1912-38; Clerk, Privy Council, 1923-38).
HARDING, Sir Edward GCMG, KCB (1880-1954). Educ. Dulwich Coll.; Ox., Hertford – PUS, Dominions Off., 1930-40.
HARDINGE, Rt. Hon. Lord Hardinge of Penshurst (Formerly Sir Charles) KG, GCB,

GCSI, GCMG, GCIE, GCVO, ISO, PC (1858-1944). Educ. Harrow; Camb., Trinity – PUS, FO, 1906-10, 1916-20.
HARDMAN, Sir Henry KCB (b. 1905). Educ. Manchester Central High; Univ. Manchester – Min. Aviation, 1961-63; MoD, 1963-66 (PUS, 1964-66).
HARRELL, Rt. Hon. Sir David GCB, GBE, KCVO, ISO, PC (1841-1939). Educ. RN Sch., Gosport – Under Sec., Irish Off., 1893-1902.
HARRIS, Sir Charles GBE, KCB (1864-1943). Educ. Bradford GS; Ox., Balliol – Jt. Perm. Sec. (Finance), War Off., 1920-24.
HARROP, Sir Peter KCB (b. 1926). Educ. King Edward VII, Lytham; Camb., Peterhouse – 2nd Perm. Sec., DoE, 1981-86.
HART, Graham H. CB (b. 1940). Educ. Brentwood Sch.; Ox., Pembroke – Dept. Health, 1992-.
HAWES, Sir Benjamin KCB (1797-1862). Educ. Dr. Carmalt's Sch., Putney – Deputy (Perm.) Sec., War Off., 1851-54; PUS, War Off., 1857-62.
HAWTON, Sir John KCB (1904-83). Educ. Emanuel Sch.; Camb., St. John's – Min. Health, 1951-60.
HAY, Robert W. (1756-1861). Educ. Ox., Christ Church – PUS, Colonial Off., 1825-36.
HAYES, Sir Brian GCB (b. 1929). Educ. Norwich Sch.; Camb., Corpus Christi – MAFF, 1979-83; Dept. Industry, 1983; DTI, 1983-89 (Jt. Perm. Sec., 1983-85).
HEATH, Sir Frank (1863-1946). Educ. Westminster; Univ. Coll., London; Strasbourg – Secy., DSIR, 1916-27.
HEATH, Sir Thomas KCB, KCVO (1861-1940). Educ. Caistor GS; Clifton Coll.; Camb., Trinity – Jt. Perm. Sec., HM Treasury, 1913-19.
HEISER, Sir Terence GCB (b. 1932). Educ. Windsor County Boys' Sch.; Birkbeck Coll., London – DoE, 1985-92.
HELMORE, Sir James KCB, KCMG (1906-72). Educ. St. Paul's; Ox., New Coll. – Min. Materials, 1952; Min. Supply, 1953-56.
HELPS, Sir Arthur KCB (1813-75). Educ. Eton; Camb., Trinity – Clerk, Privy Council, 1860-75.
HELSBY, Sir Laurence (Lord Helsby) GCB, KBE (1908-78). Educ. Sedbergh; Ox., Keble – Min. Labour, 1959-62; Jt. Perm. Sec., HM Treasury and Head of Home Civil Service, 1963-68.
HENLEY, Sir Douglas KCB (b. 1919). Educ. Beckenham County Sch.; LSE – 2nd Perm. Sec., HM Treasury, 1972-76.
HERBECQ, Sir John KCB (b. 1922). Educ. High Sch. for Boys, Chichester – 2nd Perm. Sec., CSD, 1975-81.
HERBERT, (Rt. Hon.) Sir Robert GCB, (PC) (1831-1905). Educ. Eton; Ox., Balliol – PUS, Colonial Off., 1871-92 (Acting PUS, Colonial Off., 1899).
HERON, Sir Conrad KCB, OBE (b. 1916). Educ. South Shields Sec. Sch.; Camb., Trinity – Dept. Employment, 1973-76 (2nd Perm. Sec., 1973).
HERRIES, Sir Charles KCB (1815-83). Educ. Eton; Camb., Trinity – Chm. Bd. Inland Revenue, 1877-81.
HIGHTON, John E. CB (1884-1937). Educ. Queen's Park Sch., Glasgow; Royal Tech. Coll., Glasgow; Univ. Glasgow – PUS, Scottish Off., 1937.
HILDRED, Sir William CB, OBE (1893-1986). Educ. Boulevard Sch., Hull; Univ. Sheffield – Dir.-Gen., Min. Civil Aviation, 1941-46.
HILL, Sir Rowland KCB (1795-1879). Educ. Hill Top Sch., Birmingham – Secy., Post Off., 1854-64 (Secy. to Postmaster-Gen., 1846-54).
HILLHOUSE, Sir Russell KCB (b. 1938). Educ. Hutchesons' GS, Glasgow; Univ. Glasgow – PUS, Scottish Off., 1988-.
HIRTZEL, Sir Arthur KCB (1870-1937). Educ.Dulwich Coll.; Ox., Trinity – PUS, India

Off., 1924-30.
HITCHMAN, Sir Alan KCB (1903-80). Educ. St. Bartholemew's GS, Newbury; Camb., Downing – Min. Materials, 1951-52; Min. Agriculture and Fisheries, 1952-59 (MAFF, 1955-59).
HOCKADAY, Sir Arthur KCB, CMG (b. 1926). Educ. Merchant Taylors'; Ox., St. John's – 2nd PUS, MoD, 1976-82.
HOLDERNESS, Sir Thomas, Bart. GCB, KCSI (1849-1924). Educ. Cheltenham Coll.; Ox., Univ. Coll. – PUS, India Off., 1912-19.
HOLLAND, Sir Geoffrey KCB (b. 1938). Educ. Merchant Taylors'; Ox., St. John's – 2nd Perm. Sec., Dept. Employment (MSC), 1986-87; Perm. Sec., Dept. Employment, 1988-93; DFE, 1993-94.
HOLMES, Sir Maurice GBE, KCB (1885-1964). Educ. Wellington Coll.; Ox. Balliol – Bd. Education, 1937-45 (Min. Education, 1944-45).
HOPKINS, (Rt. Hon.) Sir Richard GCB, (PC) (1880-1955). Educ. King Edward's Sch., Birmingham; Camb., Emmanuel – Chm. Bd. Inland Revenue, 1922-27; Controller, Finance and Supply, HM Treasury, 1927-32; 2nd Secy., HM Treasury, 1932-42; Perm. Sec., HM Treasury and Head of Civil Service, 1942-45.
HOPWOOD, (Rt. Hon.) Sir Francis (Lord Southborough) GCB, GCMG, GCVO, KCSI, (PC) (1860-1947). Educ. Louth – BoT, 1901-07; PUS, Colonial Off., 1907-11.
HORE, Sir Adair KBE, CB (1874-1950). Educ. Merchant Taylors'; Ox., St. John's – Min. Pensions, 1935-41.
HOWELL THOMAS, Lt.-Col. Sir Charles KCB, KCMG (1874-1943). Educ. Camb., Queens' – Min. Agriculture and Fisheries, 1927-36.
HOYER MILLAR, Sir Frederick (Lord Inchyra) GCMG, CVO (1900-89). Educ. Wellington Coll.; Ox., New Coll. – PUS, FO, 1957-61.
HUGHES, Sir Trevor KCB (b. 1925). Educ. Ruthin Sch. – Welsh Off., 1980-85.
HUME, James Deacon (1774-1842). Educ. Westminster – Jt. Perm. Sec., BoT, 1829-40.
HUNT, Sir John (Lord Hunt of Tanworth) GCB (b. 1919). Educ. Downside; Camb., Magdalene – 2nd Perm. Sec., Cabinet Off., 1972-73; Cabinet Secy., 1973-79.
HURCOMB, Sir Cyril (Lord Hurcomb) GCB, KBE (1883-1975). Educ. Oxford High Sch.; Ox., St. John's – Secy., Min. Transport, 1927-37; Dir.-Gen., Min. Shipping, 1939-41; Perm. Sec., Min. Transport, 1941-46 (Dir.-Gen., War Transport, 1941-45).
HURST, Sir Alfred KBE, CB (1884-1975). Educ. Market Bosworth; Camb., Emmanuel – PUS, Min. Mines, 1940-42.

INCE, Sir Godfrey GCB, KBE (1891-1960). Educ. Reigate GS; Univ. Coll., London – Min. Labour and Nat. Service, 1944-56.
INCHYRA, Lord – see HOYER MILLAR, Sir Frederick.

JAMES, Henry, L. CB (b. 1919). Educ. King Edward VI Sch., Birmingham – Dir.-Gen., COI, 1974-78.
JAMES, (Rt. Hon.) Sir Morrice (Lord Saint Brides) GCMG, CVO, MBE, (PC) (1916-90). Educ. Bradfield; Ox., Balliol – PUS, Commonwealth Off., 1968.
JARRETT, Sir Clifford KBE, CB (b. 1909). Educ. Dover County Sch.; Camb., Sidney Sussex – Admiralty, 1961-64; MPNI, 1964-66; Min. Social Security, 1966-68; DHSS, 1968-70.
JEFFREY, Sir John KCB, CBE (1871-1947). – PUS, Scottish Off., 1933-37.
JENKINS, Sir Gilmour KCB, KBE (1894-1981). Educ. Rutlish Sch.; Univ. London – Control Office for Austria and Germany, 1946-47; Jt. PUS, FO, 1947; Perm.

Sec., Min. Transport, 1947-59 (Transport and Civil Aviation, 1953-59).
JOHNSTON, Sir Alexander GCB, KBE, (1905-94). Educ. George Heriot's Sch.; Univ. Edinburgh – Chm. Bd. Inland Revenue, 1958-68.
JONES, Sir James KCB (b. 1914). Educ. Glasgow High; Univ. Glasgow; Ox., Univ. Coll. – (2nd) Secy., DoE, 1970-72; Perm. Sec., DoE, 1972-75.

KAY-SHUTTLEWORTH, (Sir) James, Bart. (1804-77). Educ. Leaf Square GS, Pendleton; Univ. Edinburgh – Secy., Education Dept., 1839-49.
KEARNS, Sir Frederick KCB, MC (1921-83). Educ. Burnley GS; Ox., Brasenose; RMC, Sandhurst – 2nd Perm. Sec., MAFF, 1973-78.
KEKEWICH, Sir George KCB (1841-1921). Educ. Eton; Ox., Balliol – Bd. Education, 1890-1903 (Education Dept., 1890-1900).
KEMP, Sir Peter KCB (b. 1934). Educ. Millfield Sch.; RNC, Dartmouth – 2nd Perm. Sec., Cabinet Off. (OMCS), 1988-92.
KILBRACKEN, Lord – see GODLEY, Sir Arthur.
KING, Sir Alexander KCB (1851-1942). – Secy., Post Off., 1911-14.
KING, Sir Geoffrey KCB, KBE, MC (1894-1981). Educ. Felsted – Min. Nat. Insurance, 1951-53; MPNI, 1953-55.
KING, Sir Richard KCB, MC (b. 1920). Educ. King's Coll. Sch., Wimbledon – ODA (FCO), 1973-76 (Min. Overseas Development, 1974-76).
KIRKPATRICK, Sir Ivone GCB, GCMG (1897-1964). Educ. Downside – PUS, FO (German Section), 1949; PUS, FO, 1953-57.
KNOX, (Rt. Hon.) Sir Ralph KCB, (PC) (1836-1913). Educ. Dublin, Trinity – PUS, War Off., 1897-1901.

LACK, Thomas – BoT, 1810-36 (Jt. Perm. Sec., 1829-36).
LAITHWAITE, Sir Gilbert GCMG, KCB, KCIE, CSI (1894-1986). Educ. Clongowes; Ox., Trinity – PUS, CRO, 1955-59.
LAMB, Sir John KCB (1871-1952). Educ. Univ. Aberdeen – PUS, Scottish Off., 1921-33.
LAMBERT, (Rt. Hon.) Sir John KCB, (PC) (1815-92). Educ. Downside – LGB, 1871-82 (Jt. Perm. Sec., 1871-76).
LANG, Sir John GCB (1896-1984). Educ. Aske's Haberdashers' – Admiralty, 1947-61.
LANKESTER, Sir Timothy KCB (b. 1942). Educ. Monkton Combe Sch.; Camb., St. John's – ODA (FCO), 1989-94; DFE, 1994-.
LARCOM, Sir Thomas, Bart. KCB (1801-79). Educ. RMA, Woolwich – Under Sec., Irish Off., 1853-68.
LAZARUS, Sir Peter KCB (b. 1926). Educ. Westminster; Ox., Wadham – Dept. Transport, 1982-85.
LEACH, Lieut.-Col. Sir George KCB (1820-1913). Educ. Privately; RMA, Woolwich – Bd. Agriculture, 1889-92.
LE CHEMINANT, Peter CB (b. 1926). Educ. Holloway Sch.; LSE – 2nd Perm. Sec. (MPO), Cabinet Off., 1983-84.
LEE, (Rt. Hon.) Sir Frank GCMG, KCB, (PC) (1903-71). Educ. Brentwood Sch.; Camb., Downing – Min. Food, 1949-51; BoT, 1951-59; Jt. Perm. Sec., HM Treasury, 1960-62.
LEITCH, Sir George KCB, OBE (b. 1915). Educ. Wallsend GS; Univ. Durham – Perm. Sec. and Chief Exec. (Procurement), MoD, 1972-75.
LEITH-ROSS, Sir Frederick GCMG, KCB (1887-1968). Educ. Merchant Taylors'; Ox., Balliol – Dir.-Gen., Min. Economic Warfare, 1939-42 (Jt. Dir.-Gen., 1940-42).
LE MARCHANT, Sir Denis, Bart. (1795-1874). Educ. Newcastle-on-Tyne Sch.; Eton;

Camb., Trinity – Jt. Perm. Sec., BoT, 1836-41, 1848-50.
LENNOX PEEL, Sir Charles KCB (1823-99). Educ. Privately – Clerk, Privy Council, 1875-98.
LEVENE, Sir Peter KBE (b. 1941). Educ. City of London Sch.; Univ. Manchester – Chief Exec. (Procurement), MoD, 1985-91.
LIDDELL, Sir Adolphus KCB (1818-85). Educ. Eton; Ox., Christ Church – PUS, Home Off., 1867-85.
LIESCHING, Sir Percivale GCMG, KCB, KCVO (1895-1973). Educ. Bedford Sch.; Ox., Brasenose – Min. Food, 1946-48; PUS, CRO, 1949-55.
LINDSAY, Rt. Hon. Sir Ronald GCB, GCMG, CVO, PC (1877-1945). Educ. Winchester – PUS, FO, 1928-30.
LINGEN, Sir Ralph (Lord Lingen) KCB (1819-1905). Educ. Bridgenorth; Ox., Trinity – Secy., Education Dept., 1849-69; Perm. Sec., HM Treasury, 1869-85.
LITTLE, Sir Alexander KCB (1895-1977). Educ. Oundle; Camb., Caius – Dir.-Gen., Post Off., 1949-55.
LITTLER, Sir Geoffrey KCB (b. 1930). Educ. Manchester GS; Camb., Corpus Christi – 2nd Perm. Sec., HM Treasury, 1983-88.
LLEWELLYN SMITH, Sir Hubert GCB (1864-1945). Educ. Bristol GS; Ox., Corpus Christi – BoT, 1907-19 (Jt. Perm. Sec., 1915-19).
LLOYD, Sir Thomas GCMG, KCB (1896-1968). Educ. Rossall; RMA, Woolwich; Camb., Gonville and Caius – PUS, Colonial Off., 1947-56.
LLOYD JONES, Sir Richard KCB (b. 1933). Educ. Nottingham High; Ox., Balliol – Welsh Off., 1985-93.
LOCKSPEISER, Sir Ben KCB (1891-1990). Educ. Grocers' Sch.; Camb., Sidney Sussex – Secy., DSIR, 1949-56.
LODGE, Thomas CB (1882-1958). Educ. Liverpool Inst.; Camb., Trinity – Min. Shipping, 1919-20.
LORD, Alan CB (b. 1924). Educ. Rochdale High; Camb., St John's – 2nd Perm. Sec., HM Treasury, 1975-77.
LOVELOCK, Sir Douglas KCB (b. 1923). Educ. Bec Sch. – Chm. Bd. Customs and Excise, 1977-83.
LOWE, Air Chief Marshal Sir Douglas GCB, DCF, AFC (b. 1922). Educ. Reading Sch. – Chief Exec. (Procurement), MoD, 1982-83.
LUCAS, Edward (1787-1871). Educ. Harrow; Univ. Edinburgh; Ox., Christ Church – Under Sec., Irish Off., 1841-45.
LUGARD, (Rt. Hon.) Sir Edward GCB, (PC) (1810-98). Educ. RMC Sandhurst – PUS, War Off., 1861-71.
LUSHINGTON, Sir Godfrey GCMG, KCB (1832-1907). Educ. Rugby; Ox., Balliol – PUS, Home Off., 1885-92.
LUSHINGTON, Vernon (1832-1912). Educ. Rugby; Camb., Trinity – Admiralty, 1869-77.

MABERLY, Lieut.-Col. William L. (1798-1885). Educ. Eton; Ox., Brasenose – Clerk, Bd. Ordnance, 1833-34; Secy., Post Off., 1836-54 (Jt. Secy., 1846-54).
MACDONALD, Sir Kenneth KCB (b. 1930) Educ. Hutchesons' GS; Univ. Glasgow – 2nd PUS, MoD, 1988-90.
MACDONALD, Norman H. (1806-57). Educ. Charterhouse; Ox., Oriel – Under Sec., Irish Off., 1840-41.
MACDONNELL, Rt. Hon. Sir Antony (Lord MacDonnell) GCSI, KCVO, PC (1844-1925). Educ. Queen's Coll., Galway – Under Sec., Irish Off., 1902-08.
McDONNELL, Hon. Sir Schomberg GCVO, KCB (1861-1915). Educ. Eton; Ox., Univ.

Coll. – Secy., Off. Works, 1902-12.

MACGREGOR, Sir Evan GCB, ISO (1842-1926). Educ. Charterhouse – Admiralty, 1884-1907.

MACGREGOR, John (1797-1857). – Jt. Perm. Sec., BoT, 1840-47.

MACHTIG, Sir Eric GCMG, KCB, OBE (1889-1973). Educ. St. Paul's; Camb., Trinity – PUS, Dominions Off., 1940-48 (Jt. PUS, CRO, 1947-48).

McINTOSH, Dr Malcolm K. (b. 1945). Educ. Telopea Park; Australian National Univ. – Chief of Defence Procurement, MoD, 1991-.

MACLEOD, Sir Reginald, 27th Chief of Clan, KCB (1847-1935). Educ. Harrow; Camb., Trinity – PUS, Scottish Off., 1902-08.

MACMAHON, Rt. Hon. James, PC (1865-1954). Educ. Christian Brothers' Sch., Armagh; St. Patrick's Coll., Armagh; Blackrock Coll., Dublin – PUS, Irish Off., 1918-22.

MACPHERSON, Sir John GCMG (1898-1971). Educ. George Watson's Coll., Edinburgh; Univ. Edinburgh – PUS, Colonial Off., 1956-59.

MAFFEY, Sir John (Lord Rugby) GCMG, KCB, KCVO, CSI, CIE (1877-1969). Educ. Rugby; Ox., Christ Church – PUS, Colonial Off., 1933-37.

MAITLAND, Sir Donald GCMG, OBE (b. 1922). Educ. George Watson's Coll., Edinburgh; Univ. Edinburgh – PUS, Dept. Energy, 1980-82.

MAKINS, Sir Roger (Lord Sherfield) GCB, GCMG (b. 1904). Educ. Winchester; Ox., Christ Church – Jt. Perm. Sec., HM Treasury, 1956-59.

MALLET, Sir Louis CB (1823-90). Educ. Privately – PUS, India Off., 1874-83.

MANZIE, Sir Gordon KCB (b. 1930). Educ. Royal High Sch., Edinburgh; LSE – Chief Exec., (PSA), DoE, 1984-90.

MARKHAM, Sir Henry KCB (1897-1946). Educ. Repton Sch.; Ox., Corpus Christi – Admiralty, 1940-46.

MARRE, Sir Alan KCB (1914-90). Educ. St. Olave's and St. Saviour's GS, Southwick; Camb., Trinity Hall – 2nd Perm. Sec., DHSS, 1968-71.

MARSHALL, Sir Robert KCB, MBE (b. 1920). Educ. Sherborne; Camb., Corpus Christi – (2nd) Secy., DTI, 1970-73 (Mintech, 1970); 2nd Perm. Sec., DoE, 1973-78.

MARWOOD, Sir William KCB (1863-1935). Educ. Tonbridge; Camb., Trinity – Jt. Perm. Sec., BoT, 1916-19; Secy., Min. Transport, 1921-23.

MASTERTON-SMITH, Sir James KCB (1878-1938). Educ. Harrow; Ox., Hertford – Jt. Secy., Min. Labour, 1920-21; PUS, Colonial Off., 1921-24.

MAUD, Sir John (Lord Redcliffe-Maud) GCB, CBE (1906-82). Educ. Eton; Ox., New Coll. – Min. Education, 1945-52; MFP, 1952-58 (Min. Power, 1957-58).

MAUDE, Sir John KCB, KBE (1883-1963). Educ. Rugby; Ox., Exeter – Min. Health, 1940-45.

MAXWELL, Sir Alexander GCB, KBE (1880-1963). Educ. Plymouth Coll.; Ox., Christ Church – PUS, Home Off., 1938-48.

MEADE, Hon. Sir Robert GCB (1835-98). Educ. Harrow; Ox., Exeter – PUS, Colonial Off., 1892-97.

MELVILLE, Sir Harry KCB (b. 1908). Educ. George Heriot's, Edinburgh; Univ. Edinburgh – Secy., DSIR, 1956-65.

MELVILLE, Sir Ronald KCB (b. 1912). Educ. Charterhouse; Camb., Magdalene – 2nd Perm. Sec., MoD, 1963-66 (2nd PUS, 1964-66); Perm. Sec., Min. Aviation, 1966-67; (2nd) Secy., Mintech, 1967-70; Aviation Supply, 1970-71; CSD, 1971-72.

MERIVALE, Herman CB (1806-74). Educ. Harrow; Ox., Oriel, Trinity – PUS, Colonial Off., 1848-60; PUS, India Off., 1860-74.

MIDDLETON, Sir Peter GCB (b. 1934). Educ. Sheffield City GS; Univs. Sheffield and

Bristol – HM Treasury, 1983-91.
MILNE, Sir David GCB (1896-1972). Educ. Daniel Stewart's Coll.; Univ. Edinburgh – PUS, Scottish Off., 1946-59.
MILNER, Sir Alfred (Viscount Milner) KG, GCB, GCMG (1854-1925). Educ. Abroad; King's Coll., London; Ox., Balliol – Chm. Bd. Inland Revenue, 1892-97.
MITCHELL, Sir Derek KCB, CVO (b. 1922). Educ. St. Paul's; Ox., Christ Church – 2nd Perm. Sec., HM Treasury, 1973-77.
MITFORD, Sir Algernon (Lord Redesdale) GCVO, KCB (1837-1916). Educ. Eton; Ox., Christ Church – Secy., Off. Works, 1874-86.
MONCK, Sir Nick KCB (b. 1935). Educ. Eton; Camb., King's; Univ. Pennsylvania – 2nd Perm. Sec., HM Treasury, 1990-93; Perm. Sec., Dept. Employment, 1993-.
MONRO, Sir Hector KCB (1861-1949). Educ. Repton; Camb., Clare Coll. – LGB, 1910-19 (Jt. Perm. Sec., 1919).
MONTEATH, Sir David KCB, KCSI, KCMG, CVO, OBE (1887-1961). Educ. Clifton Coll.; Ox., Trinity – PUS, India Off. and Burma Off., 1941-47; PUS, Burma Off., 1947-48.
MOORE, Henry Ponsonby – see DROGHEDA, 10th Earl.
MORANT, Sir Robert KCB (1863-1920). Educ. Winchester; Ox., New Coll. – Bd. Education, 1903-11; 1st Secy., Min. Health, 1919-20 (Jt. Perm. Sec., LGB, 1919).
MORRISON, Sir Nicholas KCB (1918-81). Educ. Cheltenham Coll.; Camb., Clare Coll. – PUS, Scottish Off., 1973-78.
MORTON, Sir Wilfred KCB (1906-81). Educ. Hutchesons' GS; Univ. Glasgow – Chm. Bd. Customs and Excise, 1965-69.
MOSELEY, Sir George KCB (b. 1925). Educ. High Sch., Glasgow; St. Bees, Cumberland; Ox., Wadham - DoE, 1980-85 (2nd Perm. Sec., 1980-81).
MOTTRAM, Richard C. (b. 1946). Educ. King Edward VI Camp Hill Sch., Birmingham; Univ. Keele – 2nd Perm. Sec., Cabinet Off. (OMCS), 1992; Perm. Sec., Cabinet Off. (OPSS), 1992-95; PUS, MoD, 1995-.
MOWATT, (Rt. Hon.) Sir Francis GCB, ISO, (PC) (1837-1919). Educ. Winchester; Harrow; Ox., St. John's – HM Treasury, 1894-1903 (Jt. Perm. Sec., 1902-03).
MUELLER, Dame Anne DCB (b. 1930). Educ. Queen Mary's High, Banbury; Sch. of St. Helen and St. Katherine, Abingdon; Wakefield Girls' High; Ox., Somerville – 2nd Perm. Sec. (MPO) Cabinet Off., 1984-87; 2nd Perm. Sec., HM Treasury, 1987-90.
MUIR, Sir Edward KCB (1905-79). Educ. Bradfield Coll.; Ox., Corpus Christi – Min. Works, 1956-65 (MPBW, 1962-65).
MUNDY, Godfrey C. (d. 1860). – PUS, War Off., 1854-57.
MURRAY, Sir Evelyn KCB (1880-1947). Educ. Eton; Ox., Christ Church – Secy., Post Off., 1914-34; Chm. Bd. Customs and Excise, 1934-40.
MURRAY, Rt. Hon. Sir George GCB, GCVO, ISO, PC (1849-1936). Educ. Harrow; Ox., Christ Church – Chm. Bd. Inland Revenue, 1897-99; Secy., Post Off., 1899-1903; Perm. Sec., HM Treasury, 1903-11 (Jt. Perm. Sec., 1903-07).
MURRAY, Sir Herbert KCB (1829-1904). Educ. Ox., Christ Church – Chm. Bd. Customs, 1890-94.
MURRAY, Sir Oswyn GCB (1873-1936). Educ. Oxford High; Ox., Exeter – Admiralty, 1917-36.
MURRIE, Sir William GCB (1903-94). Educ. Abroad; Harris Academy, Dundee; Univ. Edinburgh – PUS, Scottish Off., 1959-64.
MUSGRAVE, Sir Cyril KCB (1900-86). Educ. St. George's Coll., London – Min. Supply, 1956-59.

NAIRNE, (Rt. Hon.) Sir Patrick GCB, MC, (PC) (b. 1921). Educ. Radley; Ox., Univ. Coll. – 2nd Perm. Sec., Cabinet Off., 1973-75; Perm. Sec., DHSS, 1975-81.
NATHAN, Lieut.-Col., Rt. Hon. Sir Matthew GCMG, PC (1862-1939). – Secy., Post Off., 1909-11; Chm. Bd. Inland Revenue, 1911-14; Under Sec., Irish Off., 1914-16; Perm. Sec., Min. Pensions, 1916-19.
NEALE, Sir Alan KCB, MBE (b. 1918). Educ. Highgate; Ox., St. John's – 2nd Perm. Sec., HM Treasury, 1971-72; Perm. Sec., MAFF, 1973-78.
NEWSAM, Sir Frank GCB, KBE, CVO (1893-1964). Educ. Harrison Coll., Barbados; Ox., St. John's – PUS, Home Off., 1948-57.
NICHOL, Sir Duncan CBE (b. 1941). Educ. Bradford GS; Univ. St. Andrews – Chief Exec., NHS Management Exec., Dept. Health, 1989-94.
NICHOLLS, Sir George KCB (1781-1865). Educ. Helston GS, Newton Abbot – Secy., Poor Law Bd., 1847-51.
NICHOLSON, Sir Walter KCB (1876-1946). Educ. St. Paul's; Ox., Balliol – Secy., Air Ministry, 1920-30.
NICOLSON, Rt. Hon. Sir Arthur, Bart. (Lord Carnock) GCB, GCMG, GCVO, KCIE, PC (1849-1928). Educ. Rugby; Ox., Brasenose – PUS, FO, 1910-16.
NIELD, Sir William GCMG, KCB (1913-94). Educ. Stockport GS; Ox., St. Edmund Hall – PUS, DEA, 1968-69; Perm. Sec., Cabinet Off., 1969-72; Northern Ireland Off., 1972-73.
NIEMEYER, Sir Otto GBE, KCB (1883-1971). Educ. St. Paul's; Ox., Balliol – Controller Finance, HM Treasury, 1922-27.
NOTT-BOWER, Sir Edmund KCB (1853-1933). Educ. Cheltenham Coll. – Chm. Bd. Inland Revenue, 1914-18.

OLIVIER, (Rt. Hon.) Sir Sydney (Lord Olivier) KCMG, CB, (PC) (1859-1943). Educ. Lausanne; Kineton Sch.; Tonbridge Sch.; Ox., Corpus Christi – Bd. Agriculture and Fisheries, 1913-17.
OMMANNEY, Sir Montagu GCMG, KCB, ISO (1842-1925). Educ. Cheltenham Coll.; RMA, Woolwich – PUS, Colonial Off., 1900-07.
OTTON, Sir Geoffrey KCB (b. 1927). Educ. Christ's Hospital; Camb., St. John's – 2nd Perm. Sec., DHSS, 1979-86.
OVERTON, Sir Arnold KCB, KCMG (1893-1975). Educ. Winchester; Ox., New Coll. – BoT, 1941-45; Min. Civil Aviation, 1947-53.
OWEN, Sir Hugh GCB (1835-1916). – LGB, 1882-98.

PACKER, Richard J. (b. 1944). Educ. City of London Sch.; Univ. Manchester – MAFF, 1993-.
PADMORE, Sir Thomas GCB (b. 1909). Educ. Central Sch., Sheffield; Camb., Queens' – 2nd Secy., HM Treasury, 1952-62; Perm. Sec., Min. Transport, 1962-68.
PALLISER, (Rt. Hon.) Sir Michael GCMG, (PC) (b. 1922). Educ. Wellington Coll.; Ox., Merton – PUS, FCO and Head of Diplomatic Service, 1975-82.
PARKER, Sir Harold KCB, KBE (1895-1980). Educ. Aske's Haberdashers' – Min. Pensions, 1946-48; MoD, 1948-56.
PARKINSON, Sir Cosmo GCMG, KCB, OBE (1884-1967). Educ. Epsom Coll.; Ox., Magdalen – PUS, Colonial Off., 1937-40. 1940-42; (PUS, Dominions Off., 1940).
PART, Sir Antony GCB (1916-90). Educ. Harrow; Camb., Trinity – MPBW, 1965-68; BoT, 1968-70; DTI, 1970-74; Dept. Industry, 1974-76.
PARTRIDGE, Sir Michael KCB (b. 1935). Educ. Merchant Taylors'; Ox., St. John's – 2nd Perm. Sec., DHSS, 1987-88; Perm. Sec., DSS, 1988-.

PAUNCEFOTE, (Rt. Hon.) Sir Julian (Lord Pauncefote of Preston, Gloc.) GCB, CGMG, (PC) (1828-1902). Educ. Abroad; Marlborough – PUS, FO, 1882-89.
PELHAM, Sir Henry KCB (1876-1949). Educ. Harrow; Ox., Balliol – Bd. Education, 1931-37.
PENNEFATHER, Richard (1800-49). Educ. Eton; Ox., Balliol – Under Sec., Irish Off., 1845-46.
PERRY, Sir David KCB (b. 1931). Educ. Berkhamsted; Camb., Pembroke – Chief Exec. (Procurement), MoD, 1983-85; Chief Defence Equipment Collaboration, MoD, 1985-87.
PETCH, Sir Louis KCB (1913-81). Educ. Preston GS; Camb., Peterhouse – 2nd Secy., HM Treasury, 1966-68; 2nd Perm. Sec., CSD, 1968-69; Chm. Bd. Customs and Excise, 1969-73.
PETERSON, Sir Arthur KCB, CVO (1916-86). Educ. Shrewsbury; Ox., Merton – PUS, Home Off., 1972-77.
PHILIPPS, Trenham W. (1794-1855). – Secy., Off. Works, 1852-54.
PHILLIPPS, (Rt. Hon.) Samuel March (PC) (1780-1862). Educ. Charterhouse; Camb., Sidney Sussex – PUS, Home Off., 1827-48.
PHILLIPS, Sir Frederick GCMG, CB (1884-1943). Educ. Aske's Sch.; Camb., Emmanuel – 2nd Secy., HM Treasury, 1942-43.
PHILLIPS, G Hayden CB (b. 1943). Educ. Cambridgeshire High; Camb., Clare Coll.; Yale Univ. – Dept. National Heritage, 1992-.
PHILLIPS, Sir Thomas GBE, KCB (1883-1966). Educ. Machynlleth County Sch.; Ox., Jesus – Secy., Min. Labour, 1935-44 (Perm. Sec., Min. Labour and Nat. Service, 1939-44); Perm. Sec., Min. Nat. Insurance, 1944-48.
PHINN, Thomas (1814-66). Educ. Eton; Ox., Exeter – 2nd (Perm.) Sec., Admiralty, 1855-57.
PILE, Sir William GCB, MBE (b. 1919). Educ. Royal Masonic Sch.; Camb., St. Catharine's – PUS, DES, 1970-76; Chm. Bd. Inland Revenue, 1976-79.
PITBLADO, Sir David KCB, CVO (b. 1912). Educ. Strand Sch.; Camb., Emmanuel – Min. Power, 1966-69; Perm. Sec. (Industry) Mintech, 1969-70; (2nd) Perm. Sec., CSD, 1970-71.
PITTAR, Sir Thomas KCB, CMG (1846-1924). – Chm. Bd. Customs, 1903-08.
PLAYFAIR, Sir Edward KCB (b. 1909). Educ. Eton; Camb., King's – PUS, War Off., 1956-59; Perm. Sec., MoD, 1960-61.
PLIATZKY, Sir Leo KCB (b. 1919). Educ. Manchester GS; City of London Sch.; Ox., Corpus Christi – 2nd Perm. Sec., HM Treasury, 1976-77; Perm. Sec., Dept. Trade, 1977-79.
PORTER, George R. (1793-1852). – Jt. Perm. Sec., BoT, 1847-52.
POWELL, Sir Richard GCB, KBE, CMG (b. 1909). Educ. Queen Mary GS, Walsall; Camb., Sidney Sussex – MoD, 1956-59; BoT, 1960-68.
POYNTON, Sir Hilton GCMG (b. 1905). Educ. Marlborough; Ox., Brasenose – PUS, Colonial Off., 1959-66.
PRESSLY, Sir Charles KCB (1794-1880). Educ. Warminster; Midhurst – Chm. Bd. Inland Revenue, 1856-62.
PRESTON, Sir Peter KCB (b. 1922). Educ. Nottingham High – ODA (FCO), 1976-82 (Min. Overseas Development, 1976-79).
PRICE, Sir Norman KCB (b. 1915). Educ. Plaistow GS – Chm. Bd. Inland Revenue, 1973-76.
PRIMROSE, (Rt. Hon.) Sir Henry KCB, CSI, ISO, (PC) (1846-1923). Educ. Trinity Coll., Glenalmond; Ox., Balliol – Secy., Off. Works, 1886-95; Chm. Bd. Customs, 1895-99; Chm. Bd. Inland Revenue, 1899-1907.

PROCTOR, Sir Dennis KCB (1905-83). Educ. Harrow; Camb., King's – Min. Power, 1958-65.
PROVIS, Sir Samuel KCB (1845-1926). Educ. Univ. London; Camb., Queens' – LGB, 1898-1910.
PUGH, Sir Idwal KCB (b. 1918). Educ. Cowbridge GS; Ox., St. John's – Welsh Off., 1969-71; 2nd Perm. Sec., DoE, 1971-76.

QUINLAN, Sir Michael GCB (b. 1930). Educ. Wimbledon Coll.; Ox., Merton – Dept. Employment, 1983-88; PUS, MoD, 1988-92.

RADFORD, Sir Ronald KCB, MBE (b. 1916). Educ. Southend-on-Sea High; Camb., St. John's – Chm. Bd. Customs and Excise, 1973-77.
RADLEY, Sir Gordon KCB, CBE (1898-1970). Educ. Leeds Modern Sch.; Faraday House Electrical Eng. Coll., London – Dir.-Gen., Post Off., 1955-60.
RAMPTON, Sir Jack KCB (1920-94). Educ. Tonbridge Sch.; Ox., Trinity – (2nd) Secy., DTI, 1972-74; PUS, Dept. Energy, 1974-78.
RAMSAY, Sir Malcolm KCB (1871-1946). Educ. Winchester; Ox., New Coll. – Controller Establishments, HM Treasury, 1919-21.
RAWLINSON, Sir Anthony KCB (1926-86). Educ. Eton; Ox., Christ Church – 2nd Perm. Sec., Dept. Industry, 1976-77; 2nd Perm. Sec., HM Treasury, 1977-83; Perm. Sec., Dept. Trade, 1983; Jt. Perm. Sec., DTI, 1983-85.
RAYNER, (Sir) Derek (Lord Rayner) (b. 1926). Educ. City Coll., Norwich; Camb., Selwyn – Chief Exec., (Procurement) MoD, 1971-72.
REDCLIFFE-MAUD, Lord – see MAUD, Sir John.
REDESDALE, Lord – see MITFORD, Sir Algernon.
REDINGTON, Sir Thomas KCB (1815-62). Educ. Oscott Coll.; Camb., Christ's Coll. – Under Sec., Irish Off., 1846-52; Secy., Bd. Control, 1852-56.
REW, Sir Henry KCB (1858-1929) – Secy., Min. Food, 1916-17.
RICKETT, Sir Denis KCMG, CB (b. 1907). Educ. Rugby; Ox., Balliol, All Souls – 2nd Secy., HM Treasury, 1960-68.
RIDDLESDELL, Dame Mildred DCB, CBE (b. 1913). Educ. St. Mary's Hall, Brighton; Bedford Coll., Univ. London – 2nd Perm. Sec., DHSS, 1971-73.
RIDGEWAY, (Rt. Hon.) Sir West GCB, GCMG, KCSI, (PC) (1844-1930). Educ. St. Paul's – Under Sec., Irish Off., 1887-93.
RITCHIE, Sir Richmond (1854-1912). Educ. Eton; Camb., Trinity – PUS, India Off., 1910-12.
ROBINSON, Sir Arthur GCB, GBE (1874-1950). Educ. Appleby GS; Ox., Queen's – Secy., Air Ministry, 1917-20; Secy., Min. Health, 1920-35 (1st Secy., 1920-25); Jt. Secy., Min. Supply, 1939-40.
ROBINSON, Sir Percival KCB (1887-1949). Educ. Winchester; Camb., Pembroke – Min. Works, 1943-46.
ROGERS, (Rt. Hon.) Sir Frederic, Bart. (Lord Blachford) GCMG, (PC) (1811-89). Educ. Eton; Ox., Oriel – PUS, Colonial Off., 1860-71.
ROGERS, Sir Philip GCB, CB, CMG (1914-90). Educ. William Hulme's GS, Manchester; Camb., Emmanuel – 2nd Perm. Sec., HM Treasury/CSD, 1969-70; Perm. Sec., DHSS, 1970-75.
ROLL, Sir Eric (Lord Roll of Ipsden) KCMG, CB (b. 1907). Educ. Abroad; Univ. Birmingham – PUS, DEA, 1964-66.
ROMAINE, William Govett CB (1815-93). Educ. Camb., Trinity – 2nd (Perm.) Sec., Admiralty, 1857-69.
ROWAN, Sir Leslie KCB, CVO (1908-72). Educ. Abroad; Tonbridge; Camb., Queens' –

Off. of Min. Economic Affairs, 1947; 2nd Secy., HM Treasury, 1947-49, 1951-58.
ROWLANDS, Sir Archibald GCB, MBE (1892-1953). Educ. Penarth County Sch.; Univ. Coll., Wales; Ox., Jesus – Min. Aircraft Production, 1940-43; Min. Supply, 1946-52.
RUGBY, Lord – see MAFFEY, Sir John.
RUSSELL, George – Secy., Off. Works, 1868-74.
RYDER, Sir George KCB (1838-1905). Educ. Privately – Chm. Bd. Customs, 1900-03.
RYRIE, Sir William KCB (b. 1928). Educ. Abroad; Heriot's Sch., Edinburgh; Univ. Edinburgh – 2nd Perm. Sec., HM Treasury, 1980-82; Perm. Sec., ODA (FCO), 1982-84.

SAINT BRIDES, Lord – see JAMES, Sir Morrice.
SANDERSON, Lord Sanderson of Armthorpe (Formerly Sir Thomas) GCB, KCMG, ISO (1841-1923). Educ. Eton – PUS, FO, 1894-1906.
SANDFORD, Rt. Hon. Sir Francis (Lord Sandford) KCB, PC (1824-93). Educ. Glasgow High Sch.; Grange Sch.; Univ. Glasgow; Ox., Balliol – Secy., Education Dept., 1870-84; PUS, Scottish Off., 1885-88.
SARGENT, Sir Orme GCMG, KCB (1884-1962). Educ. Radley – PUS, FO, 1946-49.
SCHOLAR, Michael C. CB (b. 1942). Educ. St. Olave's GS, Bermondsey; Camb., St. John's; Univ. California, Berkeley – Welsh Off., 1993-.
SCOTT, Sir Harold GCVO, KCB, KBE (1887-1969). Educ. Sexey's Sch., Bruton; Camb., Jesus – Secy., Min. Home Security, 1942-43; Perm. Sec., Min. Aircraft Production, 1943-45.
SCOTT, Sir Robert GCMG, CBE (1905-82). Educ. Queen's Royal Coll., Trinidad; Ox., New Coll. – MoD, 1961-63.
SCOTT, Sir Russell KCB, CSI, ISO (1877-1960). Educ. Manchester GS; Ox., Wadham – Controller Establishments, HM Treasury, 1921-32; PUS, Home Off., 1932-38.
SCOTT-MONCRIEFF, Sir Colin KCSI, KCMG (1836-1916). Educ. Edinburgh Acad.; Military Coll., Addiscombe; Univ. Edinburgh – PUS, Scottish Off., 1892-1902.
SELBY-BIGGE, Sir Amherst, Bart. KCB (1860-1951). Educ. Winchester; Ox., Christ Church – Bd. Education, 1911-25.
SELF, Sir Henry KCB, KCMG, KBE (1890-1975). Educ. Bancroft's Sch., Woolwich; Univ. London – Min. Production, 1942-43; Min. Civil Aviation, 1946-47.
SERPELL, Sir David KCB, CMG, OBE (b. 1911). Educ. Plymouth Coll.; Ox., Exeter Coll.; Univ. Toulouse – 2nd Perm. Sec., BoT, 1966-68; 2nd Secy., HM Treasury, 1968; Perm. Sec., Min. Transport, 1968-70; DoE, 1970-72.
SHACKLETON, Sir David KCB (1863-1938). Educ. Elementary Sch., Haslingdon – Secy., Min. Labour, 1916-21 (Jt. Secy., 1920-21).
SHARP, Dame Evelyn (Baroness Sharp of Hornsey) GBE (1903-85). Educ. St. Paul's Girls' Sch.; Ox., Somerville – MHLG, 1955-66.
SHAW LEFEVRE, Sir John, Bart. KCB (1797-1879). Educ. Eton; Camb., Trinity – Jt. Perm. Sec., BoT, 1841-48.
SHEEPSHANKS, Sir Thomas KCB, KBE (1895-1964). Educ. Winchester; Ox., Trinity – MTCP, 1946-51; MHLG, 1951-55.
SHERFIELD, Lord – see MAKINS, Sir Roger.
SMIETON, Dame Mary DBE (b. 1902). Educ. Perse Sch.; Wimbledon High; Bedford Coll., Univ. London – Min. Education, 1959-63.
SMITH, Sir Frank GCB, GBE (1879-1970). Educ. Royal Coll. of Science – Secy., DSIR, 1929-39.
SOUTHBOROUGH, Lord – see HOPWOOD, Sir Francis.
SPEARMAN, Sir Alexander, Bart. (1793-1874). – Assist. (Perm.) Sec., HM Treasury,

1836-40.
SPEED, Sir Eric KCB, KBE (1895-1971). Educ. Christ's Hospital; Ox., St. John's – PUS, War Off., 1942-48.
STEPHEN, Rt. Hon. (Sir) James (KCB), PC (1789-1859). Educ. Privately; Camb., Trinity Hall – PUS, Colonial Off., 1836-48.
STEPHENSON, Sir William KCB (1811-98). Educ. Private Sch. – Chm. Bd. Inland Revenue, 1862-77.
STEVENSON, Sir Matthew KCB, CMG (1910-81). – Min. Power, 1965-66; MHLG, 1966-70.
STEWART, Sir Findlater GCB, GCIE, CSI (1879-1960). Educ. Brisbane Acad., Largs.; Univ. Edinburgh – PUS, India Off., 1930-42.
STEWART, Hon. James H.K. (1783-1836). Educ. Charterhouse; Camb., Trinity – Assist. (Perm.) Sec., HM Treasury, 1828-36.
STEWART, J. Moray CB (b. 1938). Educ. Marlborough; Univ. Keele – 2nd PUS, MoD, 1990-.
STOWE, Sir Kenneth GCB, CVO (b. 1927). Educ. County High, Dagenham; Ox., Exeter – PUS, Northern Ireland Off., 1979-81; Perm. Sec., DHSS, 1981-87.
STRACHAN, Valerie P.M. CB (b. 1940). Educ. Newland High, Hull; Univ. Manchester – Chm. Bd. Customs and Excise, 1993-.
STRANG, Sir William (Lord Strang) GCB, GCMG, MBE (1893-1978). Educ. Palmer's Sch.; Univ. Coll., London; Sorbonne – PUS, FO, 1947-53 (German Section, 1947-49).
STRATH, Sir William KCB (1906-75). Educ. Girvan High; Univ. Glasgow – Min. Supply, 1959; Min. Aviation, 1959-60.
STREET, Sir Arthur GCB, KBE, CMG, CIE (1892-1951). Educ. County Sch., Sandown; King's Coll., London – PUS, Air Ministry, 1939-45; Perm. Sec., Control Off. for Germany and Austria, 1945-46.
SULIVAN, (Rt. Hon.) Laurence (PC) (1783-1866). Educ. Hackney Sch.; Univ. Edinburgh; Camb., St. John's – Dep. (Perm.) Sec., War Off., 1826-51.
SYMONDS, Sir Aubrey KCB (1874-1931). Educ. Bedford Sch.; Ox., Univ. Coll. – Bd. Education, 1925-31.

TENTERDEN, Lord, 3rd Baron KCB (formerly Abbot, Charles Stewart Aubrey) (1834-82). Educ. Eton – PUS, FO, 1873-82.
THOMAS, Sir Inigo GCB (1846-1929). Educ. Marlborough – Admiralty, 1907-11.
THOMPSON, (Rt. Hon.) Sir Ralph KCB, (PC) (1830-1902) – PUS, War Off., 1878-95.
THORNTON, Sir Peter KCB (b. 1917). Educ. Charterhouse; Camb., Gonville and Caius – (2nd) Secy., DTI, 1972-74; Perm. Sec., Dept. Trade, 1974-77 (2nd Perm. Sec., 1974).
TICKELL, Sir Crispin GCMG, KCVO (b. 1930). Educ. Westminster; Ox., Christ Church – ODA (FCO), 1984-87.
TILLEY, Sir John KCB (1813-98). Educ. Private Sch., Bromley – Secy., Post Off., 1864-80.
TINDALE, Lawrence V. CBE (b. 1921). Educ. Upper Latymer Sch., Hammersmith – 2nd Perm. Sec., DTI, 1972-74.
TIZARD, Sir Henry GCB (1885-1959). Educ. Westminster; Ox., Magdalen – Secy., DSIR, 1927-29.
TREND, Rt. Hon. Sir Burke (Lord Trend) GCB, CVO, PC (1914-87). Educ. Whitgift; Ox., Merton – 2nd Secy., HM Treasury, 1960-62; Cabinet Secy., 1963-73.
TREVELYAN, Sir Charles, Bart. KCB (1807-86). Educ. Taunton GS; Charterhouse; Haileybury – Assist. (Perm.) Sec., HM Treasury, 1840-59.

TRIBE, Sir Frank KCB, KBE (1893-1958). Educ. Clifton Coll.; Ox., Trinity – Min. Reconstruction, 1942; MFP, 1942-45; Min. Aircraft Production, 1945; Min. Food, 1945-46.
TROUP, Sir Edward KCB, KCVO (1857-1941). Educ. Elementary Sch.; Univ. Aberdeen; Ox., Balliol – PUS, Home Off., 1908-22.
TRYON, Rear Admiral Sir George (1832-93). Educ. Eton – Admiralty, 1882-84.
TURNBULL, Andrew CB, CVO (b. 1945). Educ. Enfield GS; Camb., Christ's Coll. – 2nd Perm. Sec., HM Treasury, 1993-94; Perm. Sec., DoE, 1994-.
TURNER, Sir George KCB, KBE (1896-1974). Educ. Rotherham GS – PUS, War Off., 1949-56.
TYRRELL, (Rt. Hon.) Sir William (Lord Tyrrell) GCB, GCMG, KCVO, (PC) (1866-1947). Educ. Privately; Univ. Bonn; Ox., Balliol – PUS, FO, 1925-28.

UNWIN, Sir Brian KCB (b. 1935). Educ. Chesterfield Sch.; Ox., New Coll.; Yale Univ. – Chm. Bd. Customs and Excise, 1987-93.

VANDEPEER, Sir Donald KCB, KBE (1890-1968). Educ. Strand Sch.; King's Coll., Univ. London – Min. Agriculture and Fisheries, 1945-52.
VANSITTART, (Rt. Hon.) Sir Robert (Lord Vansittart) GCB, GCMG, MVO, (PC) (1881-1957). Educ. Eton – PUS, FO, 1930-38.
VEREKER, John M.M. CB (b. 1944). Educ. Marlborough; Univ. Keele – ODA (FCO), 1994-.
VIVIAN, John (1818-79). Educ. Eton – PUS, War Off., 1871-78.

WADDINGTON, Rt. Hon. Horatio PC (1799-1867). Educ. Charterhouse; Camb., Trinity – PUS, Home Off., 1848-67.
WALKER, Sir Michael GCMG (b. 1916). Educ. Charterhouse; Ox., New Coll. – ODA (FCO), 1971-73.
WALL, Sir John (Lord Wall) OBE (1913-80). Educ. Wandsworth Sch.; LSE – Dep. Chm. Post Office Bd., 1966-68.
WALPOLE, Sir Spencer KCB (1839-1907). Educ. Eton – Secy., Post Off., 1893-99.
WARD, Col. Sir Edward, Bart. GBE, KCVO, KCB (1853-1928). Educ. Private Sch. – PUS, War Off., 1901-14 (Secy., 1904-14).
WARDALE, Sir Geoffrey KCB (b. 1919). Educ. Altrincham GS; Camb., Queens' – 2nd Perm. Sec., DoE, 1978-80.
WASS, Sir Douglas GCB (b. 1923). Educ. Nottingham High; Camb., St. John's – HM Treasury, 1973-83 (2nd Perm. Sec., 1973-74; and Jt. Head of Home Civil Service, 1981-83).
WAVERLEY, Viscount – see ANDERSON, Sir John.
WAY, Sir Richard KCB, CBE (b. 1914). Educ. Polytechnic Secondary Sch., London – PUS, War Off., 1960-63; Perm. Sec., Min. Aviation, 1963-66.
WELBY, (Rt. Hon.) Sir Reginald (Lord Welby) GCB, (PC) (1832-1915). Educ. Eton; Camb., Trinity – HM Treasury, 1885-94.
WEST (Rt. Hon.) Sir Algernon GCB, (PC) (1832-1921). Educ. Eton; Ox., Christ Church – Chm. Bd. Inland Revenue, 1881-92.
WETHERALL, Sir Edward KCSI, CB (1815-69). Under Sec., Irish Off., 1868-69.
WHISKARD, Sir Geoffrey KCB, KCMG (1886-1957). Educ. St. Paul's; Ox., Wadham – Min. Works, 1941-43; MTCP, 1943-46.
WHITMORE, Sir Clive GCB, CVO (b. 1935). Educ. Sutton GS; Camb., Christ's Coll. – PUS, MoD, 1983-88; PUS, Home Off., 1988-94.
WICKHAM, Henry L. (1789-1864). Educ. Westminster; Ox., Christ Church – Chm.

Bd. Stamps and Taxes, 1838-48.
WICKS, Sir Nigel KCB, CVO, CBE (B. 1940). Educ. Beckenham and Penge GS; Portsmouth Coll. of Tech.; Univ Camb.; Univ. London – 2nd Perm. Sec., HM Treasury, 1989-.
WILSON, Sir Arton KBE, CB (1893-1977). Educ. Central Foundation Sch., London – Min. Pensions, 1948-53.
WILSON, Sir Geoffrey KCB, CMG (b. 1910). Educ. Manchester GS; Ox., Oriel – Min. Overseas Development, 1968-70.
WILSON, Sir Horace GCB, GCMG, CBE (1882-1972). Educ. Kurnella Sch., Bournemouth; LSE – Secy., Min. Labour, 1921-30; Perm. Sec., HM Treasury and Head of Civil Service, 1939-42.
WILSON, Sir John KCB (1915-93). Educ. Bradfield; Camb., Gonville and Caius – 2nd PUS, MoD, 1972-75.
WILSON, Richard T.J. CB (b. 1942). Educ. Radley; Camb., Clare Coll. – DoE, 1992-94; PUS, Home Off., 1994-.
WILSON, Brig.-Gen. Sir Samuel GCMG, KCB, KBE (1873-1950). Educ. Privately; RMA, Woolwich – PUS, Colonial Off., 1925-33.
WILSON SMITH, Sir Henry KCB, KBE (1904-78). Educ. Royal GS, Newcastle upon Tyne; Camb., Peterhouse – MoD, 1947-48; 2nd Secy., HM Treasury, 1948-51.
WINGFIELD, Sir Edward KCB (1834-1910). Educ. Winchester; Ox., New Coll. -- PUS, Colonial Off., 1897-1900.
WINNIFRITH, Sir John KCB (1908-93). Educ. Westminster; Ox., Christ Church – MAFF, 1959-67.
WINTOUR, Ulick Fitzgerald CB, CMG (1877-1947). Educ. Winchester -- Secy., Min. Food, 1917-18.
WOOD, John (1790-1856) – Chm. Bd. Excise, 1838-49; Chm. Bd. Inland Revenue, 1849-56.
WOODFIELD, Sir Philip KCB, CBE (b. 1923). Educ. Dulwich Coll.; King's Coll., Univ. London – PUS, Northern Ireland Off., 1981-83.
WOODS, Sir John GCB, MVO (1895-1962). Educ. Christ's Hospital; Ox., Balliol – Min. Production, 1943-45; BoT, 1945-51.
WRIGHT, Sir Patrick (Lord Wright of Richmond) GCMG (b. 1931). Educ. Marlborough; Ox., Merton – PUS, FCO and Head of Diplomatic Service, 1986-91.
WYNNE, John A. (1801-65). Educ. Winchester; Ox., Christ Church – Under Sec., Irish Off., 1852.

Bibliography

Aberbach, J., Putnam, R.D. and Rockman, B.A. (1981) *Bureaucrats and Politicians in Western Democracies*, Harvard University Press, Cambridge, Massachusetts.
Adonis, A. (1993) *Making Aristocracy Work: The Peerage and the Political System in Britain 1884-1914*, Oxford University Press, Oxford.
Alderman, R.K. and Carter, N. (1992) 'The logistics of ministerial reshuffles', *Public Administration*, 70, pp. 519-34.
Alderman, R.K. and Cross, J.A. (1979) 'Ministerial reshuffles and the civil service', *British Journal of Political Science*, 9, pp. 41-65.
Alt, J.E. (1975) 'Continuity, turnover and experience in the British cabinet 1868-1970', in Herman, V. and Alt, J.E. (eds.) *Cabinet Studies: A Reader*, Macmillan, London, pp. 33-54.
Amery, L.S. (1953) *My Political Life – Vol. II: War and Peace, 1914-1929*, Hutchinson, London.
Anderson, O. (1967) *A Liberal State at War: English Politics and Economics During the Crimean War*, St. Martin's Press, New York.
Armstrong, J.A. (1973) *The European Administrative Elite*, University Press, Princeton.
Armstrong, R. (1988) 'Taking stock of our achievements', in Peat, Marwick McLintock/Royal Institute of Public Administration (eds.) *Future Shape of Reform in Whitehall*, RIPA, London, pp. 11-21.
Armstrong, W. (1970) *Professionals and Professionalism in the Civil Service*, London School of Economics and Political Science, London.
Asquith, H.H. (1928) *Memories and Reflections* (2 vols.), Cassell, London.
Assheton (1944) *Report of the Committee on the Training of Civil Servants* (Assheton Committee), P.P. 1943-4 (Cmnd. 6525), iii.
Avon, Earl of (Anthony Eden) (1962) *The Eden Memoirs: Facing the Dictators*, Cassell, London.

Bagehot, W. (1928) *The English Constitution*, Oxford University Press, London.
Bagehot, W. (1974) 'Physics and politics', in Stevas, N. St. J. (ed.), *The Collected Works of Walter Bagehot – vol. 7*, The Economist, London, pp. 13-144.
Bahlman, D.W.R. (ed.) (1972) *The Diary of Edward Walter Hamilton 1880-1885* (2 vols.), Clarendon, Oxford.
Bahlman, D.W.R. (ed.) (1993) *The Diary of Sir Edward Walter Hamilton 1885-1906*, University of Hull Press, Hull.
Balogh, T. (1959) 'The apotheosis of the dilettante', in Thomas, H. (ed.), *The Establishment*, Anthony Blond, London, pp. 83-126.
Barberis, P. (1994) 'Permanent secretaries and policy making in the 1980s', *Public Policy and Administration*, 9, 1, pp. 35-48.
Barberis, P. (1995) 'Next Steps: consequences for the core and central departments', in O'Toole, B.J. and Jordan, A.G. (eds.), *Next Steps: Improving Management in Government?*, Dartmouth, Aldershot, pp. 99-117.
Barnett, C. (1986) *The Audit of War: The Illusion and Reality of Britain as a Great Nation*, Macmillan, Basingstoke.
Barrow, J. (1847) *An Autobiographical Memoir*, John Murray, London.
Bellamy, C. (1988) *Administering Central-Local Relations 1871-1919: The Local Government Board in its Fiscal and Cultural Context*, Manchester University Press, Manchester.
Beloff, M. (1975) 'The Whitehall factor: the role of the higher civil service 1919-39', in Peele, G. and Cook, C. (eds.), *The Politics of Reappraisal 1918-39*, Macmillan, London, pp. 209-31.
Benn, T. (1979) *Arguments for Socialism*, Jonathan Cape, London.
Benn, T. (1980) 'Manifestos and Mandarins', in Royal Institute of Public Administration (ed.), *Policy and Practice: The Experience of Government*, RIPA, London, pp. 57-78.
Beveridge, W. (1920) *The Public Service in War and Peace*, Constable, London.
Birch, A.H. (1964) *Representative and Responsible Government: An Essay on the Constitution*, Allen and Unwin, London.
Blackstone, T. and Plowden, W. (1988) *Inside the Think Tank: Advising the Cabinet 1971-1983*, Heinemann, London.
Blakeley, B.L. (1972) *The Colonial Office 1868-1892*, Duke University Press, Durham N.C.
Boyd, D. (1973) *Elites and their Education: The Educational and Social Background of Eight Elite Groups*, National Foundation for Educational Research, Windsor.
Boyd-Carpenter, J. (1980) *Way of Life: The Memoirs of John Boyd-Carpenter*, Sidgwick and Jackson, London.
Boyle, Lord (1980) 'Ministers and the administrative process', *Public Administration*, 58, pp. 1-12.
Bray, A.J.M. (1988) 'The clandestine reformer: a study of the Rayner scrutinies', *Strathclyde Papers on Government and Politics No. 55*, University of Strathclyde, Glasgow.
Brett, M.V. (ed.) (1934, 1938) *Journals and Letters of Reginald Viscount Esher 1870-1930* (4 vols.), Ivor Nicholson and Watson, London.
Bridges, E. (1950) *Portrait of a Profession: The Civil Service Tradition*, Cambridge University Press, London.
Bridges, E. (Lord) (1964) *The Treasury*, George Allen and Unwin, London.
Brown, G. (1972) *In My Way: The Political Memoirs of Lord George-Brown*, Penguin, Harmondsworth.
Bullock, A. (1967) *The Life and Times of Ernest Bevin – Vol. II: Minister of Labour 1940-*

45, Heinemann, London.
Bullock, A. (1983) *Ernest Bevin: Foreign Secretary 1945-1951*, Heinemann, London.
Bunbury, H. and Titmuss, R.M. (eds.) (1957) *Lloyd George's Ambulance Wagon – Being the Memoirs of William J. Braithwaite 1911-1912*, Methuen, London.
Butler, R. (1988) *Government and Good Public Management – Are They Compatible?*, Institute of Personnel Management, London.
Butler, R. (1990) *New Challenges or Familiar Prescriptions* (Redcliffe-Maud Memorial Lecture), PA Consulting Group/Royal Institute of Public Administration, London.

Cabinet Office (1991) *The Citizen's Charter: Raising the Standard* (Cm. 1599), HMSO, London.
Cabinet Office (1992) *Questions of Procedure for Ministers*, Cabinet Office, London.
Cabinet Office (1993) *Next Steps Agencies in Government – Review 1993* (Cm. 2430), HMSO, London.
Cabinet Office (1994) *The Civil Service: Continuity and Change* (Cm. 2627), HMSO, London.
Cabinet Office (1995) *The Civil Service: Taking Forward Continuity and Change* (Cm. 2748), HMSO, London.
Cairncross, A. and Watts, N. (1989) *The Economic Section 1939-1961: A Study in Economic Advising*, Routledge, London.
Campbell, J. (1993) *Edward Heath: A Biography*, Jonathan Cape, London.
Cannadine, D. (1990) *The Decline and Fall of the British Aristocracy*, Yale University Press, New Haven.
Carey, P. (1984) 'Management in the civil service', *Management in Government*, 39, pp. 81-5.
Carlton, D. (1970) *MacDonald versus Henderson: The Foreign Policy of the Second Labour Government*, Macmillan, London.
Carrington, P. (1989) *Reflect on Things Past: The Memoirs of Lord Carrington*, Collins, London.
Castle, B. (1973) 'Mandarin power', *Sunday Times*, 10 June.
Castle, B. (1980) *The Castle Diaries 1974-76*, Weidenfeld and Nicolson, London.
Castle, B. (1984) *The Castle Diaries 1964-70*, Weidenfeld and Nicolson, London.
Castle, B. (1993) *Fighting All The Way*, Macmillan, London.
Chapman, L. (1979) *Your Disobedient Servant: The Continuing Story of Whitehall's Overspending*, Penguin, Harmondsworth.
Chapman, R.A. (1984) *Leadership in the Civil Service: A Study of Sir Percival Waterfield and the Creation of the Civil Service Selection Board*, Croom Helm, London.
Chapman, R.A. (1988) *Ethics in the British Civil Service*, Routledge, London.
Chapman, R.A. and Greenaway, J.R. (1980) *The Dynamics of Administrative Reform*, Croom Helm, London.
Chester, N. (1981) *The English Administrative System 1780-1870*, Clarendon, Oxford.
Chipperfield, G. (1994) 'The civil servant's duty', *Essex Papers in Politics and Government No. 95*, University of Essex, Colchester.
Chorley, R.S.T. (1944) 'Some thoughts on the civil service', *Agenda*, 3, 4 (November), pp. 109-26.
Christoph, J.B. (1975) 'Higher civil servants and the politics of consensualism in Britain', in Dogan, M. (ed.), *The Mandarins of Western Europe: The Political Role of Top Civil Servants*, Sage, London, pp. 25-62.
Civil Service Commission (CSC) (1979) *Civil Service Commissioners' One Hundred and Twelfth Annual Report – 1978*, HMSO, London.

Civil Service Department (CSD) (1969) *First Report of the Civil Service Department*, HMSO, London.
Clark, A. (1993) *Diaries*, Weidenfeld and Nicolson, London.
Clarke, R. (1971) *New Trends in Government*, HMSO, London.
Cockett, R. (1994) *Thinking the Unthinkable: Think Tanks and the Economic Counter-Revolution, 1931-1983*, Harper Collins, London.
Collinge, J.M. (1979) *Foreign Office Officials 1782-1870*, University of London Institute of Historical Research, London.
Colvin, I. (1965) *Vansittart in Office: An Historical Survey of the Origins of the Second World War*, Victor Gollancz, London.
Commissioners for Fees etc. (1786) *First Report of the Commissioners Appointed to Inquire into the Fees, Gratuities, Perquisites and Emoluments Received in Public Offices*, P.P. 1806 (HC 309) VII.
Committee of Public Accounts – *see* Public Accounts Committee.
Committee on National Expenditure (1918) *Second Report From the Select Committee on National Expenditure*, P.P. 1917-8 (HC 151), iii.
Cooper, F. (1987) 'Select committees – a view from a witness', *Contemporary Record*, 1, 1, pp. 16-7.
Couzens, K. (1985) 'The principle of public service', in Royal Institute of Public Administration (ed.), *Politics, Ethics and Public Service*, RIPA, London, pp. 43-51.
Cromwell, V. (1960) 'An incident in the development of the permanent under-secretaryship of the Foreign Office', *Institute of Historical Research Bulletin*, 33, pp. 97-113.
Cromwell, V. and Steiner, Z. (1984) 'Reform and retrenchment: the Foreign Office between the wars', in Bullen, R. (ed.), *The Foreign Office 1782-1982*, University Publications of America, Frederick, Maryland, pp. 85-108.
Crosland, S. (1983) *Tony Crosland*, Coronet Books, Hodder and Stoughton, London.
Cross, J.A. (1977) *Sir Samuel Hoare, a Political Biography*, Jonathan Cape, London.
Crossman, R.H.S. (1975) *The Diaries of a Cabinet Minister – Vol. I: Minister of Housing, 1964-66*, Hamish Hamilton and Jonathan Cape, London.
Crossman, R.H.S. (1977) *The Diaries of a Cabinet Minister – Vol. III: Secretary of State for Social Services 1968-70*, Hamish Hamilton and Jonathan Cape, London.
Cubbon, B. (1993) 'The duty of the professional', in Chapman, R.A. (ed.), *Ethics in Public Service*, Edinburgh University Press, Edinburgh, pp. 7-13.
Cubbon, B. (1994) Memorandum of evidence to the Treasury and Civil Service Committee – *Fifth Report, Session 1993-94: The Role of the Civil Service – Vol. III, Appendices to the Minutes of Evidence*, HC 27 – III, pp. 108-10.

Dahl, R. (1970) *Modern Political Analysis*, 2nd. edn., Prentice-Hall, Englewood Cliffs, NJ.
Dale, H.E. (1941) *The Higher Civil Service of Great Britain*, Oxford University Press, Oxford.
Dale, H.E. (1956) *Daniel Hall: Pioneer in Scientific Agriculture*, John Murray, London.
Dalton, H. (1957) *The Fateful Years: Memoirs 1931-1945*, Frederick Muller, London.
Daunton, M.J. (1985) *Royal Mail: The Post Office Since 1840*, Athlone Press, London.
Davidson, R. (1972) 'Llewellyn Smith, the Labour Department and government growth 1886-1909', in Sutherland, G. (ed.) *Studies in the Growth of Nineteenth Century Government*, Routledge and Kegan Paul, London, pp. 227-62.
Davidson, R (1985) *Whitehall and the Labour Problem in Late-Victorian and Edwardian Britain*, Croom Helm, London.

Davie, M. (1977) 'Mandarins at bay – a glimpse from the past', *Observer Review*, 30 October.
Davies, A. and Willman, J. (1991) *What Next? Agencies, Departments and the Civil Service*, Institute of Public Policy Research, London.
Demetriadi, S. (1921) *Inside a Government Office*, Cassell, London.
Dicey, A.V. (1914) *Lectures on the Relation Between Law and Public Opinion During the Nineteenth Century*, 2nd edn., Macmillan, London.
Dickie, J. (1992) *Inside the Foreign Office*, Chapmans, London.
Dilkes, D. (ed.) (1971) *The Diaries of Alexander Cadogan 1938-1945*, Cassell, London.
Donajgrodzki, A.P. (1972) 'New roles for old: the Northcote-Trevelyan Report and the clerks of the Home Office 1822-48', in Sutherland, G. (ed.), *Studies in the Growth of Nineteenth Century Government*, Routledge and Kegan Paul, London, pp. 82-109.
Donoughue, B. (1987) *Prime Minister: The Conduct of Policy Under Harold Wilson and James Callaghan*, Jonathan Cape, London.
Dunnett, J. (1961) 'The civil service administrator and the expert', *Public Administration*, 39, pp. 223-37.

Edwards, R. Dudley (1994) *True Brits: Inside the Foreign Office*, BBC, London.
Efficiency Unit (1988) *Improving Management in Government: The Next Steps – Report to the Prime Minister*, HMSO, London.
Efficiency Unit (1993) *Career Management and Succession Planning Study* (Oughton Report), HMSO, London.
Ellis, E.L. (1992) *T.J.: A Life of Thomas Jones, CH*, University of Wales Press, Cardiff.
Englefield, D. (ed.) (1984) *Commons Select Committees – Catalysts for Progress*, Longman, London.
Estimates Committee (1958) *Sixth Report, 1957-58, together with the proceedings of the committee and evidence – Treasury Control of Expenditure*, HC 254 – I.
Estimates Committee (1965) *Sixth Report, 1964-65 – Recruitment to the Civil Service*, HC 308.
Expenditure Committee (1977a) *Eleventh Report, 1976-77: The Civil Service, Vol. I – Report* (English Report), HC 535 – I.
Expenditure Committee (1977b) *Eleventh Report, 1976-77: The Civil Service, Vol. II (parts I and II) – Minutes of Evidence*, HC 535 – II.

Faber, G. (1958) *Jowett: A Portrait with Background*, Harvard University Press, Cambridge, Massachusetts.
Fallon, I. (1993) *The Paper Chase: A Decade of Change at the DSS*, Harper Collins, London.
Finer, S.E. (1952) *The Life and Times of Sir Edwin Chadwick*, Methuen, London.
Fisher, N. (1973) *Iain Macleod*, André Deutsch, London.
Fitzroy, A. (1925) *Memoirs* (2 vols.), Hutchinson, London.
Foot, M. (1973) *Aneurin Bevan: A Biography – Vol. II: 1945-1960*, Davis-Poynter, London.
Foreign Office (1943) *Proposals for the Reform of the Foreign Service*, P.P. 1942-3 (Cmd. 6420), xi.
Foster, W. (1917) 'The India Board 1784-1858', *Transcripts of the Royal Historical Society*, 11 (3rd series), pp. 61-85.
Fowler, N. (1991) *Ministers Decide: A Personal Memoir of the Thatcher Years*, Chapmans, London.
Fraser, P. (1973) *Lord Esher: A Political Biography*, Hart-Davis, McGibbon, London.

Fry, G.K. (1969) *Statesmen in Disguise: The Changing Role of the Administrative Class of the British Home Civil Service 1853-1966*, Macmillan, London.

Fry, G.K. (1979) *The Growth of Government : The Development of Ideas about the Role of the State and the Machinery and Functions of Government in Britain since 1780*, Frank Cass, London.

Fry, G.K. (1986) 'The British career civil service under challenge', *Political Studies*, 34, pp. 533-55.

Fry, G.K. (1993) *Reforming the Civil Service: The Fulton Committee on the British Home Civil Service 1966-1968*, Edinburgh University Press, Edinburgh.

Fulton (1968) *The Civil Service – Vol. I: Report of the Committee 1966-68* (Fulton Report) (Cmnd. 3638), HMSO, London.

Gee, O. (1954) 'The British war Office in the later years of the American wars of independence', *Journal of Modern History*, 26, pp. 123-36.

Gerth, H.H. and Mills, C. Wright (eds.) (1948) *From Max Weber: Essays in Sociology*, Routledge and Kegan Paul, London.

Gilbert, M. (1991) *Churchill: A Life*, Heinemann, London.

Goldsworthy, D. (1971) *Colonial Issues in British Politics 1945-1961: From 'Colonial Development' to 'Wind of Change'*, Oxford University Press, Oxford.

Goodman, G. (1984) *The Awkward Warrior. Frank Cousins: His Life and Times*, 2nd edn., Spokesman Books, Nottingham.

Gore-Booth, P. (1974) *With Great Truth and Respect*, Constable, London.

Gosling, R. and Netley, S. (1990) *Bridging the Gap: Secondments Between Government and Business*, RIPA, London.

Greaves, H.R.G. (1947) *The Civil Service in the Changing State*, George G. Harrop, London.

Greenaway, J.R. (1983) 'Warren Fisher and the transformation of the British Treasury 1919-1939', *Journal of British Studies*, 33, pp. 125-42.

Greenaway, J.R. (1985) 'Parliamentary reform and civil service reform: a nineteenth century debate reassessed', *Parliamentary History*, 4, pp. 157-69.

Greenaway, J.R., Smith, S. and Street, J. (1992) *Deciding Factors in British Politics: A Case-Studies Approach*, Routledge, London.

Greenhill, D. (1993) *More By Accident*, 2nd edn., Wilton 65, York.

Greenleaf, W.H. (1983) *The British Political Tradition – Vol. I: The Rise of Collectivism*, Methuen, London.

Greenleaf, W.H. (1987) *The British Political Tradition – Vol. III (Parts 1 and 2): A Much Governed Nation*, Methuen, London.

Greer, P. (1994) *Transforming Central Government: The Next Steps Initiative*, Open University Press, Buckingham.

Grigg, J. (1978) *Lloyd George: The People's Champion 1902-11*, Methuen, London.

Grigg, J. (1985) *Lloyd George: From Peace to War 1912-1916*, Methuen, London.

Guillemard, L. (1937) *Trivial Fond Records*, Methuen, London.

Guttsman, W.L. (1963) *The British Political Elite*, MacGibbon and Kee, London.

Haines, J. (1977) *The Politics of Power*, Coronet, Hodder and Stoughton, London.

Ham, A. (1981) *Treasury Rules: Recurrent Themes in British Economic Policy*, Quartet Books, London.

Hamilton, H.P. (1951) 'Sir Warren Fisher and the public service', *Public Administration*, 29, pp. 3-38.

Hancock, W.K. and Gowing, M.M. (1949) *British War Economy*, HMSO, London.

Harris, J. (1977) *William Beveridge: A Biography*, Clarendon, Oxford.

Harris, J. (1982) 'Bureaucrats and businessmen in British food control 1916-19', in Burk, K. (ed.) *War and the State: The Transformation of British Government 1914-1919*, George Allen and Unwin, London, pp. 135-56.
Harris, J.S. and Garcia, T.V. (1966) 'The permanent secretaries: Britain's top administrators', *Public Administration Review*, 26, 1, pp. 31-44.
Harrod, R.F. (1951) *The Life of John Maynard Keynes*, Macmillan, London.
Hawes, D. (1993) *Power on the Back Benches? The Growth of Select Committee Influence*, School of Advanced Urban Studies, Bristol.
Headey, B. (1974) *British Cabinet Ministers: The Roles of Politicians in Executive Office*, George Allen and Unwin, London.
Healey, D. (1989) *The Time of My Life*, Michael Joseph, London.
Henderson, N. (1984) *The Private Office: A Personal View of Five Foreign Secretaries and of Government from the Inside*, Weidenfeld and Nicolson, London.
Henderson, N. (1994) *Mandarin: The Diaries of an Ambassador 1969-1982*, Weidenfeld and Nicolson, London.
Hennessy, P. (1988) 'Profile: Sir Robert Armstrong', *Contemporary Record*, 1, 4, pp. 28-31.
Hennessy, P. (1989) *Whitehall*, Secker and Warburg, London.
Hennessy, P. and Hague, D. (1985) 'How Adolf Hitler reformed Whitehall', *Strathclyde Papers on Government and Politics No. 41*, University of Strathclyde, Glasgow.
Heseltine, M. (1990) *Where There's a Will*, Arrow Books, London.
Hey, C.G. (1989) *Rowland Hill: Victorian Genius and Benefactor*, Quiller Press, London.
Hill, H.W. (1940) *Rowland Hill and the Fight for Penny Post*, Frederick Warne, London.
Hill, C. (Lord) (1964) *Both Sides of the Hill: The Memoirs of Charles Hill*, Heinemann, London.
HM Treasury (1919) *Final Report of the Committee of Inquiry into the Organisation and Staffing of Government Offices* (Bradbury Report), P.P. 1919 (CMD. 62), xi.
HM Treasury (1961) *Control of Public Expenditure* (Plowden Report) (Cmnd. 1432), HMSO, London.
HM Treasury (1989) *The Financing and Accountability of Next Steps Agencies* (Cm. 914), HMSO, London.
HM Treasury (1991) *Competing for Quality: Buying Better Public Services* (Cm. 1730), HMSO, London.
HM Treasury (1993) *Civil Service Management Code*, HM Treasury/Cabinet Office, London.
Holmes, M. (1951) 'Sir Amherst Selby-Bigge', *The Times*, 30 May.
Honey, J.R. de S. (1977) *Tom Brown's Universe: The Development of the Victorian Public School*, Millington, London.
Horne, A. (1989) *Macmillan 1957-1986: Vol. II of the Official Biography*, Macmillan, London.
Hoskyns, J (1983) 'Whitehall and Westminster: an outsider's view', *Parliamentary Affairs*, 36, pp. 137-47.
Howe, G. (1994) *Conflict of Loyalty*, Macmillan, London.
Hubbock, D. (1988) 'Sir Richard Clarke – 1910-1975. A most unusual civil servant', *Public Policy and Administration*, 3, 1, pp. 19-34.
Hughes, E. (1958) 'Sir James Stephen and the anonymity of the civil servant', *Public Administration*, 36, pp. 29-36.
Hunt, J. (1987) Commentary on G.W. Jones, 'The United Kingdom', in Plowden, W. (ed.) *Advising the Rulers*, Blackwell, Oxford, pp. 66-70.
Hutton, J. (ed.) (1885) *Selections from the Letters and Correspondence of Sir James Bland-*

Burges, John Murray, London.

Ingham, G. (1984) *Capitalism Divided? The City and Industry in British Social Development*, Macmillan, Basingstoke.

Inglis, F. (1993) 'So farewell then, citizen servant', *Times Higher Education Supplement*, 6 August.

Jay, P. (1968) Memorandum No. 132 to the Fulton Committee – *Fulton Evidence, Vol. V (Part II)*, HMSO, London, pp. 929-38.

Jay, P. (1985) 'Pontius or Ponting: public duty and public interest in secrecy and disclosure', in Royal Institute of Public Administration (ed.), *Politics, Ethics and Public Service*, RIPA, London, pp. 69-92.

Jenkins, H. and Jones, D.C. (1950) 'Social class of Cambridge alumni of the 18th and 19th centuries', *British Journal of Sociology*, 1, pp. 93-116.

Jenkins, R. (1991) *A Life at the Centre*, Macmillan, London.

Jenkins, S. (1975) 'The dame hits back – Evelyn Sharp interviewed by Simon Jenkins', *Sunday Times*, 5 October.

Jessel, D. (1980) 'Mandarins and ministers', *The Listener*, 11 December, pp. 774-5.

Johnson, N. (1981) 'Writing about public administration – the search for common ground', *Public Administration*, 59, pp. 127-38.

Johnson, P. (1991) *The Birth of the Modern: World Society 1815-1830*, Harper Collins, London.

Jones, G.W. (1976) 'The prime ministers' secretaries: politicians or administrators?', in Griffith, J.A.G. (ed.), *From Policy to Administration: Essays in Honour of William Robson*, George Allen and Unwin, London, pp. 13-38.

Jones, G.W. (1987) 'The United Kingdom', in Plowden, W. (ed.) *Advising the Rulers*, Blackwell, Oxford, pp. 36-66.

Jones, G.W. and Donoughue, B. (1973) *Herbert Morrison: Portrait of a Politician*, Weidenfeld and Nicolson, London.

Jones, T. (1951) *Lloyd George*, Oxford University Press, London.

Judge, H. (1984) 'R.L. Morant 1863-1920', in Barker, P. (ed.) *Founders of the Welfare State*, Heinemann, London, pp. 64-6.

Kaminsky, A.P. (1986) *The India Office 1880-1910*, Mansell, London.

Kavanagh, D. and Morris, P. (1989) *Consensus Politics from Attlee to Thatcher*, Blackwell, Oxford.

Keith, A.B. (1939) *The British Cabinet System 1830-1938*, Stevens, London.

Kekewich, G. (1920) *The Education Department and After*, Constable, London.

Kellner, P. and Crowther-Hunt, Lord (1980) *The Civil Servants: An Inquiry into Britain's Ruling Class*, MacDonald, London.

Kelsall, R.K. (1955) *Higher Civil Servants in Britain from 1870 to the Present Day*, Routledge and Kegan Paul, London.

Kelsall, R.K. (1974) 'Recruitment to the higher civil service: how has the pattern changed?', in Stanworth, P. and Giddens, A. (eds.) *Elites and Power in British Society*, Cambridge University Press, Cambridge, pp. 170-84.

Kemp, P. (1984) 'A civil servant's view', in Englefield, D. (ed.) *Commons Select Committees – Catalysts for Progress*, Longman, London, pp. 55-9.

Kemp, P. (1993) *Beyond Next Steps: A Civil Service for the 21st Century*, Social Market Foundation, London.

Kent, H. (1979) *In on the Act: Memoirs of a Lawmaker*, Macmillan, London.

King, A. (1981) 'The rise of the career politician in Britain – and its consequences',

British Journal of Political Science, 11, pp. 249-85.
Knaplund, P. (1953) *James Stephen and the British Colonial System 1813-1847*, University of Wisconsin Press, Madison.
Kriegel, A.B. (ed.) (1977) *The Holland House Diaries 1831-1840: The Diary of Henry Richard Vassall Fox, Third Lord Holland, with Extracts from the Diary of Dr. John Allen*, Routledge and Kegan Paul, London.

Lambert, R. (1963) *Sir John Simon 1816-1904 and English Social Administration*, MacGibbon and Kee, London.
Lawson, N. (1992) *The View From No. 11: Memoirs of a Tory Radical*, Bantam Press, London.
Lee, M.J. (1980a) *The Churchill Coalition 1940-45*, Batsford, London.
Lee, M.J. (1980b) 'The British civil service and the war economy. Bureaucratic conceptions of the "Lessons of History" in 1918 and 1945', *Transactions of the Royal Historical Society*, 30 (5th series), pp. 183-98.
Leith-Ross, F. (1968) *Money Talks: Fifty Years of International Finance*, Hutchinson, London.
Lewis, R.A. (1952) *Edwin Chadwick and the Public Health Movement 1832-1854*, Longman, Green and Co., London.
Linklater, M. and Leigh, D. (1986) *Not With Honour: The Inside Story of the Westland Scandal*, Sphere Books, London.
Lisle-Williams, M. (1984) 'Merchant banking dynasties in the English class structure: ownership, solidarity and kinship in the City of London, 1850-1960', *British Journal of Sociology*, 35, pp. 333-62.
Lloyd, C. (1970) *Mr Barrow of the Admiralty: A Life of Sir John Barrow*, Collins, London.
Lowe, R. (1982) 'The Ministry of Labour 1916-19: a still, small voice?', in Burk, K (ed.) *War and The State: The Transformation of British Government 1914-1919*, George Allen and Unwin, London, pp. 108-34.
Lowe, R. (1986) *Adjusting to Democracy: The Role of the Ministry of Labour in British Politics 1916-1939*, Clarendon, Oxford.
Lowe, R. (1993) *The Welfare State in Britain Since 1945*, Macmillan, Basingstoke.
Lowe, R. and Roberts, R. (1987) 'Sir Horace Wilson, 1900-1935: the making of a mandarin', *The Historical Journal*, 30, pp. 641-62.
Lukes, S. (1974) *Power: A Radical View*, Macmillan, London.

McDonald, O. (1992) *The Future of Whitehall*, Weidenfeld and Nicolson, London.
MacDonnell (1913) *Third Report of the Royal Commission on the Civil Service 1912-15* (MacDonnell Report) (Cmd. 6739-40) P.P. 1913, xviii.
MacDonnell (1914) *Fourth Report of the Royal Commission on the Civil Service 1912-15* (MacDonnell Report) (Cmd. 7338-40) P.P. 1914, xvi.
MacDougall, D. (1987) *Don and Mandarin: Memoirs of an Economist*, John Murray, London.
Mackenzie, N. and Mackenzie, J. (1984) *The Diary of Beatrice Webb – Vol. 3 1905-1924: The Power to Alter Things*, Virago, London.
MacLeod, R. (ed.) (1988) *Government and Expertise: Specialists, Administrators and Professionals, 1860-1919*, Cambridge University Press, Cambridge.
Macmillan, H. (1969) *Tides of Fortune 1945-55*, Macmillan, London.
Mallalieu, J.P.W. (1942) *"Passed to You, Please": Britain's Red-Tape Machine at War*, Victor Gollancz, London.
Mallet, B. (1905) *Sir Louis Mallet: A Record of Public Service and Political Ideas*, James Nisbet, London.

Marindin, G.E. (ed.) (1896) *Letters of Frederic Lord Blachford: Under Secretary of State for the Colonies 1860-71*, John Murray, London.
Marlowe, J. (1976) *Milner: Apostle of Empire*, Hamish Hamilton, London.
Marsh, D. and Rhodes, R.A.W. (eds.) (1992) *Policy Networks in British Government*, Clarendon, Oxford.
Marwick, A. (1973) *The Deluge: British Society and the First World War*, Macmillan, London.
Massey, A. (1993) *Managing the Public Sector: A Comparative Analysis of the UK and the USA*, Edward Elgar, Aldershot.
Meacher, M. (1979) 'Whitehall's short way with democracy', in Coates, K. (ed.) *What Went Wrong: Explaining the Fall of the Labour Government*, Spokesman Books, Nottingham, pp. 170-86.
Metcalfe, L. and Richards, S. (1984) 'The impact of the Efficiency Strategy: political clout or cultural change?' *Public Administration*, 62, pp. 439-54.
Metcalfe, L. and Richards, S. (1990) *Improving Public Management*, 2nd edn., Sage, London.
Meynell, A. (1988) *Public Servant, Private Woman: An Autobiography*, Victor Gollancz, London.
Middlemas, K. (ed.) (1969) *Thomas Jones: Whitehall Diary, Vol. 1 1916-1925*, Oxford University Press, London.
Middlemas, K. (1991) *Power, Competition and the State – Vol. 3: The End of the Postwar Era: Britain Since 1974*, Macmillan, Basingstoke.
Middlemas, K. and Barnes, J. (1969) *Baldwin: A Biography*, Weidenfeld and Nicolson, London.
Middleton, C.R. (1974) 'John Backhouse and the origins of the permanent undersecretaryship for foreign affairs: 1828-1842', *Journal of British Studies*, 8, 2, pp. 24-45.
Middleton, C.R. (1977) *The Administration of British Foreign Policy 1782-1846*, Duke University Press, Durham N.C.
Miliband, R. (1969) *The State in Capitalist Society: The Analysis of the Western System of Power*, Weidenfeld and Nicolson, London.
Miliband, R. (1982) *Capitalist Democracy in Britain*, Oxford University Press, Oxford.
Mills, C. Wright (1956) *The Power Elite*, Oxford University Press, New York.
Ministry of Reconstruction (1918) *Report of the Machinery of Government Committee* (Haldane Committee) (Cd. 9230), HMSO, London.
Monypenny, W.F. and Buckle, G.E. (1929) *The Life of Benjamin Disraeli, Earl of Beaconsfield* (2 vols.), John Murray, London.
Morgan, K.O. (1979) *Consensus and Disunity: The Lloyd George Coalition Government 1918-1922*, Clarendon, Oxford.
Morgan, K.O. (1984) *Labour in Power 1945-1951*, Oxford University Press, Oxford.
Morton, W.W. (1963) 'The Plowden Report: the management functions of the Treasury', *Public Administration*, 41, pp. 25-35.
Mosca, G. (1939) *The Ruling Class* (ed. Livingstone, A.), McGraw-Hill, New York.
Murray, Lady (1940) *The Making of a Civil Servant: Sir Oswyn Murray GCB, Secretary of the Admiralty, 1917-1936*, Methuen, London.

Nairne, P. (1982) 'Some reflections on change', *Management in Government*, 37, pp. 70-82.
Nairne, P. (1983) 'Managing the DHSS elephant: reflections on a giant department', *Political Quarterly*, 54, pp. 243-56.
Nairne, P. (1990) 'The Civil Service "Mandarins and Ministers"', *Wroxton Papers in*

Politics – Series A, Paper A6, Phillip Charles Media, Barnstable.
Nairne, P. (1994) 'Reflections on retirement', *Public Policy and Administration*, 9, 1, pp. 3-6.
National Oral Archive Transcripts (NOA Tr.) – interviews with Sir Charles Cunningham (29 May 1980); Lord Inchyra (14 June 1980); Sir Cyril Musgrave (11 August 1980); Sir Arthur Peterson (4 November 1980); Sir Hilton Poynton (7 May 1980); and Sir Richard Way (21 and 31 July 1980). All interviews conducted by Anthony Seldon. Tapes and transcripts lodged in the British National Oral Archive, London School of Economics and Political Science.
Naylor, J.F. (1984) *A Man and an Institution: Sir Maurice Hankey, the Cabinet Secretariat and the Custody of Cabinet Secrecy*, Cambridge University Press, Cambridge.
Northcote-Trevelyan (1854) *Report on the Organisation of the Permanent Civil Service*, (Cmd. 1713), P.P. 1854, xxvii.
Norton-Taylor, R. (1985) *The Ponting Affair*, Cecil Woolf, London.

Office of Public Service and Science (OPSS) (1993) *Realising Our Potential: A Strategy for Science, Engineering and Technology* (Cm. 2250), HMSO, London.
O'Halpin, E.J. (1987) *Decline of the Union: British Government in Ireland 1892-1920*, Gill and Macmillan, Dublin.
O'Halpin, E.J. (1989) *Head of the Civil Service: A Study of Sir Warren Fisher*, Routledge, London.
Osborne, D. and Gaebler, T. (1992) *Reinventing Government: How the Entrepreneurial Spirit is Transforming the Public Sector*, Addison-Wesley, Reading, Massachusetts.
O'Toole, B.J. (1990) 'T.H. Green and the ethics of senior officials in British central government', *Public Administration*, 68, pp. 337-52.
O'Toole, B.J. and Jordan, A.G. (eds.) (1995) *Next Steps: Improving Management in Government?*, Dartmouth, Aldershot.

Parris, H. (1969) *Constitutional Bureaucracy: The Development of British Central Administration Since the Eighteenth Century*, George Allen and Unwin, London.
Part, A. (1990) *The Making of a Mandarin*, André Deutsch, London.
Peden, G.C. (1979) *British Rearmament and the Treasury 1932-1939*, Scottish Academic Press, Edinburgh.
Pellew, J. (1982) *The Home Office 1848-1914: From Clerks to Bureaucrats*, Heinemann, London.
Perkin, H.J. (1969) *The Origins of Modern English Society 1780-1880*, Routledge and Kegan Paul, London.
Perkin, H.J. (1989) *The Rise of Professional Society: England Since 1880*, Routledge, London.
Peters, G. (1986) 'Burning the village: the civil service under Reagan and Thatcher', *Parliamentary Affairs*, 39, pp. 79-97.
Peters, G. (1989) *The Politics of Bureaucracy*, 3rd edn., Longman, London.
Pimlott, B. (1985) *Hugh Dalton*, Jonathan Cape, London.
Pimlott, B. (1992) *Harold Wilson*, Harper Collins, London.
Playfair (1875) *Reports of the Commission of Inquiry into the Civil Service* (Playfair Reports) (Cmd. 1113), P.P. 1875, xxiii.
Playfair, E. (1965) 'Who are the policy-makers?', *Public Administration*, 43, pp. 260-8.
Playfair, E. (1968) Memorandum No. 138 to the Fulton Committee – *Fulton Evidence*, Vol. V (Part II), HMSO, London, pp. 995-7.
Pliatzky, L. (1982) 'Don't throw away the over 50s', *The Times*, 9 December.

Pliatzky, L. (1984) 'Mandarins, ministers and the management of Britain', *Political Quarterly*, 55, pp. 23-38.
Pliatzky, L. (1989) *The Treasury Under Mrs Thatcher*, Blackwell, Oxford.
Plowden, W. (1985) 'What prospects for the civil service?', *Public Administration*, 63, pp. 393-414.
Plowden, W. (ed.) (1987) *Advising the Rulers*, Blackwell, Oxford.
Plowden, W. (1994) *Ministers and Mandarins*, Institute for Public Policy Research, London.
Plowden, W.J.L., Deakin, N.D. and Mayall, J.B.L. (1968) Memorandum No. 139 to the Fulton Committee – *Fulton Evidence, Vol. V (Part II)*, HMSO, London, pp. 998-1005.
Pollard, S. (1984) *The Wasting of the British Economy*, 2nd edn., Croom Helm, London.
Pollard, S. (1989) *Britain's Prime and Britain's Decline: The British Economy 1870-1914*, Edward Arnold, London.
Pollitt, C. (1993) *Managerialism and the Public Services*, 2nd edn., Blackwell, Oxford.
Ponting, C. (1985) *The Right to Know: The Inside Story of the Belgrano Affair*, Sphere Books, London.
Ponting, C. (1989) *Whitehall: Changing the Old Guard*, Unwin Hyman, London.
Preston-Thomas, H. (1909) *The Work and Play of a Government Inspector*, Blackwood, Edinburgh.
Prior, J. (1986) *A Balance of Power*, Hamish Hamilton, London.
Public Accounts Committee (PAC) (1920) *First, Second, Third and Fourth Reports from the Committee of Public Accounts, Session 1920*, HC 231 (incorporating HC 54, HC 88 and HC 182).
Public Accounts Committee (PAC) (1921) *Third Report from the Committee of Public Accounts, Session 1921*, HC 212.
Public Accounts Committee (PAC) (1984), *Twenty-Sixth Report from the Committee of Public Accounts, Session 1983-84 – Fraud in the Property Services Agency; the Wardale Report; System Controls in District Offices*, HC 295.
Public Accounts Committee (PAC) (1987) *Thirteenth Report from the Committee of Public Accounts, Session 1986-87 – The Financial Management Initiative*, HC 61.
Public Accounts Committee (PAC) (1990) *Second Special Report from the Committee of Public Accounts, Session 1989-90 – Accounting Officer Memorandum*, HC 527.
Public Accounts Committee (PAC) (1994a) *Eighth Report from the Committee of Public Accounts, Session 1993-94 – The Proper Conduct of Public Business*, HC 154.
Public Accounts Committee (PAC) (1994b) *Seventeenth Report from the Committee of Public Accounts, Session 1993-94 – The Pergau Hydro-Electric Project*, HC 155.
Pyper, R. (1991) *The Evolving Civil Service*, Longman, London.

Reader, W.J. (1966) *Professional Men: The Rise of the Professional Classes in Nineteenth-Century England*, Weidenfeld and Nicolson, London.
Redcliffe-Maud, J. (1981) *Experiences of an Optimist: The Memoirs of John Redcliffe-Maud*, Hamish Hamilton, London.
Redesdale, Lord (1915) *Memoirs* (2 vols.), Hutchinson, London.
Re-organisation Papers (1855) *Papers Relating to the Re-organisation of the Civil Service* (Cmd. 1870), P.P. 1854-5, xx.
Rhodes James, R. (1963) *Rosebery: A Biography of Archibald Philip, Fifth Earl of Rosebery*, Weidenfeld and Nicolson, London.
Richards, D. (1993) 'Appointments in the higher civil service: assessing a "Thatcher effect"', *Strathclyde Papers in Government and Politics No. 93*, University of Strathclyde, Glasgow.

Richter, M. (1964) *The Politics of Conscience: T.H. Green and His Age*, Weidenfeld and Nicolson, London.
Riddell, P. (1993) *Honest Opportunism: The Rise of the Career Politician*, Hamish Hamilton, London.
Ridley (1887) *First Report of the Royal Commission on Civil Establishments* (Ridley Report) (Cmd. 5226), P.P. 1887, xix.
Ridley (1888) *Second Report of the Royal Commission on Civil Establishments* (Ridley Report) (Cmd. 5545), P.P. 1888, xxvii.
Ridley, F.F. (1985) 'Political neutrality and the British civil service: Sir Thomas More and Mr Clive Ponting v. Sir Robert Armstrong and the Vicar of Bray', in Royal Institute of Public Administration (ed.) *Politics, Ethics and Public Service*, RIPA, London, pp. 31-42.
Roll, E. (1985) *Crowded Hours*, Faber and Faber, London.
Rose, N. (1978) *Vansittart: Study of a Diplomat*, Heinemann, London.
Rose, R. (1991) 'The political economy of cabinet change', in Vibert, F. (ed.) *Britain's Constitutional Future*, Institute of Economic Affairs, London, pp. 45-72.
Roseveare, H. (1969) *The Treasury: The Evolution of a British Institution*, Allen Lane, The Penguin Press, London.
Roseveare, H. (1973) *The Treasury 1660-1870: The Foundations of Control*, George Allen and Unwin, London.
Roskill, S. (1972) *Hankey: Man of Secrets – Vol. II, 1919-1931*, Collins, London.
Ross, J.M. (1984) 'What next minister? Another way of looking at the civil service', *Studies in Public Policy 127*, Centre for the Study of Public Policy, University of Strathclyde, Glasgow.
Royal Institute of Public Administration (RIPA) (1987) *Top Jobs in Whitehall: Appointments and Promotions in the Senior Civil Service – Report of an RIPA Working Group*, RIPA, London.
Rubinstein, W.D. (1986) 'Education and the social analysis of British elites 1880-1970', *Past and Present*, 112, pp. 163-207.
Rubinstein, W.D. (1993) *Capitalism, Culture and Decline in Britain*, Routledge, London.
Russell-Smith, E. (1974) *Modern Bureaucracy: The Home Civil Service*, Longman, London.

Sadler, M. (1932) *Modern Art and Revolution*, Hogarth Press, London.
Sainty, J.C. (1972) *Treasury Officials 1660-1870*, Athlone Press/University of London Institute of Historical Research, London.
Sainty, J.C. (1974) *Officials of the Board of Trade 1660-1870*, Athlone Press/University of London Institute of Historical Research, London.
Sainty, J.C. (1975) *Home Office Officials 1782-1870*, Athlone Press/University of London Institute of Historical Research, London.
Salter, A. (1961) *Memoirs of a Public Servant*, Faber and Faber, London.
Sanitary Commission (1869), *Second Report*, P.P. 1871, xxx.
Scott, H. (1959) *Your Obedient Servant*, André Deutsch, London.
Scott, J. (1991) *Who Rules Britain?*, Polity Press, Oxford.
Searing, D.D. (1994) *Westminster's World: Understanding Political Roles*, Harvard University Press, Cambridge, Massachusetts.
Searle, G.R. (1972) *The Quest for National Efficiency: A Study in British Politics and Political Thought 1899-1914*, Blackwell, Oxford.
Searle, G.R. (1993) *Entrepreneurial Politics in Mid-Victorian Britain*, Clarendon, Oxford.
Sedgemore, B. (1980) *The Secret Constitution: An Analysis of the Political Establishment*, Hodder and Stoughton, London.

Selby, W. (1953) *Diplomatic Twilight 1930-1940*, John Murray, London.
Seldon, A. (1981) *Churchill's Indian Summer: The Conservative Government 1951-55*, Hodder and Stoughton, London.
Select Committee on Miscellaneous Expenditure (1848) *Report on Miscellaneous Expenditure*, P.P. 1847-48 (HC 543), xviii.
Select Committee on Official Salaries (1850) *Report*, P.P. 1850 (HC 611) xv.
Select Committee on Procedure (1990a) *Second Report, Session 1989-90: The Working of the Select Committee System – Vol. I, Report*, HC 19-I.
Select Committee on Procedure (1990b) *Second Report, Session 1989-90: The Working of the Select Committee System, Together with Proceedings, Minutes of Evidence etc. (Vol. II)*, HC 19-II.
Self, P. (1972) *Administrative Theories and Politics*, George Allen and Unwin, London.
Selleck, R.J.W. (1994) *James Kay-Shuttleworth: Journey of an Outsider*, Woburn Press, Ilford.
Skelsey, P.M. (1957) 'Civil liberties', in Watson, G. (ed.) *The Unservile State: Essays in Liberty and Welfare*, George Allen and Unwin, London, pp. 54-87.
Smith, F. (1923) *The Life and Work of Sir James Kay-Shuttleworth*, John Murray, London.
Snelling, R.C. and Barron, T.J. (1972) 'The Colonial Office and its permanent officials 1801-1914', in Sutherland, G. (ed.) *Studies in the Growth of Nineteenth Century Government*, Routledge and Kegan Paul, London, pp. 139-66.
Steiner, Z. (1969) *The Foreign Office and Foreign Policy 1898-1914*, Cambridge University Press, Cambridge.
Stone, D. (1993) 'Think tanks: independent policy research institutes in the USA, UK and Australia'. Unpublished Ph.D. thesis, Australian National University, Canberra.
Stowe, K. (1992) 'Good piano won't play bad music: administrative reform and good governance', *Public Administration*, 70, pp. 387-94.
Strachey, L. and Fulford, R. (eds.) (1938) *The Greville Memoirs 1814-1860* (6 vols.), Macmillan, London.
Strauss, E. (1961) *The Ruling Servants: Bureaucracy in Russia, France – and Britain?*, George Allen and Unwin, London.

Taylor, A.J.P. (1964) 'Lloyd George: rise and fall', in Taylor, A.J.P. (ed.) *Politics in Wartime and Other Essays*, Hamish Hamilton, London, pp. 123-49.
Taylor, A.J.P. (1965) *English History 1914-1945*, Clarendon, Oxford.
Taylor, H. (1885) *Autobiography 1800-1875*, Longmans, Green and Co., London.
Theakston, K. (1987) *Junior Ministers in British Government*, Blackwell, Oxford.
Theakston, K. (1988) 'Saboteurs or scapegoats? The civil service and Labour governments', *Contemporary Record*, 2, 2, pp. 11-4.
Theakston, K. (1992) *The Labour Party and Whitehall*, Routledge, London.
Theakston, K. (1993) 'Evelyn Sharp (1903-85)', *Contemporary Record*, 7, 1, pp. 132-48.
Theakston, K. and Fry, G.K. (1989) 'Britain's administrative elite: permanent secretaries 1900-1986', *Public Administration*, 67, pp. 129-47.
Thomas, R. (1978) *The British Philosophy of Administration: A Comparison of British and American Ideas 1900-1939*, Longman, London.
Tilley, J. and Gaselee, S. (1933) *The Foreign Office*, G.P. Putnam, London.
Tomlin Evidence (1930-31), *Minutes of Evidence Taken Before the Royal Commission on the Civil Service (1929-31)*, HMSO, London.
Tomlin (1931) *Report of the Royal Commission on the Civil Service 1929-31* (Tomlin Report) (Cmd. 3909), P.P. 1930-31, x.
Torrance, J.R. (1968) 'Sir George Harrison and the growth of bureaucracy in the early

nineteenth century', *English Historical Review*, 83, pp. 52-88.
Treasury and Civil Service Committee (TCSC) (1980) *First Report, Session 1980-81 – The Future of the Civil Service Department*, HC 54.
Treasury and Civil Service Committee (TCSC) (1986a) *Seventh Report, Session 1985-86 – Civil Servants and Ministers: Duties and Responsibilities, vol. I – Report*, HC 92-I
Treasury and Civil Service Committee (TCSC) (1986b) *Seventh Report, Session 1985-86 – Civil Servants and Ministers: Duties and Responsibilities, vol. II – Annexes, Minutes of Evidence and Appendices*, HC 92-II.
Treasury and Civil Service Committee (TCSC) (1986c) *First Report, Session 1986-87 – Ministers and Civil Servants*, HC 62.
Treasury and Civil Service Committee (TCSC) (1988a) *Duties and Responsibilities of Civil Servants in Relation to Ministers*, (Session 1987-88) HC 370-i.
Treasury and Civil Service Committee (TCSC) (1988b) *Eighth Report, Session 1987-88 – Civil Service Management Reform: The Next Steps – Vol. II: Annexes, Minutes of Evidence and Appendices*, HC 494-II.
Treasury and Civil Service Committee (TCSC) (1989) *Fifth Report, Session 1988-89 – Developments in the Next Steps Programme*, HC 348.
Treasury and Civil Service Committee (TCSC) (1993) *Sixth Report, Session 1992-93 – The Role of the Civil Service: Interim Report – Vol. II, Minutes of Evidence and Appendices*, HC 390-II.
Treasury and Civil Service Committee (TCSC) (1994a) *Fifth Report, Session 1993-94 – The Role of the Civil Service – Vol. I*, HC 27-I.
Treasury and Civil Service Committee (TCSC) (1994b) *Fifth Report, Session 1993-94 – The Role of the Civil Service – Vol. II, Minutes of Evidence*, HC 27-II.
Turner, J (1980) *Lloyd George's Secretariat*, Cambridge University Press, Cambridge.

Vansittart, R. (Lord) (1958) *The Mist Procession*, Hutchinson, London.

Walden, G. (1983) 'On your bikes at the top', *The Times*, 5 August.
Wallas, G. (1908) *Human Nature in Politics*, Constable, London.
Ware, A. (1981) 'The concept of manipulation: its relation to democracy and power', *British Journal of Political Science*, 11, pp. 163-81.
Wass, D. (1983) 'The public service in modern society', *Public Administration*, 61, pp. 7-20.
Wass, D. (1984) *Government and the Governed* (BBC Reith Lectures, 1983), Routledge and Kegan Paul, London.
Wass, D. (1985) 'The civil service at the crossroads', *Political Quarterly*, 56, pp. 227-41.
Watt, D.C. (1965) *Personalities and Policies: Studies in the Formulation of British Foreign Policy in the Twentieth Century*, Longmans, Green and Co., London.
West, A. (1908) *One City and Many Men*, Smith, Elder, London.
West, A. (1920) *Contemporary Portraits: Men of My Day in Public Life*, T. Fisher Unwin, London.
Wheare, K.C. (1954) *The Civil Service and the Constitution*, University of London, Athlone Press, London.
Wiemann, F.W. (1971) 'Lloyd George and the struggle for the Navy estimates of 1914', in Taylor, A.J.P. (ed.) *Lloyd George: Twelve Essays*, Hamish Hamilton, London, pp. 71-91.
Wiener, M.J. (1981) *English Culture and the Decline of the Industrial Spirit*, Cambridge University Press, Cambridge.
Williams, P. (1979) *Hugh Gaitskell: A Political Biography*, Jonathan Cape, London.
Williams, P. (ed.) (1983) *The Diary of Hugh Gaitskell 1945-1956*, Jonathan Cape,

London.
Williams, S. (1980) 'The decision makers', in Royal Institute of Public Administration (ed.) *Policy and Practice: The Experience of Government*, RIPA, London, pp. 79-102.
Williams, W. (1989) 'Central government capacity and the British disease', *Parliamentary Affairs*, 42, pp. 250-64.
Willson, F.M.G. (1959) 'The routes of entry of new members of the British cabinet, 1868-1958', *Political Studies*, 7, pp. 222-32.
Willson, F.M.G. (1970) 'Entry to the cabinet 1959-1968', *Political Studies*, 18, pp. 236-8.
Wilson, J. (1973) *CB: A Life of Sir Henry Campbell-Bannerman*, Constable, London.
Wilson, S.S. (1975) *The Cabinet Office to 1945*, HMSO, London.
Woods, J. (1954) 'Treasury control', *Political Quarterly*, 25, pp. 370-81.
Woolton, Lord (1959) *The Memoirs of the Rt. Hon. the Earl of Woolton*, Cassell, London.
Wright, M (1969) *Treasury Control of the Civil Service 1854-1874*, Clarendon, Oxford.
Wright, M. (1972) 'Treasury control 1854-1914', in Sutherland, G. (ed.) *Studies in the Growth of Nineteenth Century Government*, Routledge and Kegan Paul, London, pp. 195-226.
Wright, M. (1977) 'Ministers and civil servants: relations and responsibilities', *Parliamentary Affairs*, 30, pp. 293-315.
Wright, M. (1988) 'City rules OK? Policy community, policy network and takeover bids', *Public Administration*, 66, pp. 389-410.

Young, H. (1990) *One of Us: A Biography of Margaret Thatcher*, Pan Books, London.
Young, H. and Sloman, A (1982) *No, Minister: An Inquiry into the Civil Service*, BBC, London.
Young, K. (1963) *Arthur James Balfour: The Happy Life of the Politician, Prime Minister, Statesman and Philosopher 1848-1930*, G. Bell, London.

Ziegler, P. (1993) *Wilson: The Authorised Life of Lord Wilson of Rievaulx*, Weidenfeld and Nicolson, London.
Zifcak, S. (1994) *New Managerialism: Administrative Reform in Whitehall and Canberra*, Open University Press, Buckingham.

Index

Aberdeen University, 101
accountability, 22-3, 62-74, 89, 152, 220-2, 228-9
Addington, Henry (Lord Sidmouth), 5
Addington, Henry Unwin, 46
Administrative Class, 98, 101, 102, 128, 136, 138-9, 142, 208-9; *see also* Class 1 clerkships
Administrative Reform Association, 149
Admiralty, 5-6, 47, 56, 64, 80, 159, 190
Agriculture, Board of, 82, 121
Agriculture (Fisheries and Food), Ministry of, 123, 127, 131, 172-3, 189, 196
Air Ministry, 56, 64, 190
Aircraft Production, Ministry of, 83
Alfred, Montague, 68-9, 71, 139, 151, 159
Allen, Sir Douglas, 15, 126-7, 169-70, 179, 184-5
Allen, Sir Philip, 126
Amery, Leo, 123
Anderson, Sir John (1858-1918), 21
Anderson, Sir John (Visc. Waverley), 82, 123, 157-8, 173, 218
Andrew, Revd. Sir Herbert, 191

Andrews, Sir Derek, 172
anonymity, xvi, 9-12, 16-7, 22-3, 24-5, 76-7, 88, 148, 203, 211, 215
aristocracy, 110-3, 116-7, 208; *see also* heterogeneity
Armstrong Memorandum, 26, 222, 225
Armstrong, Sir Robert, 15-6, 51, 106, 114, 219
Armstrong, Sir Thomas, 114
Armstrong, Sir William, 14-5, 16, 32, 49-50, 126-7, 206
Asquith, H.H., 149
Association of First Division Civil Servants, 26, 169, 229
Attlee, Clement, Attlee governments, 29, 125, 194, 206, 223-4
Aust, George, 4
Avon, Earl of, *see* Eden, Sir Anthony

Babington Smith, Sir Henry, 131
Backhouse, John, 4
Bagehot, Walter, xv, 231
Baillie Hamilton, William, 113, 159
Baldwin Council, *see* Council of Financial Officers
Baldwin, Stanley, 19, 194

Balfour, A.J., 10
Balliol College, Oxford, 100
Balogh, Thomas, 150
Bancroft, Sir Ian, 15, 27, 127, 170, 231
Bank of England, 106
Barnes, Sir George, 20
Barnett, Correlli, 201-2
Barrow, Sir John, 5-6
Beale, Sir John, 121
Beaverbrook, Lord, 18
Benn, Tony, xv, 56, 69-70, 226
Bevan, Aneurin, 40, 125
Beveridge, Sir William, 33, 149
Bevin, Ernest, 32, 124, 223-4
Birrell, Augustine, 156-7
Bishop, Sir Frederick, 209
Bland-Burges, Sir James, 4
boards, *see under individual function* (e.g. Inland Revenue, Board of)
Boer War, 17
Bowyer, Sir Eric, 39, 69
Boyle, Edward, 39
Bradbury Committee, 122
Bradbury, Sir John, 12, 37
Brett, Reginald, *see* Esher, 2nd Visc.
Bretton Woods, 216
Bridges, Sir Edward, 14, 18, 59, 66, 83, 88, 106, 114, 124-6, 151, 168, 190, 218
Bridges, Robert, 114
Brittain, Sir Herbert, 190
Brittan, (Sir) Leon, 76
Brook, Sir Norman, 14, 18-9, 37, 83, 124-5, 135, 151, 190, 218
Brown, George, 32, 134
Brown, Sir Max, 190
Brown, Sir Patrick, 159
Burke, Thomas, 6
Burns, Sir Terence, 57, 72, 101, 104, 152
business people (in Whitehall), 115-6, 149-52, 159, 208
Butler, R.A., 40, 126, 208, 212, 223-4
Butler, Sir Robin, 15-6, 31, 60-1, 76, 106, 131, 141, 190, 219, 228

Cabinet Office, 17-20, 83, 129, 134-7, 175, 190, 196-7, 205
    Economic Section, 13, 19
    MPO, 15, 51, 53
    Occupational Health Service, 53
    OMCS, 53, 129
    OPSS, 53-4, 171
    Secretariat, 17-8
cabinet secretary(ship), 15, 17-20, 82, 124, 190, 226; *see also* head(ship) of the (home) civil service
Caccia, Sir Harold, 48
Cadogan, Sir Alexander, 11, 66, 110, 124
Caines, Eric, 170
Caines, Sir John, 191
Caines, Karen, 51
Callaghan, James, Callaghan government, 73, 126-7, 133, 152, 194, 216, 230
Cambridge University, 99-100
Campbell-Bannerman, Sir Henry, 40, 121, 211
Carey, Sir Peter, 44, 69, 127, 190
Cary, Sir Michael, 190
Castle, Barbara, 29, 32, 39, 88, 126
Cavendish, Lord Frederick, 6
Central African Federation (CAF), 212
Central Policy Review Staff (CPRS), 19
Centre for Policy Studies, 38
Chadwick, Sir Edwin, 7-8, 10, 16, 81, 110, 211
Chamberlain, Austen, 24
Chamberlain, Joseph, 10, 80, 121
Chamberlain, Neville, 11, 13, 16, 47, 124, 150, 206, 212
Channon, Paul, 197
Chapman, Leslie, 72
Chapman, Richard, 170
Charterhouse, 106
Chipperfield, Sir Geoffrey, 61
Churchill, Sir Winston, 10, 11, 14, 19, 36, 122-5, 157, 194
Citizen's Charter, 52
civic universities, 100-1; *see also* 'Oxbridge'; universities
Civil Service College, 53
Civil Service Commission(ers), 100, 106
Civil Service Department (CSD), 14-5, 135
Civil Service Management Code, 26, 222
Clarendon schools, 104-6, 108; *see also* schools
Clarke, Sir Richard, 49, 212
Class 1 clerkships, 98, 100, 208-9; *see also* Administrative Class
clerical grades, 48, 101, 107, 139, 209
Clifford, Sir Hugh, 123
Clynes, J.R., 82
Cohen, Sir Andrew, 157, 212

Colonial Office, xv, 6-7, 46-7, 64, 81, 120-1, 123, 125, 150, 155, 185
Committee of Imperial Defence (CID), 17-8
Committee on National Expenditure (1918), 122
Committee of Public Accounts, *see* Public Accounts Committee
Committee on Public Monies, 63
Commons, House of, *see* Parliament; select committees
Comptroller and Auditor General, 63, 69
Conservative Party, Conservative governments, xviii, 8, 109, 111-2, 127, 157, 192, 217; *see also* under name of leader (e.g. Major, John)
constitution, 6-12, 23-9, 157, 204, 211, 220-32; *see also* anonymity; ministerial responsibility; neutrality
Continuity and Change (Cm. 2627), 53
contracting out, 52-4, 89
Control, Board of, 5
Cooper, Sir Frank, 71
Council of Financial Officers (Baldwin Council), 65
Cousins, Frank, 126
Craik, Sir Henry, 13
Crawford, Lord, 121
Creech Jones, Arthur, 125
Creedy, Sir Herbert, 122
Croham, Lord, *see* Allen, Sir Douglas
Crossman, Richard, 28, 30, 32, 39, 74, 81, 85, 126
Crowe, Sir Eyre, 66, 99, 123, 211-2
Cubbon, Sir Brian, 36, 59, 73, 184-5, 213-4
Cuckney, (Sir) John, 152, 159
Cumin, Patrick, 148
Cunningham, Sir Charles, 38-9, 48, 83-4, 126
Curzon, Lord, 123
Customs (and Excise), Board of, 155, 175, 189

Dale, H.E., xvi, 204
Dalton, Hugh, 11, 29-30, 87, 124-5
Dalyell, Tam, 12
Daniel, Sir Goronwy, 112
Dean, Sir Maurice, 126, 189, 191
Defence, Ministry of (MoD), 12, 56, 129, 131, 190, 197
    procurement, 151-2, 160, 190
delegation, decentralization, 51-2, 60, 77-8, 82, 84, 228
democracy, democratic government, 9, 14, 24, 92, 205-7, 214, 220, 226-7
departments, *see under individual functions* (e.g. Health, Ministry of)
departmental view, 39, 58-9, 205
departmentalism, 4-7, 64, 80, 119-22, 154-5, 182
Derx, Donald, 128, 218
Dicey, A.V., xviii
Digby, Revd. Kenhelm, 113
Digby, Sir Kenhelm, 113
diplomatic service, 12-3, 83, 99, 162-3, 171
Disraeli, Benjamin, 109, 120, 148
Dougherty, Sir James, 156
Douglas, Sir William, 40, 125
Drogheda, Earl of, 110
Drummond, Sir Eric, 124
Dunnett, Sir James, 169

Economic Affairs, Department of (DEA), 14, 19, 134
Economic Warfare, Ministry of, 110, 124
Eden, Sir Anthony, 11, 13, 124-6
Education Act, 1944, 208, 212
Education and Science, Department of (DES), 32, 191, 216
Education Department (of the Privy Council), 8, 10, 46, 81, 148, 155, 182
Education, Department for (DFE), 190-1, 197
Education, Ministry of, 191
Efficiency Unit, 50-2, 170
Elgin, Lord, 121
Emmerson, Sir Harold, 113, 209
Employment Committee (House of Commons), 77
Employment, Department of, 128, 189; *see also* Labour, Ministry of
English Report (1977), *see* Expenditure Committee
Environment, Department of the (DoE), 51, 127-9, 139, 163
Esher, 1st Visc., 114
Esher, 2nd Visc., 114, 120-1, 157
Estimates Committee (House of Commons), 66-7

ethics, code of, 26-7, 229; *see also* public service ethic
Eton College, 106
European Economic Community (EEC), 127, 212
European Union (EU), 162, 224-5
executive agencies, 20, 52, 54-5, 60-1, 72-3, 89-91, 152, 221
executive grades, 48, 101, 107, 139, 209
Expenditure Committee (House of Commons), 15, 169, 179, 186
expenditure, public, 63, 66-7, 205, 212
expertise, professional, 40-1, 102-4, 158-60, 207
Export Credits Guarantee Department (ECGD), 74

Fabian Society, 89, 157
Falklands war, 12
Farrer, Sir Thomas, 80, 120, 211
Fell, David, 159, 163
Fergusson, Sir Donald, 39, 123, 131
Financial Management Initiative (FMI), 51
Financial Management Unit (FMU), 51
First Division Association (FDA), *see* Association of First Division Civil Servants
First World War, xviii, 64, 98, 149-50, 175, 206, 211
Fisher, Sir Warren, 12-4, 18-9, 35-6, 64-7, 71-2, 122-4, 126, 129, 135, 155, 167-8, 170, 175-6, 207, 210-2, 218, 223
Fitzroy, Sir Almeric, 18
Fleming, Henry, 120
Flemming, Sir Gilbert, 191
Floud, Sir Francis, 123
Food, Ministry of, 121
Forber, Sir Edward, 100
Foreign and Commonwealth Office (FCO), 20, 36, 88, 106, 163, 189
Foreign Office (FO), 4-5, 11-2, 32, 46-9, 64, 66, 82-3, 99, 106, 110, 121, 123-4, 185, 211-3
fragmentation (in the civil service), 19, 38-41, 60, 77-8, 90, 141-2, 198, 221-2
Franks, Sir Oliver, 125
Fraser, Sir Bruce, 126, 191
Fraser, William, 4
Fuel and Power, Ministry of (MFP), 39
Fulton Committee, Fulton Report, 14, 44, 49-50, 52, 88-9, 92, 102, 126, 139, 152, 169-71, 178, 207

Gaebler, T., 91
Gainer, Sir Donald, 99
Gaitskell, Hugh, 39, 125
Gater, Sir George, 47, 124, 150
German, Sir Ronald, 173
Gillmore, Sir David, 159
Gladstone, Herbert, 121
Gladstone, W.E., 40, 63, 80, 120, 148-9, 192
Godber, Joseph, 127-8
Godley, Sir Arthur, 46, 114, 149, 185
Godley, John, 114
Golding, John, 77
Goldman, Sir Samuel, 104
Gore-Booth, Sir Paul, 213
Goschen, George, 156
Goulburn, Frederick, 109
Goulburn, Henry, 109
Greater London Council, 83, 161
Green, T.H., 100
Greenhill, Sir Denis, 87, 98
Gregson, Sir Peter, 190-1
Griffin, Robert, 120
Grigg, Sir James, 157-8
Guillemard, Sir Laurence, 80

Haldane Committee (1918), 18, 122
Haliburton, Sir Arthur, 40
Hall, Admiral, 6
Hall, Sir Daniel, 121
Hamilton, Sir Edward, 106
Hamilton, Sir Horace, 185
Hamilton, Sir Robert, 6
Hammond, Sir Edmund, 114
Hammond, George, 4-5, 114
Hankey, Sir Maurice, 17-9, 82, 124, 155, 157-8, 211-2
Harcourt, Sir William, 28
Hardinge, Sir Charles, 110
Hardman, Sir Henry, 173
Harris, Lord (Ralph), 38
Harrison, Sir George, 5
Harrop, Sir Peter, 163
Harrow School, 106
Hawton, Sir John, 67
Hay, Robert 6
Hayes, Sir Brian, 127-8, 134
Head, Antony, 125

head(ship) of the (home) civil service, 12-7, 19-20, 36, 122-9, 175-6, 226; *see also* cabinet secretary(ship)
Healey, Denis, 127
Health, Department of, 56
Health, General Board of, 8
Health, Ministry of, 40, 125
Health and Social Security, Department of (DHSS), 127-8, 186
Heath, Edward, Heath government, 15, 32, 36, 206, 216
Heath, Sir Frank, 104
Heiser, Sir Terence, 128-9, 139
Helmore, Sir James, 48
Helsby, Sir Laurence, 14, 104, 126, 189
Henderson, Arthur, 30, 123-4
Henderson, Sir Nicholas, 34
Hennessy, Peter, xv, 141, 148, 150, 161, 165, 210
Herbecq, Sir John, 15
Heseltine, Michael, 30, 51, 76, 129, 197
heterogeneity, social decomposition, 34, 110-7, 204-5, 210, 218; *see also* aristocracy
Hildred, Sir William, 101
Hill, Charles, 25, 28
Hill, Sir Rowland, 7-8, 16, 110, 211
Hitchman, Sir Alan, 67, 172-3
Hitler, Adolf, 11, 16
Hoare, Sir Samuel, 11, 124
Hoare-Laval pact, 11
Holland, Sir Geoffrey, 191
Holmes, Edmond, 10
Holmes, Sir Maurice, 10, 212
Home Office 4, 7, 24, 38-9, 46-8, 64, 80, 82-3, 103, 121, 124, 126, 155, 159-61, 189, 204, 212, 221
Honey, J.R. de, 104
Hopkins, Sir Richard, 13, 74, 185
Hopwood, Sir Francis, 121
Hoskyns, Sir John, 38, 151, 183
Housing and Local Government, Ministry of (MHLG), 25, 28-9, 47, 126
Howard, Michael, 24, 221
Howe, Sir Geoffrey, 25, 127
Howell Thomas, Sir Charles, 123
Hoyer Millar, Sir Frederick, 49, 67, 83
Hunt, Sir John, 213
Hurcomb, Sir Cyril, 40, 218

Ibbs Report, 44, 51-3, 72, 152; *see also* executive agencies; Next Steps
Ibbs, Sir Robin 51-2
impartiality, *see* neutrality
Ince, Sir Gilbert, 124
India Office, 9, 46, 149, 155, 157, 185
Industry, Department of, 69, 127-8, 190-1; *see also* Trade and Industry, Department of
Industry Act, 1972, 69
Information, Central Office of (COI), xvii, 160
Inland Revenue, Board of, 155-6, 173, 175, 189
Insolvency Agency (DTI), 74
Institute of Economic Affairs (IEA), 38
interdepartmental transfers, 66, 135, 166-80, 207-8
International Monetary Fund (IMF), 162, 216
Irish Office, 6, 121, 156-7, 173
Iron and Steel Board, 83

Jackson, Andrew, 51
Jenkin, Patrick, 68-9, 127-8, 134
Jenkins, Kate, 51
Jenkins, Roy, 38-9, 99, 126
Johnson, Nevil, 88
Jones, Thomas, 19
Jowatt, Benjamin, 100

Kay-Shuttleworth, Sir James, 7-8, 46, 81, 110
Kearnes, Sir Frederick, 172
Keeler, Christine, 34
Kekewich, Sir George, 10, 109
Kekewich, Samuel, 109
Kemp, Sir Peter, xvi, 32-3, 54, 77, 89, 129
Keynes, J.M., 13
Kirkpatrick, Sir Ivone, 99
Knox, Sir Ralph, 40
Knutsford, Lord, 120

Labour, Ministry of, 13, 113, 123-4, 131, 157; *see also* Employment, Department of
Labour Party, Labour governments, 112, 157, 194; *see also* under name of leader (e.g. Wilson, Harold)
Lack, Thomas, 5
Lambert, Sir John, 41, 46, 120
Lang, Sir John, 67

278 The Elite of the Elite

Lankester, Sir Tim, 70, 224
Laski, Harold, 150
Law, Andrew Bonar, 18, 121
Lawson, Nigel, 127
Leach, Sir George, 184
Lee, Sir Frank, 212, 218
Leith-Ross, Sir Frederick, 124
Lenox-Conyngham, George, 46
Levene, Sir Peter, 151, 159
Lewis, Matthew, 5
Liberal Party, Liberal governments, xviii, 109, 111-2, 149, 157, 175, 204, 206
Lindsay, Sir Robert, 99, 110
Lingen, Sir Ralph, 64, 120, 182
Llewellyn Smith, Sir Hubert, 206
Lloyd, Sir Thomas, 125
Lloyd George, David, 10, 18-9, 37, 65, 112, 121-3, 149
Local Government Board, 41, 46, 120, 204
loyalty, 26-7, 29-30, 75-6, 206, 222-7, 229-32; *see also* constitution
London County Council, 124, 150
London University, 101
Lowe, Robert, 120
Lucas, Edward, 156
Lushington, Sir Godfrey, 114
Lushington, Stephen, 114
Lushington, Vernon, 114

Maberly, Col. Walter, 7
MacDonald, J. Ramsay, 40, 82, 123-4, 157
MacDonnell, Sir Antony, 121
MacDonnell Commission (Royal Commission on the Civil Service 1912-15), 100, 122, 149, 167
McDonnell, Sir Schomberg, 157
Macleod, Iain, 113
Macmillan, Harold, 14, 34, 37, 39, 126, 192, 212-3, 223-4
Major, John, Major governments, 41, 89-90, 183, 192, 217-8, 224, 227-9
Makins, Sir Roger, 125, 190
Mallalieu, J.P.W., 202
Mallet, Sir Louis, 9
managed economy, xviii, 175
management, 140; *see also* Financial Management Initiative
   accounting, 49, 68-9, 72, 87
   output indicators, 51
   performance targets, 49, 51
   personnel, career, 57, 87, 169-71, 175
   strategic, 55, 58, 90-1
Management Information Systems for Ministers (MINIS), 51
managerialism, 44-5, 47-54, 91
Manzie, Sir Gordon, 139
market testing, *see* contracting out
mass media, 16, 36-7, 57, 68, 86
Masterton-Smith, Sir James, 123, 131
Maud, Sir John, 35, 37
Maxwell, Sir Alexander, 124, 212
Meade, Richard, 114
Meade, Sir Robert, 114, 120
Melville, Lord, 5
Merchant Taylors' School (Northwood), 106
meritocracy, 95-6, 116-7, 133, 137-40, 209-10
Middleton, Sir Peter, 72, 101, 104
Milner, Sir Alfred, 156
ministerial reshuffles, 27, 29, 192-4
ministerial responsibility, 9, 23, 62, 81-2, 152, 220-2, 226-7; *see also* constitution
ministries, *see under individual function* (e.g. Transport, Ministry of)
Mitford, Sir Algernon, 109, 114, 120, 157
Mitford, Henry, 114
Monck, Sir Nick, 106
Montague, Lord Robert, 203
Monteath, Sir David, 114
Monteath, Sir James, 114
Morant, Sir Robert, 10, 121, 155, 206, 211
Morris, Charles, 77
Morrison, Herbert, 40, 124, 150
Morton, Sir Wilfred, 168-70
Moseley, Sir George, 127
Mottram, Richard, 129
Mount, Ferdinand, 38
Mowatt, Sir Francis, 10-11, 25, 120, 211
Mueller, Dame Anne, 138
Mundella, A.J., 148
Munich agreement, 16
Munitions, Ministry of, 149
Murray, Sir Evelyn, 114
Murray, Revd. George, 113
Murray, Sir George, 113-4
Murray, Sir Herbert, 113-4
Murray, Sir Oswyn, 47
Musgrave, Sir Cyril, 20, 67-8, 71, 83, 209

Nairne, Sir Patrick, 31, 56, 73, 84, 127, 186
National Audit Act, 1983, 70
National Audit Office, 63, 70-1
National Board for Prices and Incomes (NBPI), 162
National Economic Development Council (NEDC), 162
National Insurance Commission, 10, 121, 149, 175
Neale, Sir Alan, 173
Nettleship, R.C., 100
neutrality, impartiality, 76-7, 147-8, 152, 157, 165, 229-32; *see also* anonymity; constitution; public service ethic
Next Steps, 33, 51-2, 54-6; *see also* executive agencies; Ibbs Report
Nield, Sir William, 104, 157
Noel-Baker, Philip, 39
North Atlantic Treaty Organization (NATO), 162
Northcote, Sir Stafford, 7, 109, 167
Northcote-Trevelyan Report (1854), 9, 109, 137, 148, 154, 167, 169, 171, 178, 207
Northern Ireland Office, 131

Office of the Minister for Economic Affairs, 19, 131, 182
Official Secrets Act, 12, 25
Olivier, Sir Sydney, 82, 157
Ommanney, Sir Montagu, 121
open competition, xviii, 96, 98, 106, 109, 116, 136, 138, 148, 151, 154; *see also* patronage; recruitment
open government, 16, 213, 218
Organization for Economic Co-Operation and Development (OECD), 162
Osborne, D., 91
Osmotherly Rules, 75, 77
Oughton Report (1993), 170-1
Overseas Development, Ministry of, 157
Overseas Development Administration (ODA, FCO), 70
'Oxbridge', xvi, 100-2, 108, 208
Oxford University, 97-101

Padmore, Sir Thomas, 29, 32, 39, 125-6, 190
Parkinson, Cecil, 197

Parliament, 22, 62-78, 83, 156-8, 220-1, 224-7; *see also* political connections; Public Accounts Committee; select committees
Parris, Henry, 3
Part, Sir Antony, 56, 69-70, 126, 164, 184-5, 225
Partridge, Sir Michael, 55, 69
patronage, 9, 148-9, 153-4, 156; *see also* open competition; recruitment
Patten, John, 191
Peel, Sir Robert, 8, 119, 192
Pensions and National Insurance, Ministry of (MPNI), 39
Pergau Dam project, 70, 224
permanent secretaries
    as accounting officers, 62-73, 87, 90, 223-4
    age (years), 130-2, 142, 182-4
    appointment of, 119-30
    careerists, 120-2, 147-55, 171-2, 182
    definition of, xvii
    and their departments, 42-3, 44-61, 66, 73, 75-8, 82, 140, 210-1, 215, 221-2
    development of office of, 6-12
    education of, 97-108, 208-10
    interdepartmental activities of, 31, 86-8, 225-6
    and ministers, 7-8, 16, 22-43, 47, 56-7, 67, 68-70, 75-7, 85, 89-91, 111-3, 129-30, 133-4, 172, 195-8, 203-7, 210-9, 221-7
    non-careerists, 103-4, 148-52, 155-60, 208
    origins of office of, 3-6
    and policy-making, 7-12, 24-9, 36-43, 67, 73, 84-5, 87, 90, 202-4, 210-4
    remuneration of, 20-1, 89-90, 151, 180
    social origins of, 108-16
    women, 138, 209
    working patterns, workload, 27-8, 46-7, 65, 68, 80-8, 215
permanent under-secretary, xviii; *see* permanent secretaries
Perry, Sir Michael, 20
Peterson, Sir Arthur, 48, 83-4, 161, 186-7
Phoenix Park murders, 6
Pile, Sir William, 32, 191, 216

Pirie, Madsen, 38
Playfair, Sir Edward, 39, 125, 183, 186
Playfair Commission (1875), 167
Pliatzky, Sir Leo, 151, 157, 183
Plowden, William, 89, 184
Plowden Committee (1961), 44, 66, 168-9
Policy Unit (No. 10 Downing St.), 19, 38
political connections, 4, 108-10, 120, 156-8
Pollard, Sidney, 170
Ponting, Clive, Ponting Affair, 12, 26, 222
Poor Law Board, 8, 156-7
Portland, Lord, 5
Post Office, 7-8, 21, 64, 131, 173
Powell, Sir Richard, 67
Power, Ministry of, 161
Poynton, Sir Hilton, 151
prime minister, 19, 36, 119-22, 125-9, 133, 226
    PM's private office, 35, 130-4
Primrose, Sir Henry, 80
Prior, James, 128
Prison Service, 221
private offices, private secretaries, 34-5, 130-4, 136-7, 148-9
Privy Council (Office), xvii, 18, 21, 81
Proctor, Sir Dennis, 161
Profumo, John, 34
Property Services Agency (PSA, DoE), 68-9, 139, 160
Prothero, Rowland, 121
Public Accounts Committee (PAC), 51, 62-5, 67-75, 92, 228
Public Expenditure Survey Committee (PESC), 212
public service ethic, public service tradition, 14, 54, 60, 76, 100, 114-5, 152, 210, 227-9; *see also* ethics, code of
Pugh, Sir Idwal, 33

Questions of Procedure for Ministers, 24, 229; *see also* Armstrong Memorandum; ethics, code of

Rawlinson, Sir Anthony, 106
Rayner, Sir Derek, 50-2, 152, 159, 190
recruitment, 9, 46, 100-1, 104, 153-4; *see also* open competition; patronage
Recruitment and Assessment Services (RAS), 53
Redcliffe-Maud, Lord, *see* Maud, Sir John
Redesdale, Lord, *see* Mitford, Sir Algernon
Redington, Sir Thomas, 156
Reinventing Government, 91
Riddlesdell, Dame Mildred, 138
Ridley, F.F., 220
Ridley, Nicholas, 197
Ridley Report (Royal Commission on Civil Establishments, 1887-90), 63-4, 167
Ritchie, C.T., 10
Rogers, Sir Frederic, 46
Roll, Sir Eric, 104
Rosebery, Lord, 120, 149
Rowan, Sir Leslie, 131, 182, 190
Rowlands, Sir Archibald, 48, 83
Royal Institute of Public Administration (RIPA), 89
Royal Ordnance Factories, 53
Rugby School, 106
Runciman, Walter, 10
Russell, Lord John, 81, 120

Sadler, Sir Michael, 41
St. John's College, Cambridge, 100
St. Paul's School, 106
Salter, Arthur, 80
Sandys, Duncan, 125
Sargent, Sir Orme, 99
schools, xvi, 99, 104-8, 208-10; *see also* Clarendon Schools; Eton etc.
Scientific and Industrial Research, Department of (DSIR), 103-4
Scott, Sir Harold, 47
Scott Inquiry (1993-95), 16-7, 70, 205
Scottish Office, 189, 196
second permanent secretary(ship), 20-1
Second World War, 49, 83, 98, 150-1, 158, 206
secondments, 160-5, 180, 208
Selborne, Lord, 121
Seldon, Arthur, 38
Select Committee on Official Salaries (1850), 119
Select Committee on Procedure (1990), 77
select committees, 62, 74-7, 90, 218; *see also* Parliament; Public Accounts

Committee
Self, Sir Henry, 173
Senior Appointments Selection Committee (SASC), 86, 126-9, 141, 176
Senior Salaries Review Body (SSRB), 20
Shackleton, Sir David, 157
Sharp, Dame Evelyn, 25, 28-9, 39, 47, 66, 85, 126, 138, 209, 218-9
Shawcross, Sir Hartley, 125
Sheepshanks, Sir Thomas, 39
Sherman, Sir Alfred, 38
Shrewsbury School, 106
Simon, Sir John, 41
Smieton, Dame Mary, 138
Social Security, Department of, 55, 69
specialist grades, 48, 101, 103-4, 107, 139, 207, 209; see also expertise
Speed, Sir Eric, 134
Spycatcher trial, 16-7
Stamp, Josiah, 41
Stanley, Lord, 7
Stephen, (Sir) James, 7, 46, 81, 114
Stevenson, Sir Matthew, 126
Stowe, Sir Kenneth, 127-8, 131, 223
Strachen, Valerie, 138
Strauss, Norman, 38
Suez campaign, 212-3
Supply, Ministry of, 48, 67-8, 83

Tariff Reform League, 10
Taylor, Sir Henry, xv
Tebbit, Norman, 197
Technical Co-Operation, Department of, 157
Technology, Ministry of (Mintech), 49, 103
temporary advisers, 31, 37-8, 56, 150-1, 217
Thatcher, Margaret, Thatcher governments, 15, 24-5, 31-2, 50, 73, 89, 127-8, 133, 183, 194, 206, 214-8, 228
think tanks, 37-8
Thompson, Sir Ralph, 40
Thornton, Sir Peter, 190
Tindale, Laurence, 159
Tomlin Commission (Royal Commission on the Civil Service, 1929-31), 122, 167, 169
Trade, Board of, 5, 21, 80, 120, 124-5, 156-7, 204, 211
Trade (and Industry), Department of (DTI), 103, 190-1, 197
Trades Union Congress, 157
Transport, Ministry of, xvii, 29, 39-40, 126
Treasury and Civil Service Committee (TCSC, House of Commons), 15, 26, 76-7, 170, 228-9, 231
Treasury, HM, 5, 7, 10, 12-5, 18, 21, 36, 40, 51, 53, 57, 63-7, 69-72, 80-1, 101, 106, 120-4, 127, 129-31, 134-7, 152, 155, 168, 175, 182, 189-90, 205-6, 212
Trend, Sir Burke, 14, 19, 126
Trevelyan, Sir Charles, 7, 81, 113, 167, 211; see also Northcote-Trevelyan Report
Trinity College, Cambridge, 100
Troup, Sir Edward, 100-1, 121, 123
Tryon, Sir George, 6, 159
Tucker, Benjamin, 5
Turnbull, Andrew, 131
Turner, Sir George, 125

United Nations (UN), 162
universities, 97-104, 208-10; see also civic universities; 'Oxbridge'

value for money, 52, 70-1
Vansittart, Sir Robert, 11-2, 25, 47, 66, 82, 99, 123-4, 211-2, 218-9, 227

Waddington, Horatio, 159
Waldegrave, William, 33
Wall, Sir John, 173
Walpole, Spencer, 109
Walpole, Sir Spencer, 109
Walters, Sir Alan, 38
War Office, 5, 34, 40, 56, 64, 122-3, 125, 134, 158-9, 185, 190
Wardale, Sir Geoffrey (Wardale Report on the PSA), 68-69
Wass, Sir Douglas 15, 25, 33, 188
Way, Sir Richard, 34, 98-9, 125, 134, 187, 209
Webb, Beatrice, 82, 149
Weber, Max, 82, 90, 203
Welby, Sir Reginald, 63-4, 106
welfare state, xviii
West, Sir Algernon, 80
Westland Affair, 76
Westminster School, 106
Whitmore, Sir Clive, 24, 131, 184-5

Wicks, Sir Nigel, 131, 159
Wiener, Martin J., 209
Wilson, Harold, Wilson governments, 19, 36, 38, 126, 133, 172, 194, 216
Wilson, Sir Horace, 13, 15-6, 123-4, 206, 212
Wilson, Richard, 129
Wilson, Sir Samuel, 123
Winnifrith, Sir John, 173

Woods, Sir John, 125, 130, 168-9
Woolton, Lord, 124
Works, Office of, xvii, 109, 120, 156-7
World Bank, 162
Wright, Peter, 16
Wyndham, George, 121
Wynne, John, 156

Yes, Minister, Yes, Prime Minister, xvi